Roman Catholicism and Modern Science

ROMAN CATHOLICISM

AND

MODERN SCIENCE

A History

Don O'Leary

continuum

NEW YORK • LONDON

2006
The Continuum International Publishing Group Inc
80 Maiden Lane, New York, New York 10038

The Continuum International Publishing Group Ltd
The Tower Building, 11 York Road, London SE1 7NX

Continuum Publishing is committed to preserving ancient forests and natural
resources. We have elected to print this title on 30% postconsumer waste recycled
paper. As a result, this book has saved:
9 trees
438 lbs of solid waste
3,976 gallons of water
6.6 million BTUs of total energy
861 lbs of greenhouse gases
Continuum is a member of Green Press Initiative, a nonprofit program dedicated to
supporting publishers in their efforts to reduce their use of fiber obtained from
endangered forests. For more information, go to www.greenpressinitiative.org.

Library of Congress Cataloging-in-Publication Data

O'Leary, Don, 1955-
  Roman Catholicism and modern science : a history / Don O'Leary.
    p. cm.
  Includes bibliographical references and index.
  ISBN-13: 978-0-8264-1868-5 (hardcover : alk. paper)
  ISBN-10: 0-8264-1868-6 (hardcover : alk. paper)
  1. Religion and science. 2. Catholic Church—Doctrines. I. Title.

BX1795.S35O44 2006
261.5'5088282—dc22

                            2006023343

Contents

Acknowledgments

I AM GRATEFUL TO BERNARD LIGHTMAN (YORK UNIVERSITY, Toronto) and Ernan McMullin (formerly of the University of Notre Dame) for their advice on a number of important issues, ranging from conflict and harmony theses to arguments for the existence of God. In particular I wish to express thanks to Aileen Fyfe, National University of Ireland, Galway. Her recommendations persuaded me to revise—very substantially—the contents and structure of the first chapter. Patrick Hannon, St. Patrick's College, Maynooth, directed me to a number of important sources of discourse in Catholic bioethics for which I am grateful. I am indebted to Frank Oveis, senior editor at Continuum International, for his astute observations and very helpful suggestions. Finally, I wish to record my gratitude to my family, Kate, Karen, Kevin, Sarah, and Claire, for the serene conditions of home life that made it so much easier to write this book.

DON O'LEARY
UNIVERSITY COLLEGE CORK
22 JANUARY 2006

Introduction

DOCTRINES OF THE ROMAN CATHOLIC CHURCH ARE NOT confined to the religious domain but extend beyond it to cognate disciplines in the social and natural sciences. The social teaching of the church, for example, although based on theology, must take account of economics, sociology, and political science if it is to set out clear and realistic guidelines for the pursuit of social justice—a core element of the Christian imperative to love one's neighbor as oneself. Similarly, the doctrine of creation cannot ignore cosmology, physics, chemistry, geology, and biology without sacrificing credibility. To talk about the handiwork of an omnipotent and omniscient Creator while ignoring the laws and processes of nature established by the Creator would not be credible. The church is, therefore, bound to pronounce on issues that impinge directly, or indirectly, on the domain of natural science—and it has done so for centuries.

The interaction between Christianity and science from the patristic era to the twentieth century is the subject of many scholarly works in history. However, after the Galileo affair, attention is directed mainly toward Protestantism. Historical studies of Roman Catholicism and science after the 1640s are relatively few and highly specialized, thus permitting only a very fragmented view of the subject.[1] Therefore, there is a pressing need for extensive historical analyses of Catholic attitudes toward science after Galileo. This book will be mainly concerned with the response of the Roman Catholic Church to developments in the natural sciences from about 1800 to the dawn of the twenty-first century.

Roman Catholicism and science have often been regarded as incompatible with each other. Certainly, tensions and contradictions have arisen between them. This should not be surprising in view of the ancient and medieval origins of Catholic thought. The church relied primarily on the

Bible and on the works of Greek philosophers, interpreted by theologians from the early Christian era onward, when constructing or defining those doctrines that impinged on the natural sciences. It would have been remarkable—perhaps even miraculous—if no major difficulties were encountered in reconciling Catholic doctrine with modern scientific discoveries.[2] Does an awareness of this then lead one, inevitably, to conclude that there is an inherent conflict between Catholicism and science? The church's condemnation of the Copernican hypothesis and the Galileo affair seem to offer the most impressive examples of conflict. However, when these historical events are carefully examined in detail, the element of conflict between Catholicism and science is greatly reduced.

The ecclesiastical authorities committed a grievous error of judgment in 1616 when they imposed censorship on the Copernican hypothesis. But there were strong mitigating circumstances. Copernicanism created a number of theological, exegetical, philosophical, and scientific difficulties that the ecclesiastical authorities could not simply ignore. It seemed difficult to reconcile the Copernican hypothesis with the discipline of theology, regarded as preeminent among the sciences.[3] There was also concern about Copernicanism because it seemed irreconcilable with a literal reading of some scriptural passages.[4] This in turn was seen as a challenge to church authority. The Council of Trent, in its fourth session (8 April 1546), had declared that no one has a right to decide on a meaning of scripture contrary to the church's interpretation, or even different from the unanimous teaching of the church fathers. This declaration was issued in response to Martin Luther's doctrine concerning the private interpretation of scripture.[5] Those who expressed support for the Copernican hypothesis were placing themselves dangerously close to the Protestant position where there was much emphasis on the individual's right to interpret scripture.

There were other major objections to be overcome. Could a physical model, revealing the true geography of the universe, be constructed on the basis of mathematical astronomy? Not according to Aristotelian natural philosophy, which then prevailed in the universities! In the medieval hierarchy of the sciences, mathematics was inferior to physics. Copernicus based his hypothesis on mathematics, which contradicted a basic principle of physics. This higher discipline dictated that a simple body can have only one kind of motion associated with it. This in turn was not compatible with the earth's orbit around the sun and simultaneous rotation on its axis.[6]

Even if Galileo had been able to prove scientifically the mobility of the earth, he would still have faced a major epistemological obstacle. Both Catholic and Protestant theologians maintained that it was not possible to ascertain the truth about the cosmological system with certainty through the medium of the physical sciences. Only God knew the underlying dynamics of celestial motion. Furthermore, those astronomers who did support the heliocentric hypothesis were in a minority. Therefore, when the Inquisition formally condemned heliocentrism as heretical and false in 1616, it seemed to have the weight of evidence decisively in its favor, in science as well as in theology. For members of the Inquisition it was a choice between biblical certainties and unfounded scientific speculation.[7]

If it is conceded that, historically, there is an element of conflict in the relationship between Roman Catholicism and science on the basis of the Copernican controversy, then it can be strongly argued that conflict is not the defining characteristic of that relationship. Maurice A. Finocchiaro observed that many churchmen supported Galileo while many scientists were critical of him. He argued that there were disagreements in both religion and science and that the real conflict occurred between progressive and conservative opinions from both camps.[8] The notion of a historical conflict between Catholicism and science is further diminished by the observations of John Brooke, Geoffrey Cantor, and David C. Lindberg that Galileo's loyalty to the church was widely acknowledged, even by his critics.[9]

Although Galileo's stance on the Copernican hypothesis was vindicated, it is somewhat misleading to see the controversy simply in terms of right and wrong or truth versus error. Galileo was excessively critical of some of those who were not persuaded by heliocentricism and this almost certainly alienated potential supporters.[10] Although his observations showed that the old astronomy of Aristotle and Ptolemy was faulty, this did not prove the heliocentric idea. The Danish astronomer Tycho Brahe (1546–1601) had proposed a third, and credible, alternative in 1588.[11] Furthermore, Galileo, although a brilliant scientist, was not infallible. He believed that the tides were caused by a combination of the earth's daily rotation on its axis and its orbit around the sun. This, he believed, was evidence for the motion of the earth. He was wrong.[12]

The Galileo affair is outside the main period of interest of this book. Nevertheless, it merits some attention because, first, it serves as an excellent example to illustrate the complexity of the relationship between Roman Catholicism and science. Second, the exegetical principles advocated by Galileo continued to have profound implications for the inter-pretation of scripture. Third, the harsh treatment of Galileo by the eccle-siastical authorities generated debate and deeply influenced opinions in the nineteenth and twentieth centuries about the nature of the relation-ship between Catholicism and science, and, more generally, between reli-gion and science.

The error of the ecclesiastical authorities in censuring Galileo was par-ticularly damaging to the reputation of the church, and it gave those with a propensity for anti-Catholicism a splendid opportunity for denouncing it as a backward institution, opposed to science and progress. The Catholic Church, probably more than any other Christian denomination, had to contend with the assertion that theology and science were totally irreconcilable. In the late nineteenth century, the notion of "warfare" between theology and science was popularized by two books in particular. The first publication was the *History of the Conflict between Religion and Science* (1874) by John William Draper, professor of physiology at New York University. His book was a best-seller in America and in Europe.[13] The second book was *A History of the Warfare of Science with Theology in Christendom* (1896), written by Andrew Dickson White, who served as presi-dent of Cornell University.[14] White's book originated from two earlier works: the text of a lecture entitled "The Battlefields of Science" and a slim volume, *The Warfare of Science*, published in the 1870s. Draper's book in particular was bitterly critical of the Roman Catholic Church. Its his-tory, he argued, was "steeped in blood" because, unlike the Protestant churches, it had used the civil power to brutally enforce its demands. Draper anticipated that the intellectual basis of religious faith would be undermined by the "spirit of the age." His harsh depiction of Pope Pius IX seemed prophetic. The supposedly infallible pope was "fulminating" his anathemas from the Vatican despite "the most convincing proofs of his manifold errors." Roman Catholicism was doomed. Unlike Protestantism it was hopelessly irreconcilable with science.[15] Draper's book, not surpris-ingly, was placed on the Vatican's Index of Forbidden Books in 1876.[16]

Catholic apologists, aware that this notion of conflict between theology and science could greatly damage the credibility of the church, proposed a harmony thesis to counter it. They argued that Galileo was the architect of his own downfall: his impetuosity, his arrogance, and his provocative criticism of other scholars had alienated many potential allies. He had attempted to impose the Copernican hypothesis on the church without presenting conclusive proof. They pointed to his erroneous proof of the tides and drew unfavorable comparisons between him and Kepler. Some even went so far as to argue that Galileo's presentation of Copernican theory was false because he had persisted with the notion of circular planetary orbits when Kepler had demonstrated that these orbits were elliptical. The church's error, from a conservative Catholic perspective, would not be so great if it was seen merely to suppress an unsubstantiated scientific hypothesis.[17]

In contemporary academic discourse the general tendency is to move beyond issues of conflict and harmony when attempting to elucidate the relationship between Roman Catholicism and science or, more generally, the interaction between Christianity and science. Since the 1950s, when the history of science attained the status of an academic specialist subject, there has been an increasing tendency among scholars to put forward theses that are highly nuanced and less definitive. Authors such as Charles C. Gillispie, A. Hunter Dupree, Paul H. Kocher, Giorgio de Santillana, and Richard S. Westfall argued persuasively, when discussing issues ranging from the Copernican hypothesis to Darwinism, that generalizations of either conflict or harmony fail to elucidate the complexity of the interaction between Christianity and science.[18] There is now a convergence of opinion that consolidates this view. In *Reconstructing Nature: The Engagement of Science and Religion* (1998), John Brooke and Geoffrey Cantor rejected the notion of a "master-narrative" in the history of science and religion. They challenged the commonly held belief "that there is a definitive historical account of how science and religion have been (and are) interrelated."[19]

Concepts of conflict and harmony, of course, are not mere rhetorical devices contrived by polemicists. But other themes, such as dialogue and independence, need to be considered as possible elements of the historical relationship between religion and science.[20] Furthermore, when applying these concepts, cognizance needs to be taken of their complexity and variability. Conflict, for example, may be presented as competition with or without belligerence. If harmony is discerned, then it is important to ascertain whether religion is influencing science or science is influencing religion. In the context of Roman Catholicism, and more specifically with reference to the Galileo affair, Maurice A. Finocchiaro proposes an examination of events within a conceptual framework of conservative and progressive attitudes—but not in a definitive sense. The main thrust of his argument is the need to avoid oversimplification.[21]

In this book, the study of Roman Catholicism and science is treated with the above considerations in mind. Therefore, readers will not be surprised to learn that the relationship between Roman Catholicism and science is too complex to be defined simply in terms of conflict or harmony. Generally, the study will proceed chronologically but there will be some departure from this to enhance clarity of discussion and in instances where developments occur in parallel. Scientific issues are examined on the basis of their impact on Catholic theology and the interpretation of scripture. Evolution is discussed more than any other topic in science because it was the greatest source of contention and was frequently associated with anti-Catholic opinions. A range of other topics also receive attention, including developments in geology, the philosophy of science, the professionalization of science, agnosticism, the association of anti-Catholicism and science, the historical criticism of the Bible, intellectual freedom in relation to faith and ecclesiastical authority, the tension and conflict between ultraconservative and progressive thinking in Roman Catholicism, the nature of Catholic dogmas vis-à-vis science, the Pontifical Academy of Sciences, what science has to say about the existence of God, and Catholic bioethics.

The subject matter of Roman Catholicism and science, for the period in question, is so vast that no single volume could address its many facets in depth. Some questions are beyond the scope of inquiry simply because the information required does not exist. There is, for example, very little, if any, statistical data about the opinions of Catholic scientists concerning those aspects of their church's doctrine that were called into question because of modern scientific theories. The information on record is probably not even remotely adequate. In the absence of evidence, it is reasonable to speculate. First, most Catholic scientists would not have familiarized themselves with the details of Vatican pronouncements and therefore would not have held informed opinions. Second, those Catholic scientists who disagreed would, in the vast majority of cases, have kept silent out of fear of or out of deference to ecclesiastical authority. St. George Jackson Mivart, who will feature prominently in this work, was a notable exception.

There are other areas of historical inquiry that are potentially more fruitful. There is, for example, much to be discovered about the extent to which ecclesiastical authorities influenced the teaching of science in Catholic schools and universities, especially from the mid-nineteenth century onward. Catholic attitudes toward science will vary from one country to another. Every Catholic community, especially at the national level, has had its own unique experience of modern science.[22] David N. Livingstone's study of Presbyterian responses to Darwinism in Edinburgh, Belfast, and Princeton serves as an excellent example of different attitudes within Christian denominations. Local circumstances have played a very important role in determining attitudes.[23] Relatively little is known about Catholic responses to Darwinism.[24] This study will throw some light on this topic.

It would not be prudent for any author to attempt the enormous task of ascertaining the impact of modern science on Roman Catholic opinions on a country-by-country basis. The main purpose of this book is to elucidate the response of the universal Roman Catholic Church to modern science in general terms. The approach to the subject matter is not intentionally geographical. Two main sources of information are examined. Official church documents are studied, ranging in authoritative status from the declarations of general councils to the pastoral letters of provincial synods.[25] The response of the Vatican to modern science is of central importance, especially when cognizance is taken of the enormous centralization of power that occurred in the late nineteenth century. In ecclesiastical terms the pope reigned as an absolute monarch, especially after the promulgation of infallibility in 1870. Pope John Paul II wielded enormous power, even if it was mostly in a restraining or negative capacity. Despite his poor health and advanced years, he was still able to obstruct, apparently with little effort, much-needed and much-demanded reforms pertaining to such issues as priestly celibacy and the role of women in the church.

Generally, it is reasonable to take the pope's view as representative of official church policy or as an expression of church doctrine. There is, of course, a distinction to be made between the pope and the Vatican in this regard, but the significance of such a distinction is greatly diminished by the consonance between the pronouncements of the papacy and those of the Roman curia. This is not to argue that the Vatican can be simply equated with the pope when discussing church policies and doctrines. It is not assumed that the pope is always in full control and immune to competing factional influences. For example, in the 1890s Pope Leo XIII, enfeebled by advanced years, was unable to keep the ultraconservative faction of the curia in check, and this played a major role in conditioning the institutional church's attitude toward evolutionary theory (see chapter 5). In the 1960s there is yet another example of factional influences at work. Cardinal Alfredo Ottaviani and his conservative allies played a key role in influencing the drafting of the papal encyclical *Humanae Vitae* (1968), with disastrous consequences for the Roman Catholic Church.

In the late twentieth century numerous protests were made against the excessive centralization of power in the Vatican. Bishops sought a greater role in governing the church. Appeals were made for greater autonomy for local churches and for less intervention from Rome.[26] Pope John Paul II did not make any concessions to demands for the decentralization of power.[27] His voice was, and continued to be, the voice of the institutional church. But the official teaching of the Roman Catholic Church does not always find broad acceptance among Roman Catholics. The most outstanding example is the extremely low level of awareness and commitment to Catholic social teaching.[28] There is probably a far greater awareness of another example, that is, the widespread defiance of the papal prohibition on artificial means of contraception. When Paul VI's *Humanae Vitae* reiterated the church's traditional stance on this matter, many Catholic women who were otherwise loyal to the church chose to use the contraceptive pill. Some Catholics even left the church in protest. The notion of papal infallibility was called into question in some quarters. If the pope was wrong about the pill, then perhaps he could be wrong on other matters also. Comparisons were made with the errors of the church in dealing with Galileo and the Copernican hypothesis.[29] The error of 1968 was probably far more damaging to the reputation of the magisterium than the errors of the seventeenth century, because the issue of birth control extended beyond intellectual concerns to an issue of central importance to the quality of life of ordinary Catholics.

This study will not be confined to an examination of ecclesiastical pronouncements. It will explore Catholic opinions in a broader sense. The published works of Catholic authors will constitute the second main source for ascertaining Catholic attitudes.[30] These will be discussed in a broad context, taking cognizance of the social, political, and intellectual developments that influenced dialogue between Catholic theology and modern science. For example, although the theory of biological evolution, as elaborated by Charles Darwin, intensified the difficulty of harmonizing science and scripture, this alone does not give a satisfactory explanation of the reluctance of ecclesiastical authorities to accept it as a valid scientific theory. Some of the most ardent supporters of the evolutionary concept, most notably Thomas Henry Huxley and John Tyndall, were stridently critical of religious belief and probably exerted considerable influence when they campaigned for the liberation of science from external influences. They were also known for their anti-Catholic views, and it is likely that their opinions discouraged the Catholic acceptance of biological evolution, especially as proposed by Darwin. Furthermore, the views of Huxley and Tyndall are also particularly important because they help to explain the difficulties and tensions between faith and reason. They provide a rationalist background for discussing Catholic attitudes toward science. An explanation confined to only one side of a debate would certainly be inadequate.

As indicated earlier, the pronouncements of councils, popes, and bishops do not necessarily represent the perceptions and attitudes of the broader Catholic community. Although geological discoveries and evolutionary theories made it increasingly difficult for some Christians to sustain adherence to a literal interpretation of the Bible, it is impossible to quantify, with reasonable accuracy, the extent to which theoretical science undermined religious belief and trust in the scriptural narratives. Religious faith is a subjective phenomenon, and it is not possible for historians to measure precisely the strength of religious beliefs.[31] Statistics provide very little information. Furthermore, reliable statistics of religious practice are very scarce for many areas of Europe, and where such data does exist, it is open to different interpretations.[32] Until the late twentieth century there were no opinion polls providing a mass of information about religious beliefs and practices.

In the absence of extensive statistical data, historians have had to rely on their own intuitions, a careful analysis of relevant documents, and tentative extrapolations. Since the 1980s historians have become increasingly aware of the importance of statistical information in reaching more reliable conclusions. On this point, Alvar Ellegård's *Darwin and the General Reader* (1958) was ahead of its time. Ellegård's objective was to describe and analyze the influence of Darwin's theory of evolution on British public opinion from 1859 to 1872. With this in mind he searched through 115 British newspapers, magazines, and journals to find relevant articles and reviews. Ellegård was very much aware of the limitations of his study. Readers of the press were not a representative cross-section of the community, because there was a disproportionately higher number of readers among the wealthier and more educated classes. The assumption that periodicals represented, to a large extent, the opinions and beliefs of their readers was, and still is, very much open to question. Journalists, reviewers, and polemicists often made unsubstantiated claims about the opinions of their contemporaries. Most writers knew the beliefs of a small number of people and all too frequently did not perceive the error of generalizing from their limited information. Furthermore, they were usually biased and often made assertions about the opinions of the public to support their own arguments rather than impartially seeking the truth.[33]

Ellegård was aware of the uncertainties of drawing conclusions about public opinion on the basis of press opinion, but he believed that, despite the difficulties and limitations of such an undertaking, press articles and reviews offered the best source material of all those available.[34] In this present study articles and books by Catholic apologists give some indication of the attitude toward science among Catholics. It can be argued that, for most of the period under discussion—from the 1860s to the late twentieth century—there was a strong correlation between the outlook of Catholic authors and the broader Catholic community. The institutional church, especially through the educational system, exerted a powerful influence over the beliefs and attitudes of the laity. However, it is most likely that some writers, determined to defend traditional religious beliefs against modern philosophy, historical studies, and science, tended to overestimate the dangers posed by intellectual innovations. Therefore, the uncertainties identified by Ellegård are applicable to this work also.

There is a risk of exaggerating the impact of scientific theories on public opinion if consideration is not taken of the probability that the effects of socioeconomic changes were greater than those of intellectual developments. For example, the corrosive effect of population movement on religious beliefs and practices is likely to have been more extensive than that of the publication of Darwin's *Origin of Species* (1859).[35] Generally, controversies provoked by the polemical exposition of scientific ideas did not reach center stage in the public consciousness.

Scientific theories, in contrast to the dogmas of religion, did not provoke wars. Disputes between scientists did not lead to the organization of mass movements or to the formation of powerful political parties. Nevertheless, scientific endeavor, more than any other cultural activity, has influenced the course of history, and it will continue to do so. Its impact on religious belief is the subject of endless intellectual discourse, but it is remarkable how Roman Catholicism has received so little attention, considering its central role in the development of Western civilization and its present status as the largest religious organization on earth, with approximately one billion members. In view of all this, it can be argued that a broad-ranging study of the complex relationship between Roman Catholicism and science is long overdue.

1

From Galileo to Darwin

Galileo's Exegesis

A S A LOYAL CATHOLIC AND A DEDICATED SCIENTIST, GALILEO felt compelled to do his best to prevent an error of judgment that would do harm to both the church and science. It was for this reason that he wrote his *Letter to the Grand Duchess Christina* (1615), which is the main source of his views on how science should influence the interpretation of scripture. His treatise was profoundly influenced by the works of St. Augustine, especially *De Genesi ad Litteram* ("On the Literal Interpretation of Genesis").[1]

In his *Letter to the Grand Duchess Christina*, Galileo proposed five exegetical principles—although not in the formal style given below.

1. *Principle of Prudence.* One should be aware that different interpretations of the biblical text may be possible when attempting to ascertain the meaning of a difficult scriptural verse. An erroneous and dogmatic reading of scripture may damage the credibility of the scriptural texts generally.

2. *Principle of Priority of Demonstration.* When a demonstrated truth about natural science contradicts a particular interpretation of scripture, then an alternative interpretation of scripture must be sought. This was based on the commonsense concept that two truths cannot contradict each other.

3. *Principle of Priority of Scripture.* If an apparent contradiction arises between an unproven, but reasonable, assertion about nature and a scriptural verse, then the literal interpretation of scripture should be retained until the scientific assertion is demonstrated. A question arises here, which of course was of central importance in the Coper-

nican debate: If a scriptural verse is open to a number of interpretations, then should it not be permissible to adopt a well-supported but unproven scientific claim to arrive at a particular interpretation?

4. *Principle of Accommodation.* The biblical texts were written with the intellectual capacities of the intended audience in mind. This principle took cognizance of the inadequacies of language in describing or explaining the complex realities that are frequently beyond human comprehension. It was argued by Galileo, in reference to *De Genesi ad Litteram*, that God, acting through human writers, did not wish to teach men about nature when this was of no relevance to salvation. The purpose of scripture was to teach people how to gain admission to heaven, not to inform them about the shape of the heavens.

5. *Principle of Independence.* Scripture is primarily concerned with human salvation; therefore, scriptural texts should not be used to reach decisions on controversial issues in the natural sciences. Science and religion belong to, and are competent in, two distinct domains of knowledge. Science is concerned with the factual domain of natural phenomena; religion is concerned with faith and the supernatural.[2]

The *Letter to the Grand Duchess Christina* is an extremely complex document and has elicited widely varying assessments from different authors. Some have claimed that Galileo's exegetical principles are consistent with one another and that the Principle of Priority of Scripture is not even expressed in the *Letter*. Other writers argue to the contrary, claiming some degree of inconsistency, or at least tension.[3] For example, it could be argued that if we are to be guided by Independence and Accommodation then there would be no need for Priority of Demonstration and Priority of Scripture because the demonstration of scientific hypotheses would be deemed irrelevant to theological issues. But, given the circumstances of his time, Galileo could not have set aside Priority of Demonstration and Priority of Scripture without arousing the antagonism of the theologians.[4]

Cardinal Robert Bellarmine, the most influential and highly respected theologian of his time, viewed science and scripture in a different light. He argued that the Copernican system that Galileo and others were defending should be regarded as a mere hypothesis, not an established fact, because it would be "a very dangerous thing, likely not only to irritate all scholastic philosophers and theologians, but also to harm the Holy Faith by rendering Holy Scripture false."[5] His long campaign against heresy, inside and outside the church, hardened his attitude against those who would reinterpret scripture on the basis of new discoveries in natural science. Although Bellarmine accepted the possibility that scripture would have to be revised in the light of demonstrated conclusions in science, he set limits to inquiry—this may be referred to as the Principle of Limitation.[6] He argued that all factual statements in scripture were not revisable. He stated, for example, that it would be "heretical" to deny that Abraham had two children, to claim that Jacob did not have twelve, or to reject the virgin birth of Christ. Significantly, none of these examples was of relevance to issues that stimulated an interaction between religious and scientific thought—reference to some aspect of the Genesis account of creation would surely have been more appropriate. From Bellarmine's point of view it was not sufficient to argue that a scriptural reference to an astronomical phenomenon was not a matter of faith because, if it was not so "as regards the topic," it was so "as regards the speaker"—because biblical verses were inspired by the Holy Spirit and issued through the medium of the prophets and apostles.[7] This was a major error of judgment by Bellarmine. Although he seems to have considered the possibility that scripture would have to be reinterpreted in the event of a "true demonstration" of a mobile earth and a stationary sun, he effectively closed the door on compromise and reconciliation between faith and science by grossly overextending the domain of faith. Such a hard-line position would eventually prove unsustainable.

Bellarmine's opinions rather than Galileo's represented the official church position. On 5 March 1616 the Congregation of the Index issued a public decree, declaring that the motion of the earth and the stationary position of the sun, as taught by Copernicus, were false and contrary to scripture. When Galileo published his advocacy of Copernicanism in 1632, he provoked a censorious response from the ecclesiastical authorities. The circulation of his *Dialogue on the Two Chief World Systems, Ptolemaic and Copernican* was prohibited and Galileo was put on trial before the Inquisition in June 1633. He conceded that he had been "judicially instructed" by the Holy Office to "abandon completely the false opinion that the sun is at the center of the world and does not move and the earth is not the center of the world and moves, and not to hold, defend, or teach this false doctrine in any way whatever, orally or in writing." He confessed that he had transgressed this judicial instruction, and, wishing to remove the suspicion of heresy "rightly conceived" against him, he declared, "with a sincere heart and unfeigned faith I abjure, curse, and detest the above-mentioned errors and heresies."[8]

The physical sciences in Italy went into sharp decline shortly after the death of Galileo.[9] The institutional church had the resources to police the faith and repress unacceptable ideas. These included magic and astrology, and their condemnation in turn led to action being taken against those who practiced chemistry and chemical medicine. Not surprisingly, very few Catholics undertook research in these branches of science. In the seventeenth century by far the main contribution came from Protestants.[10]

The Catholic authorities were mainly concerned with combating Protestant heresies. The formidable system of censorship, centered on the Congregations of the Index and the Holy Office, had not been established primarily to deal with works of natural philosophy, which might present undesirable implications for theology. Nevertheless, natural philosophers such as Girolamo Cardano, Giambattista della Porta, Francesco Patrizi, Bernardino Telesio, Tommaso Campanella, and Giordano Bruno all suffered at the hands of ecclesiastical censors. It was in this atmosphere of ecclesiastical vigilance that the French Catholic philosopher and mathematician René Descartes (1596–1650) felt vulnerable. In his treatise *Le Monde*, he declined to make use of Aristotle's ideas about substantial forms and natural kinds. He followed the Copernican hypothesis in proposing a theory of the origins and functioning of the solar system. After the trial of Galileo and the censorship of Copernicanism, however, he was concerned about how his work would be judged and decided to withhold it from publication. His system of thought—Cartesian philosophy—was elaborated in his *Discourse de la Méthode* (1637), the *Meditationes de Prima Philosophia* (1641), and the *Principia Philosophiae* (1644). He stressed the mechanistic view of the natural world, which even then was gaining acceptance in intellectual circles. In the *Principia Philosophiae* he gave an extensive account of his metaphysical and philosophical theories, including the Copernican hypothesis, which was cautiously presented as an explanatory method rather than as literally true. It was his theory of matter, however, rather than Copernicanism, that created difficulties for him with the ecclesiastical authorities. It clashed with the Thomistic exposition of the miracle of the Eucharist. He attempted to reconcile his ideas about matter with transubstantiation, but the outcome was eventually found to be unsatisfactory and thirteen years after his death his *Meditationes* was placed on the Index of Prohibited Books.

Measures were taken to suppress Cartesian philosophy, but these met with only limited success. The church authorities also took action to suppress ideas about atomism and the plurality of worlds, but apart from these initiatives it expressed little interest in the works of contemporary science. The majority of published works were not adversely affected by the system of censorship. Nevertheless, scholars were aware of the threats of censorship and inquisitorial intervention, and this probably did much to curtail the spirit of inquiry, especially in Italy.[11]

In western Europe there was a movement of intellectual life toward the north, away from the older Catholic centers of learning such as Padua and Paris that had become associated with the censorship of free thought. In countries such as Holland and England the Copernican texts of Galileo, Johannes Kepler (1571–1630), and Philip van Lansbergen (1561–1632) were disseminated to a rapidly expanding readership and met with increasing approval.[12] However, a note of caution is necessary here. John Hedley Brooke, in his *Science and Religion* (1991), warns against overstating the suppressive effects of Index and Inquisition initiatives. Italian scholars continued to make valuable contributions to a broad range of disciplines, including logic, mathematics, and medicine. The Congregation of the Index did not isolate Italian scholars from their European contemporaries. Prohibited books were acquired and read where intellectual considerations took priority over the demands of ecclesiastical censorship. Furthermore, only a relatively small number of works concerned with the natural sciences were placed on the Index.[13] Roman Catholics continued to make important contributions to the progress of science, despite the restrictions imposed by the institutional church.[14] They also had to contend with the iconoclastic ideas of Enlightenment philosophies that proposed a secularized, anthropocentric universe as an alternative to a traditional theocentric one. In response, some devout Catholic scientists attempted, from different viewpoints and with different methodological approaches, to harmonize the latest developments in science with Catholic apologetics.[15]

New Interpretations

The quest for harmonization had proved to be extremely difficult. The outcome of Galileo's trial in 1633 was still a problem for the church as science moved inexorably against it. Isaac Newton's *Philosophiae Naturalis Principia Mathematica* (1687) superseded Aristotelian physics and bolstered arguments for heliocentricism, which was modified on the basis of Johannes Kepler's three laws of planetary motion. The old geocentric idea was overturned, including that of Tycho Brahe. In 1728 the discovery of the aberration of starlight by the English astronomer James Bradley (1693–1762) provided strong scientific evidence of the earth's orbit around the sun. This discovery became widely known in Italian scientific circles in 1734. Although Aristotelian physics and the Tychonic system were discredited, this did not mean that the Copernican system was conclusively proven—but it was proven beyond reasonable doubt. The need to reinterpret scripture was felt with greater intensity in Rome. But how was the church to retreat from its decree of 1616 which declared that Copernicanism was opposed to scripture? The church could admit its error openly and decisively change its position. Or it could act quietly, minimally, and gradually to safeguard its prestige, to avoid embarrassment, and to protect the tranquil acquiescence of the faithful. It chose the second option.[16]

In 1741 the Holy Office gave permission for the publication of the first almost complete edition of the works of Galileo—including the *Dialogue* but excluding the *Letter to the Grand Duchess Christina*. In 1757, under the pontificate of Pope Benedict XIV (1740–1758), the church took another step in reconciling its position with the astronomy of its time. In its list of forbidden books, published the following year, the Congregation of the Index did not reiterate the decree of 1616, which ruled against the mobility of the earth. This should have led to the simultaneous omission of books by Copernicus, Diego de Zuñiga, Paolo Antonio Foscarini, Kepler, and Galileo. But this did not occur. The omission of the decree of 1616 did not mean that it was formally revoked. No further significant measures to address this matter were taken until the early nineteenth century.

The church was reactive rather than proactive. In 1820 Canon Giuseppe Settele (1770–1841), professor of astronomy at the University of Rome, sought permission to publish the second volume of his *Elements of Optics and Astronomy*.[17] He intended to present the Copernican system as a thesis rather than as a hypothesis. Settele was granted permission in 1822 to have his work published only after he made it clear to his readership that the Copernican system was revised because of the errors, inconsistencies, and incomplete observations in its earlier state of development. This implied that the church had not committed an error in 1616 when the hypothesis in question was so defective as to merit censorship.[18] Another thirteen years passed before Galileo's *Dialogue* and a number of other Copernican books were removed from the Index of Forbidden Books. Three years later (1838) the observation of stellar parallax by the German astronomer and mathematician Friedrich Wilhelm Bessel (1784–1846) and the experiments of the French physicist Jean Foucault (1819–1868) offered further compelling evidence for the Copernican system.[19]

The removal of Copernican books from the Index did not resolve the Copernican problem for the church, nor did it undermine the basis for controversy in future decades.[20] However, the reinterpretation of scripture arising from the acceptance of Copernican astronomy was a simple matter in comparison to other issues raised by progress in the natural sciences. For example, reconciling reason with the story of the Flood was a long-standing problem. Apparently, the biblical narrative was intended to be understood in a literal sense. The words of Genesis seemed clear enough when describing the Flood : "the waters rose and increased greatly on the earth . . . and all the high mountains under the entire heavens were covered. . . . Every living thing on the face of the earth was wiped out. . . . Only Noah was left, and those with him in the ark" (Gen. 7:18–23 New International Version). Patristic and medieval theologians had taken these words of Genesis literally and believed that the Flood was universal. It seemed quite plausible to them because they had to make provision for only a few hundred species in their calculations and it was generally taken for granted that all animal species could be found in one geographical area. The story of the Flood, however, seemed more and more incredible as new discoveries were made in geography, zoology, and geology after the Middle Ages. The discovery of America stretched the literal interpretation of Genesis to the breaking point. After the European voyages of discovery by Christopher Columbus, Vasco da Gama, Amerigo Vespucci, Ferdinand Magellan, and others, the number of known species rose to thousands. Many of these were unique to regions remote from southwestern Asia. For example, marsupials were found only in Australia; giraffes, chimpanzees, and zebras were indigenous to Africa; and America was the exclusive domain of armadillos and llamas. It did not seem reasonable that animals from extremely remote lands could have traveled or been brought to the ark. Furthermore, the volume of the ark was hopelessly inadequate for the needs of thousands of animals, many of them dangerous carnivores.[21]

Christian authors, both Catholic and Protestant, began to question the traditional understanding of the Flood.[22] The teaching authority of the Catholic Church did not take a definite position on this biblical story. This gave Catholic scholars freedom to disagree on a range of issues. For example, was the Flood universal, or did it extend only to areas of human habitation? Was it brought about through the agency of natural causes, or was it a miracle? Did it significantly change the surface of the earth? Did the earth have a long antediluvian history?

Both Catholic and Protestant writers struggled with these questions and constructed hypotheses based on the biblical narratives. Notable examples of such theologically inspired enterprise include the *Natural and Moral History of the Indies* (1590) by the Jesuit missionary priest José de Acosta (1540–1600); *The Sacred History of the Earth* (1680) by Thomas Burnet (c. 1635–1715); and *An Essay toward a Natural History of the Earth* (1695) by John Woodward (1665–1728). However, all attempts to reconcile the Flood with scientific observations led to nonliteral interpretations of Genesis. Nevertheless, natural philosophers in the eighteenth century generally did not deny the historicity of the Flood. Galileo's belief that the Bible should be reinterpreted on the basis of scientific facts seems to have been shared by the majority of authors.[23]

Throughout the eighteenth century, increased geographical exploration and European colonization led to the discovery of thousands of animal and plant species new to Western science. With the discovery of so many new forms of life, the idea that a pair of each species could have been accommodated in the ark was rendered extremely implausible. By the 1770s leading intellectuals had abandoned the idea of an ark in the literal sense.[24] In addition to the problematical findings of biology, geology, and geography, there was an additional formidable question to be addressed. Where did all the water come from to cause such a global catastrophe? The volume required to cover the highest mountains was at variance with physical geography. It was of course possible that God specially created water to destroy almost all terrestrial animal life and that afterwards he eliminated the surplus quantity. Yet there was no evidence for such an assumption, either in scripture or in science. There was very little support among biblical scholars for such an idea. There was no doubt about God's ability to perform such a miracle—his omnipotence was not in question—but the weakness of the argument was that it was contrary to the known laws of nature and was completely devoid of evidence.

The idea of a universal flood was simply untenable. By the middle of the nineteenth century the vast majority of those who wrote about the subject believed that the inundated region was only the plain of Mesopotamia. The Principle of Accommodation was invoked to facilitate a reinterpretation of Genesis. Many Catholic exegetes argued that the Flood covered only that part of the earth inhabited by humans. There was no basis, however, for such a contention in scripture, where no distinction was made between animal and human life.[25] By the late nineteenth century it was clearly evident from studies in geology, archaeology, history, ethnology, and linguistics that the entire human race (excepting of course Noah and his family) was not destroyed by the Flood. The American

Catholic priest John Augustine Zahm discussed this topic in detail in his book *Bible, Science, and Faith* (1894).

Zahm acknowledged that the church fathers and theologians were almost unanimous in teaching that the Flood was universal.[26] Was it permissible to reject their teaching and propose a contrary opinion? The declarations of the Council of Trent and the First Vatican Council asserted that, in matters of faith and morals, it was not permissible to interpret the Bible "contrary to the unanimous consent of the Fathers" (p. 141). Zahm argued that questions about the universality of the deluge were not directly concerned with faith and morals and were only incidental to the substance of the faith. Therefore, traditional theological consensus was not binding on this issue. More than one interpretation of scripture was possible in this instance—the church had not defined its position on the question (p. 148).

In the context of the consensus of theologians, there was a fundamentally important distinction to be made between mere opinion and immutable articles of faith (pp. 149–50). Zahm concluded on the basis of these arguments that the Flood covered only a relatively small portion of the earth's surface. This interpretation seemed inconsistent with the biblical text, where universal expressions had been used without restraint: ". . . all life under the heavens, every creature that has the breath of life in it. Everything on earth . . . all living creatures . . . every kind of creature . . . all the high mountains under the entire heavens . . . every living thing . . ." (Gen. 6:17–7:23). In the Old Testament universal terms were frequently used instead of particular terms. The authors of scripture used hyperbole with little if any inhibition (pp. 135–39). Noah and his family had observed the Flood destroying all animals and people around them and concluded that all the earth was flooded. The Holy Spirit did not see fit to enlighten Moses—scientifically—when he was writing for posterity (p. 159). The purpose of the story was to give an account of God's chosen people, not to write the history of the world (pp. 159–61). All this seemed remote from what was, apparently, the real meaning of the biblical text. But Zahm's work was not censored. It was permissible to depart from the literal meaning of scripture when reason demanded it—and the demands of reason were heavy and varied, especially concerning the Book of Genesis.

Geology and Revelation

From the late eighteenth century to the early decades of the nineteenth century, geology emerged as a newly defined branch of science with a

heavy emphasis on empiricism and a marked tendency to reject grand theories, including those that invoked the supernatural. When James Hutton
(1726–1797) wrote his *Theory of the Earth* (1795), he strictly confined his
explanation to natural processes in accounting for geological features. His
method was contrary to physicotheology because it could not be used to
support the idea of a God who was constantly intervening. Furthermore,
Hutton made no effort to harmonize his findings with the biblical account
of creation.[27]

The "uniformitarianism" proposed by Charles Lyell (1797–1875) was
similar to Hutton's outlook, but it had a much greater volume of supporting evidence. He argued that the geological processes observed now were
the same as in the past, and he stressed that the slow-acting forces of erosion and deposition needed a vast time scale to bring about the formation
of the earth's surface. This meant that the earth was many millions of years
old rather than the few thousand allowed for by the genealogies of Genesis. His *Principles of Geology* (1830–1833) exerted a powerful influence on
contemporary scientific thought. In view of his developmental approach
to geology, it might have been reasonable to expect that Lyell would have
quickly gravitated toward the acceptance of an evolutionary process in
biology—he did not. Instead, he continued to accept, until the early
1860s, that God's intervention was necessary for the origin of every living
species. Despite his religious views, however, he rejected physicotheology
and called for the liberation of geology from the cosmogony of Moses.[28]
His work effectively undermined diluvial geology.

The account of creation needed to be reexamined in the new light of
geological discoveries. The English clergyman and geologist William
Buckland (1784–1856) responded vigorously and imaginatively to the
challenge. He was already well known for his attempts to reconcile geology and Genesis. His *Geology and Mineralogy Considered with Reference to
Natural Theology* was published in 1836 as the sixth volume in the *Bridge-
water Treatises*. He proposed two novel ideas: first, the "gap" hypothesis—
the notion of an indefinite length of time between the creation of the
universe and the first of the Mosaic Days; and second, the "day-age"
hypothesis—the idea that the Mosaic Days represented indefinite periods
of time. Buckland preferred the gap hypothesis. Its great advantage over
the day-age hypothesis was that it did not require any manipulation or
altering of the text to make it fit with scientific observations. Most of the
earth's geological history could be intercalated between the beginning of
the universe and the first Mosaic Day. Scripture was silent about this

period of time; therefore there could be no contradiction between geology and the creation narrative.[29]

Buckland's treatise did not permanently dissipate Christian concerns about geology. From 1844 to 1863 over sixty books were published that addressed the issue of reconciliation between geology and Genesis. The Catholic contribution was disproportionately small. No Catholic book in the English language was issued until the English-language translation of Abbé A. Sorignet's *Sacred Cosmogony* (1854) was published in 1862. Sorignet's book bluntly asserted that geology lacked sound evidence when it was not in harmony with scripture.[30] But geological findings, inimical to a literal interpretation of Genesis, were too well established to be swept aside and dismissed as mere speculation. The American Catholic priest Clarence Augustus Walworth (1820–1900) expressed views sharply at variance with Sorignet's in his book *The Gentle Skeptic* (1863).[31] He believed that Sorignet's biblical literalism was undermined by science, and he argued that the six days of creation were not really days but were instead metaphorical expressions used as a means to classify the works of creation. Walworth's book received good reviews from the American Catholic press, and it proved to be popular. It was reprinted in 1867 and 1875.

From Walworth's perspective respect for science was respect for reason, which in turn was of crucial importance to the credibility of his Christian faith. The Irish Catholic theologian Fr. Gerald Molloy (1834–1906) shared a similar attitude. His book *Geology and Revelation* (1870) was based on a series of nine articles published in the *Irish Ecclesiastical Record* from 1867 to early 1869.[32] Molloy was acutely aware that throughout Europe, especially in England, there was a widely held belief that recent scientific discoveries contradicted parts of scripture. This misunderstanding needed to be addressed, and his book was written with this in mind. In the preface, Molloy made it clear that the geological material in his book was based entirely on the published work of others, not on his own original research. He relied heavily on two volumes by Charles Lyell —*Principles of Geology* and *The Elements of Geology* (1838).[33]

Molloy started with the unassailable premise that truth does not contradict truth. Thus, he had nothing to fear from science, geological or otherwise. But there was widespread misunderstanding that geology was at variance with the Book of Genesis. Molloy's primary objective, therefore, was to impart to the "simple-minded faithful" that God was the author of both the Book of Nature and the Book of Revelation—there could be no contradiction. This emphasis was necessary because the enemies of the church had stridently asserted that the known facts of geology were incompatible with a belief in scripture (pp. 2–3).

Molloy identified two points of contact between revelation and geology, concerning (1) the antiquity of the earth, and (2) the antiquity of humanity. Geologists had demonstrated, beyond reasonable doubt, that the age of the earth was much older than the six to eight thousand years apparently allowed for by the Bible. It was imperative for theologians, therefore, to reinterpret scripture in the light of known geological facts.

Molloy's analysis was well balanced, and he did not refrain from criticizing those who championed the cause of religion. He claimed that grave misunderstandings had arisen because of the errors of both geologists and theologians. In their respective disciplines they had misinterpreted the record of the rocks and the text of the Bible. Many devout Christians, therefore, had ignored the findings of this popular subject—which had attained the status of a mature science based on a sound methodology (pp. 5, 9–10). Furthermore, there was a tendency by some religious writers to criticize geologists for not making explicit reference to God's omnipotence in the course of elaborating their findings. Molloy dismissed their critical remarks as "unphilosophical." The beauty and complexity of nature were the outcome of secondary causes (i.e., natural laws) which affirmed the existence of a great First Cause. By exploring the earth's crust and elucidating natural processes, geologists revealed the handiwork of the Creator and were innocent of the charge of "impiety" (pp. 153–54).

Molloy argued that God worked through natural causes and that these were amenable to observation, study, and verification. Fossils were "Nature's hieroglyphics," and it was the business of scientists to use these objects to cast light on natural history (pp. 208–9). Molloy set himself the task of explaining the most important features of geological theory that commanded a broad consensus among geologists. This was a prerequisite for any attempt to reconcile geology with revelation. He believed that it would be "a mistaken and mischievous course" to deny what had been proven by careful research (pp. 157–58). Those Christians who used the Bible to refute the known facts of science lost credibility with well-informed unbelievers who might otherwise give serious consideration to the scriptural texts. Thus, they unintentionally did a great disservice to the cause of religion (pp. 326–29).

Molloy argued that the Bible did not indicate the age of the earth. But it did seem to reveal, on the basis of Old Testament genealogies (from Adam to Jesus Christ), that the origin of humanity was "comparatively recent"—somewhere between six and eight thousand years (pp. 316–21). For centuries it had been taken for granted that after the creation of the universe God immediately set about preparing it for human benefit. His task, it was believed, took six days to complete, culminating in the creation of Adam and Eve. Thus, there was very little difference between the age of humans and the age of the earth. This outlook, in Molloy's opinion, was perfectly reasonable in the absence of modern scientific knowledge. Now that the world was "ringing with the wonderful discoveries of Geology" it was time for a closer look at scripture (pp. 322–23). But this was a precarious undertaking. In challenging a cherished view of the world, Molloy anticipated that he might be accused of "irreverence" toward the Bible. In his defense he stated that the Roman Catholic Church had made no final judgment on the issues he addressed (p. 326). Furthermore, he invoked the teachings of eminent scholars of the church to stress his adherence to Roman Catholic doctrine. In his opinion, the preponderance of scholarly opinion, ancient and modern, protected him against charges of theological error (pp. 323–24, 343). Confident of his position, he then proceeded to elaborate his findings.

Molloy pointed to two events described in Genesis. Genesis 1:1 states: "In the beginning God created the heavens and the earth." Genesis 1:3, describing the first Mosaic Day, states: "And God said, 'Let there be light,' and there was light." Scripture did not reveal what length of time elapsed between these two divine acts. Therefore, there was a period of indefinite duration between the creation of the earth and the beginning of the Mosaic Days. Catholics were at liberty to believe that the earth was host to a great diversity of life forms in this era. In addition to this point, Molloy contended that it was permissible to represent the six days of creation as long periods of time. His hypothesis presented a number of problems. For example, plants and animals could not have existed without light before the Mosaic Days. From Genesis it appears that light was not created until the beginning of the first day. Molloy answered this difficulty by speculating that light did exist before the first day but at the close of the indefinitely long period "the earth was waste and empty and darkness was upon the face of the deep" (Gen. 1:2)—hence the need for God to restore this vital source of energy (pp. 346–48).

The Book of Genesis did not give a concise account of natural history, and there were major difficulties in reconciling it with the findings of science. However, Molloy argued that a book should be judged by the purpose that it was meant to serve. Genesis was not written to teach natural science—it was to serve the spiritual needs of God's chosen people. The inspired author, it was contended, did not lead his readers into error—he simply left them in ignorance of events that were deemed irrelevant to their needs. The purpose of the author was to impress upon the Hebrews that God was the creator of everything (pp. 348–49). An elaborate account of geology, botany, and zoology was of little interest to "a rude and uncultivated race of men" who were inclined to indulge in idolatrous practices (pp. 394–95, 398).

Contrary to popular opinion, there had been a lack of consensus among the church fathers on the meaning of the Mosaic Days (pp. 352–53). Therefore it was deemed permissible to abandon the literal meaning of the word "day" to bring scripture into harmony with modern science (pp. 354–55, 383–84). On this basis it seemed that there was a similarity between the order of creation set forth in Genesis and the sequence of events evident from the geological record. However, this view had severe limitations. Genesis was but a very brief description of creation, and not all important natural processes and events were evident from the geological record (pp. 384–94). Thus, the scheme of correlating the Mosaic Days with geological periods could only be defended as a legitimate hypothesis, not as an established truth (p. 396).

Molloy put forward two hypotheses for consideration: the gap theory and the day-age theory. In his opinion the geological record did not indicate a preference for one of these in particular. Neither hypothesis could be proved, but what was provided was a framework to build on, so that science could be reconciled with scripture (pp. 396–97). Molloy did not claim to have originated the gap and day-age theories. This placed him in a precarious position. He was treading as lightly as possible on Catholic theological sensitivities. In view of the antipathy between Catholicism and Protestantism in Ireland, it would not be prudent to give full credit to Buckland—an Anglican priest—and other Protestant writers. Molloy referred to Hugh Miller's *Testimony of the Rocks* (1857), Thomas Chalmers's *Evidences of the Christian Revelation*, and one or more unnamed publications by Pye Smith concerning the Bible and geology. He downplayed the role of Protestant authors, adding their names after his Catholic sources as if they were merely supplementary.

Molloy's Catholic sources included the *Twelve Lectures on the Connection between Science and Revealed Religion* (1836) by Cardinal Nicholas Patrick Wiseman (1802–1865), the leading English Catholic apologist, who was later elevated to the rank of cardinal archbishop of Westminster; *Cosmogonia Naturale Comparata col Genesi*, by John Baptist Pianciani, S.J., published by the ultraconservative *Civiltà Cattolica*; and *Prælectiones Theologicæ* by Giovanni Perrone, S.J., theologian at the Gregorian University in Rome. Catholic and Protestant authors were divided about which hypothesis to accept, although not on a denominational basis. Chalmers and Pye Smith, like Buckland, expressed preference for the gap hypothesis. Pianciani and Miller chose the day-age hypothesis. Molloy followed Wiseman's lead and declined to choose one over the other. Both hypotheses were of equal merit. It was even permissible to accept both hypotheses together.[34] In his closing statements Molloy acknowledged that he had not studied the antiquity of humankind in the context of reconciling recent geological discoveries with the Bible. This was a task he would undertake if circumstances provided the opportunity.[35]

The Vatican had come to terms with the theological implications of modern geological theory. A letter indicating papal approval of *Geology and Revelation* was published in the *Irish Ecclesiastical Record* (1870).[36] Twenty-five years later Molloy attended the first academic meeting of the newly formed Maynooth Union, which was held as part of the centenary celebrations of St. Patrick's College, Maynooth. In his lecture entitled "The Historical Character of the First Chapter of Genesis," he referred to his book *Geology and Revelation*. He told his clerical colleagues that he had received "many" letters from "friendly critics," some "of high standing and authority," objecting to the idea that the six days of creation represented long periods of time. However, opinions had changed in the intervening years, and the views that he had expressed in 1870 were "generally accepted" in 1895.[37] It was clear that progress in the natural sciences compelled allegorical interpretations of scripture in some instances. However, there were limits to exegetical flexibility, especially in conservative Catholic circles, where there was stubborn resistance to the idea that the story of Adam and Eve should be understood in a nonliteral sense because of the extension of evolutionary theory to humankind. According to the Maynooth professor Walter McDonald, Molloy did some work for a second book on the "*Antiquity of Man*; but, having satisfied himself on certain points, thought it more prudent to keep his conclusions to himself. He had no taste for martyrdom."[38] The Roman Catholic Church was extremely reluctant to concede that the Genesis account of human origins was not literally true—despite the fact that precedents had been established for accepting nonliteral rather than literal interpretations of scripture. However, before discussing the church's attitude toward human evolution in depth it will be necessary to give some attention to the theory itself, and the background to it, as a basis for such a study.

Darwin

In the 1850s there was a growing suspicion in British society that natural science posed a threat to the integrity of scripture and to the dignity of humankind.[39] However, before 1858, the year when Brixham Cave (in southern England) was scientifically excavated, there was very little evidence to suggest that the history of humankind extended far beyond six thousand years. Although geology had demonstrated the great age of the earth, it contributed very little to the elucidation of human history. The discoveries at Brixham Cave changed all this; estimates of the antiquity of humankind were revised upwards out of all proportion to traditional calculations. It was clear from the findings that humans once lived among animals that had long since succumbed to extinction. The six-thousand-year estimate of human history, based on the Bible, was no longer sustainable. It seemed possible that humans might have existed before Adam and Eve.[40]

The theory of biological evolution was greatly strengthened by the publication of *The Origin of Species* by Charles Darwin (1809–1882) in November 1859. The response to this book throughout Europe was one of intense interest and it had an enormous impact on a broad spectrum of thought, including science, philosophy, economics, political theory, and theology. Darwin, aware of how sensitive human evolution was, chose not to discuss it, although the implications of his theory were quite apparent. The only relevant statement he made was, "Light will be thrown on the origin of man and his history."[41] He thought it necessary to direct attention to more technical matters so that evolutionary theory could be discussed more freely. It was not until 1871 that his book *The Descent of Man and Selection in Relation to Sex* was published.

Some concerned Christians found it difficult to reconcile evolution with their faith, and many were quite shocked by it.[42] The earlier discoveries in astronomy and geology had created difficulties for maintaining the biblical cosmogony as set forth in Genesis. But the churches had yielded the minimum necessary on both of these issues, and the story of humankind was not called into question. Darwin's theory had far more serious implications because it impacted on the early history of the human species, which in turn was closely associated with important Christian concepts such as original sin, atonement, and redemption.[43]

The idea of natural selection in particular created a major problem because it seemed to undermine the teleological argument for the existence of God (i.e., the argument from design). It was now claimed that organisms were exquisitely adapted to their environment, not because they had been designed in a particular way but because only well-adapted creatures survived. Darwin believed that the argument from design elaborated in William Paley's *Natural Theology* (1802), which to him had seemed so conclusive, was no longer sustainable because of the discovery of natural selection. Therefore, he could not turn to science for evidence of God's existence and, confessing his poor abilities in philosophy, he was effectively left with no basis for belief. He concluded that it was beyond the limits of the human intellect to know with certainty whether God existed or not, and he resigned himself to agnosticism.[44]

Darwin overestimated the adverse impact of his theory on natural theology. The kind of natural theology that had been popularized by John Ray and William Paley was overturned because their outlook was based on the assumption that the universe was static—as if the work of creation had been finished at a particular period or moment in time. According to them, natural structures and species, designed by God, were permanent and immutable. This view of nature, held by many Protestants, became increasingly untenable as evidence accumulated to indicate a changing universe. The fossil record revealed the extinction of some species and the emergence of new ones, over vast periods of time. Extinction seemed to indicate wastefulness, imperfection, and a process of trial and error in God's creative enterprise. Darwin's theory brought all this, and suffering, into sharper focus, with its ruthless struggle for existence—through which only the "fittest" survived.[45] But it did not destroy the credibility of natural theology generally. In Roman Catholicism, and in some branches of Protestantism (especially Anglicanism), natural theology proved to be quite resilient. Catholic theologians made the point that only the fifth of St. Thomas Aquinas's proofs for the existence of God was directly affected by natural selection. St. Thomas had argued that natural agents, acting consistently and harmoniously, indicated a purpose in nature that is determined by a supernatural intelligence. His fifth argument proved to be far less rigid, and therefore much more adaptable, to evolutionary theory than the natural theology of Ray and Paley.[46]

Roman Catholicism was far less reliant on natural theology than Protestantism. The eminent English Catholic theologian John Henry Newman (1801–1890) even went so far as to argue for the almost complete isolation of science and theology. In his *Idea of a University*, Newman asserted that these disciplines relied on different methods—"induction is the instrument of Physics, and deduction only is the instrument of Theology." The Baconian method and theology did not "correspond." Theology was concerned with supernatural knowledge; science was confined to the natural domain. There was a limited degree of intersection, but Newman concluded: "it will be found, on the whole, that the two worlds and the two kinds of knowledge respectively are separated off from each other; and that, therefore, as being separate, they cannot on the whole contradict each other."[47] Newman acknowledged that the Bible had in a number of instances, especially in Genesis, "advanced beyond its chosen territory." But this did not worry him because the Roman Catholic Church had not yet formally defined the many scriptural verses in question. Therefore, Catholic theology, from this perspective, had nothing to fear from progress in the natural sciences.[48] Newman wrote little about human evolution and does not seem to have been very troubled by it. In 1863 he declared that "it is as strange that monkeys should be so like men, with no historical connection between them, as that there should be no course of facts by which fossil bones got into rocks . . . I will either go whole hog with Darwin, or, dispensing with time and history altogether, hold not only the theory of distinct species but that also of the creation of fossil bearing rocks."[49]

Many of those who publicly questioned the philosophical and methodological basis of Darwin's theory were motivated mainly by its religious implications. Religious beliefs probably generated the main stimulus for interest among the general public, and all too frequently there was little effort devoted to an objective assessment of the factual evidence.[50] Most of those who were prepared to accept evolutionary theory did so only when they believed that there was a place for God as an omnipotent guiding force.[51]

Darwin, deeply worried about the possibility of an adverse response to *The Origin of Species*, was careful to win the support of a few eminent scientists to ensure that his theory was not dismissed before it received a fair hearing. His supporters included Charles Lyell, Joseph Dalton Hooker (1817–1911), and Thomas Henry Huxley (1825–1895). They were not reticent about publishing their views. Huxley, although skeptical of Darwin's mechanism of natural selection, was an enthusiastic exponent of evolution because of his eagerness for naturalistic explanations. Known as "Darwin's bulldog," he wrote *Zoological Evidence as to Man's Place in Nature* (1863). Charles Lyell cautiously changed his mind about evolution and his work *The Geological Evidence of the Antiquity of Man* (1863) was clearly supportive of Darwin.

Darwin was content to let them confront the hostile reactions of those who were religiously conservative. His *Origin of Species* played a major role in persuading the majority of scientists to support evolutionary theory. By the end of the 1860s the majority of biologists had come to accept that new species had originated from older ones by a process of transmutation.[52]

2

Religion and Science in Victorian Britain

Conflict—Real and Imaginary

INSTITUTIONAL CHANGE AND THEORY FORMATION IN SCIENCE do not occur independently of social and political conditions. Intellectual trends in Victorian society, internal and external to the scientific community, favored the broad acceptance of Darwinism and elevated the status of science and scientists. Darwin's theory was used to justify a broad spectrum of social and political ideologies. The middle classes, who had prospered from industrialization, were attempting to gain political power from the landed aristocracy, and evolutionary theory provided them with a strong ideological argument. In some quarters social reform was seen as an extension of evolutionary change, and both were regarded as inherently progressive. In the middle of the nineteenth century, *laissez-faire* capitalism was at its height in Britain. Darwin was not impervious to the ideas, biases, and attitudes of his social environment, and his intellectual horizons extended beyond the realm of the natural sciences. That he was in touch with the social philosophy of his time is indicated by his familiarity with the works of Adam Smith and other political economists who advocated social reform based on free enterprise.

Darwin came from a prosperous middle-class background. His family had gained wealth through their own efforts, and they did not agree with the privileges of the aristocracy. Their commitment was to the free-enterprise system, which had served them so well. Darwin's concept of constant struggle in nature was analogous to the competitive ethos of Victorian capitalism. Another kind of struggle was also in progress. In the

19

third quarter of the nineteenth century many outspoken Victorian scientists had entered the scientific community from the periphery of middle-class society and from outside the main social and intellectual institutions of England. Their opposition to the *status quo* was motivated by professional and ideological considerations. Men such as Huxley and the Irish physicist John Tyndall (1820–1893) were highly talented and ambitious and sought recognition from both their scientific peers and from the general public.[1] They challenged the traditional intellectual elite, particularly the clergy. Their popular writings and public lectures brought science into the arena of public debate and gained some support for their cause.

Huxley, Tyndall, and other scientists endeavored to establish science as a new source of authority in Western society. In this context Darwinism can be seen as a great secularizing force in the nineteenth century.[2] Scientific naturalism served as an ideological basis and justification for the professionalization of science in Britain. Ideas were based on empirical data, and the study of nature was founded mainly on three major scientific theories, namely, the atomic theory of matter, the conservation of energy, and evolution. Many scientists believed that these three theories made possible a complete explanation of nature, including humankind. This outlook combined neatly with the professional interests of the scientific advocates. In some quarters it seemed that the clergy no longer served a useful purpose in society.

In Britain, the proponents of scientific autonomy were greatly assisted by developments within the Church of England. A tendency developed, mainly owing to the Oxford Movement, whereby the clerical vocation was redefined on a distinctly religious basis.[3] As the professional scientists gained more influence within the scientific community, they effectively marginalized the clerical amateurs. This was particularly evident in the British Association for the Advancement of Science, which had been founded in the 1830s. Contributions from the clergy, and from other non-scientists, became increasingly unwelcome. The growing autonomy of science, and the advancement of professional standards in its various disciplines, facilitated the objectives of Huxley and others to rid science of clerical interference so that scientific research could be pursued, unfettered by the dogmas of religion. Huxley expressed his "untiring opposition to that ecclesiastical spirit, that clericalism which, in England, as everywhere else, and to whatever denomination it may belong, is the deadly enemy of science."[4]

In promoting their cause Huxley and his colleagues argued, both implicitly and explicitly, that their practical, enlightened, and altruistic goals stood in stark contrast to what appeared to be the narrow denominational interests of the clergy. Professional scientists, in opposition to Anglican ecclesiastical authorities, represented themselves as the superior educational party whose aspirations and self-interest harmonized with the economic, medical, industrial, and military requirements of an imperial nation.

The attainment of a large measure of control over the educational system by professional scientists was seen as crucial for the advancement of science. This would lead to an increase in the applications of science throughout society and would enhance employment prospects for science graduates. Professional scientists stood to gain power and prestige. Their demands included the teaching of science as determined by professional scientists and an end to theological tests in the universities. Furthermore, they opposed denominational control over the school boards. Their endeavors inevitably brought them into conflict with those religious denominations that exercised considerable influence and control over educational institutions, especially Anglicans and Roman Catholics.

The anticlericalism of Huxley and other scientists is understandable when cognizance is taken of the fact that the clergy exercised enormous influence and power through the pulpit, the educational system (including the universities), and the bench of bishops. Scientists and other professionals including, for example, physicians and engineers, constituted an emerging heterogeneous group of workers, possessing relatively little wealth or prestige. They resented what they considered the unjustified interference of the clergy and ecclesiastical authorities in practical matters pertaining to their professional domain.[5] Huxley believed that it was unreasonable to leave the training of science teachers to colleges that were under the control of church authorities, because students in these institutions were obliged to spend half of their time "grinding into their minds . . . tweedle-dum and tweedle-dee theological idiocies," and the other half was spent "cramming them with boluses of other things to be duly spat out on examination day."[6]

The members of the "X Club" (formed on 3 November 1864) were united by their "devotion to science, pure and free, untrammelled by religious dogmas."[7] The club included Thomas Huxley, Joseph Dalton Hooker, Herbert Spencer (1820–1903), John Tyndall, George Busk, Edward Frankland, John Lubbock, Thomas Hirst, and William Spottiswoode. Membership in the club was not based on professional status in science—Busk, Lubbock, and Spottiswoode were amateurs. The criterion was a devotion to scientific research free of religious dogmas.[8] Although the club membership numbered only nine, it proved to be of major significance. All of the members supported Darwin's theory and were rising to positions of power and influence. Collectively, they came to exert considerable power within scientific circles in Britain. Furthermore, through their popular books and lectures, they succeeded in gaining some degree of acceptance for their ideas beyond the scientific community.

In pursuance of their objectives, Huxley and his colleagues constructed a conflict thesis, portraying religion, based on faith, in opposition to science based on fact. This manifestation of hostility toward religion was not unique to Britain. In France science was used as an ideological weapon against the church by militant republicans—this was part of a much larger struggle between church and state for control over the educational system (especially the university sector).[9] The most influential exponent of evolution in Germany, Ernst Haeckel (1834–1919), insisted that Christianity could not be reconciled with Darwinian evolution. The German materialists warmly welcomed Darwinian theory in their struggle against the Christian churches. G. Seidlitz (1875) believed that science, especially Darwinism, could be used as a powerful ideological weapon against the Lutheran Protestants and ultramontane Catholics. David Friedrich Strauss, in his *Der Alte und der neue Glaube* (1872), expressed views on Darwinism that were hostile to Christianity. Although he acknowledged that Darwin's theory was still incomplete, he maintained that it held an "irresistible attraction" for those who hungered for truth and intellectual freedom. He declared that philosophers and "critically-minded theologians" had been unable to expel the supernatural because of their inability to discover a natural process to replace it. Darwin had come to their rescue. He had "opened a door" through which it was now possible to "thrust the supernatural into eternal banishment."[10] It seemed that Darwin had made disbelief in the supernatural world credible.

Two books in particular helped to popularize the notion that there was a conflict between religion and science. These were John William Draper's *History of the Conflict Between Religion and Science* (1874); and Andrew Dickson White's *A History of the Warfare of Science with Theology in Christendom* (1896), published in a series of editions from the 1870s. Frequent assertions by strident evolutionists significantly influenced popular opinion.[11] Roman Catholicism was often singled out for attack by those who extrapolated evolutionary theory beyond the natural sciences. This was especially true of Britain where anti-Catholicism was rife for reasons that had little to do with science.

Anti-Catholicism and Science

In the early decades of the nineteenth century, Roman Catholicism in Britain was socially and politically marginalized, numerically weak, and educationally disadvantaged. It could not have been reasonably feared as a serious threat to the primacy of Protestantism. However, the Catholic Church benefited enormously from a number of changes from mid-century onwards. From the late 1840s their numbers grew rapidly, as thousands of Catholics from Ireland fled famine and poverty. Many Irish Catholics traveled from Britain to the United States of America, Canada, and Australia; but tens of thousands settled in Britain. In English society there was a tendency to compare them with African Negroes, who were, allegedly, "thoroughly sunk in ignorance, idolatry, and moral degradation."[12] The Irish were regarded as intemperate, thriftless, dirty, diseased, idle, superstitious, and strongly inclined toward criminal behavior. Walter L. Arnstein, in reference to racial and religious prejudice in Victorian society, observed (although acknowledging some degree of oversimplification and exaggeration) that "Victorian Englishmen looked upon both Roman Catholics and Irishmen as inferior to themselves, and when Irishmen turned out to be Roman Catholic, as they generally did, then Englishmen considered them doubly inferior."[13] Irish Catholics were a liability on their church in England because of their pressing need for social services on a vast scale. However, in time they played a major role in transforming the Roman Catholic population of Britain into a numerically significant, disciplined, and assertive minority.[14]

As Catholicism prospered in Britain, its doctrines gained the confidence of a number of eminent intellectuals, most notably John Henry Newman, the leading figure of the Oxford Movement in the Church of England. In 1850 Pope Pius IX, in response to expanding Catholic numbers, restored the hierarchy of England and Wales (and Scotland in 1878). He appointed Nicholas Wiseman as cardinal archbishop of Westminster and the first Catholic primate since the Reformation. Wiseman's tactless remarks at his elevation provoked anti-Catholic rioting in England, hostile sermons from Anglican pulpits, and an outpouring of anti-papal rhetoric. But anti-Catholicism was never far from the surface. In the early 1870s fears of a powerful Irish political movement under the leadership of Roman Catholic priests, and concerns about the emergence of an educational system under the control of a church tainted by Catholic ritualistic practices, exacerbated anti-Catholic sentiment.[15]

Papal dogmatism served to intensify the prejudice against Roman Catholicism that was so prevalent in Protestant societies—not least in Victorian Britain. After the publication of the *Syllabus of Errors* in 1864, the general perception, especially in England, was that the pope had rejected all the principles and liberties of contemporary civilization. Furthermore, liberal Catholics were very disconcerted by the papal pronouncements.[16] In 1870 there was another resurgence of hostility against the papacy because of the declarations made by the First Vatican Council. (The *Syllabus of Errors* and the First Vatican Council will be discussed in the next chapter.) British Protestants reacted angrily against the lofty claims of the papacy, and this intensified their suspicions of Cardinal Paul Cullen and the Irish Catholic hierarchy, who were among the most ardent supporters of ultramontanism.[17]

The British statesman William Gladstone, leader of the Liberal Party and four times prime minister between 1868 and 1894, was outraged by the Vatican decrees.[18] He claimed that Rome had "refurbished and paraded anew every rusty tool she was fondly thought to have disused. . . . That no one can now become her convert without renouncing his moral and mental freedom, and placing his civil loyalty and duty at the mercy of another" and "that she [Rome] has equally repudiated modern thought and ancient history."[19] These statements were so deeply resented in Ireland that Gladstone, then in opposition, wrote a sixty-six-page pamphlet in support of his views. It was published in 1874 under the title *The Vatican Decrees in Their Bearing on Civil Allegiance: A Political Expostulation.* Gladstone devoted considerable attention to the decrees of the Vatican Council concerning papal infallibility and obedience to the pope, which, in his opinion, were subversive of the civil allegiance that Roman Catholics owed to their nation-state.[20] The pamphlet received favorable reviews from most English and Scottish newspapers, and in the first two months 145,000 copies were sold.[21] However, the Vatican decrees, and Gladstone's *Expostulation*, did not provoke anti-papal agitation comparable to that of 1850–1851, when the Catholic hierarchy was formally restored by Pope Pius IX.[22]

Anti-Catholicism in Britain was sometimes remarkably effective in uniting aristocrats and laborers, Anglicans and nonconformist Protestants, right-wing Tories and left-wing Liberals in a common cause. Anti-Catholic views were quite common in intellectual circles—both Protestant and secular. Notable examples of anti-Catholic rhetoric can be found in Herbert Spencer's and Edward Taylor's denunciation of priestcraft, William Clifford's strident anticlericalism, and the critical articles of

Leslie Stephen on English religion in American journals. Tyndall, Huxley, Spencer, and other proponents of scientific naturalism became prominent among those who publicly opposed Roman Catholicism.[23]

Huxley's anti-Catholicism was clearly evident in his speeches to the London School Board, and his extreme criticism of the English Catholic scientist St. George Jackson Mivart. However, despite his contempt for Roman Catholicism, Huxley had a peculiar respect for it. About 1873 he visited Ireland's leading seminary, St. Patrick's College, Maynooth. He viewed it as the most important institution for the training of Catholic priests in the United Kingdom of Great Britain and Ireland. He regarded Catholic priests as worthy opponents, unlike the "comfortable" defenders of Anglicanism and Protestant Dissent. They were trained to know their business and to do it effectively. The professors of the college—"learned, zealous, and determined men"—had agreed to a candid exchange of opinions. They talked with Huxley—"like outposts of opposed armies during a truce—as friendly enemies." He was informed by the college professors that the Roman Catholic Church had survived many dangers over the centuries, and they confidently declared that it would not be destroyed by its enemies. Seminarians were being systematically trained so that they would be able to rise to the challenge of refuting contemporary criticisms of Christianity.

Huxley expressed his deep respect for an organization that so vigorously confronted its enemies, and he wished that other religious bodies were so well prepared for battles of the intellect. Liberal thinkers were in "very loose order" and, in his opinion, contemporary freethinkers all too frequently used their freedom to express nonsense. A strong and determined enemy would compel those who were not shackled to religious dogmas and authority to organize and discipline themselves for the struggle ahead.[24]

The friction between Catholic conservatism and modern scientific theories was frequently represented by anticlerical scientists as an issue of intellectual freedom struggling against religious obscurantism and censorship. They, and many of their contemporaries, believed that if religious and intellectual liberty were to be promoted and protected then it was imperative to work toward the demise of Roman Catholicism. Tyndall and Huxley, continental anticlericals, positivists in Latin America, Ralph Ingersoll, and other American freethinkers expressed this idea. However, many of those who advocated anti-Catholicism were not consistently liberal in their views and sometimes supported illiberal causes such as Bismarck's *Kulturkampf*, British rule in Ireland, and the opposition of

American Protestants to the immigration of European Catholics. These and other manifestations of anti-Catholicism elicited strident support from scientific communities in various countries.[25]

In Britain, the Church of England, claiming that it was promoting a learned theology, represented itself as a safeguard against the dangers of Roman Catholicism. However, those with a secular outlook, including irreligious scientists, were among those who questioned its ability to fulfill this role. They aspired to take over the role of the Church of England as the leading educators of the nation.[26] In working toward their objective they associated anti-Catholic polemics with the advancement of science. This proved to be very advantageous because it enabled them to tap into popular anti-papal opinion in Britain.[27] The Roman Catholic Church, especially under Pope Pius IX, was viewed as an institution exercising the most extreme form of religious repression over its members. The *Syllabus of Errors* and the assertion of papal infallibility were not the only sources of antagonism. The power of the Roman Catholic Church in Ireland was deeply resented by some scientists. Catholicism in Ireland was seen as a great obstacle to science and therefore to progress. Ireland was regarded as an integral part of the British state and, from the perspective of Victorian scientific naturalism, it epitomized the potential of ecclesiastical authority to stifle the progress of a nation.[28]

Huxley and Tyndall

In Britain the adverse impact of Darwin's theory on religion was exacerbated by the close interdependence between religion and science that had been constructed on a foundation of natural theology. If Darwin was correct, then life could be explained without recourse to God's design and purpose. Theology would be expelled from its last foothold in the natural sciences. Accidental variations and natural causes alone could be used to explain progressive changes. Darwinism thus exposed the inherent dangers arising from an extensive intellectual domain claimed by both religion and science and made it easier for Huxley to promote his conflict hypothesis.[29] He used extremely provocative rhetoric, as the following quotation will indicate.

> Extinguished theologians lie about the cradle of every science as the strangled snakes beside that of Hercules; and history records that whenever science and orthodoxy have been fairly opposed, the latter has been forced to retire . . . bleeding and crushed, if not annihilated; scotched, if not slain.[30]

In June 1860, Huxley had clashed publicly with the Anglican bishop Samuel Wilberforce on the issue of evolution. A popular misunderstanding, fostered by the supporters of scientific rationalism, was that Huxley discredited the antievolutionary arguments of Wilberforce. Scientific rationality was supposed to have triumphed over traditional superstition —but there was no clear victor on that occasion.[31] The controversy arising from *The Origin of Species* was not predominantly a confrontation between clergymen and scientists. It was more of a confrontation between religious and irreligious scientists.[32] Many scientists were men of faith, and some of the clergy believed in Darwin's theory. The reaction of theologians to *The Origin of Species* was just as varied as the reaction among scientists.[33] Furthermore, a number of scientists objected to evolution on a scientific basis and had some justification for doing so (scientific objections to Darwinism will be discussed later). Huxley's notion of conflict was an exaggeration, and an oversimplification, of the complex relationship between religion and science, but it served his purpose and that of his like-minded colleagues. The polemical stance helped scientists to assert their independence from external influence that had dictated, in the past, how science should be applied to social problems.[34]

Huxley earned a reputation as a witty writer and debater, and he enjoyed great popularity among the working-class men who attended his public lectures. His talent for simplifying extremely complex concepts enabled him to communicate the basic tenets of evolutionary theory to those who were uneducated or poorly educated. His lectures played a major role in publicizing the idea of evolution, and the journalists who attended some of his rather simplistic expositions spread the message of science to a much broader audience.

It is important to emphasize at this point that Huxley's crusade for science was motivated by considerations far greater than those pertaining to professional interests. The pursuit of truth was of paramount importance to him. From his perspective the dogmas of Christianity, such as the infallibility of the Bible, were not self-evident. He acknowledged that people had the right to believe what they liked, but he argued that

> every man should be able to give a reason for the faith that is in him . . . it is the fundamental axiom of modern science. . . . In matters of the intellect, follow your reason as far as it will take you, without regard for any other consideration . . . do not pretend that conclusions are certain which are not demonstrated or demonstrable. This I take to be the agnostic faith. . . .[35]

Although Huxley believed that there was no evidence for the existence of God, this did not lead him to embrace atheism, because it was "on purely philosophical grounds untenable."[36] However, if religious belief was not substantiated, then the imperative of intellectual integrity could only lead one to decline acceptance of such belief even if this decision should "wreck morality and insure our own damnation several times over." But he did not fear that society would be torn apart by immoral behavior sim-ply because of the discovery that biblical narratives were mythical rather than historical. On the contrary, his understanding of history convinced him that goodness did not emerge from falsehood.[37]

Huxley was not hostile to religion in all its manifestations. Religion as spiritual aspiration and as a basis for morality was not offensive to him. He even supported the reading of the Bible in the educational system (free of theology and subject to corrections) because it served to inculcate moral values.[38] But the rejection of religious faith, he believed, did not necessar-ily lead to immoral behavior. His personal life served as a good example in support of such an opinion.

His opposition to religious faith was provoked by his perception of its dogmatic theology, its hierarchical authority, its unhistorical assertions, and its unscientific pronouncements. Huxley argued that "the books of ecclesiastical authority" were contrary to science on numerous issues con-cerning the origins of the universe, the beginning of life, and human his-tory. He anticipated that the theologians would be forced to "surrender" or to retreat by the advances of science. Their long-term position was "hopelessly untenable."[39] He envisaged that the "Christian Heathen" of Britain and Ireland would be converted to "the true faith" by "scientific missionaries."[40] Science was nothing more than "trained and organised common sense,"[41] based on observation, experiment, and evidence rather than on dogmatic authority. In emphasizing its crucial importance, he argued that modern civilization would not have developed without progress in science and that Britain's status as a leading nation was depen-dent on its benefits.

John Tyndall, like Huxley, played a prominent role in promoting the liberalization of science and in advancing its professional status. As a physicist he rose to prominence in British science, becoming professor at the Royal Institution of Great Britain in 1854. He played a leading role in the X Club. His views merit close attention because of his central role in the controversies concerning the relationship between religion and sci-ence. Physics, in his opinion, was not merely an instrument of material prosperity. Like other branches of science it represented a noble pursuit of truth. In order to be a successful physicist it was absolutely essential to cultivate an attitude of honest receptivity and a willingness to discard preconceived ideas, no matter how cherished, if they were found to contradict newly discovered facts. Thus, physics was an agent of high intellectual culture.[42]

Tyndall, like Darwin and Huxley, was an agnostic. Agnosticism, in this Victorian context, was a variant of skepticism based on Kantian epistemology, German transcendentalism, and English empiricism.[43] Tyndall, like Huxley, was willing to engage in debate with those of any religious persuasion, including spiritualists. Spiritualism had become popular in Victorian society from the mid-1860s. In many homes throughout Britain attempts were made to contact the disembodied spirits of those who had died. A number of eminent figures, including Alfred Russel Wallace, were interested in this phenomenon. In his essay "Science and the Spirits," Tyndall gives an account of his experience when he accepted an invitation to attend a *séance* in London. It served only to consolidate his cynicism toward claims of supernatural phenomena. He believed that spiritualists were "beyond the reach of proof" because they had succumbed to "the weed of superstition" and did not wish to be enlightened. After this disheartening experience, further invitations were extended to him, but the "spirits" did not improve with further acquaintance. Thus he concluded that "no baser delusion ever obtained dominance over the weak mind of man."[44]

Tyndall was harshly critical of the clergy because, through their control of the educational system, they sometimes obstructed the application of scientific remedies to concrete problems. In the 1860s he publicly questioned the efficacy of prayer. Special prayers for the alleviation of such problems as poor harvests and cattle plague tended to consolidate ignorance rather than stimulate a rational and active response. Investigations of the real causes of scarcity and disease were neglected while a "delusive reliance" on supernatural intervention predominated.[45] Tyndall therefore believed that the superstitions of the clergy and their claims concerning the natural sciences were not harmless—they were perceived as obstacles to progress.[46]

Miracles were placed in the same category as witchcraft and magic, and all these were presented as part of a superstitious mentality that had hindered progress and had instigated crimes against humanity in the name of Christianity and justice. But modern science, he believed, was making it more difficult to sustain belief in miraculous events.[47] Despite all this, Tyndall, as an agnostic, could not absolutely rule out the possibility of miracles. If an omnipotent being created the universe he was capable of interfering with or suspending the laws of nature. In a strict logical sense, consistent with agnosticism, Tyndall could not affirm or deny the occurrence of miracles. However, he asserted that no one else could either, because the power of the Almighty was not evident from nature and could only be attributed to the human imagination. Thus,

> the pictorial representations of the Deity, the bodies and wings of cherubs and seraphs, the hoofs, horns, and tail of the Evil One, the joys of the blessed, and the torments of the damned, have been elaborated from materials furnished to the imagination by the senses. It behoves you and me to take care that our notions of the Power which rules the universe are not mere fanciful or ignorant enlargements of human power. (p. 38)

Tyndall, notwithstanding his vigorous assaults on religious belief, was not blind to what science was unable to achieve. For example, could the human mind be explained totally in purely physical terms, without recourse to a spiritual dimension? Tyndall speculated that there might be a correlation between physicochemical actions in the brain and mental processes. However, he realized his inherent inability as a scientist to explain the human mind. Even if science could identify and elaborate on the connections between brain biochemistry and different states of mind, this would only amount to empirical association—the underlying nature of the connection would not be elucidated. Two classes of phenomena, fundamentally different from each other, were separated by a chasm that defied logical explanation—hence Tyndall's exhortation: "Let us lower our heads, and acknowledge our ignorance, priest and philosopher, one and all" (pp. 87–88).

On 16 September 1870 Tyndall spoke about the "Scientific Use of the Imagination" at a conference organized by the British Association in Liverpool. Despite his trenchant criticisms of traditional religious thinking, he had sustained a friendly relationship with a small number of clergymen, and he paid tribute to those members of the clergy who had changed their views on scripture in the light of scientific discoveries (p. 129). Furthermore, he displayed a rather transient sensitivity to Christian faith, which he acknowledged as an important antecedent of contemporary culture. Enlightened clergymen were valued allies because they had an important role to play in making the public mind more receptive to new ways of thinking consistent with the tenets of modern science (p. 6).

The question of human origins aroused intense interest. In attempting to provide answers concerning cosmology and human origins it was deemed absolutely necessary to repress dogmatic assertions. Intellectual freedom was to be encouraged, which would transcend narrow empiricism and embrace speculation—subject to rational discourse (p. 128). In common with Huxley and other first-generation Darwinists (including Darwin), Tyndall saw biological evolution as part of a far greater cosmic process. He defended the evolutionary hypothesis, which maintained that all forms of life—even the human mind itself—"were once latent in a fiery cloud." Thus, "all our philosophy, all our poetry, all our science, and all our art—Plato, Shakespeare, Newton and Raphael—are potential in the fires of the sun" (p. 131). Tyndall was led to the outer boundary of speculative science. The origin of the nebular cloud, which was thought to have formed the universe, was not, and could not, be explained by science. Therefore, the "ultimate" mystery of the universe remained untouched by the physical sciences. Evolutionary theory, he believed, was quite compatible with the "virtues" of Christianity. It did "nothing more than transport the conception of life's origin to an indefinitely distant past" (p. 133). Tyndall acknowledged that there was much uncertainty about various aspects of evolutionary theory and was mindful of the limitations of science. Science was a search for truth based on the "uniformity" or laws of nature. It could neither prove nor disprove the existence of God and was therefore as far removed from the atheist as from the theist (pp. 132–34). God, if God existed, was not evident in nature.

Tyndall's Belfast Address and the Irish Catholic Bishops

On 19 August 1874 Tyndall delivered his famous Belfast address. At the time he was president of the British Association for the Advancement of Science. The controversy stimulated by his presidential address to the British Association was much greater than that arising from the polemical encounter of Huxley and Wilberforce, and it may even rank as the most important confrontation between religious apologists and the proponents of agnostic science in Victorian Britain.[48] For this reason the address, and the events surrounding it, deserve detailed discussion here.

Tyndall was deeply distrustful of Roman Catholicism and regarded it as detrimental to intellectual freedom. He believed that his native country, Ireland, served as a particularly good example of how the Roman Catholic Church could obstruct the progress of science, much to the detriment of society. On 29 November 1873 "a Memorial addressed, by Seventy of the Students and Ex-students of the Catholic University in Ireland, to the

Episcopal Board of the University" highlighted concerns about the mismanagement and defective educational system of the institution. This document, which "appeared for a moment" and then "unaccountably vanished from public view," did not escape Tyndall's attention.[49] Strong views were expressed about the neglect of science. It was claimed that the lecture list of the university did not include the name of even one professor or lecturer of the natural sciences for the faculty of arts. The signatories strenuously argued their case. They claimed that if science did not receive due attention then the university could not hope to rise to a position of prominence among the educational institutions of the country. Furthermore, the neglect of science was

> to be regretted, as it has afforded a very plausible argument to the enemies of the Catholic University, who never tire of repeating that the Catholic Church is the enemy of science. . . . Now, this is, of course, a sneer; but we are sorry to say it is a sneer with a sufficient gilding of truth to give it currency. We do not know of any reply to such taunts so conclusive as the foundation of a great school of science in the University. No one can deny that the Irish Catholics are miserably deficient in scientific education. That deficiency is extremely galling to us. In a commercial sense it involves a loss to us, while in a social and intellectual sense it is a positive degradation.[50]

The future of the institution was under threat if this deficiency persisted, but there was a much greater issue to be addressed. Scientific studies were regarded as preeminent and were a potent weapon in the hands of "infidel" writers whose objective it was to discredit the biblical texts. This threat to the faith was to be counteracted by educated Catholics who would use science to defend scripture. Therefore, in reference to the poor scientific education of Catholics, the signatories declared:

> We are determined that such inferiority shall exist no longer. If scientific training be unattainable in their own University, Irish Catholics will seek it at Trinity or the Queen's Colleges, or they will study for themselves the works of Haeckel, Darwin, Huxley, Tyndall, and Lyell.[51]

The protestors then called upon the bishops, as a matter of urgency, to recruit competent teachers of science but the bishops did not respond positively. This incident was to deeply influence Tyndall's Belfast address.

Tyndall traced the history of science from its rudimentary state in ancient Greece to the modern discoveries of the nineteenth century. Christianity, he believed, had stifled the advancement of science for centuries.[52] The stagnation of Western intellectual thought was overcome gradually, starting with the Copernican discoveries, and the new astronomy was underpinned by the philosophies of Bacon and Descartes. Progress continued and was consolidated by the scientific revolution that gave rise to Newtonian physics and the empirical philosophy of John Locke. This in turn formed the basis of nineteenth-century science. Tyndall's historical perspective was not unusual among eminent scientists. It was based on the published work of the Enlightenment *philosophes*, and especially on *The Intellectual Development of Europe* (1862) by John W. Draper.[53] His understanding of history, therefore, supported his contention that scientists should "wrest from theology, the entire domain of cosmological theory."[54]

Tyndall argued that nature should be studied without recourse to teleology—it was to be liberated from "the meddling of the gods."[55] Deities were to be displaced by the "grand generalisations" of science (pp. 180–81). These included the conservation of energy, the conservation of matter, and the theory of evolution expounded by Darwin, Wallace, Huxley, and other scientists. Science had its limitations, however: for example, it was "utterly incongruous" that the interactions and combinations of "dead" atoms could give rise to sensations, thoughts, and emotions (pp. 167–68, 193–95). Darwin's theory had its weaknesses, and it did not attempt to explain how primordial life originated (pp. 179, 189). Tyndall, confronted with these insurmountable problems, realized that there were two choices: invoke the notion of creative acts, or radically change current ideas pertaining to matter (p. 189). Determined to expel God from scientific thinking, he chose the latter option.

Working within the constraints of empiricism proved too restrictive for Tyndall; therefore he resorted to speculation in place of the supernatural. Speculation might lead to error, but it was still justified if it was consistent with scientific thought (pp. 191–92, 194, 200). The avoidance of dogma would leave scientific theories open to correction. Tyndall emphasized that speculation was an important element of scientific research; he declared:

> Believing, as I do, in the continuity of nature, I cannot stop abruptly where our microscopes cease to be of use. Here the vision of the mind authoritatively supplements the vision of the eye. By a necessity engendered and justified by science I cross the boundary of the experimental evidence, and discern in . . . Matter . . . the promise and potency of all terrestrial Life. (p. 191)

He attributed to matter what was commonly attributed to God, and by doing so he was certain to provoke a hostile reaction. But, anticipating this, he still did not refrain from expressing his opinions. He was aware that the religious element of human nature was a powerful force. For the masses it offered a degree of comfort and assurance in the face of adversity. Tyndall's friend Huxley had been confronted with the comforting allure of religion but had deprived himself of its potential benefits. Tyndall also declined to seek sanctuary in the embrace of religion because he felt unable to "purchase intellectual peace at the price of intellectual death" (p. 200). He exhorted his readers to adopt the same position.

Tyndall acknowledged that science did not answer all the intellectual needs of humanity. Nor did it penetrate the veil imposed by the nebular cloud—what lay beyond it was a mystery. In his concluding remarks Tyndall urged that "the Mystery" from which the universe had emerged should be discussed without fear of bigotry (p. 201). However, this conciliating exhortation was more than offset by his aggressive assertions against religious beliefs. Religion had no place in the domain of "objective knowledge," and it was the duty of those who exerted influence over public opinion to do their utmost to prevent it from reasserting its "despotic sway" over the human intellect (p. 196). Tyndall was cautiously optimistic about the future. Science was a transforming influence in the world, its impact would increase with time. Even Ireland, in the throes of a religious revival, offered some hope to the Irish physicist.

> I should look upon the mild light of science breaking in upon the minds of the youth of Ireland, and strengthening gradually to the perfect day, as a surer check to any intellectual or spiritual tyranny which may threaten this island, than the laws of princes or the swords of emperors. (p. 197)

The Irish Catholic hierarchy, understandably, was offended by such statements, but the antagonized response extended far beyond the boundaries of Irish Catholicism. Tyndall's presidential address provoked an outcry from both Catholics and Protestants inside and outside of Ireland. His views were already well known, but on this occasion his contentious statements received far more attention because he was president of a prestigious scientific organization.[56]

The Irish Catholic bishops did not remain silent about Tyndall's quest for truth, nor about the scientific speculations of many of his colleagues. On 14 October 1874 they issued a pastoral letter, written by Bishop Patrick Francis Moran (1830–1912) of Ossory (1872–1884) and later archbishop of Sydney (1884–1911). Moran was a protégé and nephew of the first Irish cardinal, Paul Cullen. He was chosen to write this document because he was the only signatory who had some scientific knowledge and training. It is also noteworthy that Moran, like Tyndall, was born in Leighlinbridge, Co. Carlow, Ireland, and was educated by the teacher John Conwill, who had also taught Tyndall.[57] The bishops declared that the professors of materialism had, "under the name of Science, obtruded blasphemy upon this Catholic nation."[58] Tyndall was clearly the main target of their denunciation. His agnostic pronouncements, and those of other scientists, were perceived as a direct threat to the faith.

The bishops argued that if man was only a product of the interplay of physicochemical laws, then he was a mere "conscious automaton." The soul was supplanted by the nervous system, and liberty was nothing more than an illusion as humans responded to the irresistible impulses of natural laws. This, if widely accepted, had dire implications for the welfare of humanity. The bishops asserted that if there was no free will then there could be no moral responsibility, no sin, no holiness, and hence no justifiable punishment for criminal offenses. Man would be little more than a "brute," bereft of moral dignity, devoid of charity and self-sacrifice, and with little inclination toward duty. All this would lead to social disintegration accompanied by a "universal unchaining of all the worst passions ravenous for satisfaction" (pp. 593–94).

The Irish Catholic bishops relied on the Dogmatic Constitution on the Catholic Faith for theological guidance, referring to it as the "Charter of Catholic Science." This document enunciated the fundamental principle that it is not possible for conflict to arise between religion and science— when both are properly understood (pp. 602–4). The bishops quoted extensively from Newman's lecture "Christianity and Physical Science," given at the School of Medicine at the Catholic University of Ireland (pp. 596–98). On that occasion Newman emphasized the Baconian method, which effectively limited the scope of science and reduced the probability of conflict with theology.[59] The bishops, mindful of the central importance of Baconian methodology in the practice of science, used it to their advantage. They stressed the distinction to be made between the unproven claims of some scientists from the proven findings of science in general. On this basis they believed that theories concerning spontaneous generation, natural selection, and "other favourites of the hour" were unsubstantiated and unscientific.[60] They asserted that modern science, dominated by materialistic thinking, had exceeded its proper limits by constructing a new cosmogony. Science per se did not support materialistic theories. It was not the purpose of science to put forward theories of cosmogony—it was to investigate facts. Science was to be circumscribed. It was to ascertain, compare, and classify natural phenomena with reference to the laws of nature. It was not to go beyond the examination of cause and effect. The physicist, in his capacity as a physicist, was not to hypothesize about external influences on the universe—science had nothing to say about the subject (pp. 596–97).

The agnosticism expressed by Tyndall was inimical to the faith of Catholics and Protestants alike. A common threat should have brought them closer together, but this did not happen in Ireland. Tyndall's address served only to exacerbate mutual antagonism. The Catholic bishops were critical of Protestantism, seeing it a facilitator of materialistic influences in the educational system. Tyndall's address stiffened their resolve to gain firm control over that part of the system which was to serve the needs of Catholics. They were concerned that public opinion did not distinguish materialistic opinions from the substantiated findings of scientific research. Thus, in an age of "unparalleled hostility" toward the Catholic Church, there was a danger that the pronouncements of the materialists would lead "weak minds," especially those of Irish youth, to perdition (pp. 595–96, 604, 608). The bishops noted that Tyndall had been quite explicit about his expectation that scientific education—of the "godless" variety—would gradually detach the youth of Ireland from the Catholic faith (p. 606). Therefore, they were more determined than ever to secure for Irish Catholics an educational system under episcopal authority, where science would be "explained according to the mind of the Church" (pp. 604–7). Ironically, Tyndall's Belfast address served the hierarchy's interests. This is most clearly evident when, in reference to his aspirations, they declared:

> They justify to the full the determination of Catholic Ireland not to allow her young men to frequent Universities and Colleges where Science is made the vehicle of Materialism. They rebuke the indifference of those who may be tempted to grow slack in the struggle for a Catholic system of education. They serve to convince of their error those well meaning men who are reluctant to believe that the Chairs of Science in Ireland are ever converted into pulpits, whence infidelity and irreligion are disseminated. (pp. 606–7)

A columnist for *The Times* (31 October 1874) was quick to note the astuteness of the hierarchy. It was observed that Tyndall had unwittingly served the interests of the Catholic bishops by being so forthright. The "simple people" had suffered "a kind of scare" and the bishops—not handicapped by simplicity—had been quick to take advantage of it. They were now able to impress upon the Catholic laity, with greater effectiveness, the grievous dangers to the faith posed by secular education, particularly the "godless" nondenominational Queen's Colleges of Cork, Belfast, and Galway. This in turn served the cause of securing a system of education under their control where science would be tightly controlled and purged of materialistic tendencies.[61]

In Protestant-dominated Belfast, the Catholic hierarchy's assertion that strictly limited science to facts derived from experiment and observation provoked some harsh criticism on the grounds that it contradicted scripture. Reverend Robert Watts, professor of systematic theology at Assembly's College (also known as Presbyterian College) was sharply critical of both Tyndall's speech and the pastoral letter of the Irish Catholic bishops. On 23 August he excoriated the views of Tyndall when he delivered a sermon at Fisherwick Place Church. His attack on Tyndall's address was reported in the Presbyterian newspaper *The Witness* (28 August 1874). The sermon was so popular that it was reissued as a pamphlet. Five thousand copies were reported sold in the first month. The reprint of his pamphlet, entitled "Atomism: Dr. Tyndall's Atomic Theory of the Universe Examined and Refuted" (1875), included an appendix that castigated the pastoral letter of the Catholic bishops. Watts opposed the restriction of science to the empirical domain and its separation from religion. This, he claimed, would lead to the secularization of science. Furthermore, it was contrary to scripture, which declared that "the Word of God enjoins it upon men as a duty to infer the invisible things of the Creator from the things that are made." Therefore Watts maintained that the attitude of the Catholic hierarchy in this matter was contrary to the Bible.[62] This was not clearly the case. The opinion of Watts was almost certainly based on Romans 1:20; however, the Irish Catholic bishops did take cognizance of this scriptural verse when they quoted *De Fide Catholica* (Dogmatic Constitution on the Catholic Faith [1870]).[63] Evidently, they read it with philosophy in mind rather than looking to science for direct evidence of God's existence.

Meanwhile, Tyndall had remained defiant in the face of adversity. His "Apology for the Belfast Address" (1874) was an apologia rather than an apology; it reaffirmed what he had said in Belfast. He denied the charge of atheism,[64] but, as an agnostic, he remained adamant that God, if he existed, was beyond human reach and had no place in scientific thought. Tyndall embraced the nebular hypothesis as elaborated by Immanuel Kant, Pierre Simon de Laplace, and William Herschel. He envisaged the potency for life in the primordial universe and did not see any need for the creative power of a deity to explain it. But could not God, from outside the nebula, guide its development and infuse it with a great diversity of life forms? Tyndall had little time for this argument and declared

As far as the eye of science has hitherto ranged through nature, no intrusion of purely creative power into any series of phenomena has ever been observed. The assumption of such a power to account for special phenomena, though often made, has always proved a failure. It is opposed to the very spirit of science. (p. 209)

This view was, apparently, tainted by dogmatism—a fault reprehensible to Tyndall. Therefore, mindful of this danger, he qualified his statements: his refusal to accept the theistic hypothesis was not based on an assertion supported by fact; rather it was a protest against an assumption of something that was, in reality, unknowable. Genesis had been discredited by geology; it was a "poem, not a scientific treatise" (p. 210).

Tyndall castigated the "extravagances" and "foolish notions" of religious life and defended his foray into the domain of theology, arguing that when an eminent presidential predecessor of his expressed views supportive of religion no protest was made about trespassing on theological territory (p. 207). He claimed the same right of intrusion. Natural history was a progressive process and so also was science—destined to lift humanity out of ignorance while enhancing the quality of life. The human mind, dependent on matter and resident in the nervous system, would mold the moral and intellectual dimension of human nature. Did such a dependency of mind on matter degrade humanity? Tyndall thought not. Matter and mind could be raised to a higher level by liberation from ignorance (pp. 218–19); however, the defenders of faith obstructed progress.

The Irish Catholic bishops were singled out for special attention. Tyndall had read the article in *The Times* (31 October 1874), which caused him to see their pastoral letter of 14 October in a new light. In his opinion the bishops were "usually too wise to confer notoriety upon an adversary by imprudently denouncing him" (p. 210). This lent credence to the opinion expressed in *The Times* that the bishops had used the Belfast address to their advantage. However, this pungent insight did not give him cause for regret because his primary objective was not to diminish the power of the Irish Catholic bishops—it was to liberate science from restrictive external influences, especially emanating from organized religion. He had studied the pamphlet dated November 1873, issued by the students and ex-students of the Catholic University in Ireland, and quoted it extensively in making the point that Irish Catholics were "writhing under the sense of their inferiority in science" (p. 212). According to Tyndall, the signatories should not have been surprised by the conspicuous absence of Irish Catholics in the upper echelons of the natural sciences because they ought to have known that their complaint issued forth from "free and cultivated minds wherever a Priesthood exercises dominant power" (p. 213). A similar complaint had been made with reference to the Catholics of Germany. The "Jesuitical system" had "crushed out of Catholics every tendency to free mental productiveness," especially in countries where ultramontanism had become deeply entrenched. Ireland and Spain were most deeply affected, but Tyndall noted that "the Irish intellect is beginning to show signs of independence" (pp. 213–14). He was wrong. Throughout the following decades the bishops were remarkably successful in consolidating their control over the minds of the Catholic majority. The ultramontanism, so abhorrent to Tyndall, was triumphant and remained undiminished up to the 1960s—long after he had "melted into the infinite azure of the past." Furthermore, his tendency for polemics made it more difficult for scientists and clergymen to reach a compromise. The Irish Catholic bishops remained vigilant and inordinately defensive. In September 1875 they renewed their condemnation of wayward science when they castigated "the assaults of infidelity and the contradictory wranglings of so-called scientific theories."[65] However, they had little to fear from Tyndall. Although he was highly influential abroad,[66] he exerted little influence in his native country.[67]

Catholicism and Evolutionary Theory in the English-Speaking World

The ultramontane variant of Irish Catholicism prospered not only in Ireland but far beyond the shores of that troubled country. Irish Catholicism played a central role in the development and expansion of the Roman Catholic Church in English-speaking countries such as Scotland, England, the United States of America, most of Canada, Australia, New Zealand, and South Africa.[68] It is very likely that Irish Catholic priests and bishops serving in these new environments strongly influenced the outlook of their congregations on a wide range of issues, including the theory of evolution. As Tyndall preached the gospel of agnosticism at Belfast, Cardinal Cullen was sending "a steady stream of protégés, imbued with his own ultramontane and combative brand of Irish Catholicism" to Australia and New Zealand.[69] The general tendency of Catholics in these countries was to reject evolutionary theory or ignore it, especially when Darwinism featured as an element of strident anti-Catholicism. Furthermore, a number of other conditions probably militated against the acceptance of evolution. In the case of New Zealand, in the 1880s, newly arrived

Catholics were so preoccupied with the building of churches, schools, seminaries, and other facilities that they had very little time for intellectual pursuits. Besides, many of these Catholics were poorly educated and probably did not know about the contentious issues at the interface of science and religion.[70]

Evolutionary theory fared little better among Catholics in England. In the 1860s it seems that the majority of English Catholics did not know how to respond to Darwin's theory and reacted "with a sort of inarticulate horror." The dominant tendency was to remain silent.[71] By the 1880s there was apparently very little change in outlook. St. George Jackson Mivart discovered, with very few exceptions, "a condemnation of evolution, if not of science, based upon ignorance and prejudice" among the English Catholic laity.[72] John Henry Newman, in correspondence with Mivart, defended Catholic priests who were frequently confronted with the troublesome implications of modern scientific theories. Newman argued that priests were in the front line of an ongoing battle with unbelief. They were poorly trained for such a role because they did not have sufficient time to educate themselves in the natural sciences, especially concerning theories that were difficult to harmonize with the Bible. The weakness of this argument is that it did not take cognizance of the fact that science was neglected in the seminaries.[73] Newman maintained that the skeptical and unfriendly attitude of priests toward "the whole scientific movement" was reinforced by the use of theories rather than facts in finding fault with biblical texts. The tendency of priests, therefore, was to wait for these theories to be discredited by scientific research rather than expending intellectual energy in overturning error.[74]

The intellectual condition of American Catholicism was probably far less developed than that of English Catholicism. The Catholic Church in the United States of America (like its counterpart in England) was mainly an immigrant church in the mid-nineteenth century, and many of its members, for the most part from Ireland, Germany, Poland, and Italy, were impoverished and poorly educated. Very few had the leisure time and the scientific background to publish their views on evolution. Generally, American Catholics were too busy attending to the practical needs of life —building homes, setting up schools, and starting up businesses—to cultivate a sustained interest in evolution. The clergy were preoccupied with pastoral duties. Furthermore, the Civil War (1861–1865) had greatly impeded the development of intellectual debate. Catholic intellectuals were mainly concerned with enhancing conditions for the preservation of the faith, and they had little confidence in science, or even in natural theology, as a significant beneficial influence.[75] Therefore, it should not be surprising that American Catholicism did not produce an expert on evolutionary theory comparable in stature to Mivart or Asa Gray.[76]

In the 1870s the anti-Catholic views expressed by John William Draper, John Tyndall, and Thomas Henry Huxley all received wide circulation. The anti-Catholic polemics of these and a number of other eminent evolutionists served only to reinforce reactionary attitudes among Catholics; however, the Catholic response to evolutionary theory was not simply one of rejection. The attitude of American Catholics toward evolution, and more generally toward science, was more complicated. The historian William J. Astore, in his analysis of American Catholic attitudes toward evolution and cognate topics from 1845 to 1875, concluded that Catholics firmly believed their church possessed the truth and that this truth, of a transcendental nature, formed the basis of evaluating other forms of knowledge. Only the church could ascertain the real meaning of scripture. If scientific theories contradicted Catholic doctrine, then they were decisively rejected. Those that could be reconciled with the church's teaching—for example, geological theories that indicated that the earth was millions of years old—were either conditionally accepted or tolerated. There was also a resistance to scientific theories that seemed to diminish or eliminate God's role in nature, such as Darwin's idea of natural selection.[77]

Orestes Augustus Brownson (1803–1876), possibly the most influential American Catholic apologist from 1845 to 1875, vigorously opposed the evolutionary concept. The reluctance of Catholics to accept Darwin's theory was influenced considerably by a confluence of ideologies either hostile to, or incompatible with, Roman Catholicism. The Darwinian idea of the "survival of the fittest" was extended to the social sciences—hence the term "social Darwinism," which was used to address a range of controversial issues such as free trade, imperialism, and racial extermination. The association of social Darwinism with nativism—a social movement dedicated to the defense of Anglo-Saxon privilege in the United States, and unambiguously anti-Catholic—was understandably perceived by Catholics as offensive, morally unsound, and threatening in a personal sense.[78] However, in the late 1870s and early 1880s paleontological discoveries, biological publications, and lectures by scientists and by popularizers of science, all tended to make evolutionary theory more acceptable.[79]

The American Catholic response to evolution was influenced by objectives that seemed mutually antagonistic. The result was that opinions were frequently tentative, inconsistent, and unclear. American Catholics wished to reconcile their religious beliefs not only with science but also with mainstream American culture and intellectual life. In doing so they had to struggle with the major difficulty of not stepping beyond what was deemed to be theologically permissible.[80] Some succeeded, but very few went so far as to openly agree with Darwin. The biologist William Seton (1835–1905) was a notable exception. He wrote passionately in favor of Darwinism, and, although he won few converts, it is likely that he persuaded some of his co-religionists at least to consider the probability of non-Darwinian evolution. Seton observed with satisfaction the popularization of evolutionary theory by the Jesuit priest and entomologist Erich Wasmann. The opponents of evolution were still very strong in American Catholicism, but they lost their dominant position in the years from 1890 to 1905.[81]

Agnosticism and Religious Revival

John Tyndall, Thomas Henry Huxley, Herbert Spencer (1820–1903), Leslie Stephen (1832–1904), and William Clifford (1845–1879) were the most influential agnostics in Victorian Britain. By the 1890s Clifford was dead, and those who were still alive were old and tired, and increasingly marginalized. The agnostic movement was in marked decline. Its philosophical complexity had greatly impeded its acceptance among the masses. Values and perspectives formed in the social and intellectual milieu of the late nineteenth century were decisively shattered in the early years of the twentieth century.[82]

In Britain the diminution of religious faith occurred not mainly because of an attack on religion by agnostics and other skeptics but, ironically, as a consequence of the most intense religious crusade that the nation had experienced since the seventeenth century. The historian Frank M. Turner has argued that the propagation of doubt and unbelief was mainly due to the excesses of the religious revival and the bitterness generated by conflict between and within Christian denominations, which influenced the political and educational systems and the social life of the national community.[83] After the undermining of the Anglican confessional state, the Church of England was compelled to compete in the religious marketplace. Increased competition led to a resurgence of religious commitment, not just in the Anglican Church but also in the other Christian denominations. The evangelical Christian movement also contributed significantly to the intensity of British religious life.

In nineteenth-century Britain, religion had been used to provide moral legitimacy for the existing social and political order. This was very much influenced by a reaction to the French Revolution, the policies of which were anticlerical and sometimes even anti-Christian. British scientists, many of them clergymen, had written extensively on natural theology to argue that a correct understanding of science and philosophy led one not toward political revolution and atheism but rather toward support for the existing social and political order and reverence for God.

Religion became associated with a growing number of personal and public issues. It became more and more intrusive, and many people felt compelled to reassess their thinking about the nature and meaning of their religious beliefs. A religion less intrusive and not so demanding would have been easier to isolate from contentious social and intellectual issues. Under these circumstances it would have been less likely to be tested and found inadequate. In the late nineteenth century there was considerable alienation, especially among urban workers, from institutional religion. Church attendance declined, and unquestioning respect for the clergy was less widespread.

Doubters and unbelievers of every hue did, of course, play a significant role in eroding the influence of religious faith. Religious doubt was frequently expressed as a central theme in novels and plays throughout the nineteenth century, and this reached its peak in the 1880s and 1890s.[84] Belief in the inerrancy of the Bible seems to have declined sharply in the last half of the nineteenth century, owing mainly to "scientific" historical criticism.[85] Samuel Taylor Coleridge's *Confessions of an Inquiring Spirit* (1840), George Eliot's translations of both David Friedrich Strauss's *Life of Jesus* (1846) and Ludwig Feuerbach's *Essence of Christianity* (1854), and Ernest Renan's *Life of Jesus* (1863), all contributed very substantially to a diminution of the belief that scripture was free of error.[86] The outcome of all these developments was that intense religiosity existed side by side with skepticism and unbelief.

The natural sciences, in contrast to the mixed fortunes of religion, enjoyed a growing prestige. The application of science in medicine, manufacturing, and engineering led to improvements in the standard of living of most people; and the rapid growth of knowledge that it brought enticed people to worship at new shrines. The vast accumulation of scientific knowledge and the pronouncements of scientists influenced the perceptions and beliefs of ordinary men and women.[87] Huxley, Tyndall, and Spencer had relegated God to the Unknown, beyond scientific investigation and human knowledge. In some quarters evolution was no longer just a mere scientific hypothesis but an explanation of the world. It was applied to the social sciences and profoundly influenced social and economic theory formation. Evolutionary theory, in combination with other scientific discoveries, technical innovations, and improved standards of living, created conditions where the notion of progress found popular acceptance.

The idea of progress could be used to argue for or against religion. From a liberal theological perspective evolution led to the development of higher mental powers and to the emergence of moral sensibilities. This in turn facilitated spiritual progress. Therefore, evolution could be seen as supportive of, rather than contrary to, the belief that humans were divinely created. As indicated above, however, Huxley and his supporters viewed progress as the outcome of natural laws working without any sign of divine intervention.[88]

There were genuine difficulties in reconciling Darwinian evolution with divine purpose or design in nature. Random genetic variation and natural selection, giving rise to the suffering and death of innumerable unfit organisms, seemed very much opposed to any sense of divine purpose. The scientific naturalism of Huxley and Spencer could only have exacerbated Christian fears about the materialistic implications of Darwinism.[89] It was in this intellectual milieu that the custodians of Christian faith felt vulnerable. This in turn provoked in Roman Catholicism, as in other Christian denominations, a hostile and defensive response.

3

A Church under Siege

Pope Pius IX and the *Syllabus of Errors*

THE FRENCH REVOLUTION (1789–1799) GENERATED POWERFUL ideological forces that exerted a profound influence on political, economic, social, and intellectual developments in Europe. Principles such as religious toleration, civil equality, freedom of the press, and liberal ideas about education clashed with the church's traditional perception of its responsibility for the spiritual, moral, and educational welfare of its membership. In the early nineteenth century a liberal anticlerical movement kept the ideals of the Revolution alive. Some liberals even wished for the elimination of religious faith because they believed it was incompatible with reason and they regarded it as an obstacle to social and political progress.

The French Revolution led to a polarization of Catholic opinion. Some Catholics wished to support moderate liberal ideas. These included Fr. Félicité de Lamennais, Archbishop Félix Dupanloup of Orléans, and Count Charles de Montalembert in France, Dr. Ignatz von Döllinger in Germany, and Lord John Acton in England. The ultramontanists were resolutely opposed to liberal reforms and expressed their ultraconservative views through such newspapers as *Civiltà Cattolica* (Rome) and *L'Univers* (Paris). In matters of doctrine they were narrow-minded, intolerant, and aggressive. They made extravagant claims for papal authority and denounced other Catholics whose views they regarded as insufficiently papalist. Those who were prominent in the ultramontane movement included Louis Veuillot (France), William George Ward (England), and Juan Donoso Cortés (Spain). The majority of the Italian and Spanish bishops, and many of the French, German, and British bishops, were also in the ultramontane wing of the church.[1]

The papacy reacted to the revolutionary changes sweeping Europe by attempting to preserve the traditional alliance between the church and conservative regimes. It ignored those Catholics who pointed out that the church was too closely associated with an archaic political system and was, as a consequence, losing contact with a large sector of its membership who were becoming increasingly alienated from the old order. Pope Leo XII (reigned 1823–1829) rejected even moderate liberal proposals. He stifled freedom of the press and suppressed liberal influences in the Papal States. Pope Gregory XVI (reigned 1831–1846) condemned the principles of separation of church and state, freedom of religion, and freedom of the press in his encyclical *Mirari Vos* (1832). The dominant trait of papal policy from 1823 to 1878 was one of intransigence.[2] An institution so politically, economically, and socially conservative was not likely to be progressive, flexible, and innovative when responding to intellectual challenges in theological matters.

Intellectual trends in nineteenth-century Europe created grave problems not only for the papacy but also for the Christian churches in general. The rationalism of the Enlightenment fostered a distrust of authority and tradition in matters of intellectual enquiry and asserted that truth could be acquired only through reason, observation, and experiment. Great advances in the study of ancient Egyptian, Assyrian, Babylonian, and Greek literature indicated the need for a fresh approach to biblical interpretation. From about the 1840s onwards the findings of biblical scholars demolished many traditional beliefs about the historical accuracy of the scriptural narratives.

The Bible was no longer studied as if it was literally true and directly inspired by God. This "higher criticism" of the Bible, originating in Germany, was generally undertaken with a reverential Christian attitude. But there was also a tendency for it to lead toward humanism and away from Christianity, as in, for example, *The Essence of Christianity* (1841) by Ludwig Feuerbach. In England, biblical criticism was embraced by a group of liberal Anglicans including Thomas Arnold. The publication of *Essays and Reviews* in 1860 brought the ideas of biblical criticism to public attention and provoked a hostile reaction from the conservatives. Bishop Samuel Wilberforce, who was prominent in castigating the essayists, believed that the Church of England was being attacked from two directions at once: revealed theology was being eroded by biblical criticism, while belief in natural theology was being whittled away by evolutionary theory. The controversy generated by *Essays and Reviews* overshadowed the smaller debate about *Darwin's Origin of Species*, published in the previous year.[3]

Those who were well informed about biblical criticism, geology, and evolutionary theory found it increasingly difficult to sustain a belief in the literal interpretation of scripture. New concepts and discoveries were no longer confined to the intellectual elite. The rapid growth of mass literacy and cheap printing facilitated the dissemination of ideas deemed inimical to the Catholic faith. Skepticism and anticlericalism became widespread.[4] The Roman Catholic Church reacted aggressively to these developments. But the papacy, probably mindful of the church's mistake in condemning Galileo, was careful not to issue *ex cathedra* declarations against modern scientific theories (especially concerning evolution) which seemed to undermine the authority of scripture.[5]

The earliest indication of Catholic ecclesiastical opinion concerning the theory of human evolution is to be found in a decree of the Provincial Council of Cologne, passed in 1860. It declared:

> Our first parents were immediately made by God. Hence, we declare openly opposed to Holy Scripture and to the Faith the opinion of those who go so far as to say that man, so far as his body is concerned, was produced by the spontaneous transformation of the less perfect into the more perfect, successively, ultimately ending in the human.[6]

The council did not rule out completely the application of evolutionary theory to humankind. The key word here is "spontaneous"—the notion of nonteleological evolution was rejected. God's "immediate" intervention had to be postulated so that Adam could attain the status of a "rational soul." It was permissible to hypothesize that divine intervention could accelerate the process of evolution while at the same time not undermining the causality of physical laws.[7]

The decree of Cologne was not reiterated by any other ecclesiastical provincial council, nor was it endorsed by the supreme teaching authority of the church. Therefore, it had no significant impact on the universal church. Although the papacy refrained from making any dogmatic statements about evolutionary theory, it was not reticent about declaring its contempt for many of the other ideas and values of modern civilization.

Pope Pius IX was the longest reigning pope in history (1846–1878). At the beginning of his pontificate he earned a liberal reputation when he granted amnesties to political prisoners, set up commissions to reform procedures in civil and criminal law, and announced a development program for railways in the Papal States. In 1847 he established the Pontificia Accademia dei Nuovi Lincei. The purpose of the Academy was to promote scientific research and to advise the government of the Papal

States on scientific issues.[8] All this occurred against a background of political instability. The very existence of the Papal States was threatened by the *Risorgimento*, the movement to establish an independent united Italy.

In the revolutionary atmosphere of November 1848, the pope's prime minister, Pellegrino Rossi, was assassinated. Several days later Pius was forced into exile and fled to the Kingdom of Naples. These bitter experiences purged him of any genuine liberal tendencies he may have had. He became firmly convinced that the principles of the French Revolution represented the main threat to the entire moral, social, and religious order. He condemned the errors of modern civilization in his allocution *Quibus quantisque malorum* (20 April 1849) and urged loyal Catholic authors to write in defense of the church. His call was answered in the Catholic press in France, Germany, Spain, Belgium, England, Italy, and Central America. In Rome a number of Jesuits responded energetically to the papal request and founded *Civiltà Cattolica* in 1850.[9] This ultraconservative journal was dedicated to the defense of both the church and the papacy. In that same year the pope's political power was restored by the military intervention of France, and on 12 April he returned to Rome. Afterwards he had to confront liberalism and anticlericalism to maintain his regime.

It is likely that the political uncertainties with which Pius had to contend stiffened his resolve against modernity and made him less inclined to facilitate the harmonization of Catholic theology with the latest developments in the historical and natural sciences. He feared that the published works of Catholic intellectuals, intent on reconciling their faith with new developments in biblical criticism and natural science, would pose a serious threat to the future of the church. Ignatz von Döllinger, the most eminent Catholic historian of his time and a leading figure in liberal Catholicism, was one of a number of influential Catholic scholars who suffered papal censure. He played a leading role in organizing the Munich Congress (a gathering of mainly German theologians) in September 1863. He had already given offense to Rome by criticizing the pope's government. The pope was also displeased because the congress had been called without seeking the permission of the ecclesiastical authorities.

The main concern of the Munich Congress was to discuss the independent rights of history, philosophy, and science, and the relationship of these disciplines to both theology and ecclesiastical authority. Döllinger, in his address to the congress, praised German scholarship and drew attention to the poor standards prevailing in Italy. Furthermore, he declared that scholasticism should be regarded as a thing of the past and advocated a much greater degree of intellectual freedom in theological studies. All this was sure to anger Pope Pius IX, but he did not initially reveal his displeasure. What provoked him to act, it seems, was the activities of Döllinger's enemies in Rome, especially Cardinal Charles Auguste Reisach, formerly an archbishop of Munich. Reisach and Döllinger had disagreed on the issue of how theology should be taught to seminarians. Reisach now played a leading role in dissipating papal tolerance for Döllinger's initiative.[10] He drafted the text of the Munich Brief, which was published as the papal letter, *Tuas Libenter*, dated 21 December 1863.

In this document Pius stated that in recent times a number of German publications had been added to the Vatican's Index of Forbidden Books. He claimed that some Catholic students were relying far too much on the power of reason and were arguing for the independence of science to such an extent that their opinions were in conflict with the doctrines of the church. He insisted that Catholics were not only obliged to submit to the dogmas of the church, but they were also duty bound to accept the doctrinal decisions of the pontifical congregations and the teaching of theologians. Pius asserted the primacy of the faith over the natural sciences as follows:

> While Catholics may cultivate these sciences safely, explain them, and render them useful and certain, on the other hand they cannot do so if their natural intellect, in investigating natural truth, does not supremely venerate the infallible intellect of God as revealed in Christianity.[11]

Christianity, in this context, was of course synonymous with Catholicism—presided over by the pope. This assertion would effectively give the Catholic ecclesiastical authorities the right to curtail the speculations of Catholic scientists.

John Henry Newman believed that the Munich Brief was broadly acceptable. But he had concerns about its application, and he seemed unsure about its interpretation. In reference to that part of the document quoted above, he asked if Newton was unable to reach "useful and certain" conclusions in astronomy because of not being a Catholic. Does a scientist have to be constantly alert to the danger that the outcome of his research may lead him to conclusions that seem to contradict revelation or are incompatible with a literal interpretation of scripture? If a man's reasoning leads him to a conclusion contrary to Catholic doctrine should he then terminate his research in the absence of detecting any error in his work?

Newman made reference to the frequently expressed opinion that

Galileo had committed a major error of judgment when he involved himself in theological arguments in the course of his scientific debates. This opinion failed to allow for the fact that Galileo did not have the option of steering clear of theology when expressing his scientific opinions.[12] Newman inferred that the church was now unjustly interfering in scientific studies. He was of the opinion that the Munich Brief demanded that scientists should be ever mindful of theology in their scientific research. He did not think it correct to claim that one could write about controversial scientific theories to defend the teachings of the church against free-thinking scientists without allowing them the freedom of reasoning in their chosen discipline. However, Newman reconciled himself to the document by regarding it as an exhortation to the faithful to refrain from expressing opinions about new interpretations of scripture, arising from scientific theories, because much scientific research had yet to be done.

The pope's reaction to the proceedings of the Munich Congress put an end to plans to hold it annually. It also had an adverse impact on the liberal English Catholic scholar Lord Acton. Denied admission to Cambridge University because of his religion, he had spent eight years abroad, studying under Döllinger in Germany, who profoundly influenced his formation as a historian. In 1864 he was editor of the British periodical the *Home and Foreign Review* (previously the *Rambler*). Acton had welcomed the Munich Congress because he anticipated that it would make an important contribution to the work of clarifying how reason should relate to tradition and authority. In his opinion the outcome of the first meeting showed that the congress respected both the dogmas of the church and the independent rights of science.[13] But the Munich Brief proved too restrictive for him. This document demanded that scientific studies be circumscribed by dogma, which Catholics would naturally accept. But the pursuit of truth had also to take cognizance of the Roman Congregations —especially the Congregation of the Index—and theological opinions deemed acceptable by the hierarchy. These nondogmatic requirements were unacceptable to him and to "the conductors" of the *Home and Foreign Review*. The outcome of this was that the periodical ceased publication.[14] But worse was yet to come, namely, the *Syllabus of Errors*. Work on this document started in 1852 and was extremely slow.[15] The drafting process did not occur in isolation from political, social, and intellectual developments.

The *Risorgimento* had been defeated but not crushed after the 1848 revolution and grew in strength in the 1850s. In 1859–1860 the Papal States of Romagna, Umbria, and the Marches were annexed by the Kingdom of

Sardinia-Piedmont. Only Rome and its hinterland (the "Patrimony of St. Peter") remained under papal sovereignty, and this was under constant threat. French troops protected Rome from Italian nationalists who hoped to make the city their capital. However, under the terms of the September Convention of 1864, France agreed to withdraw its troops provided that Italy guaranteed the territorial independence of Rome under papal rule. Pius IX, distressed and angry at the loss of most of his papal territories, was bitterly critical of Emperor Napoleon III's agreement with Italy, which left his diminished political domain even more vulnerable than before. Other external threats were also evident. The church was failing dismally to adapt to a social environment that was influenced by a confluence of liberalism, socialism, nationalism, science, and Enlightenment philosophies. Liberal Catholics, especially in France and Germany, pressed for reconciliation between the church and the modern world and in doing so challenged the curia and their ultramontane co-religionists.

Liberal Catholics were once again expressing opinions that seemed to be antagonistic to the papal worldview. Pius was especially agitated by two speeches by eminent liberal Catholics in 1863. The first one, already discussed, was by Döllinger at Munich. The second speech was by Montalembert at the first Congress of Belgian Catholics at Malines in Belgium. Montalembert argued that the interests of Catholicism would be best served by religious toleration and by the church coming to terms with the modern state. The ultramontanes reacted by pressing the Vatican to take firm action against liberal Catholicism. The papacy felt compelled to reassert its authority within the church and to dispel any doubts about its attitudes on a broad range of issues. It was under these adversarial circumstances that Pius issued the *Syllabus of Errors* with the encyclical *Quanta Cura* in 1864.[16]

There was no direct connection between the *Syllabus* and the encyclical except that both documents were issued on the same date. The *Syllabus* caused the most controversy, condemning as it did many of the principles applied by scientists, social scientists, and non-Catholic biblical scholars.[17] Of all the condemned propositions, it was the eightieth that provoked the greatest sense of outrage. The proposition that the "Roman Pontiff can, and ought to, reconcile himself and come to terms with progress, Liberalism and modern civilization" was declared anathema.[18] This seemed to condemn the most cherished ideals of the nineteenth century in the democracies of western Europe. But the theological jargon of the *Syllabus* was open to misinterpretation and was unsuitable for a broad readership.[19] Furthermore, it was written mainly with Italian circumstances in mind. The eightieth condemned proposition was based on the allocution *Jamdudum Cernimus* (18 March 1861), which condemned not progress and civilization in general but the Piedmontese government's notion of these concepts. In Italy "progress, liberalism, and modern civilization" indicated the closure of convents and monasteries and the establishment of secular education. But Europeans and Americans in general did not interpret the *Syllabus* from an Italian perspective—nor was it reasonable to expect them to do so. Consequently, the Catholic hierarchies of most Western countries experienced embarrassment and difficulties with their governments and with public opinion.[20]

In anti-Catholic circles the *Syllabus* reinforced the opinion that the Roman Catholic Church was an archaic institution and an obstacle to progress. In the *Syllabus* the church had asserted the contrary view when it condemned the following propositions:

12. The decrees of the Apostolic See and of the Roman congregations impede the true progress of science.

13. The method and principles by which the old scholastic doctors cultivated theology are no longer suitable to the demands of our times and to the progress of the sciences.[21]

The church was defended against the encroachments of philosophy and cognate disciplines, and the primacy of religion over reason was upheld. The following propositions were regarded as anathema.

8. As human reason is placed on a level with religion itself, so theological must be treated in the same manner as philosophical sciences.

9. All the dogmas of the Christian religion are indiscriminately the object of natural science or philosophy; and human reason, enlightened solely in an historical way, is able, by its own natural strength and principles, to attain to the true science of even the most abstruse dogmas; provided only that such dogmas be proposed to reason itself as its object.[22]

Pius then proceeded to assert the authority of the church over philosophy. The propositions condemned were:

10. As the philosopher is one thing, and philosophy another, so it is the right and duty of the philosopher to subject himself to the authority which he shall have proved to be true; but philosophy neither can nor ought to submit to any such authority.

11. The Church not only ought never to pass judgement on philosophy, but ought to tolerate the errors of philosophy, leaving it to correct itself.

14. Philosophy is to be treated without taking any account of supernatural revelation.[23]

57. The science of philosophical things and morals and also civil laws may and ought to keep aloof from divine and ecclesiastical authority.[24]

Philosophy and science were closely related, what pertained to philosophy in this context also applied to science.

Science had to be controlled. In its unfettered state it was perceived to be a danger to the faith. However, the main threat to the future of the church was not seen to originate from the actions of independent-minded scientists. The ecclesiastical authorities were more concerned about liberals, socialists, freemasons, and atheists, who exploited the materialistic presentation of science to undermine the church, politically and otherwise. The press was a powerful medium for disseminating their ideas— but the Catholic Church was not without influence here. Pope Pius IX praised a number of periodicals for their staunch support, including *Le Monde* and *L'Univers* (Paris), *Bien Public* (Gand, Belgium), *Osservatore Cattolico* (Milan), *Osservatore Cattolico* (Bologna), and the *Archivio Ecclesiastico* (Florence). He reserved his greatest commendation for the Jesuit authors of *Civiltà Cattolica*. On 12 February 1866 he issued the brief (papal letter) *Novissimum Supremi Nostri*, which created a literary college under their direction. This distinction was a reward for loyal service. For sixteen years these Jesuits, motivated by "unadulterated Popery," had submitted their work at regular intervals to the pope for inspection and had "embraced every opportunity of knowing and fulfilling his wishes."[25] They were to wield inordinate power and influence in the closing years of the nineteenth century and were resolutely against evolution, even when Catholic authors proposed it as God's *modus operandi*.

In 1864 the *Origin of Species*, translated into Italian by Giovanni Canestrini and L. Salimbeni, was published in Modena. In the same year the professor of zoology at Turin University, Filippo De Filippi, delivered his lecture "L'uomo e le scimmie," which led to an impassioned public debate. These two events made Darwinian theory much more widely known in Italy. The controversy that followed De Filippi's lecture provoked religious opposition to evolutionary theory because of the thorny issue of man's primitive origins. In the 1860s in Italy, the emergence of Italian positivism, the materialistic presentation of evolution, and the extrapolation of Darwinian concepts to human society all contributed to a polarization of attitudes. In 1869 an exceptionally bitter debate, probably the most controversial of the decade, took place between the Russian physiologist Alexander Herzen and the Catholic poet N. Tommaseo. It epitomized the conflict that was occurring at the time between scientific and religious attitudes.[26]

In Vatican circles, Darwinism was perceived as part of a conglomeration of ideas regarded as contrary to the church's traditional teaching.[27] It was associated with anticlericalism, not just in Italy but also in France and Spain.[28] Darwinism clearly generated apprehension in some Catholic circles. For example, in June 1876 a synod appointed by Archbishop José María de Urquinaona y Bidot of the Canary Islands denounced a treatise on natural history that expressed approval of the works of Darwin and Haeckel. The censorship imposed by the ecclesiastical authorities was motivated by a fear that evolutionary ideas that contradicted scripture, especially the doctrines of original sin and the redemptive promise of the Messiah, would lead to apostasy and the overthrow of the status quo. The freedom of thought associated with materialism and the acceptance of the evolutionary hypothesis would "deny to the poor the hope of eternal glory." Thus, "the poor man, denuded of his religious beliefs, would curse his poverty and ready his knife for the rich."[29] The institutional church had much to lose. All this was at a time when major scientific advances were occurring with increasing rapidity, greatly enhancing the prestige and influence of science. Catholic scholarship, in stark contrast to the progress of science, was extremely poor during the pontificate of Pius IX. There were very few centers of scholarship outside of Germany whose achievements could be compared favorably with those of Protestants and rationalists.[30] The poor condition of Catholic scholarship provoked a French cleric to remark that "it is not by reciting the Rosary that Renan . . . can be refuted."[31] The church was clearly at a disadvantage in defending itself when some scientists went beyond the boundaries of their discipline to dismiss it as a backward institution founded on dogmas of blind faith.

The First Vatican Council

It had been about three centuries since the Roman Catholic Church had convened a council, and some prelates believed that such an assembly would provide an opportunity to reaffirm Catholic principles while at the same time enhancing the spiritual and ecclesiastical power of the papacy. Immediately after the publication of the *Syllabus of Errors* in 1864, Pius IX informed the cardinals in strict secrecy of his intention to hold a general council. On 8 December 1869 Vatican Council I was convened. The pope presided over the council, and there was little freedom for debate. The issue of papal infallibility received a disproportionate amount of attention.[32] Bishops were not granted permission to originate motions. Two commissions served this purpose, but the minority liberal wing of the episcopate was excluded from these. The rules of procedure were heavily biased in favor of those who supported papal infallibility. Furthermore, dissenting bishops were subjected to intimidation, and sometimes bribery was used to change their views.[33]

The decision to convoke a council had also been influenced by the threats to the church posed by naturalism and rationalism.[34] The Vatican Council issued declarations about the existence of God and the relationship between faith and reason. The Dogmatic Constitution on the Catholic Faith, promulgated in the third session of the council (24 April 1870), declared that:

> God, the source and end of all things, can be known with certainty from the consideration of created things, by the natural power of human reason: ever since the creation of the world, his invisible nature had been clearly perceived in the things that have been made.[35]

This statement, inspired by Romans 1:20, was consistent with the teaching of St. Thomas Aquinas and was in opposition to the older Augustinian belief that there was no unaided knowledge of God.[36] The declaration seemed to indicate that it was possible to be sure of the existence of God through unaided human reason. It repudiated fideism—a belief that deprecated the role of reason in the acquisition of religious knowledge, that is, basing knowledge of God entirely on faith. In 1855 the Holy Office had declared that the use of reason comes before faith and, assisted by revelation and grace, leads to it.[37]

The Vatican Council defended Catholic faith against what was perceived to be the false claims of science and philosophy, and it asserted the primacy of Catholic theology. Some statements from the dogmatic constitution are particularly worth quoting in this context.

> Even though faith is above reason, there can never be any real disagreement between faith and reason. . . . God cannot deny himself, nor can truth ever be in opposition to truth. The appearance of this kind of specious contradiction is chiefly due to the fact that either the dogmas of faith are not understood and explained in accordance with the mind of the church, or unsound views are mistaken for the conclusions of reason. . . . all faithful Christians are forbidden to defend as the legitimate conclusions of science

those opinions which are known to be contrary to the doctrine of faith, particularly if they have been condemned by the church; and furthermore they are absolutely bound to hold them as errors . . . faith delivers reason from errors and protects it.[38]

Furthermore, it stated:

If anyone says that it is possible that at some time, given the advancement of knowledge, a sense may be assigned to the dogmas propounded by the church which is different from that which the church has understood and understands: let him be anathema.[39]

The inerrancy of scripture was upheld. All the books of the Old Testament and the New Testament—"with all their parts"—were to be regarded as free of error because they were written under the inspiration of the Holy Spirit, and, therefore, God was their author. To eliminate any doubts about what books might or might not be covered by this dogmatic declaration, reference was made to the first decree of the fourth session of the Council of Trent (8 April 1546), which listed all the sacred books. All these were included in the old Latin Vulgate edition of the Bible.[40]

The council indicated that the church would not attempt to interfere with the principles and methodologies of academic disciplines, provided that they did not "become infected with errors by conflicting with divine teaching, or, by going beyond their proper limits, intrude upon what belongs to faith and engender confusion."[41] This statement indicated some degree of flexibility by the teaching authority of the church, but this was not forthcoming. In the upper echelons of Catholic power there was little tolerance even for a version of human evolution that allowed a place for God in the process. In one of the council's documents the theory of humankind's animal origins was described as evil and incompatible with human dignity.[42] However, the council did not have enough time to examine and define the relationship between evolutionary theory and Catholic theology. It was terminated abruptly in July 1870 because of political tensions caused by the outbreak of the Franco-Prussian War.

Although the First Vatican Council did not issue any definitive statements against evolution, there was, nevertheless, much hostility toward it among Catholic prelates. Pope Pius IX's stern opposition to it became very clear in 1877 when he praised Constantin James's book *Du Darwinisme, ou l'homme-singe* (later editions in 1882 and 1892 were published under a slightly different title). This book was a scurrilous attack on Darwin and on other evolutionists and contained within its covers words of wholehearted approval by the pope.[43]

Evidently, the pope was displeased about the spread of Darwinism in Italy. In 1875 Darwin had been made Foreign Member of the Reale Accademia dei Lincei. Three years later Thomas Huxley received the same honor. In 1879 Darwin was awarded the Bressa Prize by the Turin Royal Academy. These events give some indication of the favorable reception of Darwinism in some sectors of Italian society. In the late nineteenth century Darwin's published works were becoming more and more accessible and were also increasingly the subject of critical review. From 1871 to 1890 the Unione Tipografica-Editrice Torinese published Italian translations of Darwin's major works, and from 1892 those of Ernst Haeckel, the most eminent Darwinist in Germany. The biologists Filippo De Filippi, Michele Lessona, Paolo Mantegazza, and Giovanni Canestrini played a central role in making Darwin's theory known throughout Italy. They promoted its acceptance in the universities and among Italian scientists. A large sector of the Italian public was also familiar with evolutionary theory. This was due mainly to naturalists and evolutionist philosophers who had, since the 1860s, written books and given lectures with nonprofessionals in mind.

Darwin was widely respected in Italy, and many Italian Catholics accepted the general theory of evolution. Despite all this, his concept of natural selection gained very limited support. There were a number of reasons for this, including (1) the reaction against the arrogance of those naturalists associated with Darwinism who asserted their competence to explain all reality on a materialistic basis; (2) the rejection of humankind's uniqueness; and (3) the repudiation of teleology. Natural selection was regarded as too circumscribed. It could not explain the origin of life itself; it was deemed unsatisfactory as an evolutionary mechanism; and it relied excessively on the element of chance. By 1880, in a broader European context, there had been many scientific objections to Darwin's proposed mechanism of evolution. Furthermore, there was some apprehension about the application of Darwin's theory to the social sciences, especially concerning the moral implications of the principle of "survival of the fittest."[44]

The general theory of evolution had created theological difficulties for the Roman Catholic Church, but this issue was not uppermost in the mind of Pope Pius IX, especially in 1870. Two months after the end of the First Vatican Council the forces of the *Risorgimento* entered Rome. After the invasion of the city, Pius regarded himself as a prisoner and never traveled outside the Vatican again. The last remnants of his temporal power had been obliterated. A relatively minor consequence of Italian unification was the split in the Accademia Pontificia dei Nuovi Lincei. Benedetto Viale-Prelà, president of the Academy and physician to the pope, withdrew from the institute with a group of scientists. They did not recognize the legitimacy of the new state and reorganized under the previous name of the Accademia Pontificia dei Nuovi Lincei. Those academics who supported the Italian state, and the secularization of culture, renamed their institute the Accademia Nazionale dei Lincei.[45]

After the loss of the Papal States, papal power within the Roman Catholic Church continued to increase. This was due very much to the decree of papal infallibility arising from the proceedings of the Vatican Council. The bishops lost their independence and were effectively relegated to the status of papal officials. Rome tightened its grip over theological developments to such an extent that the ascendancy of Thomism was greatly enhanced and no new theological trends were possible without the approval of the Vatican. The power of the curia, the administrative system of the pope, was also greatly increased.[46]

The process of centralization occurred at a time when the Catholic Church was experiencing remarkable renewal and growth. There was a rapid increase in the numbers of those joining religious orders, and new religious orders were founded. Many of these orders were dedicated to working in schools, hospitals, and a variety of other institutions. Local churches came increasingly under the control of the papacy, especially in the United States of America, where the Catholic population was rapidly expanding. The drive toward centralization did not stop when Pius IX died on 7 February 1878.

The Biblical Question: Inspiration and Error

Pius IX was succeeded by Gioacchino Pecci, who took the name of Leo XIII. Leo became the second longest reigning pope in history (1878–1903). He was as authoritarian as his predecessor and insisted on the trappings of monarchy. During his pontificate, papal intervention was extended and consolidated right down to the lower echelons of the church.[47] He intervened with national episcopates, increased the authority of his nuncios, and directed religious orders to locate their headquarters in Rome. This growth of power was facilitated by the ultramontane movement, which dominated late-nineteenth-century Catholicism. Ultramontane theology was extremely dogmatic, antirationalist, and papalist in its outlook. Those who favored it promoted a "ghetto" mentality, seeking to protect the faithful masses against Protestant and rationalist ideas. Their piety was repugnant not only to Protestants but also to liberal English Catholics.[48]

Leo was not a liberal and had contributed to the idea of issuing a comprehensive condemnation of all the sinful ideas of the modern age, which led to the publication of the *Syllabus of Errors*. The written works of St. Thomas Aquinas, in sharp contrast to the philosophy of the Enlightenment, formed the basis of his outlook. This was indicated on 4 August 1879, when he issued *Aeterni Patris*. The encyclical indicated the program that he intended to pursue throughout his pontificate, and its purpose was to promote the Aristotelian-Scholastic philosophy as expounded by St. Thomas Aquinas (Thomism). Leo's support of Thomism encouraged the most conservative elements of the curia to suppress, or to at least discourage, any ideas that were different from their own. A culture of intolerance developed that became associated with Thomism.[49]

The pope believed that the political and social evils of his time were based on philosophical and theological errors. These errors were traced back to the Reformation and, according to Leo, had penetrated deep into Western society.[50] Thomism was promoted to protect the church against the onslaught of secular philosophy, Protestant subjectivism, rationalism, and science. It was intended to demonstrate that Roman Catholic doctrine did not contradict modern scientific findings.[51] But Leo still tended to perceive scientists as enemies of the church. The church genuflected to reason, but it was intolerant of individualism, which is essential to the scientific ethic.[52] Furthermore, the polemical tendencies of some eminent scientists, especially in Britain and Germany (notably John Tyndall, Thomas Huxley, Ernst Haeckel, Ludwig Büchner, Carl Vogt, and Jacob Moleschott), probably made it much more difficult for the papacy to reconcile itself with the modern scientific theories of the late nineteenth century.[53]

Belief in religion was regarded as unscientific in some quarters. In western Europe nonreligious views of the world spread beyond elite groups, and for many science offered the exclusive path to truth and progress and was thought to serve as a sound basis for everyday living. Some of those who advocated antireligious science also engaged in radical politics. In Germany there was a tendency among Social Democrats to embrace a synthesis of Marx and Darwin for the purpose of constructing a total explanation of the natural and social world.[54] In Italy, Leo XIII, like his predecessor, had refused to acknowledge the legitimacy of the new Italian state and prohibited Catholics from participating in general elections.

Many scientists did not conform to the pope's wishes and were politically active, sometimes with remarkable success. Quintino Sella, for example, served as prime minister and was later elected president of the Accademia Nazionale dei Lincei in 1874. Numerous scientists had fought for Italian statehood and served on commissions for the reform of education; some of them were elected to the national parliament. Political and scientific activities were seen to be closely connected. Political action, cultural reform, and the advancement of science were all seen as vital elements of the process of modernization, which was regarded as essential for national resurgence. All this was strikingly different from the conservative Catholic view of the ideal scientist whose faith kept his reason in check. Scientists were not supposed to participate in controversies external to their discipline, especially those that were concerned with social, philosophical, and moral questions.[55] Frequently, they did not measure up to the devout stereotype of conservative Catholicism, and this in turn led to the belief that they were enemies of the church.

On 10 January 1890 Leo issued the encyclical *Sapientiae Christianae*. In this document he protested against what he regarded as the hostility of scientists. Writing in the context of a war against the church, Leo observed that many of nature's secrets had yielded to the initiatives of scientists. There was nothing intrinsically wrong with this. Nevertheless, an unfortunate consequence of scientific progress, from his perspective, was that scientists had

> become possessed with so arrogant a sense of their own powers, as already to consider themselves able to banish from social life the authority and empire of God. . . . from nature, they maintain, we must seek the principle and rule of all truth. . . . they deny all revelation from on high, and all fealty due to the Christian teaching of morals as well as all obedience to the Church.[56]

Leo was aware that the unfriendly disposition of many scientists toward the church fomented anticlericalism. This was a major reason for his decision to found the Vatican Observatory in 1891. Leo declared:

> In taking up this work we have become involved not only in helping to promote a very noble science . . . but we have in the first place put before ourselves the plan . . . that everyone might see that the Church and its Pastors are not opposed to true and solid science, whether human or divine, but that they embrace it, encourage it, and promote it with the fullest possible dedication.[57]

In the late nineteenth century, theological difficulties arising from scientific progress were exacerbated by discoveries in archaeology and history. These developments seemed to underpin rationalist interpretations of the biblical texts. In this context the Bible could be regarded as unhistorical as well as unscientific. Some Catholics reacted by refusing to make any concessions to the modern criticism of the Bible. Others argued that the book was entirely concerned with religious values and saw few points of contact, if any at all, between it and the sciences. The outstanding advantage of the isolationist position was that it would render Genesis invulnerable to new discoveries in both the physical and historical sciences.

It was relatively easy for the magisterium to anathematize the ideas of non-Catholics who were stridently critical of its doctrines about the Bible. However, a much greater problem, which called for intellectual resourcefulness and tact, was how to respond to highly respected theologians within the church who questioned what Catholic doctrine on scripture really meant and how it could be credibly maintained in the light of history and science. The views of two eminent Catholic scholars, Bishop William Clifford of Clifton (Britain), and Cardinal John Henry Newman, and the opinions of their critics, will be examined here to illustrate the theological difficulties facing the Roman Catholic Church in the late nineteenth century.

In 1881 Bishop Clifford proposed, in the *Dublin Review*, a radical hypothesis for the express purpose of liberating the creation narratives from the troublesome implications of modern science. He maintained that all attempts to reconcile the first chapter of Genesis with the established findings of science had proved unsuccessful when the sacred text was regarded as a historical narrative. The period theory, which viewed the days of creation as indefinite periods of time, was popular among Christian apologists, but Clifford argued at length against it on the basis that it was becoming more and more inconsistent with new discoveries in geology. He observed that Charles Lyell's *Principles of Geology* had demonstrated the continuous action of secondary causes in nature and that, generally, processes of change and development were gradual rather than abrupt. Therefore, he concluded that there was no basis for the vast time scale of creation to be divided into six or any other number of distinct periods.

It was not the purpose of the Bible to teach science. It was not evident from scripture that Moses, or any of the other sacred writers, had received divine revelation about astronomy, geology, or any other branch of the natural sciences. There was no reason to believe that Moses was a geologist. Had an examination of Genesis "ever led to the discovery of a single geological fact?" Apparently not! Therefore, a revelation that reveals nothing would be useless and, by implication, would not be included in the sacred text as such. Clifford did not go so far as to claim that there were no connections between religion and science, nor did he wish to devalue the works of those who attempted to reconcile scripture with modern theories. Nevertheless, he observed that a major problem in establishing harmony between scripture and science was the continual changes in scientific theories, especially in geology. This meant that any conclusions reached would be, at best, tentative. Clifford then proceeded to argue that the first thirty-four verses of Genesis (the first chapter and the first three verses of the second chapter) were a sacred hymn and were not meant to be read as history—unlike the rest of the book. These verses were a preface to Genesis and were not really part of the book itself. The verses in question were written by Moses to honor the works of the one true God in order to counteract the influence of idolatrous practices propagated by Egyptian priests.[58]

The bishop's article provoked some controversy, especially through the pages of the English Catholic periodical the *Tablet*.[59] An English priest, John S. Vaughan, observed that, with the exception of the *Tablet* correspondence, there was little interest in Clifford's article in England; but abroad several critical reviews were published in France, Germany, Italy, and Belgium. Vaughan quoted several European authors "of eminence" as a counterweight to the "exalted" and "illustrious" status of the bishop.[60] The purpose of this exercise was to gain the confidence of his readers.

Vaughan argued that if contradictions were perceived to exist between science and scripture, then these were apparent rather than real. Science, especially geology, was at an early and very imperfect state of development. Contradictions would dissolve in the face of new discoveries and improved methods of investigation. All this was gratuitously optimistic. Vaughan was aware of the "tardiness" of his article in the *Dublin Review*. He had reluctantly entered the debate because he believed that Clifford's opinion had not been adequately addressed in Britain and Ireland. However, his contribution was not without merit. He conceded that it was not the purpose of scripture to teach science, but he insisted that, where there were points of contact, truthful accounts had to be given. This required sacred writers to use "natural truths and scientific facts" rather than "absurdities and trifles" when narrating the history of God's creative actions. Clifford's initiative was ultimately self-defeating; he had defended Genesis against the onslaught of modern science, but in doing so had destroyed its credibility as a divinely inspired text.[61]

Clifford did not let Vaughan's critique pass unanswered. He was not impressed by the list of authors ranged against him because none of them had asserted that his hypothesis was contrary to the authoritative teaching of the Roman Catholic Church. Neither was he impressed by such defensive generalizations as "truth does not contradict truth," or that the contradictions between science and scripture were merely apparent rather than real, or that science (especially geology) was still in an early and imperfect state of development. He was on less solid ground when he reiterated that Moses did not teach science but simply used the scientific terminology of his day without confirming the truth or falsehood of the underlying theories.[62] This explanation was clearly not satisfactory if divine inspiration was to be maintained free of error. It seemed to admit that some scriptural verses, formerly understood to be statements of fact, were now liable to be demonstrated as factually inaccurate or totally false.

What were Catholics to believe about scripture? It is likely that the vast majority of them gave it little thought. However, those who had an extensive knowledge of their religious faith and were well informed about developments in archaeology, history, and the natural sciences had good reason to be concerned about biblical criticism and where it might lead. John Henry Newman addressed this thorny issue in the February 1884 issue of the *Nineteenth Century*. Formerly an Anglican minister, he had converted to Roman Catholicism in 1845 and was ordained a priest in 1847. His elevation to the rank of cardinal by Pope Leo XIII in 1879 indicated how highly regarded he was in the church.

Newman, now in his eighty-third year, did not calmly put pen to paper. He was provoked to do so. Claims were being made that the Catholic Church demanded of its membership an assent to views and interpretations of scripture that scientific and historical research had rendered untenable. Newman was particularly offended by Ernest Renan's assertion that the church was so uncompromising in matters of biblical criticism and history that it greatly exceeded the rigidity of the most conservative Protestant denominations. Such allegations could not be left unchallenged.

Newman accepted, of course, that all Catholics were obligated to give their assent to what had been dogmatically defined by the church. But what about novel opinions that seemed contrary to the nondogmatic teachings of the church? Newman believed that in some instances assent could be withheld but there was "a duty of silence" as in, for example, the case of Galileo. Silence should be maintained in deference to ecclesiastical authority and the need to avoid disturbing "ill-educated minds."[63] There were other considerations. If the church had not formally interpreted a verse in scripture, then it was not heretical to propose an interpretation contrary to what was generally understood, provided that there was "nothing in the act intrinsically inconsistent with the faith . . . nothing of contempt or rebellion, nothing temerarious, nothing offensive or scandalous."[64]

The Catholic attitude toward scripture embraced two dogmas: first, scripture was inspired throughout; and, second, the church was, in matters of faith and morals, the only infallible interpreter of the sacred text. Inspiration would not yield truth in the absence of infallible interpretation. A book "so complex, so unsystematic, in parts so obscure" would not be amenable to the understanding of mere individual judgment. Readers who were not enlightened by the teaching authority of the church would not be able to distinguish opinion from history, fact from vision, or what was allegorical from what was literal.[65] Such was the weakness of the Protestant position.

Newman was acutely aware that the Vatican Council had declared that the Bible was inspired throughout—but not in all respects. Inspiration was not without limits. Newman maintained that inspiration

> cannot be in every respect, unless we are bound *de fide* to believe that . . . heaven is above us, and that there are no antipodes. And it seems unworthy of Divine Greatness, that the Almighty should in His revelation of Himself to us undertake mere secular duties, and assume the office of a narrator, as such, or an historian, or geographer, except so far as the secular matters bear directly upon the revealed truth.[66]

Those facts that had a direct bearing on faith could not be dispensed with. Therefore, scripture was inspired "not only in faith and morals, but in all its parts which bear on faith, including matters of fact."[67] But not all passages in scripture, which seemed to be statements of fact, were essential for an adherence to the precepts of faith. Newman referred to these as *obiter dicta*. These were statements or phrases that Catholics were not bound to accept as part of their faith, even if such statements or phrases seemed to be literally statements of fact (e.g., Judith 1:5 and 2 Timothy 4:13). Some passages of scripture were incidental rather than doctrinal and were concerned with such unimportant details as the dog of Tobias, St. Paul's cloak, and Nebuchadnezzar's supposed kingship of Nineveh.

Such minutiae did not seem worthy of inspiration.[68] Newman was cautious in expressing his views and made it clear that they were tentative rather than dogmatic.

Professor John Healy of Maynooth (Ireland) promptly responded to Newman's notion of partial inspiration. He believed that any novice in the schools of Catholic theology who read Newman's ideas about scripture would be alarmed. The Vatican Council, he asserted, had not made any distinction between matters of faith and morals and matters of fact when it was proclaiming that all the books of the Bible, and all their parts, were inspired throughout. If the Bible was inspired throughout, then God was its principal author and, because of this, there could be no trace of falsehood or error. Falsehood would destroy the integrity of scripture.[69]

Newman's retort to Healy was printed as a private pamphlet, under the cumbersome title of *What Is of Obligation for a Catholic to Believe concerning the Inspiration of the Canonical Scriptures* (1884). He accused the Irish professor of "sharp practice" in giving a misleading account of his opinions. According to Newman, Healy's thesis was that scripture was virtually or actually inspired, not just in faith and morals as declared by the councils of Trent and the Vatican, "but in all respects, and for all purposes, and on all subjects; so that no clause all through the Bible is open to the charge of error of any kind, and that no good Catholic can think otherwise."[70]

It seems that in the upper echelons of the church there was little toleration for open debate on the delicate topic concerning errors in scripture. Healy wrote a reply to Newman's second essay, but Cardinal Edward McCabe prevented its publication in the *Irish Ecclesiastical Record*. In his unpublished essay Healy argued that Newman's concept of *obiter dicta* in scripture would destroy its authority. A major weakness in Healy's position was his denial of what had been ascertained by historical research. For example, he was adamant that Nebuchadnezzar was king of Nineveh, as stated in the Book of Judith. The insistence by historians to the contrary did not persuade him otherwise.[71]

Thoughtful Catholics were in a quandary about scripture. Not all could be so dismissive as Healy of the new research findings in history and science. The essay "Can the Scriptures Err?" by Bishop John Cuthbert Hedley of Newport (Britain) indicates that the Catholic position was not at all straightforward. Hedley's article was published in the *Dublin Review* (1888). In addressing the question of whether or not there were errors in scripture, Hedley contemplated the implications of answers in the affirmative and negative. If errors in scripture were accepted, then it would be extremely difficult to limit the boundaries of error. Furthermore, error was not compatible with divine inspiration. If error was denied, then bibli-cal scholars had to contend with the admission that many scriptural narra-tives—"in their literal and traditional sense"—were now conceded to contradict science and probably history also. However, there were ways and means open to loyal Catholics for dealing with such a distressing issue. The old Augustinian strategy was particularly useful—"if I meet anything in the text which seemeth contrary to truth, I shall unhesitatingly conclude either that the copy is faulty, or that the translation is mistaken, or that I do not understand."[72] Furthermore, some errors could be explained away by the assertion that the Bible cannot be mistaken in what it states "as its own," but infallibility does not extend to "what it quotes others as saying."[73]

The councils of Florence, Trent, and the Vatican all issued pronounce-ments on the inspiration of scripture, although Trent never actually used the word "inspiration." This term was not formally defined by the church. Hedley understood it to mean that the Holy Spirit directed or influenced the sacred writers so that the Bible was "in a special sense 'the word of God.'" Inspiration, although undefined, was held to be incompatible with error—therefore no statement by any sacred writer, presented as a "fact, judgement," or "assertion" was "absolutely and without qualification, erroneous or untrue." However, writers, being human, were not perfect and, despite the guidance of the Holy Spirit, were still imperfect conduits for God's message. It seemed that, after all, there might be errors in scrip-ture. Hedley struggled to avoid such a conclusion. Since error was incom-patible with inspiration, this would have led to the conclusion that there were uninspired parts of scripture. Partial inspiration was unacceptable—such an admission would put the Bible at the mercy of "the rationalist pack" who were "clamouring to tear it to pieces."[74]

Hedley's next line of defense was probably influenced by Bishop William Clifford's essays on Genesis. Catholics were bound to give their assent to the historical "facts" of scripture. But what were "facts" in this context? Hedley acknowledged that the assertion of such facts was not always clear. A passage that seems to be a statement of history may be a poem or an allegory, like the first chapter of Genesis. The story of the Flood was not an allegory or a poem—it was "very obscure." Indeed "obscurity" was another useful device and could endure indefinitely. But even after all this obfuscation Hedley felt compelled to admit that there were "a very large number of mistakes in details, such as names, numbers, tenses and parts of speech." In the Vulgate version of the Bible, considered "authentic" by the church, there were mistakes in names and numbers and "contradictory parallel passages." After all the assertions of infallibility, it seemed that errors were admissible, provided that they were "slight and unimportant."[75]

Hedley believed that the greatest difficulty in defending the inspiration of the Bible arose from divergences between scripture and contemporary science. If all rational arguments failed to sustain the divine inspiration of the Bible, then Catholics could always rely on their faith. Reason had to be made subservient to faith. Whatever might be proved or disproved would not make the Bible anything other than the Word of God. "Chemistry, geology, biology—even, were it possible, history herself—must be stunted, or decay or perish, if there is no way for them to flourish except on the ruins of inspiration." Scientists who conducted their work without due regard for scripture were not imbued with "the bias of faith" but rather with the bias of "unbelief and antagonism."[76] Catholic scientists, if they were loyal to the church, would be Catholics first with their critical faculties held firmly in check by the dictates of faith.

Hedley, like Clifford and Newman, was relatively liberal in his views. All three expressed their opinions cautiously and were submissive to the teaching authority of the church. However, not all Catholic scholars were able to restrain their intellects and express deference to ecclesiastical authority when required to do so. The eminent French Catholic professor and priest Alfred Loisy (1857–1940), saw the Bible in a very different light from that of orthodox Catholics. Study of the Bible was to be directed not by the dogma of inspiration but by scientific methodology. Since there was an undeniable human dimension to the writing of the scriptural texts, it was necessary to study the cultural milieu of the writers so that the truths of the sacred documents could be elucidated. Christian scholars should ascertain what the Bible had to say about itself, not what theological dogma had to say about it. Biblical studies were to be conducted on the basis of the best methods of literary and historical criticism. The doctrine of inspiration would then be revised in accordance with the findings of advanced scholarship.

Loisy lectured at the Institut Catholique de Paris. The institute's rector, Maurice de Hulst (1841–1896), shared with Loisy a commitment to the advancement of biblical studies. De Hulst, like so many other Catholic lecturers, struggled to satisfy two conflicting objectives: first, to remain loyal to Catholic dogma and to submit to the authority of the hierarchy; and, second, to foster independent scholarship.[77] On 25 January 1893 his essay entitled "La Question Biblique" ("The Biblical Question") was published to promote toleration for Loisy's teaching, which had by then fallen under suspicion. Loisy was not mentioned by name, but the article was clearly intended to represent his views. De Hulst claimed that there were three schools of thought in Catholic theology. All three were dedicated to resolving contradictions between modern scientific studies (physical and historical) and the traditional dogma of the inspiration of scripture. The right wing maintained that the Bible was completely free from error because God was its author. The left wing (*école large*) argued that inspiration covered all statements pertaining to faith and morals but conceded that errors existed in narratives concerning only history and science. And the center (*école moyenne*) sought the middle ground between the two extremes. De Hulst urged that all three schools be tolerated within the church. Loisy's views, implicitly rather than explicitly, were associated with the left wing. This reading of Loisy's views by de Hulst was a gross misrepresentation. Loisy's opinions about dogma and inspiration placed him definitively outside all three schools of thought proposed by de Hulst.[78]

De Hulst's initiative proved to be quite inept, and, instead of fostering toleration, it provoked a backlash from the traditionalists. Conservative theologians such as Joseph Brucker and Paulin Moniquet condemned de Hulst's article. Loisy was dismissed from his professorship of Holy Scripture and, on 15 November, he was deprived of his position as teacher of Hebrew and other oriental languages. In the meantime the controversy surrounding de Hulst and Loisy had been brought to the pope's attention, and he responded with the encyclical *Providentissimus Deus* ("A Most Provident God"), which was issued on 18 November 1893.

Providentissimus Deus

Leo condemned the "higher criticism" of the Bible, which he saw as yet another threat to orthodoxy.[79] His criticism of the scientific community was particularly harsh—its "detestable errors" were being "obtruded on the world as the peremptory pronouncements of a newly invented free science; a science, however, which is so far from final that they are perpetually modifying and supplementing it."[80] Evidently, he had little, if any, understanding of the inductive method in modern science.

Leo believed that educated Catholics were capable of defending themselves against the intellectual imperialism of aggressive scientists. However, he was worried about "the more ignorant masses," who were susceptible to the "deadly poison" of the enemy, which, he alleged, was administered through the medium of books, pamphlets, newspapers, and public lectures. The church had to contend with those who made use of natural science to disparage the Bible. This was "peculiarly dangerous" to the masses and especially to young people, who, if they lost confidence in scripture on one or more points, were likely to abandon it completely.[81]

The Bible is a vital part of Catholic doctrine, and Leo, therefore, felt compelled to do his utmost to defend it. This required a clarification of the church's position concerning the status and authenticity of scripture. In *Providentissimus Deus*, Leo put forward guidelines for biblical studies. His theological sources included St. Augustine's *De Genesi ad Litteram* and St. Thomas Aquinas's *Summa Theologiae*. Leo's encyclical vindicated the exegetical principles proposed in Galileo's *Letter to the Grand Duchess Christina*.[82] These principles are very much in evidence in the text. Leo referred to the same passages of St. Augustine's *De Genesi ad Litteram* as Galileo did in his *Letter to the Grand Duchess Christina*.[83] However, he carefully avoided making any explicit statement about the ongoing Galilean controversy. The papacy was still far from acknowledging explicitly the merits of Galileo's hermeneutics and defense of scientific autonomy.[84] The principles and guidelines pronounced by Leo for the interpretation of scripture can be summarized as follows:

1. *The Infallibility of Scripture.* All the books of the Bible, recognized as sacred by the church, were written under the inspiration of the Holy Ghost. No error can exist—inspiration and error are incompatible. God cannot lie. The notion of partial inspiration would have enabled the church to sidestep problems concerning the veracity of scripture arising from historical criticism and the natural sciences. The basis of this approach was to argue that, in questioning the truth or falsehood of a passage, it was important to determine not so much what God actually said but God's reason for saying it. Since the Bible was written to teach people the way to salvation, rather than to advance their knowledge of history and science, was it not correct to believe that inspiration should be confined to matters of faith and morals? Leo made it clear that the church would not tolerate this exegetical principle.[85] This was a clear condemnation of de Hulst's *école large*.

2. *The Authority of the Church.* God "delivered" the Bible to the church, and the church is the authoritative guide in the reading of scripture. The First Vatican Council reiterated the decree on scripture that had been issued by the Council of Trent. In matters of faith and morals the teaching authority of the church, in accordance with the unanimous agreement of the church fathers, was to determine the true meaning of scripture. No

Catholic is permitted to put forward a contrary interpretation of the Bible (p. 286). However, not all the opinions of the fathers have to be maintained because, when commenting on physical things, they "sometimes expressed the ideas of their own times, and thus made statements which in these days have been abandoned as incorrect" (this point had been made very strenuously by Galileo in his *Letter to the Grand Duchess Christina*[86]). Therefore it is necessary for Catholic interpreters to examine carefully "what they lay down as belonging to faith, or as intimately connected with faith—what they are unanimous in." In matters not pertaining to faith, Catholics are at liberty to hold different opinions.[87] Furthermore, it was acknowledged that some published works of non-Catholics are useful to Catholic scholars—when carefully consulted. But only the unadulterated, true meaning of scripture can be found within the church (p. 289).

3. *Principle of Prudence.* The text of the Bible is sometimes used to express things that are beyond unaided human reason. The meanings of many scriptural passages may be "most difficult and obscure," with "hidden" depths of meaning, and quite different from the literal sense (pp. 277, 285). The church has not pronounced definitely on the meaning of all scriptural passages. In view of all this, care should be taken to avoid making rash assertions (p. 294). When there is agreement among "philosophers" on something that does not contradict the Catholic faith, it is unwise for Catholics to make assertions about it on the basis of dogma. Such assertions may "give to the wise of this world an occasion of despising" the Catholic faith, because in matters of natural science, "much which has been held and proved as certain has afterwards been called in question and rejected" (p. 295).

4. *Principle of Priority of Demonstration.* When convincing proofs of a natural phenomenon are put forward, it is necessary for Catholic interpreters to show that scripture can be reconciled with it. In reference to scientists Leo stated, "whatever they can really demonstrate to be true of physical nature we must show to be capable of reconciliation with our Scriptures . . ." (p. 294). Sometimes the search for reconciliation is extremely difficult. In this context Leo reiterated the basic theological principle that the proven facts of the natural sciences, archaeology, history, and other disciplines cannot, in truth, contradict scripture; that is, truth cannot contradict truth. If a contradiction is apparent between scripture and science, then every effort must be made to eliminate it. Theologians and other experts should be consulted for the purpose of ascertaining the true meaning, or the most probable meaning, of the scriptural

passages in question (pp. 299–300). It seems, however, that Leo had deep reservations about revising scriptural interpretation on the basis of what had been demonstrated in science, because, as mentioned earlier, what had sometimes been regarded as certain was later rejected.

Leo insisted that if a "discrepancy" between science and scripture persisted, then the search for reconciliation had to continue. In these circumstances there is an error, either in the interpretation of scripture or in the scientific findings. Failure to detect the mistake requires a suspension of judgment until the problem is resolved. Leo acknowledged that the interpretation of some scriptural passages not pertaining to faith and morals had been changed as a result of careful studies. However, he also indicated his awareness of the provisional nature of scientific theory when he stated that many "objections" were directed against the Bible that "have been proved to be futile and are now never heard of" (p. 300). What he was effectively doing here was setting a very high standard—arguably an unreasonably high standard—for allowing a departure from the literal reading of some biblical verses so that scripture could be reconciled with modern science—especially evolutionary theory.

5. *Principle of Priority of Scripture.* Catholic scholars are permitted to extend their studies beyond what the church fathers have done. But they are not permitted to "depart from the literal and obvious sense, except only where reason makes it untenable or necessity requires." It was deemed necessary to restrain the "thirst for novelty and the unrestrained freedom of thought" so widespread in the late nineteenth century, which, Leo feared, could lead to errors dangerous to the faith (p. 288).

6. *Principle of Accommodation.* The Bible was not intended as a guide to natural science; it is not concerned with phenomena "in no way profitable unto salvation." Some physical events or developments were described in figurative language, similar to the popular speech at the time of writing (p. 294).

7. *Principle of Independence.* No "real discrepancy" can exist between theologians and scientists when "each confines himself within his own lines" and refrains from making rash assertions concerning the other discipline (p. 294). As mentioned earlier, Catholics were urged not to invoke dogmas of faith when involving themselves in philosophical or scientific disputes that were irrelevant to the faith.

Significantly, the tensions (if not inconsistencies) between the exegetical principles that had been expressed by Galileo are present also in *Provi-*

dentissimus Deus. The principles of Prudence and Accommodation indicate that a literal reading of scriptural verses is not always compatible with the true meaning. Why, then, should there be such a heavy emphasis on the demonstration of scientific hypotheses, as required by the Priority of Demonstration and Priority of Scripture, to permit a departure from the literal meaning of biblical verses?

Providentissimus Deus was generally regarded as too conservative.[88] Although Leo's positive attitude toward scholarship can be discerned in the encyclical, it was mostly conservative and seems to have been influenced by the reactionary Jesuit cardinal Camillo Mazzella.[89] The primacy of theology was asserted: theology did not receive its first principles from other sciences—it was based on revelation from God. Other sciences were deemed to be "her inferiors or handmaids."[90] In this context, of course, theology was regarded as a discipline determined by the teaching authority of the Catholic Church. However, Catholic theology, so circumscribed, was to prove excessively restrictive on some Catholic intellectuals who attempted to reconcile their faith with modern scientific theories.

4

Defensive Strategies

Scientific Objections to Darwin's Theory

DOGMATIC DECLARATIONS BASED ON RESTRICTIVE INTERPRETATIONS of biblical texts did not constitute an adequate response to evolutionary theories. Some Catholic apologists, in common with a number of their Protestant counterparts, evidently realized that their faith could be defended in two other ways. First, they felt compelled to reexamine biblical narratives in order to reconcile scripture with established scientific findings (this response will be examined in later chapters). Second, they expressed skepticism and disbelief of evolutionary theory on the basis that it was unscientific.[1] In France, for example, the initial rejection of Darwinism by clerical intellectuals was based on contemporary scientific objections and was not simply motivated by a rigid adherence to the text of Genesis.[2] Theologians were thus able to move outside the realm of their discipline to fight the perceived threat of science with science, thus gaining a measure of credibility for their negative stance. The critics of biological evolution raised a number of credible scientific objections to the concept of natural selection.[3] To understand their arguments it is necessary to discuss in some detail several features of evolutionary theory put forward by Darwin.

In chapter 6 of *The Origin of Species*, Darwin acknowledged that there were some major problems with his theory. But none, he claimed, was fatal to what he was proposing.[4]

1. If species were descended from other species by numerous fine gradations, why were transitional forms absent or rare? Why were species so well defined? Darwin argued that each improved form of a species tended to exterminate its predecessor by natural selection; extinction and natural

selection worked in parallel. Some transitional forms did exist, such as "flying" squirrels. These gliding species represented an intermediate between earthbound mammals and flying mammals such as bats. The existence of "flying" squirrels provided evidence for the viability of animals with limbs intermediate between legs and wings (pp. 212–13).

2. Why was there an absence of innumerable transitional forms throughout many strata of the earth's crust? Darwin believed that the probability of discovering fossilized transitional forms was considerably less than forms with fully developed features because the transitional forms would have existed in lesser numbers (p. 214). Furthermore, the fossil record was far from complete. Darwin argued that the conditions necessary for fossilization were often absent and that rock formations could not be regarded as an unbroken record of continuous deposition (p. 206). Thus, there had to be huge gaps in the fossil record. Darwin gave considerable attention to this problem, devoting the whole of chapter 9 to the "extreme imperfection" of the fossil record. He stated that the scarcity of intermediate types was probably "the most obvious and gravest objection" that could be put forward against his theory (p. 292). New discoveries did eliminate some of the gaps in the fossil record, but the many that remained persuaded some scientists to explore theories based on sudden substantial changes.

3. Natural selection seemed unable to explain the existence of millions of primitive species that were still in existence. It was argued, for example, that some mollusks had remained unchanged throughout many millions of years to the present day. The persistence of unimproved species did not seem consistent with natural selection, which was supposed to be constantly at work. It was argued that many species should be more advanced than they were. Why had no other animals evolved as far as humans? Proponents of Darwin's theory argued that natural selection had to be understood in relation to the environment and conditions of each species. A lion, for example, could be regarded as an improved form of cat. It was possible for both species to coexist in the same environment because they hunted different prey. It would not benefit cats to become more like lions because this would bring the two species into competition and the cats would initially be at a disadvantage. Therefore, the evolutionary prospects of any type of animal or plant depended heavily on an ecological niche not being already occupied by another species.

4. Organs of "extreme perfection and complication" presented a serious problem to the plausibility of natural selection.[5] That a highly intri-

cate organ like the eye might have evolved by natural selection seemed "absurd in the highest possible degree" to Darwin (p. 217). Yet, on careful reflection, he maintained that it was reasonable to believe that natural selection and numerous fine changes were quite adequate to account for its development. The evolution of organs was essential to his theory. Darwin admitted: "If it could be demonstrated that any complex organ existed, which could not possibly have been formed by numerous, successive, slight modifications, my theory would absolutely break down" (p. 219). However, he could not find any example of this.

Natural selection could only favor those characteristics and structures that were favorable to the struggle for existence. Each small change in the evolutionary process implied an advantage for the population in which it occurred. It was essential to show that each modification was advantageous in comparison with the one before it. In 1865 the Swiss botanist Karl Wilhelm von Nägeli (1817–1891) observed that there were numerous specific characteristics that did not seem to have any adaptive advantage and therefore could not have been brought about by natural selection. Darwin responded to this claim in later editions of *The Origin of Species*, suggesting that, in many cases, too little was known about the lifestyle of a species to be certain that any particular characteristic was useless. Furthermore, he argued that natural selection could sometimes be forced to develop useless organs because of their close linkage to adaptive features, a correlative effect that required that in order to improve one characteristic another trait had also to be developed. The argument from the uselessness of incipient structures was sometimes used against evolutionary theory in general and sometimes specifically against the theory of natural selection. It had its limitations, however. The vast majority of those who opposed Darwin held teleological views, and it was difficult for them to claim that any organ was really useless.

5. The argument based on independent homologies was used occasionally against the theory of natural selection. Darwin's theory seemed unable to explain the separate development of similar structures in very dissimilar species. The probability of a long series of small and accidental variations bringing about the same kind of developments more than once seemed to be extremely remote. St. George Jackson Mivart (1827–1900) argued that the similarities between the eye of the squid and the mammalian eye could not have been brought about by the randomness of natural selection. He believed that the regularities in evolution indicated that it could not be a purely natural process. In later decades those who wished

to confine their explanations to the realm of science used the term "ortho-genesis," which meant that evolution was directed by an internal regular-izing mechanism.

6. Darwin was far ahead of his time. The science of genetics had not yet emerged when his book *The Descent of Man and Selection in Relation to Sex* was published in 1871. Gregor Johann Mendel had published the results of his plant breeding experiments in 1865, but it was not until the first decade of the twentieth century that biologists realized the significance of his findings. Without knowledge of the mechanisms of inherited charac-teristics, Darwin was severely disadvantaged by an unexplained premise.[6] He was unable to explain variation within species upon which natural selection acted. Furthermore, his vulnerability to sustainable criticism became quite evident in 1867, when Fleeming Jenkin, a Scottish engineer, argued that a favorable variation would be dispersed and diluted to the point of insignificance as the advantaged individual interbred with other members of the population.

7. Darwinism seemed to contradict the laws of physics as then under-stood by Victorian scientists. In 1862 the eminent British physicist William Thomson (Lord Kelvin, 1824–1907) estimated that the age of the earth was one hundred million years at most. This was based on its rate of cooling. Darwin had relied on the vast amounts of time allowed for by Lyell's uniformitarianism because he believed evolution to be an extremely slow process. Kelvin's calculations therefore tended to under-mine the theory of natural selection, supplying theologians with "some of the best weapons for an assault on Mr. Darwin's position."[7] However, this was before the discovery of radioactivity. Radioactivity, discovered by Antoine Henri Becquerel (1852–1908) in 1896, was by far the major source of energy. This meant that the earth's internal source of heat and its external source of heat (the sun) were far greater than Kelvin had esti-mated.

Of central importance to Darwinism was the concept that simple life forms evolved into more complex life forms. This seemed to be at variance with the Second Law of Thermodynamics and the process of entropy. There was (and still is) an irreversible process at work in the universe as a whole which dissipated heat energy. The principle of entropy states that matter tends to become increasingly disordered. Biological evolution implies the opposite. In reality there was no contradiction because entropy applied only to closed systems, not to open systems like the earth's biosphere, which receives most of its energy from the sun. But those who opposed evolutionary theory misapplied the principle of entropy to refute evolution.[8]

8. One of the main criticisms of Darwin's theory was that it was not inductive; that is, it was based on assumptions rather than on facts. Darwin was accused of deserting the British scientific tradition initiated by Bacon and brought to maturity by Newton. This was true to some extent. Darwin's theory was hypotheticodeductive. He did not produce any experimental evidence to prove that any animal had, over a number of generations, given rise to an animal of a distinctly different species. His critics invoked the principle of induction to refute his findings and frequently resorted to such terms as "mere conjecture," "crude theories," "reckless speculation," and "bold theorizing."[9] Those who supported Darwin acknowledged that his hypothesis could not be directly verified, but they responded, quite reasonably, that the very long time-scale associated with the formation of a new species precluded the possibility of observing the process of transmutation. Such an argument was favored by a growing awareness that a rigid inductive methodology was unduly restrictive on scientific enterprise. In the late nineteenth century there was a greater tendency among scientists to embrace the hypotheticodeductive method. The publication of Darwin's theory coincided with this development and may have contributed to it.[10] Furthermore, ordinary readers were not persuaded by the philosophical arguments against Darwin because they were unwilling to follow the debate to such a highly abstract level.[11]

After the publication of *The Origin of Species*, the theory of evolution was consolidated. Darwin's influence reached its peak in the late 1860s and 1870s.[12] But natural selection—the mechanism of evolution elaborated by Darwin—met with increasing opposition, largely because of the scientific problems associated with it. By the 1880s few supported it.

The problems that confronted the divided school of evolutionary thought were quite formidable and were used by Catholic apologists to ward off what they perceived as the threat of evolutionary theories. There was a tendency among Catholic scientists to reject Darwin's theory because it was sometimes associated with materialism and secularism.[13] Darwin and his colleagues had put forward a scientific explanation of human origins. This seemed to denigrate man's status and was regarded by many devout Christians as intolerable. In *The Descent of Man* Darwin applied the theories of *The Origin of Species* to humans. The human was descended from some "hairy quadruped," which in turn was descended from more primitive life forms.[14] Christian fundamentalists, who resolutely adhered to a literal interpretation of Genesis, according to which God created the world in six days and six nights, saw no way of reconciling it with the idea of humankind as part of an evolutionary process that had been taking place for millions of years. Furthermore, Darwin did not concede that God played an active role in evolution. This aroused much antagonism from Catholics and Protestants alike. Thus, it was observed that

> the obvious tendency of his doctrines is—if not to eliminate creative action altogether out of the universe of mind and matter, and to reduce the order of harmony of Nature to the results of blind fortuitous forces, which would be to obliterate God altogether—at least to place the Creator at such a distance from His works that His supervision, providence, and justice may be safely ignored.[15]

There was a widespread tendency among those who were religiously conservative to denounce Darwinism. Catholic apologists, like their Protestant counterparts, were determined to retain a role for God in nature because this was essential for repelling the grim specter of a godless universe. For those who wished to reconcile their Christian faith with evolution this required finding a *via media* between the notion of a blind evolutionary process and a literal reading of scripture. St. George Jackson Mivart was to play a central role in the achievement of this objective.

Mivart's Hypothesis

The majority of eminent Catholic intellectuals whose works were published in English between 1840 and 1860 were converts to Roman Catholicism. Their educational opportunities were much greater than those of their contemporaries who were born into the faith. Consequently, their intellectual horizons tended to be much more extensive. They wished to convert non-Catholics of all persuasions. Their missionary zeal was generally reflected in their published works, the readership of which extended beyond the boundaries of the Catholic community. This tendency differed from that of writers who had been reared as Catholic, who usually confined their attention to their co-religionists. The outcome of this was that publications of intellectual converts were more likely than those of born Catholics to meet standards of scholarship prevailing outside the Catholic Church.[16]

In the late nineteenth century, Catholic converts were determined to demonstrate that their church was committed to the pursuit of truth. Those who accepted evolutionary theory and adopted the historical-critical methods of biblical criticism were particularly at risk of provoking a disciplinary or punitive response from the ecclesiastical authorities. In reference to evolutionary theory and, more generally, the harmonization of the natural sciences with theology, St. George Jackson Mivart is particularly worthy of discussion. He joined the Roman Catholic Church in 1844 when to be a Roman Catholic was a distinct impediment to upward social, economic, and political mobility. Mivart, according to his biographer, Jacob W. Gruber, became the "most ardent" and the "most articulate" of the Catholic Church's "lay reformers" in England.[17] He was one of Darwin's most eminent critics throughout the 1870s.

At the time of his conversion, the future direction of the church was very uncertain. Ultramontane and liberal views were sharply at variance with one another. Ultramontane Catholics looked to Rome for strong leadership. They believed that the pope was supreme and that his pronouncement on any issue was deserving of unquestioning obedience. In contrast to this outlook, liberal Catholicism placed greater emphasis on the freedom of individual conscience and intellect and relied far less on an infallible teaching authority. Proponents of liberal views included Ignatz von Döllinger in Germany and Sir John Acton in England. They held Catholicism to be the one true faith but it had to be in agreement with the findings of objective science. During the 1850s and 1860s liberals and ultramontanes clashed on a number of issues. The liberals represented a small minority of Catholics, and, despite the strength of their arguments, they were decisively defeated, not just in England but throughout the church. After the First Vatican Council in 1870, the supremacy of ultramontanism was unassailable. In this stifling milieu some liberal Catholics ceased their efforts to reconcile the church to the new scientific and political ideas of their age. They now redirected their intellectual energies to more secular matters. Lord Acton, for example, became preoccupied with historical studies. Döllinger refused to give his assent to the Vatican Council decrees and was excommunicated.[18] Nevertheless, Catholic liberalism was not extinguished. Pope Leo XIII was less intolerant than his predecessor, and under his pontificate the suppressive activities of the ultramontane movement were held in check.[19]

It was possible, therefore, for Mivart to sustain an optimistic outlook. In his school days he was intensely interested in science, but afterwards he studied law in London and was called to the bar in 1851. In 1859 he met Huxley for the first time, and his enthusiasm for science was rekindled. It is ironic, in view of subsequent developments, that Huxley influenced him to pursue a career in science.[20] In 1861 Mivart became a student of Huxley, and the following year, with the benefit of references from Huxley and Richard Owen, he managed to secure the position of lecturer at St. Mary's Hospital in London. The relationship between Huxley and Mivart developed into one of personal friendship, despite Huxley's contempt for Roman Catholicism. It seems typical of Huxley that he could, in his sociable activities, distinguish between the belief and the believer[21]—somewhat analogous to a virtuous Christian who distinguished between the sin and the sinner. Huxley introduced Mivart to Darwin and to a number of eminent proponents of Darwin's theory, including Joseph Hooker and George Busk.

In 1868 Mivart began to experience difficulties with the acceptance of Darwin's theory of natural selection. These difficulties were very much inspired by theological considerations. On 15 June 1869 he visited Huxley at the School of Mines and made his views known. Huxley had good reason to be concerned. Mivart's professional status had benefited greatly from Huxley's goodwill. His arguments could not be dismissed as mere theological objections masquerading as science. Furthermore, although not a member of the X Club, he had been introduced into the inner circle of Darwinians and had formed friendly relationships with Ernst Haeckel and Alfred Russel Wallace.[22]

Mivart was the only eminent Catholic scientist in England, and he was aware of the frequently repeated allegation that the Catholic Church was hostile to science and progress and that it stifled the intellectual development of its members. He was determined to challenge such claims and to prove that the church's teachings were compatible with science. Furthermore, he hoped to persuade Catholics to learn and practice science. He realized that proclamations from the Vatican were not sufficient to dispel the charge that Catholicism and science were irreconcilable (pp. 48–49).

Mivart was confronted by an apparent contradiction between the Catholic and evolutionary explanations of the universe. This was extremely difficult for him because he was devoted to both science and Roman Catholicism. His objective, therefore, was to seek reconciliation between the two. With this in mind he wrote his book *On the Genesis of Species*, which was published in January 1871. Mivart had two main objectives: first, to demonstrate scientifically that Darwin's theory was untenable and that natural selection did not explain the origin of species; and, second, to show that nothing in the evolutionary process (even Darwin's explanation of it) was necessarily in opposition to Christianity (p. 52). The objections to Darwin's theory can be categorized under six headings as follows, some of which have been already discussed.

1. *The inability of natural selection to account for the incipient stages of useful structures.* Incipient or undeveloped structures did not serve a useful purpose. An explanation of such structures required either a guiding force, planning the development of the efficiently functioning organ, or a sudden change that produced the completed organ. Mivart did not dismiss natural selection completely; he conceded a very limited role for it. Natural selection could not, by itself, explain the development and conservation of rudimentary structures—even if these structures, after numerous minute modifications, became highly advantageous in time. But it was capable, by itself, of accounting for the further development of variations that were already sufficiently advantageous to the organism to give it a competitive advantage over its rivals.

2. *The independent origin of similar structures.* Parallel developments in widely dissimilar species, on the basis of accidental variations and natural selection, seemed extremely unlikely to Mivart.

3. *The importance of saltations/macrochanges in evolution.* Mivart referred to gaps in the fossil record in support of his argument. The gross underestimation of the time allowed for biological evolution, based on the laws of physics as then understood, favored Mivart's mechanism over Darwin's. Mivart argued that transitional forms, showing minute changes, were generally absent and, furthermore, that they were absent in instances where, on the basis of deduction, they were expected to be present.

4. *The development of useless organs.* This was not consistent with natural selection. Mivart gave a number of examples, including the aborted index finger of *Perodicticus potto*, a short tailed prosimian primate.

5. *Specific stability and orthogenetic tendencies.* Natural selection was supposed to operate on indefinitely varying populations. Mivart questioned how major types maintained relative stability. There seemed to be barriers that resisted change in certain directions as well as tendencies to develop in particular ways.

6. *The unity of the organism.* Every organism is made up of parts that are interrelated and coordinated. Mivart speculated that if the internal complexity of the organism could be understood, then this might shed light on a number of developmental qualities that would in turn explain the mechanism of the evolutionary process.

Jacob W. Gruber, Mivart's biographer, concluded that all of the above arguments, supported by an extensive volume of biological data, were valid (pp. 53–56). Mivart's arguments against Darwinism were used by later generations of critics, including modern creationists. He argued that humans originated not from the blind process of natural selection but from an evolutionary process under God's guidance. He claimed that theistic evolution was "thoroughly acceptable to the most orthodox theologians."[23] In doing so he referred to the works of St. Augustine, St. Thomas Aquinas, and the Jesuit Francisco de Suarez.[24] He accepted that humans, in common with all other species, were part of the evolutionary process, but, in accordance with his Catholic faith, he reaffirmed that the human soul was directly created by God.[25]

Mivart versus the Darwinians

Despite his liberal views concerning human evolution, Mivart's book was generally well received in English Catholic circles. It was favorably reviewed in the English ultramontane periodical the *Tablet*, and in the *Dublin Review*, then under the editorship of W. G. Ward, who was the leading lay figure of ultramontane Catholicism in England.[26] The *Genesis of Species*, in addition to the favorable reviews it received in the Catholic press, also received approval in professional and popular journals, such as the *British Medical Journal*, *Nature*, and the *Saturday Review*.[27] The Darwinians were slow to react in print. Darwin, after hurriedly reading the text, wrote to Alfred Russel Wallace on 30 January 1871, expressing concern that Mivart's work would "have a most potent influence versus Natural Selection. The pendulum will now swing against us." Wallace was of the opinion that the book was "exceedingly clever" and that some of the arguments against natural selection, as the only mechanism of development, were "exceedingly strong."[28] Indeed, Mivart's criticisms were so strong that when the sixth edition of the *Origin of Species* was published in 1872, a new chapter was devoted mainly to addressing them.[29]

Mivart's arguments against natural selection had benefited considerably from his knowledge of Darwin's work in progress. He had helped Darwin with experimental material for *Variation of Animals and Plants under Domestication* (1868) and *The Descent of Man* (1871). Darwin, and those who supported him, had reason to feel aggrieved that Mivart had defected to the opposite side. However, their initial reaction to the *Genesis of Species* was tolerant and impersonal. Mivart's book had treated Darwin's theory with respect. But Mivart drastically changed his argumentative approach when he reviewed Darwin's *Descent of Man* in the conservative *Quarterly Review* in July 1871. Although written under cover of anonymity, similarities between the review and the *Genesis of Species* effectively identified Mivart as the author. The tone of the article was bitter and condemnatory, peppered with personal bias. Darwin was deeply offended and, in reference to Mivart's Catholic motivations, informed his close friend Joseph Hooker that "accursed religious bigotry is at the root of it."[30]

Huxley reacted swiftly. He regarded Mivart as "clever and not a bad fellow," but he had been "insolent" to Darwin. Public excoriation of the Darwinian apostate was planned through the medium of the popular press. Huxley set to work on a review article that was to be published under the title of "Mr. Darwin's Critics" in the *Contemporary Review*. A key objective was to undermine Mivart's presentation of Catholic theology, especially in reference to Suarez. After an intensive study of scholastic philosophy and Catholic theology, Huxley, in a letter to Joseph Hooker, declared that Suarez would have "damned" Mivart "forty times over" for the views he expressed.[31]

Huxley was quite explicit about his contempt for Catholicism, declaring that the Roman Catholic Church was the "vigorous and consistent enemy of the highest intellectual, moral, and social life of mankind."[32] In addition to the truth of evolution, one of its greatest merits, for Huxley, was that it stood in absolute opposition to the teachings of the Catholic Church.[33] It was of fundamental importance to Huxley's philosophy of science that his profession confined itself to the study of nature. He was resolutely opposed to the introduction of religious issues into scientific discourse because, if this was permitted, scientific progress would be greatly impeded by beliefs and prejudices beyond the realm of empirical investigation.

Huxley's strategy was to use Catholic theology to undermine Mivart. There was merit in his argument that Suarez's theological outlook would not have allowed Catholics the freedom to embrace evolutionary theory. But he exaggerated this to the point that objectivity was clearly compromised. Huxley did not vanquish Mivart on the issue over whether or not the philosophy of the church fathers provided for the acceptance of evolutionary theory. Nor did he adequately address the scientific arguments put forward by Mivart in the course of their debate through the medium of the press.

Mivart was surprised and distressed to learn that he was no longer considered "a loyal soldier of science" because he had committed the unforgivable offense of attempting to demonstrate that there was no real incompatibility between Christian revelation and evolutionary theory.[34] An underlying cause of his dilemma can be identified by examining the sharp differences in outlook between Mivart and the Darwinians concerning the notion of a First Cause in nature. In the course of his scientific investigations Mivart resorted too readily to the invocation of the supernatural when confronted with difficult questions. In these instances further research or a more intensive application of rational analysis would have yielded at least some additional clarification in physical or rational terms.[35] Huxley, in contrast to Mivart, maintained that the idea of a First Cause did not serve any useful purpose. He reasoned: if something is produced by a supernatural cause, how does this advance our understanding? Is it not just a grandiose way of saying that we are really clueless about the matter? An event in nature is subject to explanation when it is associated with some general law of nature. But the supposed intervention of a supernatural being—by its very nature beyond the realm of science—cannot assist in the exemplification of any law. Huxley's outlook on this matter was very similar to that of the philosophers David Hume and John Stuart Mill.[36]

Tyndall, like Huxley, did not see any merit in the concept of a First Cause or personal God in nature. He argued that such a concept did not lead to the simplification of theories. Instead, he believed that the notion of an active Creator added greatly to the difficulties and complexities of physical reality. God, as a First Cause, raised more questions than he answered. If Tyndall believed in God, then he would have a burning desire to know God's origins, God's activities, and where God lives. Tyndall was aware of the Christian response that God is eternal, that God works in all things, and that God is present everywhere. But for Tyndall this was much further removed from "common sense" than the assumption that life's origins were to be found in the vast nebular cloud that formed the universe.[37]

The sharp differences of opinion between Mivart and the Darwinians were not confined to the realm of theory. Mivart failed to understand that there was also a disciplinary or institutional dimension. Huxley and other professional scientists vigorously opposed those who were motivated to use science for religious purposes and for ecclesiastical approval. If this was tolerated, then, from their point of view, the rightful autonomy of science was compromised. Scientists had the right to choose their own epistemology, education, employment, and social function independent of religious considerations or ecclesiastical restrictions.[38]

Mivart had aroused the antagonism of the Darwinians and his relationship with them suffered, both professionally and at a personal level. Although he continued to have some social contact with Huxley and Darwin their friendship had been irreversibly damaged. The rift widened gradually. The final breach occurred in the months that followed Mivart's excessive criticism of an article on eugenics by George Darwin, son of Charles Darwin. Mivart's review, published in the July 1874 issue of the *Quarterly Review*, had slandered George. In the controversy that followed, Charles Darwin and his supporters severed their social contacts with Mivart. Furthermore, they used their formidable influence to block any efforts he made to further his career. Mivart, the Darwinian apostate, had been "excommunicated."

Catholics and Scientific Freedom

After the publication of his *Genesis of Species*, Mivart continued to advocate the notion of harmony between Roman Catholicism and science in *Man and Apes* (1873), *Contemporary Evolution* (1876), *Lessons from Nature* (1876), *Nature and Thought* (1882), and *The Origin of Human Reason* (1889). In each case he found himself at odds with the Darwinians.[39] Approval of his work by the Vatican was indicated as early as 1876, when Pope Pius IX conferred on him the degree of doctor of philosophy. This award, although signifying papal approval of Mivart's opinions, does not seem consistent with the pope's personal dislike of evolutionary theory.

Mivart's project of reconciliation met with opposition not only from the Darwinians but from Catholics also. Prominent among these was the Irish priest Fr. Jeremiah Murphy. His attention had been called to an article written by Huxley in the *Contemporary Review* for November 1871. Huxley maintained that human evolution could not be reconciled with theology. Mivart, in the conclusion of his *Lessons from Nature*, attempted to overturn this argument, but Murphy, although sympathetic with his coreligionist, believed that Huxley's obstacles to reconciliation had withstood the challenge.[40]

Murphy's arguments against evolution were published under the title of "Evolution and Faith," in the *Irish Ecclesiastical Record*. Murphy rejected the claim that human evolution was reconcilable with Catholic doctrine. His rigid conservatism was probably representative of the majority of Catholic apologists and coincided with a resurgence of ultraconservatism in the church in the 1880s. But the fact that the *Irish Ecclesiastical Record* provided a platform for the expression of an opposite opinion indicates that there was a significant minority of the clergy in favor of reconciling the idea of human evolution with Catholic doctrine. A second priest, Fr. John S. Vaughan, vigorously challenged Murphy's opinions on human evolution in a series of articles published in 1884 and 1885.[41] These literary debates took place at a time when the orthodoxy of current scientific ideas was being discussed in the popular Catholic press. The primary focus was on evolution.[42]

Mivart retired in 1884 and then had plenty of time to devote to theological studies and cognate issues. He endeavored to ease the minds of Catholics who were experiencing a number of intellectual difficulties about their faith, especially concerning issues arising from the interaction of science and religion. However, he seemed unable to write in the service of his church without stimulating controversy.[43] It would have been uncharacteristic of him if he did not respond to the obscurantism of Murphy and others. His objective was to demonstrate that Catholics enjoyed far more freedom in science than they supposed. With this in mind he wrote "Modern Catholics and Scientific Freedom," published in the July 1885 issue of the *Nineteenth Century*. He asserted that the ecclesiastical authorities in the seventeenth century had stepped outside their proper sphere and imposed an erroneous decree adversely affecting the science of astronomy. They committed an even more grievous error by basing their judgment on scripture—the interpretation of which was supposed to be within their range of competence. Furthermore, the ecclesiastical authorities had failed to express remorse on behalf of their predecessors for the misguided actions of the institutional church against Galileo.[44]

Mivart drew two conclusions from his findings. First, when ecclesiastical congregations declared that an idea concerned with science was contrary to scripture and the teaching of the church fathers, they might be in error. Second, in some instances, as in the case of Galileo, scientists had a better understanding of scripture than ecclesiastical authorities. The term "science" used by Mivart extended beyond the natural sciences to include political economy, history, and biblical criticism—everything that "comes within the reach of human inductive research, and is capable of verification."[45] Catholic scientists were then urged not to permit the pronouncements of ecclesiastical authorities to interfere with their pursuit of truth.[46]

Mivart did not rest his argument entirely on the case of Galileo when contending that scientists might understand the biblical narratives better than the church authorities. He reminded his readers of one of Fr.

Murphy's objections to the evolution of humankind. Murphy argued that "so precise, so circumstantial, is the Scriptural account of man's creation, that, if the evolution theory were true, the sacred writers, if they intended to deceive us, could not have chosen language better calculated to effect that end."[47] Mivart candidly admitted that he was at a disadvantage in challenging Murphy. He had no skill or knowledge of exegesis, but he was not overwhelmed by such a consideration because the key to enlightenment here was science, not theology. Mivart argued that Murphy's statement about deception could be applied, with equal effect, to the universality of the Flood—which, by the late nineteenth century, had been discredited by science.

Mivart acknowledged that human evolution could not be scientifically demonstrated and that the mental dissimilarities between humans and animals indicated against evolution. Nevertheless, a physical phenomenon that is incapable of demonstration is not necessarily untrue. And the anatomical, developmental, and physiological similarities between humans and animals strongly indicate a common origin. On balance it seemed that humans did evolve. This had profound implications for Mivart, because Murphy argued that Catholics were forbidden by the dogmatic imperatives of their faith to believe in human evolution.[48] Their salvation was at stake. This assertion was intolerable to Mivart. God would not have created the first humans instantly with physical features pointing strongly toward an evolutionary process. He would not test the faith of Catholics to such an extent as to endanger their eternal happiness. Furthermore, as Murphy had acknowledged, no authoritative statement by a pope or general council of the church had been issued against evolution.[49]

Mivart was aware of the difficulty of reconciling his views with the pronouncements of the encyclical *Mirari Vos* (1832), the Munich Brief, *Quanta Cura*, and the *Syllabus of Errors*. He acknowledged the possibility that the church might make a similar error to that of condemning Galileo. If the teaching authority of the church ever demanded assent to an article of faith that conflicted with truth—something supported by a "preponderance of evidence"—then authority would lose its claim to allegiance. This had already happened in matters of science because of the poor judgement exercised by the church authorities in dealing with Galileo.[50] Authority had to be justified by reason and the merit of scientific and philosophical hypotheses would be decided not by authority but by evidence. The church's authority would be limited to the relatively narrow domain of faith and morals—a proposal that was, at the time, diametrically opposed to developments which extended rather than restricted papal power and influence.

According to Mivart's biographer, Jacob W. Gruber, the article "Modern Catholics and Scientific Freedom," was the beginning of a long process of withdrawal from the church. Mivart's criticism of ecclesiastical authority, in the context of the Galileo affair, was so severe that it even exceeded that of his old antagonist, Thomas Henry Huxley. As Huxley toured Rome in early 1885 he was mindful of how Galileo had suffered at the hands of the Inquisition.[51] Months later, after returning to England, he read "Modern Catholics and Scientific Freedom" in the light of his own research on Galileo. However, instead of castigating the church authorities, he concluded, in a letter to Mivart, that "the Pope and the College of Cardinals had rather the best of it."[52]

Mivart's article was provocative and was roundly condemned by the Catholic press in Britain.[53] Murphy's response was published in the May 1886 issue of the *Nineteenth Century*. He asserted that the intellectual freedom that Mivart claimed for Catholics was not really freedom at all but "wanton license, the offspring of intellectual pride." The freedom that Mivart wished for was neither sought by loyal Catholics nor granted by the church.[54] Murphy referred to a number of papal documents to bolster his argument, including the encyclical *Quanta Cura* and two briefs addressed to the archbishop of Munich—*Inter Gravissimas* (1862) and *Tuas Libenter* (1863).[55] Furthermore, when Mivart claimed that the ecclesiastical authorities had hindered the progress of science in the seventeenth century, he was castigated by Murphy for reiterating the twelfth proposition condemned in the *Syllabus of Errors*. Murphy's opinion, rather than Mivart's, represented the dominant attitude toward science in the upper echelons of the Roman Catholic Church. Nevertheless, ecclesiastical authority did not censure Mivart. Nor was there even a hint of displeasure.

Mivart, confident of his position in the church, reiterated his views on scientific freedom under the title of "The Catholic Church and Biblical Criticism" in the July 1887 issue of the *Nineteenth Century*. However, his main focus was now on the criticism of biblical narratives from the historical rather than the natural sciences. He was pleased that the teaching authority of the church had refrained from condemning evolution, and he believed that there was no longer a danger of conflict between Catholic theology and biological science. The same could not be said for the historical sciences. It seemed very likely that historical criticism would elicit condemnation from the ecclesiastical authorities and lead to the greatest ever crisis in Christendom. He had read the works of Edouard Reuss, Bishop John William Colenso, Julius Wellhausen, and A. Kuenen. These were men whose opinions could not be lightly set aside. Therefore, he hoped that the Vatican would prudently abstain from issuing any pronouncement against modern Biblical criticism.[56]

Mivart concluded that many of the Old Testament texts were misleading in a historical sense. What was commonly thought to be history was now, on the basis of modern criticism, shown to be "mythical, legendary, or quite false." The book of Chronicles, for example, was "a thoroughly unhistorical work"; the book of Daniel was "little more than a mass of fiction"; and the book of Judith was "a mere romance" (pp. 41–42).

Mivart did not regard the leading biblical critics as infallible. Their views, like those of their counterparts in the natural sciences, were open to correction. What was of crucial significance here was his conviction that historical criticism led one much closer to the truth than traditional approaches to scripture. Choosing sides was determined on the basis of evidence. A principle of fundamental importance was the moral duty to withhold assent from a belief that was not "adequately proved," the corollary of which was to give assent to what was "evidently true" (p. 35). But would not such a principle, in view of the results of historical research, prove fatal to the Catholic faith, especially considering the church's practice of quoting scripture to bolster its authority? Mivart did not think so. The church had come to terms with the Copernican hypothesis, geological discoveries, and the theory of biological evolution. It had changed its teachings and demonstrated remarkable ability to adapt to advancements in the natural sciences. The same adaptive process would occur with biblical criticism—which was, at that point, in its "pre-Copernican" phase of development.

The works of Kuenen, Colenso, Reuss, Wellhausen, and others would cause alarm and distress initially, but when the controversy subsided, history and theology would move toward reconciliation (pp. 44–46). The church was not as vulnerable as it seemed. It was in a much stronger position that the Protestant churches because of its claim to have existed before the New Testament was written. It claimed the authority to interpret the New Testament in whatever way it deemed appropriate. Furthermore, the many works of its theologians provided it with "other bases of support" (p. 47). Mivart next referred to the idea of partial inspiration put forward by Cardinal Newman in 1884, which seemed to offer an excellent means of defense against troublesome findings in science and history. One could argue that only matters concerning faith and morals were definitely inspired. However, the word "inspiration" was not clearly defined. Inspired narratives might after all contain error. If scripture was held to be inspired—"in some undefined sense of that word"—then all difficulties that might otherwise be presented by science and history could be avoided. Catholics could put their minds at ease (p. 48). Mivart's views were, however, more novel and were expressed much less cautiously, than those of Cardinal Newman.

Mivart envisaged that the Vatican would be led by progressive Catholic opinion. What the teaching authority initially resisted, it would ultimately accept. The church's error in censoring Galileo now provided the basis for greatly extending the boundaries of Catholic intellectual freedom. Ecclesiastical authorities and theologians had no right to dictate science to scientists, nor history to historians—rather, they had a duty to be enlightened by them. The Galileo affair had effectively given the coup de grâce to assertions of authority by the Catholic hierarchy based on the "ordinary teaching" and the "consensus of theologians." Therefore, Catholic thinking could only be circumscribed by decrees of the pope, issued *ex cathedra* about faith and morals (p. 50).

Mivart was confident that inaccuracies in the Bible pertaining to science and history posed no threat to the Catholic faith. His views did not go unchallenged. In the October 1887 issue of the *Nineteenth Century*, Sir James F. Stephen responded with "Mr. Mivart's Modern Catholicism." Stephen was not Roman Catholic, nor was he sympathetic toward Roman Catholicism. He maintained that Mivart failed to grasp the implications of his arguments in his previous two articles. If Mivart acknowledged the merit of biblical criticism by Kuenen, Colenso, Reuss, and Wellhausen, why not also include the works of David Friedrich Strauss and Ernest Renan, which were so contrary to fundamental Christian beliefs? Was there an intellectually credible basis for excluding their contributions to biblical scholarship? Essential doctrines of the church concerning the birth, life, death, resurrection, and ascension into heaven of Jesus Christ were all held to be historical events, just like the accounts of creation, the formation of Eve, and the Flood. If the Old Testament stories were untrue, why should one believe the New Testament narratives? How could one still believe in Jesus Christ when the stories about him had "all the marks which distinguish poetical legends from history" and were little more than "uncertified hearsay?"[57] What basis was there for belief in the absence of sound historical evidence? Stephen argued that if the natural sciences, literary criticism, and history were allowed complete freedom, then the existence of God, the infallibility of the church, and the truth of its dogmas would all be called into question. Ecclesiastical authority and Christian faith would be undermined (pp. 588, 590).

Stephen was adamant that faith and reason were irreconcilable. Attempts to embrace both in theology led to "a double standard of truth," which was "absolutely fatal to common sense" and to "common honesty." Faith rested on the acceptance of a conclusion "without qualification" and on the basis of "imperfect" evidence. It was so radically different from scientific epistemology that Stephen questioned the ability of any rational person to think in terms of such conflicting principles (p. 591). The absolute primacy of reason in the search for truth was a basic element of his philosophy. How could one make any judgment on any controversial issue except through reason? (p. 597) But reason, if not manacled by ecclesiastical authorities, would turn Catholic theology into a "poetic fable" (p. 594). Stephen saw painful dilemmas ahead for Mivart as he fought a losing battle to reconcile his scientific outlook with his religious beliefs (p. 596).

Mivart answered Stephen's essay in December 1887, again through the medium of the *Nineteenth Century*. In "Catholicity and Reason" he maintained that faith was based on reason, not on authority, and that there was no inconsistency in accepting propositions based on both reason and faith. Reason assessed the credibility of authority and the revelation it promulgated. The authenticity of revelation was judged on the basis of whether or not it was self-contradictory and whether or not it contradicted any "self-evident truth." The absence of such contradictions did not, of course, constitute adequate proof of the credibility of divine revelation, which probably contained truths beyond the reach of "unaided" reason. If assent was to be given to any proposition, religious or otherwise, then it had to be based ultimately on "ordinary human reason."[58]

What Mivart needed was positive proof of Catholic dogma. He was satisfied that he had found it, but he chose not to give an account of his reasoning on the basis that limited space did not provide for what would be a lengthy exposition (p. 862). In this article, therefore, his objectives were limited to a demonstration that Catholicity and reason were in harmony. As a Catholic he was amenable to reasonable arguments. But what if the church declared, dogmatically, something to be true that was demonstrated by science to be false? Then Mivart would abandon his Catholic faith, provided that he was "absolutely certain of the scientific truth" under discussion (pp. 868–69).

As a man of science, in the broadest sense, Mivart was quite prepared to add Strauss and Renan to his list of biblical critics. If they proved that statements of fact pertaining to essential Catholic doctrines were untrue, then he would regard Christian faith as untenable. It was easy for him to make this concession to historical criticism because he had already placed obstacles in the way of such an unwelcome conclusion. Such obstacles would be arduous if not impossible to overcome. The supreme authority for him was the church rather than the Bible. The dogmas of the church were primarily based on the authority of the church rather than on the New Testament. He could thus concede, if necessary, that many of the New Testament narratives were unhistorical (pp. 856–58).

Mivart placed Catholic dogmas of revelation beyond the scope of inductive research in both the social and natural sciences. Therefore, it would be absurd for scientists to deny the virgin birth and resurrection of Jesus Christ on grounds of physiology, or Christ's presence in the Eucharist on the basis of chemistry. It would be meaningless to assert that the pope could not receive divine guidance when speaking *ex cathedra* because of psychological considerations, or that miracles were impossible because of the laws of nature (p. 864). Mivart had nothing to fear from Strauss, Renan, Huxley, or Tyndall. The maximum intellectual freedom could be gained for Roman Catholics at no cost to the security of their faith, which would be placed safely beyond the boundaries of rational discourse. Mivart had, in reality, avoided rather than confronted the arguments of Stephen.[59]

The intellectual freedom that Mivart claimed for himself and his fellow Catholics was very much in excess of what the institutional church was prepared to grant. Bishop John Hedley of Newport was given the onerous task of issuing a response. The bishop was acknowledged as the semi-official spokesman for the hierarchy on controversial issues, but he did not wish to engage in this controversy, probably because Mivart was a personal friend of his. Hedley was urged, "by those whom he felt bound to respect," to write an article on "Dr. Mivart on Faith and Science," which was summarized in the *Tablet* before publication in the *Dublin Review* (1887). Hedley judged some of Mivart's opinions to be "theologically wrong, erroneous and mischievous"—and, most significantly, found them to be "censurable" if "the right authority" decided to take action. He called on Mivart to retract his unorthodox views.[60] Mivart declined to do so. In his letter to Hedley, published in the *Dublin Review*, he was respectful but defiant.[61] Hedley was conciliatory, insofar as he could be, acknowledging that, in view of his published works against irreligious ideas, Mivart deserved the praise and gratitude of English-speaking Catholics.

However, he took the opportunity to caution the scientist against making assertions in matters of theology.[62]

Mivart persisted in his refusal to retract anything that he had written. Hedley, again through the medium of the *Dublin Review*, felt it necessary to reiterate the church's position. Mivart's assertion of intellectual freedom for Catholics was far too extensive and, therefore, was intolerable to the church. The Bible was not to be treated like an ancient text devoid of divine inspiration. It was not to be submitted to the judgment of those who lacked the Catholic virtues of humility and obedience. Mivart had relied too much on reason and not enough on faith.[63]

The ecclesiastical authorities in England did not formally censure Mivart. Nor did the Vatican reveal any sign of displeasure. Emboldened by such tolerance, Mivart turned his attention to another issue which led him far beyond the interface of science and theology in his search for truth, intruding deep into the realm of the latter. He naively set about the task of liberating his church from the doctrine of hell. The church, as he should have understood, would not relinquish such a belief, because it acted as a powerful device in compelling compliance. Mivart believed that for many Catholics this doctrine was the single greatest difficulty of their faith. He did not deny the existence of hell, but he argued that it was possible for its imprisoned inhabitants to find some measure of happiness there. He objected strenuously to the doctrine of hell on humanitarian as well as on theological grounds. In his quixotic attempt to enlighten the church Mivart wrote three articles on "Happiness in Hell" that were published in the *Nineteenth Century* from December 1892 to April 1893. The Vatican did not appreciate his good intentions, and on 19 July 1893 the Holy Office in Rome decreed that the three articles were to be placed on the Index of Forbidden Books. Mivart immediately submitted on the basis that none of his propositions had been condemned.[64] Four months later Pope Leo XIII's *Providentissimus Deus* was issued. Its publication was probably far more distressing to Mivart than the condemnation of his articles on hell. The encyclical dealt a bitter blow to Mivart's hope that scripture would no longer be invoked to violate the rightful autonomy of science. A more oppressive orthodoxy was emerging that was to prove inimical to his cherished hypothesis about evolution and Catholic theology.

5

The Suppression of the
Mivartian Hypothesis

Leroy and Zahm

IN EUROPE THE PROCEEDINGS OF FIVE INTERNATIONAL SCIENTIFIC
congresses of Catholics, held in Paris (1888, 1891), Brussels (1894), Fribourg (1897), and Munich (1900), indicated a complexity and diversity of views toward evolution. At the congress held in 1888 it was proposed that Catholics should oppose evolutionary theory on the basis that it was incompatible with the Catholic faith and that it contradicted the Bible. The proposal failed to gain sufficient support, and therefore it was not approved. Many Catholics were able to distinguish between the misapplication of evolution as an element of antireligious ideology and the application of evolution as a very important concept in science. The acceptance of evolution was widespread among scientists—including Catholic scientists, for example, J. B. J. d'Omalius d'Halloy, Charles Naudin, Albert Gaudry, and the Marquis Gaston de Saporta. Some of those who did not support evolution, such as Paul Maisonneuve (professor at the Catholic faculty of science in Angers), realized that the autonomy of science had to be respected and that no attempts should be made to suppress discussions about evolution.[1] Even Darwin's theory of natural selection found support among Catholics. The German Jesuit biologist Erich Wasmann defended Darwinism against the criticisms of Albert Fleischmann. Catholic supporters of Darwin did not see an inevitable conflict between natural selection and the doctrine of creation.

In the 1890s the Vatican indicated its disapproval of evolutionary theory extended to humankind. Nevertheless, there was a substantial liberalization of discourse, and this was evident from the proceedings of the fifth international congress held in Munich in 1900. There was greater confidence in speculating on the probable relationship between humans and animals on the basis of the evolutionary process. The acrimony that had frequently characterized debates concerning science and religion subsided. This was particularly evident in late-nineteenth- and early twentieth-century France. There are a number of explanations for this. A new intellectual atmosphere developed that was more favorable to religious belief. French Catholicism experienced a vigorous intellectual renewal, some of it stimulated by the Catholic universities. A qualitative improvement in Catholic higher education occurred after the establishment of Catholic institutes in Paris, Lille, Lyon, Angers, and Toulouse in the late 1870s. Science faculties were established in these institutes to counteract anticlerical scientism in the state universities. Scientists were trained here in an intellectual milieu controlled by the church.[2] Science seemed less threatening, notwithstanding the continued assaults of some scientists such as Marcelin Berthelot, Yves Delage, and Félix Le Dantec. Their ability to intensify disputes arising from the overlapping domains of religion and science was limited because Catholic apologists proved quite adept at manipulating their opponents into defensive positions through the use of scientific arguments. The widespread acceptance of evolutionary theory among Catholic biologists and anthropologists also played a major role in dissipating the tension between religion and science in French Catholicism.[3]

In France and elsewhere there was also a growing realization among perceptive Christians that the outright condemnation of evolution served only to endanger the faith rather than safeguard it. The evidence for evolution was growing rather than diminishing. Discerning apologists realized that if theologians and ecclesiastical authorities persisted in making belief in the Bible dependent on the rejection of evolution, this would eventually endanger the credibility of scripture. This motivated them to study more carefully the implications of evolution to see if it could be reconciled with scripture.[4]

Some of those who wrote and spoke in defense of their faith were confident that evolution, as a scientific hypothesis, did not pose a real threat to Catholic belief. To support their assertions of orthodoxy they studied and cited the published works of the church fathers, especially St. Augustine of Hippo (A.D. 354–430). This practice had the advantage of providing some degree of protection against the risks of ecclesiastical censorship (although it was not clear to what extent the writings of the church fathers supported arguments for or against evolution).[5] The invocation of the church fathers did not dissuade some Catholics who opposed evolutionary theory from reporting deviations from orthodoxy—real or imagined—to the church authorities in Rome. The papacy, as noted already, refrained from issuing any dogmatic statements about evolution pertaining to the physical origins of humankind. Nevertheless, the hierarchical church had other options open to it in curtailing the enthusiasm of those who, in its opinion, displayed an unhealthy tendency to advocate rash hypotheses inimical to the faith.

The reaction against evolutionary theory was strong in Italy. In the mid-1890s the church authorities in Rome became highly intolerant of evolution. This intolerance originated not from Pope Leo XIII himself but from a clique of ultraconservative and highly influential Jesuits in Rome. Their views were published in the journal *Civiltà Cattolica* and were also expressed surreptitiously to great effect. They played a pivotal role in the censorship of a number of eminent Catholic scholars in the 1890s.

In 1887 Père M. D. Leroy's *Evolution des Espèces Organiques* was published. The second edition was issued under the title *L'Evolution Restreinte des Espèces Organiques* (*Evolution Restricted to Organic Species*). The French Dominican cleric set forth a theory of human evolution that was similar to Mivart's. Leroy argued that the Bible does not rule out the evolution of the human body and that the church fathers did not write conclusively on the matter. Furthermore, he observed that the decree of the Council of Cologne, which ruled out spontaneous evolution, did not rule out evolution under God's directive power. The Cologne decree was then the only ecclesiastical edict on the subject.

Leroy argued, in reference to St. Thomas Aquinas, that it is the human soul that makes the human body specifically human. God directly created the soul and infused it into the body; therefore God effectively made the human body. Leroy took great care to maximize the retention of traditional beliefs in presenting his hypothesis. In nineteenth-century French clerical circles this cautious treatise was viewed as unorthodox, and Leroy received very little support from his clerical colleagues.[6] His book was denounced to the Holy Office (renamed the Congregation for the Doctrine of the Faith) by M. Chalmel. The consultors examined Leroy's book and found that the accusations of Chalmel were without foundation. Nevertheless Leroy was summoned to Rome in February 1895, and later that month the retraction of his treatise was published in *Le Monde* (Paris). He had been persuaded by "the competent authority" that his work was "untenable," especially in reference to the human body. Therefore, as a "docile child of the Church," he retracted what he had written and undertook to do his utmost to restrict the circulation of his book.[7] The "competent authority" was the Holy Office, and there is strong evidence to indicate that it was influenced by the authors of *Civiltà Cattolica*. The terminology in the text of its judgment against Leroy is strikingly similar to that of articles in *Civiltà Cattolica* written by the Jesuits Fr. Salvatore Brandi (1852–1915) and Fr. Francesco Salis-Seewis.[8] These writers, in common with their colleagues, wrote anonymously.

The second distinguished Catholic scholar to suffer at the hands of the ecclesiastical censors was Fr. John A. Zahm (1851–1921), a priest of the Congregation of the Holy Cross and professor of physics at the University of Notre Dame in the United States of America. In 1893 Zahm delivered five lectures on the relationship between revelation and science at the Catholic Summer School in Plattsburgh, New York. These lectures were very well attended and received wide coverage in the secular and religious press. In some quarters Zahm was regarded as the "Mivart of America" because of his progressive thinking about science and religion. Eventually these lectures formed the basis of his book *Bible, Science, and Faith* (1894). In this work he insisted that, contrary to popular opinion, Catholics had wide latitude of intellectual freedom and that the dogmas of their church did not prevent or restrain an interest in science.[9] Over the next two years he delivered popular lectures and wrote a number of journal articles on evolution and Catholic doctrine.[10]

In 1896 Zahm's book *Evolution and Dogma* was published in the United States. Shortly afterwards it was published in French and Italian. In his introduction Zahm stated his reasons for writing on the subject of evolution. He was acutely aware that agnostics and atheists were using evolutionary theory to undermine religious belief, and, in his opinion, they were enjoying considerable success. Ignorance about evolution was "dense" among American Catholics, and this made them vulnerable to adverse influences. Zahm frequently encountered "pious but timid souls" who were distressed because evolution had raised serious doubts about their faith. They were under the mistaken impression that they had to choose between evolution and faith—unaware that the church had not pronounced against evolutionary theory.[11]

In Zahm's opinion the best antidote to apostasy was education. Therefore, his objective was to educate his fellow American Catholics. In doing so he decided to adopt a *via media* between two extremes—"reprehensible" liberalism, which endangered the faith, and ultraconservatism, which stifled intellectual progress. Evolution had become associated with materialistic, agnostic, and atheistic philosophies. But the misuse of a theory did not indicate how sound or unsound it was (pp. vii–viii). Zahm felt free to evaluate evolutionary theory on its scientific merits in view of the fact that the church had not defined its position on the issue. He discussed at length the arguments for and against evolution and concluded that no satisfactory evolutionary mechanism had yet been proposed. Lamarckism and Darwinism were seriously flawed (p. 196), but evolution itself was established beyond reasonable doubt (p. 201). Zahm concluded that the "most venerable philosophical and theological authorities" of the Catholic Church supported theistic evolution (p. 312).

If evolution was to be regarded as a tenable hypothesis by Roman Catholics, how did it compare to the alternative of "special" creation? Both ideas were based on a number of assumptions. Zahm did not pretend that evolution had been conclusively proven. Nevertheless, its degree of probability was "very great." Furthermore, its great commendation was its use to explain a great variety of natural phenomena. Special creation, in contrast, had "no foundation but assumption" and could claim "no more substantial basis than certain postulates which are entirely gratuitous." The theory of special creation explained nothing in science and, by its very nature, was incapable of explaining anything. Furthermore, it tended to impede research and obstruct progress (pp. 417–19).

The issue of special creation versus evolution was regarded by Zahm as analogous to a number of other controversies at the interface of science and religion. It was clear from geology and paleontology that the six days of creation in Genesis were not literally days. It had been widely believed that the Flood, described in chapters 7 and 8 of Genesis, had covered the entire earth. This was no longer credible in view of progress in a range of disciplines, including ethnology, linguistics, prehistoric archaeology, and the interpretation of scripture. Similarly, the notion that the genealogies of Genesis could be used to date the creation of the first humans to about 4,000 B.C. had been discredited by science. Zahm believed that the notion of special creation had been similarly discredited, and he concluded that "the preponderance of probability" was "overwhelming in favor of Evolution of some kind" (pp. 419–23).

Catholics were at liberty to accept the evolution of plants and animals—but what about the evolution of humankind? Zahm asserted that there was no sound fossil evidence for human evolution (p. 351). There was much debate as to whether or not the newly discovered *Pithecanthropus erectus* ("Java man") was the "missing link" between humans and apes, but Zahm did not think so and believed it unlikely that strong evidence for human evolution would be discovered in the near future. Nevertheless, there was nothing in science that would exempt humans from the evolutionary process, and the vast majority of contemporary evolutionists had come to accept the idea of humankind's primitive ancestry.

Zahm was aware that evolutionary theory, applied to humans, might create "certain grave difficulties" in metaphysics and biblical exegesis. Such difficulties, he believed, could be overcome. Mivart's hypothesis had been publicly discussed for twenty-five years. Zahm maintained that if the *Genesis of Species* was dangerous to the faith of Catholics, as some of its critics had argued, or if it was heretical, it would have been put on the Index of Forbidden Books (p. 358). Since the book had not been condemned, it was reasonable to claim that it was not in conflict with Catholic doctrine. Nevertheless, there was still very strong ecclesiastical opposition to Mivart's hypothesis.

Zahm was, apparently, unaware that Leroy had retracted his treatise. He referred to Leroy's *L'Evolution Restreinte des Espèces Organiques*, observing that it had received the *imprimatur* of the Dominican provincial and the *censor librorum* of the Dominican order. Furthermore, he observed that the theologian Père T. R. P. Monsabré and the eminent Catholic geologist Albert de Lapparent had expressed support for Leroy's views (p. 363). There was no mention of Leroy's retraction in *Le Monde*. Zahm concluded that, whatever the verdict of science on human evolution, there could be no sustainable objection on the basis of Catholic dogma (pp. 364, 428–29).

Evolution and Dogma was an international best-seller. In the United States the response was mainly favorable. It received laudatory reviews in a number of journals such as the *Popular Science Monthly* and the *Dial*. The response of the Catholic press was mixed. *Donahoe's Magazine*, the *Messenger of the Sacred Heart*, and the weekly *Review*, edited by Arthur Preuss, all expressed strong opposition to it. The *Catholic World*, the *American Ecclesiastical Review*, the *Catholic University Bulletin*, and the *Catholic Citizen* supported it.[12]

In Europe Zahm's book received some good reviews, but not in Rome. This did not surprise the Holy Cross priest. He anticipated that the Italian and French editions would elicit a critical response from the Jesuits of *Civiltà Cattolica*. Nevertheless, he was optimistic. This proved to be an underestimation of the influence of those who were determined to see his work censored.[13] Curial officials were angry because Zahm had presented Sts. Augustine and Thomas Aquinas as evolutionists. Fr. Salvatore Brandi alleged that Zahm misunderstood Thomistic philosophy and that this led him to misapply neo-scholastic principles.[14] Zahm's book was denounced to the Congregation of the Index on 5 November 1897 by Bishop Otto

Zardetti, who served as bishop of Minnesota and later as archbishop of Bucharest. He had retired in June 1895. In his submission to the Congregation, Zardetti cited articles by Salis-Seewis in *Civiltà Cattolica*, and a review of the book by Brandi, also in *Civiltà Cattolica*. His only other supporting reference was the Latin theological manual *De Deo Creante: Praelectiones scholastico-dogmaticae* (1880) by Cardinal Camillo Mazzella. The Dominican priest Enrico Buonpensière was the only consultor asked to examine Zahm's book. The only supporting reference cited in Fr. Buonpensière's report was the review by Brandi in *Civiltà Cattolica*. He recommended that the Congregation issue a public condemnation of Zahm's book so that Catholics would be clear about what they were not to believe concerning evolutionary theory. The Congregation did not accept this proposal, choosing instead to issue a decree of personal condemnation to Zahm, channeled through the Superior General of his order. As in the case of Leroy, there was evidence to indicate that the authors of *Civiltà Cattolica* were well informed about what was happening at the Holy Office and at the Congregation of the Index.[15]

Zahm submitted to Rome and withdrew the English-language edition of his book. On 16 May 1899 he also wrote to Alfonso Galea, the Italian translator of his book, seeking assistance in having the book withdrawn from sale because he had learned from an "unquestionable authority" that the Vatican was "adverse" to its further distribution.[16] This letter was published without the author's permission in the *Gazetta di Malta* on 31 May or early June and was republished from this source by *Civiltà Cattolica* on 1 July. Shortly afterwards Zahm quietly withdrew from his role as an apologist for the church in matters at the interface of theology and science.[17]

Bonomelli and Hedley

The attitude of the church authorities in Rome had hardened against theistic evolutionary theory. As the examination of Zahm's book was in progress, Bishop Geremia Bonomelli (1831–1914) of Cremona found himself in trouble. In an appendix to his book *Seguiamo la Ragione* (1898), he had referred to the evolutionary origins of the human body as explained by Zahm. He did not condemn it, and this was regarded as an unacceptable omission. Bonomelli, unlike Leroy and Zahm, was not contacted by the Holy Office or by the Congregation of the Index. Instead he was persuaded by "friendly, kind and very competent persons" that the evolution of humankind, even as a hypothesis, was "not perfectly in conformity with the teaching of the Church."[18] He was urged to make public his repudiation of human evolution. He did so through the medium of a letter to the *Lega Lombarda* in late October 1898. The authors of *Civiltà Cattolica* reported Bonomelli's repudiation "with pleasure" and republished the full text of his letter.[19] Bonomelli's letter was published after Leroy's retraction but before Zahm's letter to the Italian translator of his book.

It was not clear at the time on whose authority the books of Leroy and Zahm had been censored. The reason for this was that the Vatican had resolutely avoided making any explicit condemnation of evolution pertaining to the human species. The published works of Charles Darwin and Jean Baptiste de Lamarck were not included in the 1,359 items added to the Vatican's Index of Forbidden Books in the nineteenth century.[20] This led to some confusion about the church's official position on the issue. The unpleasant experience of Bishop John Cuthbert Hedley of Newport (England) with *Civiltà Cattolica* provides an excellent example of such confusion. Hedley was the leading intellectual figure in the English Catholic hierarchy. In 1871 he wrote in the *Dublin Review* that to question the instantaneous or "quasi-instantaneous" creation of Adam's body from inorganic matter, and Eve's body from a rib of Adam, was "at least, rash, and, perhaps, proximate to heresy."[21] However, twenty-seven years later he had changed his mind about evolution and wrote approvingly of it in the October 1898 issue of the *Dublin Review* when reviewing Zahm's published work about Catholicism and science. Hedley did criticize Zahm on a number of points, but he maintained that Zahm's presentation of evolutionary theory did not in any way endanger the faith. It was possible for a Catholic to be a "good evolutionist without giving up one iota of his faith or his Catholic philosophy."[22]

Hedley's article on "Physical Science and Faith" was lavishly praised by the liberal Catholic newspaper *La Rassegna Nazionale* of Florence. This in turn elicited an adverse commentary from Brandi in *Civiltà Cattolica* on 7 January 1899 under the heading of "Evoluzione e domma." The retraction of Père Leroy was quoted which vaguely referred to the "competent authority." Hedley responded through the medium of the English Catholic periodical the *Tablet* (11 January 1899). He referred to his 1871 article, observing that a view that was considered "rash"—theologically speaking—need not always be considered rash. The attribution of "rashness" could be justified only if the idea in question was contrary to the consensus of theologians or was not proposed on a reasonable basis. Evidently he had been unaware of Leroy's retraction, and he assumed that the authority stated by *Civiltà Cattolica* was that of the Holy Office. Therefore he felt compelled to conclude that the Mivartian theory was no longer tenable.[23]

The Holy Office, despite the power of the ultraconservatives, had to deal sensitively with Leroy and others who had not advocated anything clearly in violation of dogma. The case against evolution was not strong enough to impose conformity in a heavy-handed manner. In the Leroy case the consultors to the Holy Office had advised against the publication of a condemnation. Leroy was a highly respected scholar in the church, and the consultors feared that such a punitive act would provoke opposition from many influential theologians. In the case of Zahm, ecclesiastical politics probably dictated a cautious policy. Several American prelates, including Cardinal James Gibbons of Baltimore, Archbishop John Ireland of St. Paul, and Bishop Denis O'Connell of Richmond, were frequently traveling between the United States and Rome. They were trying to persuade the Vatican not to condemn Zahm, and Americanism—a unique variant of Catholic liberalism that, *inter alia*, advocated the acceptance of the principle of religious liberty and the separation of church and state. They failed in both objectives. In view of the opinions of the American prelates, however, the reactionaries in Rome probably thought it prudent not to deal too severely with Zahm.[24]

Controversies about the implications of evolutionary theories for Catholic theology did not occur in isolation from other issues. In the case of Zahm the censorship of his book was not due simply to theological considerations. There were a number of complicating factors, such as Zahm's support for the liberal "Americanist" clergy in the 1880s and 1890s; the ecclesiastical power politics of ultraconservatives such as Salvatore Brandi; and the inordinate fear of Zahm's Superior General that the status of the Congregation of the Holy Cross, and its relationship with the papacy, might be endangered.[25]

The actions of the church authorities in Rome did not reflect the outlook of Pope Leo XIII. The difference between Pius IX and Leo XIII was not that one was a conservative and the other a liberal. Their aims were very similar but their means were different. Pius's attitude toward the modern world was one of intransigence and confrontation. Leo's approach was one of constructive dialogue and cautious compromise.[26] Thus, he was far more progressive than his predecessor. His encyclical *Rerum Novarum* (1891) was one of the most important papal pronouncements in modern history, and it profoundly influenced the formation of Catholic social teaching throughout the twentieth century. He endeavored to bring the church into dialogue with the modern world, which entailed challenging the modern world to reform itself in the interests of social justice as demanded by the Gospel. An essential part of the church's dialogue with modernity was to make peace with the natural sciences, history, and philosophy. Leo supported research in astronomy by modernizing the Vatican Observatory, and he promoted the study of the natural sciences at the Vatican. He made the Vatican archives accessible to scholars (even to Protestants), declaring that the church had nothing to fear from the truth. But Leo's policy of making peace with the sciences was obstructed by the Jesuits in Rome—who, incidentally, were not representative of their order in this context.[27] Two conservative Jesuit cardinals held key positions in Rome: Camillo Mazzella acted as confidential theological advisor to an aged and infirm Leo, and Andreas Steinhüber was prefect of the Congregation of the Index. In the 1890s the number of Jesuits in the curia increased significantly. Their success in influencing a reversal of papal policy was probably facilitated by Leo's advanced age. In 1895, the year of Leroy's retraction, Leo was eighty-five years of age.[28]

The Excommunication of Mivart

Hedley, Bonomelli, Leroy, and Zahm had all demonstrated their readiness to bow to the authority of Rome. Mivart was not so submissive to ecclesiastical authority and criticized the hierarchical church on a range of issues, some of which had nothing to do with the natural sciences. His articles on "Happiness in Hell," as noted earlier, had been put on the Index of Forbidden Books in 1893. For the next few years Mivart did not engage in theological controversy. He may have wished to avoid further censure from Rome, but his confidence in his own judgment was as strong as ever. The condemnation of his articles in 1893 was, he hoped, motivated by the intention to slow down, rather than prevent, the liberalization of doctrine. This proved to be naive.

As the upper echelons of the institutional church became increasingly conservative in the 1890s Mivart became embittered and disillusioned with it. In 1899 a convergence of events provoked him to denounce ecclesiastical authority and to question fundamental aspects of Christian belief. It was in that year that his articles on hell were included in the new edition of the Index. This pushed him into open repudiation of traditional dogma and defiance of Rome's ecclesiastical authority.[29] He wrote to Andreas Steinhüber, the Jesuit cardinal who was prefect of the Congregation of the Index, seeking the name of his accuser and the specific errors he was supposed to have made. The reply referred to the 1893 decree but did not provide the information he requested. He then wrote back, in August, withdrawing his earlier submission. Several weeks later he wrote a long letter to the *Times* (17 October 1899), castigating the Roman Catholic Church, especially the French bishops and the Roman Congregations, for their stance in the controversy surrounding the court martial of Alfred Dreyfus (1859–1935). Dreyfus, a Jewish officer in the French army, had been found guilty of passing military secrets to Germany. Anti-Semitic opinions were expressed in many Catholic newspapers, and Mivart deplored the fact that such opinions were not censured, especially by the French bishops. Furthermore, he asserted that the papacy had undermined its moral credibility because of the position it adopted in the Dreyfus case. Mivart, therefore, repudiated the doctrine of papal infallibility.

The repressive orthodoxy of the Catholic hierarchy provoked Mivart to become more trenchant in his criticism of the stifling authority of Rome. In 1899 he realized that he was terminally ill. He wished to know whether or not his position in the Roman Catholic Church was tenable, in view of his beliefs. Significantly, it was also in 1899 that the retractions of evolution by Catholic apologists became more widely known.[30] Mivart came to the conclusion that the church "must tolerate a transforming process of evolution, with respect to many of its dogmas, or sink, by degrees, into an effete and insignificant body, composed of ignorant persons, a mass of women and children and a number of mentally effeminate men."[31] If this vital transforming process was to be permitted, then, Mivart argued, it was necessary for the church to abandon its claim to infallibility in matters of doctrine. Neither the Bible nor the church was free of error. Mivart was determined to provoke a response from the ecclesiastical authorities, and with this in mind he bluntly stated his views.

In the first week of January 1900 two of Mivart's articles were published: "The Continuity of Catholicism" in the *Nineteenth Century*, and "Some Recent Catholic Apologists" in the *Fortnightly Review*. Mivart claimed that many Catholics were distressed because of what they believed were authoritative declarations by the church against evolution. He reiterated the views he had expressed in 1893 in his article "Modern Catholics and Scientific Freedom"—but now his criticism was unrestrained. Rome would become "the laughing-stock of the civilised world" on the issue of evolution if "some ignorant men of the Curia were not quickly muzzled." He was clearly angry about the censorship imposed on Leroy and Zahm. Leroy, like Galileo, had been "induced to solemnly tell a lie."[32] Therefore, there was not only a theological or intellectual aspect to these issues of science and theology—there was also a serious moral dimension. If members of the curia were compassionate and conscientious about the truth, they would have insisted on submission, not on recantation.

Catholics were exhorted by Mivart to reject any claim to authority in science by a Roman Congregation. He referred to the Galileo case to bolster his contention that Rome had blundered once and could never be trusted again. By this time polemical discourse about Galileo had spread from scholarly exchanges to the level of popular culture.[33] Mivart maintained that astronomy, biology, political economy, history, biblical criticism—everything within the realm of inductive research—was to be excluded from its domain of authority. Rome was admonished to "humbly accept the teaching of science, and nothing but science," and for this it should be "grateful." Yet he knew that the "absurdity" of the curia would not be easily vanquished, especially concerning human evolution—but neither would it achieve victory. The curia had not succeeded in influencing the church to authoritatively condemn evolution because, despite their disproportionate influence, the "Curialists" were as "impotent" as they were "unscrupulous and corrupt."[34]

Mivart believed that the greatest threat to the church was its utter disregard for scientific truth—especially as exhibited by the curia. The primary motive of those in the curia, according to Mivart, was to wield power over "weak credulous minds and tenderly scrupulous consciences."[35] He made it clear that, in denouncing the curia, he did not wish to impugn or tarnish the reputations of Pope Leo XIII and the "many exemplary" cardinals. He was referring to "ecclesiastics of a lower grade" who were completely devoid of "evangelising zeal."[36] He coined the term "Curialism" to express his contempt for that intolerant mind-set that was averse to justice, truth, and rational liberty in matters of religion. It was the "one dangerous and deadly foe of Catholicity," but Mivart was confident that it would be eventually defeated. Curialism was particularly associated with "the rabid Catholic party" in Italy and France, which included the authors of *Civiltà Cattolica*, Louis Veuillot, Canon Delassus, Abbé Charles Maignen, and their supporters—especially some devout anti-Dreyfussards. Mivart regarded liberal Catholicism as the antithesis of this movement, and in this context he pointed to British and American culture, which he believed was especially favorable to it. Americanism, in his opinion, was "eminently Catholic" and "profoundly displeasing to Curialism."[37]

Mivart believed that, despite the extensive influence of the curia, educated Catholics were aware of the numerous statements in the Bible that were scientifically and historically false. For example, the world was not really created in six days.[38] Eve was not formed from a rib of Adam. The story of the Flood was not true. Linguistic diversity did not arise because of God's fear that the Tower of Babel would reach to the heavens. All these statements were factually incorrect. It was "most shocking" that these and other errors were preached to adults and children as if they were true. Pope Leo's declaration, in *Providentissimus Deus*, that there were no errors in scripture, was upheld on the basis of an ingenious—but not entirely honest—distinction between "errors" and "untruths." Falsehood was endemic in the church. The prelates of the church had themselves been misled about the inerrancy of scripture. Even the pope was a prisoner of the system. Mivart was skeptical that Leo XIII was the real author of *Providentissimus Deus*. Whether he was or not was not of the greatest importance because he was "bound hand and foot" by what had been declared at the Council of Trent and the First Vatican Council.[39]

Mivart declared that his aim was to strengthen Catholicism, not to weaken it. But he had strayed so far from the precepts of Roman Catholicism that a Jesuit priest, Robert F. Clark, argued that he was not, and never had been, a Catholic. When Mivart entered the church, he did not leave his intellect at the threshold. He brought his "private judgment" with him and failed to make that "act of entire and absolute submission." Therefore, he was "in the Church, but not of it."[40] The writing of the January articles effectively marked Mivart's departure from the church—he was now a critic of Catholicism rather than a Catholic critic.[41]

Mivart aroused the enmity of ecclesiastical authority, most significantly in Westminster and the Vatican. On 9 January, Cardinal Herbert Vaughan, archbishop of Westminster and the most authoritative figure in Catholic England, sent Mivart a lengthy Profession of Catholic Faith for his signature. Vaughan very seldom acted on important matters without consulting the Vatican. He sent a file about Mivart to Cardinal Rafael Merry del Val, enclosing the two January articles, a copy of the Profession of Catholic Faith, and copies of Mivart's recent letters to him. Merry del Val was a confidant of Vaughan and a consultor for the Congregation of the Index. He personally advised the pope on the details of the case and on 13 January he informed Vaughan that Pope Leo XIII had spoken "very energetically against Mivart." Three days later Cardinal Lucido Maria Parocchi, secretary of the Holy Office of the Inquisition, and Cardinal Mieczyslaw Ledóchowski, prefect of the Congregation de Propaganda Fide, sent Vaughan the authorization to take prompt action against Mivart.[42]

Vaughan was advised that he could proceed without waiting for the formal condemnation of the two January articles, because Mivart had withdrawn his submission to the 1893 decree concerning his hypothesis about hell.

In his lengthy correspondence with Cardinal Vaughan in January 1900, Mivart explained that he had written the January articles out of "a sense of duty" and with a view to "opening as wide as possible the gates of Catholicity." The possibility that the ecclesiastical authorities might look kindly on his efforts was unrealistic—indeed it even occurred to Mivart that his aspirations might be quixotic.[43] The last shred of hope that he nurtured must surely have been dissipated by the critical response from the English Catholic press. Harshest of all was the *Tablet*, which was then under the control of Vaughan. Mivart was deeply offended because the article in question had impugned his character. He demanded a retraction and an apology before he would even consider signing the Profession of Catholic Faith.[44] Vaughan declined, rather bluntly, to facilitate Mivart on this matter. Even if he had, it would not have addressed the fundamental doctrinal differences between Mivart and the church. Vaughan's third and final demand for the signing of the profession of faith required, *inter alia*, the acceptance of the Roman Catholic Church's claim to be the supreme and infallible guardian of the Christian faith, and assent to the dogma that the Bible was free of error. To sign it would have meant utter humiliation and the abandonment of principles that Mivart had struggled for many years to uphold. Not surprisingly, therefore, he refused to sign the document and, in late January, he was deprived of access to the sacraments. He now had little to lose. His article "Roman Congregations and Modern Thought," published in the *North American Review*, called on the church to abandon its dogma of infallibility, to admit that the pronouncements of the Councils of Florence, Trent, and the Vatican were subject to correction, and to revoke the encyclical *Providentissimus Deus*.[45] Only then could Catholic doctrine evolve to embrace all scientific and religious truths, including the best of what paganism had to offer.[46] All these demands were of course anathema to the magisterium and incredibly naive.

Mivart viewed the church as a polarized institution composed of liberal and ultramontane sections. He was firmly in the liberal camp and wished for its growth and ultimate dominance. In his article "Scripture and Roman Catholicism," published in the *Nineteenth Century* (March 1900), he declared that he worked to create conditions so that those Catholics whose liberalism was most energetic and advanced could be retained within the fold. He had been optimistic about the potential of liberal

Catholicism, but in 1893 his confidence was shattered. The publication of *Providentissimus Deus* raised formidable difficulties and doubts for Mivart concerning the reconcilability of Catholicism and science. Over the next several years he struggled to overcome this problem. When he set about deliberately testing the tenability of his position in the church, his liberal friends opposed his course of action. They feared that it would provoke the wrath of the Vatican and endanger not only his position but theirs also. But Mivart persisted, arguing that they should know whether or not their status as Roman Catholics was honest and secure. The reaction to the January articles left him in no doubt—Catholic doctrine and science were diametrically opposed and no reasonable and well-educated man could join the church if he had a sound knowledge of the Catholic faith and the Bible.

Mivart was confident that he had demonstrated that Catholicism, in its present form, was intellectually untenable, but he did not expect that this would bring about any significant changes in the next few years. He perceived that the religious beliefs of the majority of humankind were based on feeling rather than on reason. Intellectual progress would gradually lead to positive developments, but this would occur in a time-scale of centuries rather than years.[47] This opinion was, most probably, of little consolation to him in the last few weeks of his life. He died on 1 April 1900, an outcast of the church he had served so diligently for most of his life. However, the Roman Catholic Church did not escape unscathed; it had lost its "only scientific man of repute" in England.[48] The Mivart affair dealt a severe blow to Catholicism in England. The condemnation of his articles and the acrimonious controversy that ensued received extensive coverage in the English secular and religious press.

The Joint Pastoral— Prelude to Antimodernism

The ecclesiastical authorities had dealt swiftly and harshly with Mivart because they perceived a growing threat to Catholicism in the form of seditious liberal influences, especially in England. A number of Catholic authors, including Émile Joseph Dillon, William Gibson (Lord Ashbourne), Richard Bagot, and Fr. William Francis Barry, were all regarded as "pseudo-Catholics or men who scarcely think as Catholics."[49] Liberal Catholics such as the Jesuit theologian Fr. George Tyrrell (1861–1909), Wilfrid Ward, and Baron Friedrich von Hügel, feared that the condemnation of Mivart would now lead to adverse developments where the ecclesiastical authorities would become less tolerant of their views.[50] Their fears were well founded.[51] From a hierarchical perspective something more than the effective excommunication of an eminent heretic was deemed necessary. The Catholic bishops were determined to make their position clear on a range of issues that had been raised by Mivart and others, especially pertaining to ecclesiastical authority. Vaughan wrote to Merry del Val, requesting advice about the best course of action to take. Merry del Val indicated that he had contacted the Jesuit authorities about the crisis. A pastoral condemnation of liberalism seemed to be the most appropriate response. The Superior General of the Society of Jesus, Luis Martín (1846–1906), appointed two Jesuit authors to write the initial draft of the pastoral letter, and he also contributed to the final editing of the document. It is highly significant that one of the two authors was Salvatore Brandi, the editor of *Civiltà Cattolica*. The second author was an American, Thomas A. Hughes, a member of the curial staff in Rome. It is likely that the Franciscan priest Fr. David Fleming played a role in the final editing of the document. He was a consultor to the Holy Office and a friend of Merry del Val's. Martín received the draft pastoral from Merry del Val on 20 November 1900 and proposed a few amendments which were accepted. Merry del Val then sent the pastoral to Vaughan for approval. Vaughan returned the document to Rome for Pope Leo XIII's approval before it was presented to the bishops of England and Wales for their signatures. Great care was taken to ensure that the Roman origins of the document were not disclosed to the public.[52]

On 29 December 1900, "The Church and Liberal Catholicism: A Joint Pastoral Letter" was published under the nominal authorship of the bishops of England and Wales. It received wide circulation when it appeared in the *Tablet* of 5 and 12 January 1901. The pastoral letter condemned ideas that had been mainly advocated by Mivart.[53] The bishops pointed out that the church was not a democracy. They observed that the loyalty of some Catholics was tainted by false principles—"insensibly imbibed by too close a contact with the world." Furthermore, some converts to Roman Catholicism had failed to shake off "the critical spirit of private judgement" which they had exercised before joining the fold.[54]

Liberalism was seen as a threat. A small number of Catholics, "wanting in filial docility," had proven their potential to "infect and unsettle the minds of many" (pp. 132–33). Some of them had risen to eminence in science and were especially dangerous. The bishops complained that the "bold assertions of men of science are received with awe and bated breath

... while the mind of the Church and her guidance are barely spoken of with ordinary patience." The pernicious influence of liberal Catholicism carried with it the threat of heresy and schism (p. 144). All this stirred the bishops to reiterate some doctrines for the guidance of the laity (p. 133). Their view of the church was of an institution divided in two. A chosen minority—the *Ecclesia docens*—consisted of the pope and the bishops in communion with him. They were, on the basis of God's authority, in supreme command of the vast majority of Catholics—the *Ecclesia discens*.

Assisted by the Holy Spirit and representing the authority of Jesus Christ, they were entrusted with the mission of teaching the doctrines imparted to them. It was usual for the *Ecclesia docens* to seek the advice of specialists in theology, philosophy, and the natural sciences, but this did not represent any erosion of its authority. No external dictation would be tolerated (p. 137).

Loyal Catholics were forbidden to publish anything on religious issues without the imprimatur of the *Ecclesia docens*—no matter how learned they were. The failure of a number of Catholics to comply with this requirement was denounced. Some Catholics, failing to gain approval from the *Ecclesia docens* for their ideas, appealed directly to public opinion through the medium of the press (p. 138). They sought to promote the acceptance of a revised Gospel based on notions of science, criticism, and modern progress.

Mivart was not explicitly referred to, but it is clear that the authors of the joint pastoral had him in mind when they were condemning modern errors. It had been argued that the *Ecclesia docens* had proven itself incompetent in defining doctrine because they did not have the benefit of knowledge that was later acquired by research. It was then erroneously concluded that Catholic dogmas were subject to change in the light of modern science. Ecclesiastical authority was challenged as claims were made for the participation of the laity in the governance of the church. However, the bishops were adamant that those who were highly educated among the laity would not ascend from the humble status of disciples to leaders. Ecclesiastical authority, rather than public opinion, would determine what was permissible and what was not (p. 139).

The excessive emphasis on authority and the denigration of private judgment were most unlikely to stimulate an influx of converts in societies professing a Protestant and liberal ethos. This was not of paramount importance for the bishops. They were primarily concerned with preserving the faith of those already within the fold. It was not sufficient for a prospective convert to assent to the articles of Catholic faith based on individual judgment. The first and most important requirement was one of submission to the authority and infallibility of the Divine Teacher in matters pertaining to faith and morals (p. 145).

Mivart had not complied with this condition. In later years he challenged the authority of the Roman Congregations on the basis that the Holy Office and the Congregation of the Index had committed a grievous error of judgment in dealing with Galileo and had, *ipso facto*, forever forfeited their right to speak authoritatively on scientific subjects. The bishops rejected this contention. They did concede that a number of novel opinions and theories advocated by scholars were initially censured by the Roman Congregations and later tolerated and even accepted. It was, they insisted, perfectly appropriate for the Holy Office to pronounce against a new interpretation of scripture if there was an insufficient weight of logic and evidence to support it. These decisions were not immutable and did not prevent Catholics from continuing their research. If fresh evidence or more convincing arguments were presented, then the *Ecclesia docens* was prepared to change its position on the disputed text (p. 141). The bishops acknowledged that the Roman Congregations were not infallible. They insisted, however, that this did not undermine their authority in doctrinal matters. Miscarriages of justice frequently occurred in civil and criminal courts, yet their authority was maintained because the legal system was able to correct its errors. This prerogative was claimed for ecclesiastical tribunals in the religious domain (p. 152).

The bishops likened the church to an organism, growing but maintaining its identity. They even used the word "evolution" to describe the developmental process. However, they hastily added that this did not imply "essential change" (p. 148). Progress in the natural sciences would not be allowed to dictate changes in dogma. The doctrines of the faith were a "Divine deposit," entrusted to the teaching authority of the church to be safeguarded, developed, and explained with infallible and divine authority (p. 149) to a docile *Ecclesia discens*.

The joint pastoral was not well received by a number of eminent English Catholics. Wilfrid Ward (1856–1916) was disturbed by its failure to take account of difficulties experienced by some Catholics who reflected deeply about their faith. The excessive emphasis on authority and strict conformity discouraged those who desired to use their talents to serve their church. In an article signed by Lord Halifax (Sir Charles Lindley Wood), but actually written by the Anglo-Irish Jesuit George Tyrrell, the joint pastoral was condemned as an expression of ecclesiastical absolutism.[55]

The reactionaries were in the ascendant. In Rome they remained so vigilant and intolerant of new ideas that even so moderate a figure as Bishop Hedley found himself in difficulties with them again. As stated earlier, Hedley had assumed that the Holy Office judged Leroy's thesis about human evolution to be untenable. However, when he wrote to the Anglican minister Rev. Spencer Jones in early 1902, he had become skeptical about this assumption. In his letter to Jones about the case of Leroy, the bishop stated that *Civiltà Cattolica* had not referred specifically to a ruling by a Roman Congregation and only spoke vaguely about authority. Since then he had received information that the condemnation of Leroy's book, "if it ever was pronounced, emanated merely from the Dominican Superior, and not from the Holy See at all."[56] Hedley's letter was published in the first edition of Jones's book, *England and the Holy See*, and in a number of Catholic and other journals. It elicited a frosty response from Fr. Brandi because it called into question the information of *Civiltà Cattolica* concerning the case of Fr. Leroy. In the journal issue of 5 April 1902 Brandi delivered his coup de grâce to Hedley's claim, asserting that the bishop was misinformed and that the authority in question was the Holy Office. Brandi then declared that "if the bishop were to write to that competent authority he will receive, we are certain, though perhaps in a confidential manner, information that it was not possible nor permissible for us to give to our readers."[57] Brandi had an unfair advantage over Hedley. He, and his colleagues at *Civiltà Cattolica*, had access to confidential information that they were not entitled to have, and they were highly influential at the Holy Office.

Brandi in particular was an influential figure. From 1893 he enjoyed a close relationship with Pope Leo XIII and Cardinal Giuseppe Melchiorre Sarto (the future Pope Pius X). Brandi, who had joined the staff of *Civiltà Cattolica* in 1891, was appointed editor in 1905. He was an ardent opponent of liberals of all persuasions and became closely associated with Cardinal Merry del Val. When Sarto was elected pope in August 1903, he chose Merry del Val as his secretary of state. The Vatican was firmly in the hands of the ultraconservatives. Merry del Val was to play a key role in continuing the crusade against liberalism. He was the main instigator of two documents, similar in style and content: the joint pastoral letter issued in the name of the English and Welsh bishops, and the antimodernist encyclical, *Pascendi Dominici Gregis* (8 September 1907).[58] This latter document, and the reaction against modernism, will be discussed in the next chapter.

6

Antimodernism

The Antimodernist Crusade

MODERNISM, IN THE THEOLOGICAL SENSE, HAS BEEN DEFINED as "the meeting and confrontation of a long religious past with a present which found the vital sources of its inspiration in anything but this past."[1] It was not a revival or direct continuation of nineteenth-century liberal Catholicism.[2] Modernists were acutely aware of divergences between Catholic theology and the latest developments in science. Generally, they tended to examine contemporary literature rather than that of thirty to forty years previously. This is not to say that they learned nothing from the works of liberal Catholics such as Döllinger or Newman. In the case of Newman, his *Essay on the Development of Christian Doctrine* (1845) addressed a topic that was central to their concerns, and some modernists, especially Alfred Loisy, found his work useful. However, from a modernist perspective Newman's concept of the development of doctrine was fundamentally flawed. Newman did not question the idea of the apostolic deposit of faith. For him the development of doctrine would be driven by deductive reasoning applied to the original revelation for the purpose of ascertaining its implications and consequences. The modernists, in contrast, put forward a number of proposals concerning the immutability and infallibility of the *depositum fidei* which were contrary to the church's teaching. Their approach to this core dogma of Catholicism was inspired by an evolutionary worldview.[3]

Modernism seems to have been a universal phenomenon, finding expression in both non-Christian religions, such as Islam and Buddhism, and in Christianity, occurring in Roman Catholicism, in the Russian Orthodox Church, and in the mainstream Protestant denominations.[4] Modernism in the Anglican Church originated in the Broad Church in

113

the late nineteenth century and manifested itself in the reformism of the Churchmen's Union for the Advancement of Liberal Thought (renamed the Modern Churchmen's Union in 1928). The connections between the modernist movements in the Anglican and Roman Catholic churches were tenuous.[5] The Congregationalists, the most liberal of the Free Churches in England, had a short-lived experience with modernism in the form of R. J. Campbell's "New Theology."

Modernism, in the context of Roman Catholicism, is a term that can be used to refer to the views expressed by Catholic scholars who adopted a critical and skeptical attitude toward the traditional doctrines of their church. It gave rise to the greatest intellectual crisis in the church since the Reformation—a crisis aggravated by the excessive emphasis on Thomism.[6] Pope Leo XIII had taken a medieval system of philosophy, based on the works of St. Thomas Aquinas, and elevated it to a dominant status in Catholic theology. A major consequence of this was that it obstructed the harmonization of Catholic doctrine with new developments in science and philosophy. Furthermore, his encyclical *Providentissimus Deus* failed either to solve or to address the serious problems arising from the ongoing process of interpreting scripture, many of which were historical in nature.[7] Scholars still experienced major difficulties and were unable to reconcile biblical texts with the discoveries of the modern age.[8] Leo recognized the need for promoting biblical studies, and on 3 October 1902, a few months before his death, he established the Pontifical Biblical Commission in Rome, which had among its objectives the observance of the guidelines laid down in *Providentissimus Deus*. The commission was given the responsibility of passing judgment on biblical questions debated by Catholic scholars, and it was to publish studies on the Bible. Furthermore, it was to ensure that the Vatican Library had adequate resources with these objectives in mind. One of its early pronouncements was the affirmation of the Mosaic authorship of the Pentateuch (the first five books of the Old Testament).[9]

Leo's policies created confidence among educated Catholics to explore new ideas that impinged directly or indirectly on their religious beliefs. This created a false sense of liberalization and encouraged some scholars to be less than cautious. Liberal Protestants had applied modern scientific methods to biblical criticism, and a number of Catholic intellectuals attempted to do the same. It was becoming increasingly evident to them that the narrow traditionalist approach to biblical studies, so rigidly upheld in the seminaries, was likely to damage the credibility of Catholic doctrine. Catholic scholars, especially in Britain, France, Italy, Germany, and Belgium, endeavored to apply secular methodologies from science, history, and sociology to the church, concerning its historical development, its disciplinary requirements, and its approach to theology and biblical studies.[10]

An issue of central importance in the modernist crisis was how to reconcile submission to ecclesiastical authority with truly independent scholarship.[11] Modernist writers were dissatisfied with neo-scholasticism, which formed the basis of their church's orthodoxy. They were concerned to harmonize Christian thought with Enlightenment ideas, and especially with the findings of history and the natural sciences that were, at the beginning of the twentieth century, commanding widespread interest and support.[12] Frequently they went far beyond the boundaries of Catholic orthodoxy. Alfred Loisy and George Tyrrell, the most eminent figures in the modernist movement, argued that the dogmas and organization of the church had developed under environmental influences and were responses to the needs of successive generations of Catholics.[13] Catholic modernists were also motivated by a desire to defend their church against criticism by Protestant writers—sometimes with unfortunate results. A notable example of this is Loisy's *L'Évangile et l'Église* ("The Gospel and the Church"), published in 1902, and written in response to Adolf Harnack's *What Is Christianity?*, which was published two years earlier. Harnack, a liberal Protestant scholar, had elaborated his views on the origins and nature of Christianity and in doing so attempted to separate Christianity from its Catholic accretions. Loisy took issue with Harnack, but in doing so he strayed beyond the boundaries of Catholic doctrine and his book was placed on the Index of Forbidden Books by the Catholic authorities in 1903.

Modernism did not represent a particular school or system of theology; instead it encompassed a diversity of opinions, aims, and aspirations held by Catholic intellectuals who held in common a desire to promote Catholic scholarship capable of defending itself against the derision of hostile scientists.[14] The papacy and the local hierarchies were concerned that the intellectual endeavors of the modernists would tend to undermine rather than support the Catholic faith as defined by the teaching authority of the church. *Providentissimus Deus* represented an attempt by Pope Leo XIII to impose limits on biblical criticism and as such was the first counteroffensive measure against the modernists.[15]

Pius X, who succeeded Leo XIII in 1903, was more aggressive in dealing with the problem. He decided to confront the modernists. Circumstances greatly favored such an initiative. Great strides in the centralization of power had occurred throughout the pontificates of Pius IX and Leo XIII. Papal control over the church had never been so strong. Furthermore, those in the upper echelons of power in the Vatican were deeply committed to a rigid traditionalist outlook in theological matters.

On 3 July 1907 the Holy Office (now the Congregation for the Doctrine of the Faith) issued the decree *Lamentabili Sane Exitu* ("A Lamentable Departure Indeed"). Pope Pius X confirmed the decree the following day. This document was somewhat similar to the *Syllabus of Errors*. It condemned sixty-five "errors" of the modernists, some of which claimed that the institutions, dogmas, and sacraments of the church were the result of an evolutionary process that was still in progress. A number of propositions were condemned in reference to the social and natural sciences. These included the following:

57. The Church has shown that she is hostile to the progress of the natural and theological sciences.

64. Scientific progress demands that the concepts of Christian doctrine concerning God, creation, revelation, the Person of the Incarnate Word, and Redemption be re-adjusted.

65. Modern Catholicism can be reconciled with true science only if it is transformed into a non-dogmatic Christianity; that is to say, into a broad and liberal Protestantism.[16]

Two months later Pius X issued the encyclical *Pascendi Dominici Gregis* ("Feeding the Lord's Flock"). This document presented modernism as a coherent school of thought, which was far from accurate. All modernists advocated revisions of Catholic doctrine, but there was a great divergence of views about this, and none of them espoused the objectives that the encyclical attributed to them. Pius X claimed that the religious philosophy of the modernists was based on agnosticism—a philosophy that asserted that human reason was incapable of discovering anything about God through the study of the physical world. Agnosticism contradicted an important finding of the First Vatican Council which stated that God could be "known with certainty by the natural light of human reason by means of the things that are made. . . ."[17] Modernism was condemned as "the synthesis of all heresies" (par. 39). The pope believed that modernism, if left unchecked, would destroy all religious belief. He viewed it as an intermediate step in a process that led from Protestantism to atheism.

Pius believed that the concept of evolution was the "principal doctrine" of the modernists. He gave considerable attention to this assertion in his encyclical. The "laws of evolution" were applied to everything, including dogmas, the Bible, the liturgy, and even faith itself. The evolutionary process in the church was driven by the need of the institution to adapt itself to the social conditions in which it was immersed. Nothing was stable, nothing was immutable (parr. 26–28). It was through an evolutionary process that dogmas would be brought into harmony with history and science (par. 38). Pius deplored all this. Although he did not explicitly refer to the biological theory of evolution, it is very likely that Pius had this in mind when he condemned its analogue in theology.

In his encyclical Pius revealed a lack of enthusiasm for the natural sciences. Although he urged that science should be studied "energetically," he immediately added the cautionary statement that this should be done without "interfering" with religious studies. Errors—"perverse" and "monstrous" ones—had arisen because the natural sciences had received so much attention at the expense of the "more severe and lofty" subjects. He dictated that the teaching of the natural sciences in the seminaries should be carried out to an extent proportionate to its relative importance and in a way that would not lead to the propagation of errors (par. 47).

The intensity of Pius's contempt for modernism, and for the modernists, is indicated by the intemperate language of *Pascendi Dominici Gregis*. For example, those who strayed from Catholic orthodoxy were "thoroughly imbued with the poisonous doctrines taught by the enemies of the Church, and lost to all sense of modesty" (par. 2); "blind they are, and 'leaders of the blind' puffed up with the proud name of science, they have reached that pitch of folly at which they pervert the eternal concept of truth" (par. 13); and "it is pride which puffs them up with that vainglory which allows them to regard themselves as the sole possessors of knowledge, and makes them . . . elated and inflated with presumption" (par. 40). It was to be the duty of those in positions of authority to employ such "victims of pride" in the "lowest and obscurest offices" so that their potential for harm would be reduced as much as possible. Those seminarians who showed signs of "the spirit of pride"—that is, who were suspected of holding modernist ideas—were to be refused entry to the priesthood (par. 40). Near the end of his lengthy encyclical Pius gave instructions for the implementation of a number of measures to protect Catholics against the pernicious effects of modernist ideas. These included a vigorous campaign of censorship, the careful selection of candidates for influential positions in seminaries, the requirement to study courses in scholastic philosophy for the awards of doctorates in theology and canon law, the prohibition of congresses of priests except by special permission of local bishops and subject to strict conditions, and the setting up of diocesan vigilance committees.

Pius deemed it essential to impose limits on the interpretation of scripture in order to protect the church against the perceived dangers of modernism. Catholic biblical scholars were obliged to submit to standard ecclesiastical procedures. In his *motu proprio* (an administrative papal bull) *Praestantia Sacrae Scripturae* (18 November 1907), he declared that all Catholics were duty bound to accept the decisions of the Pontifical Biblical Commission, just as they were under obligation to accept the decrees of the Sacred Congregations concerned with doctrine and approved of by the pope.[18] The commission was composed of several cardinals and benefited from the expertise of a number of Catholic scholars.

On 1 September 1910, Pius continued his offensive against modernism by issuing the *motu proprio Sacrorum antistitum*, obliging all clergymen to take an antimodernist oath. The obligation to take the oath was deeply resented in some quarters, especially in Germany. Resistance was so strong there, particularly in the universities, that the Vatican agreed to grant an exemption to priests who did not exercise a parochial ministry. Those who swore the oath gave their assent to a number of articles of faith, including the following:

1. The existence of God "can be known with certainty," and his existence can be "demonstrated," from the application of reason to the "visible works of creation."

2. There are "external proofs of revelation"—especially miracles and prophecies, which are amenable to the understanding of all men at all times.

3. The church was founded by the real and historical Jesus Christ.

4. There is a sacred deposit of faith which does not change over time—dogmas do not evolve.

The oath also required submission and adherence to all the declarations, prescripts, and condemnations contained in *Pascendi Dominici Gregis* and in *Lamentabili Sane Exitu*.[19] Only about forty of the clergy refused to take the oath.[20] The antimodernist oath was retained until the Congregation for the Doctrine of the Faith rescinded it in July 1967.

There was some justification in Pius's decision to confront the modernists. The published works of a number of theologians indicated that they had ventured far beyond the limits of Catholic doctrine and, in some cases, even beyond what could be reconciled with Christian thought. But the pope's response was extreme, and the offensive against heresy over which he presided often failed to discriminate between serious error and legitimate freedom of expression.[21] Pius X was not intellectually gifted and was "so ill at ease in the presence of all learning" that the Holy Office was given freedom of action in dealing with those who were regarded as modernists.[22] The curia had persuaded him that a modernist conspiracy, proliferating outward from the church in Germany, posed a major threat. His secretary of state, Rafael Merry del Val, was an ardent opponent of modernism. With the cardinal's approval, a Vatican official, Monsignor Umberto Benigni (1862–1934), organized a spy system under the name of *Sodalitium Pianum* ("The Sodality of Pius," also known as *La Sapinière*), which proliferated throughout the dioceses of Italy and beyond. Published works, sermons, speeches, and even private conversations were reported to Rome by the secret organization when it was thought that there was a departure from orthodoxy or a disagreement with papal policies. Cries of heresy emanated from the conservative Catholic press. A reign of unremitting repression and harsh censorship spread throughout the church in Europe and intensified from 1907 onward.

There was no significant danger of the Catholic masses casting aside their traditional beliefs and wholeheartedly embracing modernist ideas. Nevertheless, it was thought prudent to educate them about the heresies then in circulation. *Pascendi Dominici Gregis* seemed to be beyond the comprehension of ordinary Catholics. Therefore one of the authors of the encyclical, the Vatican theologian Fr. Joseph B. Lemius, wrote *A Catechism of Modernsim* (1908) for their edification.[23] He did so with the blessing of Pope Pius X and Cardinal Merry del Val. Lemius had spent years scrutinizing the works of contemporary Catholic authors and arranging them into an elaborate heterodox system which he believed was the basis of all that they had written. Merry del Val, in his prefatory letter to the *Catechism*, praised the volume and wrote that "the less cultured classes" were "very easy prey to all errors," especially when these were "presented under a false scientific guise."[24]

As early as 1903 well-informed observers of the curia had anticipated that the Vatican would take action against the modernists. In view of the illiberal proclivities of the hierarchy, such an initiative was not altogether surprising. What could not be confidently predicted, however, was the virulence and excesses that became so characteristic of antimodernism. The church felt threatened yet again by the modern world and reacted defensively, as it had during the pontificate of Pope Pius IX. It had lost power and property to secular institutions in European society. It had to contend with a range of ideas that challenged its core doctrines, pertaining to the nature of dogma, scriptural inerrancy, and the authority of the church. On the political front, the papacy was confronted by such hostile forces as French republican anticlericalism and Italian nationalism. The institutional church was able to do little to silence its external critics, but it was in a very strong position to take action against those whom it viewed as the enemy within. And it did so. This facilitated an increase in the centralization of power and the reaffirmation of Catholic doctrine based on a rigid adherence to scholastic philosophy. The papacy and the clerical bureaucracy at the Vatican emerged more powerful than ever when the antimodernist campaign ended.[25]

The modernist movement within the Catholic Church was not only defeated; it was exterminated. Comprised of a small number of intellectuals, lacking organization, and without popular support, it possessed little power to resist the onslaught of the antimodernists.[26] By 1911 Loisy had left the church, Tyrrell was dead, and Friedrich von Hügel (1852–1925) had ceased to participate in the modernist movement. Most of those who were prominent in modernism were either expelled from the church or submitted in order to remain within the fold. Even Catholic scholars who were professedly orthodox, such as Pierre Batiffol and Père M. J. Lagrange, found themselves in difficulties with the ecclesiastical authorities.[27] Fidelity did not guarantee safety.

In Fear of Error

Catholic authors who wrote about science at this time needed to be extremely careful when their subject matter impinged on theology. This is evident in James J. Walsh's *Popes and Science* (1908), which was published under the imprimatur of his friend Archbishop John M. Farley of New York. Walsh served as professor of the history of medicine at Fordham University. He conceded that the church's persecution of Galileo was a "deplorable mistake," but he argued that it was exceptional.[28] He contended that the idea of papal opposition to science was based mainly on an exaggeration of the Galileo case. There was also, he claimed, widespread misunderstanding about the church's supposed opposition to the practice of dissection and, more generally, to the development of the medical sciences, with which his book was mainly concerned. He believed that most of the misinformation in America about the papal opposition to medical science originated from Andrew D. White's published work *On the History of the Warfare of Science with Theology in Christendom.*

Walsh's objective was to dispel false notions about the church's opposition to science and to show that the papacy in particular had supported rather than opposed scientific progress. This was a relatively safe topic for him to address. His book was mainly concerned with pre-Reformation Europe. It is significant that he mentioned Darwin in an appendix but did not discuss his highly controversial theory. He merely stated that Darwin correctly anticipated that the majority of men of his own age and generation would not accept his theory.[29] The context for this statement is particularly interesting because it implies that Walsh approved of Darwin's theory but chose not to be explicit. Walsh argued, in reference to Jonathan Swift, that "when a true genius appears in the world, you may know him by this sign—that all the asses are in confederacy against him"—and the "asses" were as numerous in the ranks of the clergy as in other professions.[30] Sometimes they used their religion to oppose science. However, the inordinate opposition to new ideas sometimes found among the clergy was not unique to religious organizations. Walsh claimed that innovative scientists had suffered far more at the hands of their fellow scientists than from the intolerance of the clergy.[31]

Ultraconservatism was an ingrained feature of human nature, common to all cultures, Protestant and Catholic, medieval and modern. Walsh argued that, when scientists opposed new discoveries and ideas in science, they did so because they were convinced that they fully grasped the full significance of the knowledge at their disposal. To admit that important findings could be ascertained, on the basis of familiar information, by someone else would be regarded as an acknowledgment of poor observational and intellectual abilities. Professional jealousy became evident especially when a younger man made the discovery. Walsh believed that most of the opposition to progressive or new ideas came from men who were "beyond middle age." This observation had troublesome implications for those in positions of ecclesiastical authority who were "beyond middle age." Pope Pius X, for example, was seventy-three years old at the time. Walsh may have realized the adverse inferences that could be made. He stated that, although the ultraconservatives did much harm, they served the "supremely beneficial" purpose of preventing young men with rash ideas from leading society astray. This latter statement did not at all seem consistent with his lengthy discussion about the adverse effects of ultraconservatism.[32] It was somewhat ironical that Walsh dedicated his book to Pius X, a man who richly deserved the epithet of ultraconservative.

The Jesuit author Karl Alois Kneller adopted a different approach to

Walsh in seeking to demonstrate the harmony between Roman Catholicism and science. In his book *Christianity and the Leaders of Modern Science* (1911), he focused on scientists of the nineteenth century. The Christian faith of earlier scientists such as Copernicus, Galileo, Kepler, Boyle, Newton, and Linnaeus could be confidently taken for granted. But what about the faith of modern scientists, especially in view of the argument that modern science was more solidly based on facts? Kneller asserted that scientific facts posed no threat to Christianity. Rather, it was the application of modern philosophy to the facts that created the impression of conflict, and this philosophy was as unstable as any of its predecessors. Kneller's declared objective was not to propose an argument for Christianity but to repudiate the notion that there was a consensus in science against it. If there was conflict between religious belief and scientific research, then, Kneller argued, it would be most conspicuous to "minds of the first order."[33] This he failed to find.

Kneller conceded that some eminent scientists, such as Rudolf Virchow (1821–1902), Emil Heinrich Du Bois-Reymond (1818–1896), Marcelin Berthelot (1827–1907), and John Tyndall, did not believe in Christianity (p. 391). From his extensive survey of the various branches of science, however, Kneller expressed confidence in his finding that the majority of eminent scientists retained their religious beliefs.[34] Thus he was able to conclude that there was no basis for claiming that science was "intrinsically and necessarily hostile to religion" (p. 391).

Near the end of his book Kneller discussed, very briefly, the theory of evolution. He maintained that, although the theory had frequently been used to attack religious belief, it was in no way irreconcilable with theism. Even in its "more sweeping form," which was nothing more than a "pure hypothesis," it would be unreasonable not to regard it as evidence for the existence of God (p. 366). This, of course, was mere theological assertion, not a serious attempt to engage in philosophical discourse. It simply sidestepped the problems evolution posed for theology. Kneller quickly returned to his primary objective. His purpose here was not to discuss the "intrinsic validity and significance" of evolution; rather it was to ascertain how the scientific research of the pioneers of evolutionary theory influenced their religious beliefs.

Kneller argued, rather weakly, that Darwin could not be regarded as a satisfactory standard-bearer for those who were against religion. First, as an agnostic, he had never denied the existence of God. Second, he had not reflected systematically and at length about religion and its relationship with science. Third, speculative philosophy was not his forte (pp. 372–73).

However, all this did not rule out the possibility that science had led Darwin gradually from Protestantism to agnosticism.[35] Satisfied that Darwin could be pushed gently aside, Kneller then proceeded to enlist the support of a number of scientists who wrote about evolutionary theory, or whose work contributed to its development. These included Armand David (1826–1900), James Dwight Dana (1813–1895), Asa Gray (1810–1888), and Charles Lyell.[36] Kneller then concluded that scientists "of the first rank," who were evolutionists, were also able to sustain their Christian faith. This did not imply that evolution was in accordance with the facts of nature as established by scientific research (p. 386).

Kneller's finding that the majority of eminent scientists in the nineteenth century at least believed in God, if not in Christianity, did not seem consistent with his perception that it was widely believed that science was somehow inimical to Christian belief. If the majority of eminent scientists were not either irreligious or antireligious, how could such a misunderstanding have arisen? Kneller speculated that the "scientific apostles of unbelief," most notably Haeckel, Vogt, Tyndall, and Huxley, were much better than their Christian colleagues at gaining publicity and support for their views. In contrast, the "true masters of science . . . shrank from publicity" and confined their activities to academia (pp. 395–96). This adverse state of affairs was exacerbated by the omission of details concerning religious belief in the biographies of famous scientists (pp. 396–97).

Kneller was satisfied that he had demonstrated the harmony between science and religion in the "simplest" way possible—it is reasonable to infer here a certain satisfaction on his part at having avoided the pitfalls of discussing evolutionary theory and its implications for Catholic theology. Nobody, as far as he knew, had attempted to show that the majority of eminent scientists were opposed to religious belief. He was confident that such a project, if undertaken, would have been hopeless (p. 391).

The assertion of harmony between religion and science by Kneller was not based on philosophical, theological, or scientific arguments. He had started out with an assumption that seemed to guarantee success. In his introduction he stated that even if every eminent scientist rejected Christianity and embraced atheism it would only provide a "very slight" argument in favor of atheism. It would "offer no disproof of Christianity" (pp. 2–3). If Kneller is to be taken at his word, then the reverse finding— to be logically consistent—provided only "very slight" support for theism and offered no proof of Christianity. He argued that, because scientific opinion is subject to change, any consensus attained does not guarantee the truth. Furthermore, he observed that materialism, atheism, and positivism are not facts but systems of philosophy and inferences from facts that lie within the discipline of metaphysics. Scientists are not authoritative figures when reaching conclusions of this order. By arguing that science, and the opinions of scientists, counted for so little in this context Kneller unintentionally devalued his extensive study. The harmony of science and religion was, for him, a foregone conclusion, and, most importantly, a safe conclusion—no small consideration at a time when antimodernism was rife.

The Pontifical Biblical Commission

During the pontificate of Pius X (4 August 1903–20 August 1914) the internecine conflict between the integralist Catholics and progressive Catholics intensified. His successor, Benedict XV (born Giacomo della Chiesa) resolved to bring it to an end. On 1 November 1914 he issued his first encyclical, *Ad Beatissimi Apostolorum* ("At the Threshold of the Most Blessed Apostles") with this in mind. Benedict did not withdraw the condemnations of modernism by his predecessor. What he did was to call for an end to the extreme measures that had been employed against the modernists. This led to an abatement of internal conflict, but antimodernism was still a potent force and was to dominate the teaching of the church for about half a century—up to the death of Pope Pius XII in 1958.[37] Throughout this period Catholic intellectuals were severely restricted in entering into dialogue with secular scholars and scientists. They were discouraged from pursuing new avenues of inquiry in their research and from publishing their findings. In the first twenty to thirty years of the antimodernist period Catholic scholars judiciously avoided exegetical studies of a number of biblical books, especially Genesis, Joshua, Judges, and Isaiah.[38] The intensity of the antimodernist reaction effectively stifled creativity in biblical studies.

It is somewhat ironic that, in the first decade of the twentieth century, when antimodernism was at its most intense, that the church began to adopt a more tolerant attitude toward evolution. The Pontifical Biblical Commission played a very important role in this development. On 23 June 1905 it conceded that some "historical" narratives in the Bible could be interpreted allegorically or as parables. Such a departure from the strict literal or historical sense was not to be "easily or rashly admitted."[39] On 30 June 1909 it issued its decree concerning the first three chapters of Genesis. It specified the limits to which the text of Genesis could be reinterpreted. In paragraph 2 the commission addressed the following questions:

> Whether we may . . . teach that the three aforesaid chapters do not contain the narrative of things which actually happened, a narrative which corresponds to objective reality and historic truth; and whether we may teach that these chapters contain fables derived from mythologies and cosmologies belonging to older nations, but purified of all polytheistic error and accommodated to monotheistic teaching by the sacred author or that they contain allegories and symbols destitute of any foundation in objective reality but presented under the garb of history for the purpose of inculcating religious and philosophical truth; or, finally, that they contain legends partly historical and partly fictitious, freely handled for the instruction and edification of souls.

The commission answered "in the negative to each part."

In paragraph 3 of its decree the commission pointed out that there were points of contact between Genesis and "the fundamental teachings" of the church. These teachings were not subject to revision and included the following:

1. The creation of all things by God at the beginning of time.

2. The "special" creation of man.

3. The formation of the first woman (Eve) from man.

4. The unity of the human race.

5. The fall of our first parents from "their primitive state of innocence" and the promise of a future Redeemer.

However, in paragraphs 4 to 8, the commission permitted a considerable degree of latitude in the interpretation of these chapters. In paragraph 4 the commission stated that the church fathers had interpreted some scriptural passages in different ways and it was permissible for Catholics to choose from their opinions, or to propose a new opinion, subject to the exercise of prudent judgment. In paragraph 5, it was conceded that there were metaphorical expressions in the text and that a literal interpretation could not be sustained if it was found to be contrary to reason. Although the historical character of Genesis was upheld, it was acknowledged, in paragraph 6, that the fathers of the church had "prudently" applied allegorical interpretations to some passages in the first three chapters of Genesis. In paragraph 7 the commission pointed out that the author had not intended to give a scientific account of creation. When interpreting Genesis, scholars were not strictly bound to look for "scientific exactitude of expression." The importance of differentiating between scientific terminology and everyday speech, which had been pronounced upon by Pope Leo XIII in *Providentissimus Deus*, was reiterated by the Pontifical Biblical Commission. In paragraph 8 the commission deemed it permissible to interpret the Hebrew word *yom* for "day" to mean an indefinite length of time.[40] This was of major significance when arguing that God worked through secondary causes when creating the heavens and the earth. All these statements by the commission made it easier to depart from the literal meaning of scripture.

Dorlodot—Defender of Darwin

A second event in 1909 indicated a greater tolerance of evolutionary theory in Catholic clerical circles. In that year the University of Cambridge celebrated the centenary of Charles Darwin's birth and the fiftieth anniversary of the publication of his *Origin of Species*. The Catholic University of Louvain was invited to send a representative, and its Rectoral Council decided, unanimously, to accept the invitation. Canon Henri de Dorlodot, director of the university's geological institute, was selected as the representative by the Rectoral Council. The text of the speech that he delivered at Cambridge was first read and approved of by the dean of the faculty of sciences and by the professor of dogmatic theology. Therefore, the opinions he expressed were much more than merely his own. Dorlodot was generous in his praise of Darwin. He told his audience:

> It is no exaggeration to say that, in showing us a creation more grandiose than we had ever suspected it, Charles Darwin completed the work of Isaac Newton; because, for all those whose ears are not incapable of hearing, Darwin was the interpreter of the organic world; just as Newton was the voice from heaven come to tell us of the glory of the Creator, and to proclaim that the universe is a work truly worthy of His hand.[41]

This tribute to Darwin "by the first learned body of the Catholic world" was warmly received in England. The "élite" of English Catholics was pleased with the views expressed by Dorlodot, and his speech subsequently received publicity in the *Tablet*. There was, however, some criticism in Belgium of his enthusiastic participation in the celebration of Darwinism. Because of this Dorlodot felt compelled to give several lectures after returning to Belgium. These lectures formed the basis of his book *Darwinism and Catholic Thought*, published in French in 1921 and in English in 1925. Dorlodot asserted that Darwin, contrary to the views of some Catholics, had not been judged by the church to be heretical on the theory of evolution applied to humankind. To argue that *The Descent of Man* was irrelevant to the celebrations at Cambridge would not have been sustainable. If Darwin had been declared a heretic, this would have obliged Louvain to decline Cambridge's invitation.[42]

Dorlodot maintained that the purely scientific details and the physical mechanism of evolution were outside the range of theological concern when the origins of humankind were not included in the debate (pp. 3–4). He asserted that Darwin's theory, strictly as a scientific theory—that is, free of "unphilosophical" extrapolations—was concerned with explaining the role of secondary causes in the evolution of the universe and that it did not reject the ultimate action of the First Cause. Therefore Darwinian theory was not synonymous with atheistic evolution (pp. 27–28, 42). This implied that Catholics had nothing to fear from evolutionary theory. Dorlodot thus felt confident in declaring that Darwin's theory was highly probable.

There was nothing in the Bible, according to Dorlodot, that supported those who opposed the theory of the transformation of species. Furthermore, spontaneous generation was acceptable and had been taught by many of the church fathers as part of a process that was even applied to the human body (pp. 63, 89). Although there was no sustainable theological objection to the spontaneous generation of life from nonliving matter, Dorlodot believed that there was a strong scientific basis for rejecting it in view of the contemporary state of scientific knowledge—but he was not absolutely certain about this (p. 126).

He argued that Catholics were at liberty to accept the transformation of species as proposed by Darwin, on the basis of secondary causes, and without invoking additional special interventions of God in the process. This opinion put him at variance with many Catholic apologists.[43] But Dorlodot was confident that he was within the bounds of orthodoxy, and he invoked the works of St. Augustine for support. He referred extensively to *De Genesi ad litteram* in maintaining that many Catholic authors had made it possible for Darwinism to be used against Catholicism. Catholic authors had unwittingly inflicted harm on Christian belief by falsely claiming that it was not compatible with Darwin's theory. Dorlodot maintained that those non-Catholic scholars who were convinced of the truth of Darwinism would not even have considered studying religious doctrines that were presented to them as hostile to the truth.[44] Significantly, other Catholic authors had referred to St. Augustine's *De Genesi ad litteram* to make the same general point when arguing for the toleration or acceptance of novel scientific theories that presented difficulties for maintaining some traditional religious beliefs. The most notable example is Galileo's defense of the Copernican hypothesis in his *Letter to the Grand Duchess Christina* (1615).[45]

Dorlodot's robust exposition and the decree of the Pontifical Biblical Commission concerning the first three chapters of Genesis had promoted a greater acceptance of biological evolution among Catholics.[46] These developments reinforced a trend that had emerged in the late nineteenth century. It had become increasingly difficult since then for Catholics to sustain total opposition to evolutionary theory when the vast majority of scientists (including Catholic scientists) had embraced it.[47] Yet there was a strong tendency for Catholic authors to grudgingly concede the minimum. The Jesuit author Karl Frank, in the conclusion of his book *The Theory of Evolution in the Light of Facts* (1913), acknowledged that "theories of evolution will remain, since everything points to the fact that there was and is an evolution of the organic world." However, he had already taken the precaution of protecting himself against possible charges of heterodoxy. Evolutionary tendencies were put in place by God, but humankind required "a special intervention" because, "taken as a whole," no animal could be regarded as an ancestor.[48] The kind of evolution acceptable to Frank was so heavily dependent on divine intervention that it was far removed from mainstream science.[49] Another notable feature of Frank's book was its scathing criticism of Darwinism.[50]

The English Catholic scientist Sir Bertram C. A. Windle, like Karl Frank, was cautious in his approach to evolutionary theory. He was aware that those "able theological writers" who had "overconfidently" advocated Mivart's version of evolutionary theory had retracted their views after the Vatican authorities expressed their disapproval. In his book *The Church and Science* (1920) he maintained that a new interpretation of scripture could not be "freely taught" until there was conclusive proof that humans were, like all other species of life, the outcome of an evolutionary process. But Rome had still not made any definite pronouncements against the application of evolutionary theory to Adam's body. This was understandable in view of its experience with Galileo. Nevertheless, Windle argued that loyal Catholics were obligated to adjust their thinking to "the mind" of the church—even when its teaching was not put forward as immutable.[51] His thinking reflected the dominant view in the institutional church.

7

Catholicism and Science
in the Interwar Years

Salvation and Science—A Conflict of Interests?

HENRI DE DORLODOT'S WORK HAD PROMOTED A MORE PROGRESSIVE attitude toward evolution in some Catholic circles. John Butler Burke, a contributor to the *Dublin Review*, felt confident enough to write that the evolution of humankind seemed "almost certain." He then proceeded to argue that the church's competence was in the spiritual realm and that scientists should be free to engage in "unfettered speculation" in the physical domain.[1] However, there was still strong opposition to the idea of human evolution. Humphrey Johnson's *Anthropology and the Fall* (1923) gives some indication of attitudes at the root of censorious proclivities. Johnson's book was published under the imprimatur of the bishop of Birmingham. The Jesuit C. C. Martindale wrote the preface. Martindale did not approve or disapprove of the opinions of the author because he did not regard himself as professionally competent to do so. Nevertheless, he did feel it necessary to elaborate some clear guidelines for the readership. The views of anthropologists about the origins, early history, and nature of humankind were of interest to the Roman Catholic Church because a number of doctrines, especially original sin, were linked to these issues. Furthermore, the veracity of scripture—the book of Genesis in particular—was also impinged upon by anthropological studies.

Martindale observed that there was "no *a priori* reason why a Scriptural author might not write inspired fiction." The church not only acknowledged, but insisted, that some biblical passages were to be interpreted metaphorically rather than literally. Genesis 2:7 declared that God "breathed" into Adam's nostrils "the breath of life." A literal interpretation here would be heretical because it would imply the materiality of God.[2] There were well-established precedents for adopting nonliteral interpretations of Genesis. Johnson gave a number of examples. He concluded that, in the light of ethnology, anthropology, and archaeology, it was impossible to sustain a literal reading of the chronology of Genesis (pp. 29–30, 46). Furthermore, it was clear that the story of the Flood could no longer be sustained in its literal form (pp. 53–56).

In view of the above, a considerable degree of latitude in exegesis would have been reasonable to expect. Progress in biblical studies was anticipated in the light of advances in the natural sciences, archaeology, and history. But, from Martindale's point of view, a far greater consideration outweighed this prospect. The church existed for the salvation of souls and was entrusted by divine authority to teach the truth and nothing but the truth. Upholding the infallibility of scripture was an essential part of its mission. The church was not a school of science. The teaching authority, in safeguarding the "saving truths" of the church, would not allow its scholars to be "hasty" or "reckless." New opinions on the meaning of scripture would have to be "thoroughly tested" before being widely disseminated (p. xi). Catholics would not be permitted to treat the narratives of Genesis as unhistorical—as "purified Babylonian myths" (p. xii–xiii). It was feared that if new interpretations of scripture were adopted too readily on the basis of modern scientific theories this could undermine Catholic doctrine because of the evolutionary nature of science. Therefore, Catholics were exhorted to be

> extremely careful not to admit as a fact what may turn out to be fiction . . . too many theories arise, grow fashionable, and expire unlamented . . . to feel the least temptation to accept a theory because it is new and neat. The more vital the truths they believe to have been committed to them, the more scrupulously careful are they to apply the maximum test to any theory or fact which may be brought into connection with such truths. (p. vii)

The denigration of science was, therefore, to be used as a prop to sustain the maximum rigidity. This attitude failed to take cognizance of two very important points. First, traditional and widely held interpretations of scripture had been decisively overturned by scientific discoveries. Therefore, simply to dismiss science as fickle and unreliable was irrational. Second, science—in the broadest sense of the term—was constantly changing in the light of new discoveries. It was eminently sensible to propose theories for the purpose of placing a mass of data, arising from experiment and observation, in a logical framework to enhance understanding. Future research could then be focused to optimize beneficial results. It was in the nature of science to abandon, modify, or expand theories in the light of new observations. This was its strength, not its weakness.

Martindale's intention was not to defend error, but his excessively cautious stance, and that of others, effectively inhibited the correction of error—arising out of a fear that a greater error might be committed in the process. The intolerance of novel ideas expressed by him was also clearly evident in the published work of his Jesuit co-religionist H. Muckermann. In the fourth edition of his book *Attitude of Catholics towards Darwinism and Evolution* (1924), Muckermann concluded that the theory of evolution applied to humankind was "directly opposed" to the faith. Furthermore, he denied that spontaneous generation had taken place and he maintained that Darwin's evolutionary mechanism of natural selection was to be "unconditionally rejected." With evolution so circumscribed he then felt confident in declaring that it was "a harmless doctrine."[3]

Catholic resistance to the theory of evolution, although diminished, still remained strong. Catholics, of course, were not exceptional among Christians for their resistance to evolutionary theory. The opposition of Protestants to evolution, when it did occur, was motivated especially by the extension of the theory to humankind. The most dramatic manifestation of this was the Scopes trial (1925)—sometimes referred to as the "monkey trial"—in Dayton, Tennessee. John Scopes, a public school teacher, was prosecuted for breaking a law that prohibited the teaching of evolution in the classroom. By 1929 six states in the United States of America had passed anti-evolution legislation.

Generally, most of the objections leveled against evolution were focused on Darwin's mechanism of natural selection rather than on the broader theory of evolution itself. Many Catholic apologists felt confident in referring to the works of a number of leading biologists in constructing their arguments. The most eminent of these scientists was the German physiologist and philosopher Hans Driesch (1867–1941), who claimed that Darwinism was no longer tenable. A number of eminent biologists who reached a similar conclusion included Albert Fleischmann, August Pauly, Johannes Reinke, and Gustav Wolff.[4]

In Britain, popular Catholic authors such as Hilaire Belloc and G. K. Chesterton were very influential in arguing against Darwinism. Their criticisms of various aspects of evolutionary theory were based not on a literal interpretation of Genesis but on a determination to defend the Roman Catholic Church against a concept that was frequently associated with a materialistic outlook.[5] Their influence extended beyond the ranks of their co-religionists. They challenged the views of rationalist writers such as H. G. Wells in order to defend Christian values.[6] They played a major role in propagating the misleading idea that scientists had abandoned Darwinism. Contrary to this erroneous assertion, biologists gradually came to realize, in the period from about 1920 to 1950, that explanations based on genetic mutations and natural selection were not mutually contradictory. They concluded that a comprehensive explanation of biological evolution required both mechanisms of change. Natural selection operated by favoring or suppressing genes that had mutated. The fusion of these two key concepts was termed the "modern synthesis" by Julian Huxley (grandson of Thomas H. Huxley). The modern synthesis was developed on the basis of the published work of many specialists, including population geneticists, zoologists, and paleontologists. These scientists, from different national backgrounds, included Ronald Fisher, John B. S. Haldane, Ernst Mayr, George Gaylord Simpson, Sewall Wright, Sergei Chetverikov, and Theodosius Dobzhansky. Darwin's theory was consolidated on a firm foundation of experimental genetics and population statistics.

Despite their proficiency in the art of polemics, Belloc and Chesterton had a poor understanding of the natural sciences, and they were out of touch with new developments in biology.[7] This contrasted with developments in French Catholicism. Here a number of eminent scientists were also Catholic clergymen. They included Pierre Teilhard de Chardin, Robert de Sinéty, and Abbé Henri Breuil. They played an important role in bringing about a considerable degree of harmonization between Catholic opinion and evolutionary theory in general. Their influence was transmitted through Catholic faculties of science and journals.[8] Gradually it became clear that evolutionary theory per se did not pose a threat to religion. Nevertheless, Catholic authors felt the need to be extremely cautious in writing about evolution because of the possibility of a hostile response from the Vatican. Their fears were well founded.

In France differences of opinion between those who supported evolutionary theory and those who were implacably against it were particularly acrimonious. The opponents of evolution were eager to inform the Vatican about the alleged heresies of their co-religionists. Those who advocated the acceptance of evolution also appealed to the Vatican for support. It is likely that the Société scientifique de Bruxelles and its *Revue des questions scientifiques*, and three cardinals—Bourne, Maffi, and Mercier—played an important role in counteracting the opposition to evolution in the Vatican. But it seems that the anti-evolutionists, greatly assisted by

Monsignor Benigni and the antimodernist network, were still very active.[9] Concerted efforts by conservative Catholics were made to discredit evolutionists such as Canon Henri de Dorlodot and the French Jesuit priest Pierre Teilhard de Chardin (1881–1955). The conservatives attempted to persuade the Holy Office to publish a general denunciation of evolutionary theories.

Catholic scientists in France, unable to win sufficient support from the bishops, decided to take a more direct approach in gaining Vatican approval. In the summer of 1925 they organized the so-called Council of Altamira, an international gathering of scientists consisting of both clergy and laity. The scientists discussed evolution for four days, and, from these discussions, a memorandum was drafted that was sent to Pope Pius XI in an attempt to counteract the machinations of their conservative opponents. It was emphasized that the evolutionary concept was of central importance to science and that it did not pose a threat to Christianity. The authors of the memorandum, so typical of Catholic evolutionists, referred to the works of St. Augustine and other church fathers for support. It seems that the scholarly Pius XI was favorably impressed by their arguments, because it became known, through Cardinal Mercier, that no hostile action would be taken by the Vatican against the proponents of evolution provided that their findings remained "prudent and objective."[10]

Messenger's Hypothesis

Evolutionary theory in general became a relatively safe subject for Catholics to discuss, but the narrower issue of human origins was less straightforward. The theologian Rev. Ernest C. Messenger discussed this thorny issue with "a distinguished Jesuit" and was told that the question of human origins would have to be addressed again. Whoever chose to do so would risk censorship. Messenger, who had translated Canon Dorlodot's book from French to English, decided to undertake the hazardous task himself.[11]

Messenger, like Dorlodot, enjoyed substantial support for his relatively liberal views on evolutionary theory within the church. His book *Evolution and Theology: The Problem of Man's Origin* (1931) was published under the imprimatur of the bishop of Northampton, Dudley Charles Cary-Elwes. Laudatory prefaces were written by two Catholic theologians: Fr. Cuthbert Lattey, S.J., who acted as *censor deputatus* and was professor of fundamental theology at Heythrop College; and Very Rev. Charles Souvay, C.M., who was president of Kenrick Seminary in St. Louis, Missouri.

Messenger, like Dorlodot, believed that there was no scientific evidence for the spontaneous generation of life, but he did not rule it out as a possibility for two reasons. First, many scientists argued that it could have occurred when conditions on earth were very different from those in modern times. Second—and this was the preferred reason—there was a theological basis for spontaneous generation because some of the church fathers had advocated it. The transformation of species, excluding humans, was more firmly based because it was strongly supported by scientific evidence, and it was compatible with theology.[12]

The third section of Messenger's book, by far the largest, was devoted to discussing the origins of the human species. Messenger pointed out that there was no "conclusive" evidence that humans had evolved. He acknowledged that some scientific facts indicated that such a process had occurred, but the evidence was only strong enough to warrant a working hypothesis—albeit one that was "very attractive." It was, after all, "natural" to infer that humans had evolved when we accepted that all other species had been formed by an evolutionary process (p. 275).

From a theological perspective, scripture neither taught nor opposed the evolution of the human body. The church fathers were divided on the subject. Messenger did not rule out the possibility that the human body was created entirely by a natural process put in place by God, but he speculated that secondary causes alone were not adequate for its formation. He was inclined to believe that divine intervention had occurred to make the human body suitable for the "infusion" of the human soul. He was careful to emphasize that the human soul definitely did not evolve, that it came directly from God. Furthermore, philosophy confirmed that an "immaterial substance" could not come from something that was "material" (pp. 275–77).

Messenger was aware that many contemporary theologians were hostile to the application of evolutionary theory to humankind (p. 250). Their opposition, he believed, was due to an excessive adherence to the literal interpretation of the biblical texts, a failure to understand the patristic evidence, and an inflated estimation of the implications of a number of Vatican acts, both doctrinal and disciplinary (p. 275). But the theologians were not in an authoritative position—they did not form part of the "teaching" church. They served as advisers and experts who assisted in the continual progress of knowledge and understanding in the church pertaining to matters of the faith (pp. 240–41). The teaching authority consisted of the hierarchy in union with the pope—and it had not pronounced on the issue of whether or not the human body had been formed through the evolutionary process. Messenger, mindful that many Catholics were uncertain about what to believe concerning human origins, made a number of additional points about the attitude of the church.

1. Even if the primitive ancestry of the human species was proven, the Roman Catholic Church would not affirm it because it was not "her business" to make such an affirmation.

2. The church had not yet obtained adequate scientific proof and would not permit any individual representing it to assert human evolution as factual.

3. If the church did receive physical evidence as strong as, for example, the theory of gravitation elaborated by Newton, it would include the theory of human evolution in the educational programs of its institutions of advanced learning.

4. Catholics were free to promote the acceptance of such a theory by engaging in research and debate.

5. Catholics were individually free to believe in the evolution of the human body (p. 251).

Messenger stated that it was a principle of "Christian Naturalism" that God acted through secondary causes wherever and whenever possible (p. 278). He was inclined to believe that there had been at least some role for secondary causes in the formation of Adam's body—but he expressed this tentatively because of "the attitude of Ecclesiastical Authority" and, to a lesser extent, because of "the hostile attitude adopted by so many modern theologians." He anticipated that the church might pronounce, sometime in the future, that Adam's body was formed exclusively and immediately by God from inanimate matter. Catholics who believed in the evolution of humans would then be obliged to admit that their opinions were incorrect. Therefore, Messenger believed that the best choice for Catholics was to suspend judgment on the issue or at least not to accept the evolutionary concept as definitely true (p. 280). In the foreword to his book he declared his readiness to submit to the judgment of the church if anything he had written was found to be in error (p. xxiv). Messenger's statement of explicit loyalty to the teaching authority of the church was not one of excessive caution. Antimodernism was not yet a spent force in the church, although it had weakened considerably since the pontificate of Pius X.

Messenger's work was extensively reviewed. Some of these reviews were republished in a sequel to *Evolution and Theology* of which Messenger was the editor and a contributory author. Many differences of opinion were expressed in this second book, *Theology and Evolution* (1951), by the reviewers about the extent to which God used secondary causes in creating the first human couple, Adam and Eve. A comprehensive study of their views would be too long here but some of their observations and arguments merit attention.[13]

Rev. P. G. M. Rhodes, a retired professor of dogmatic theology (Oscott College), originally wrote about Messenger's book in the February 1932 issue of the *Clergy Review*. Rhodes expressed the opinion that if *Evolution and Theology* was allowed to continue on sale without ecclesiastical censure, then it would be reasonable to conclude that a "modified" evolutionary theory applicable to the human body was theologically acceptable. He believed that the published work of Catholic evolutionists, especially Messenger's book, had influenced many British Catholic pupils at secondary school level to consider seriously the possibility of human evolution. Young educated Catholics had relegated the "special creation" of plants and animals to the status of Ptolemaic astronomy. Rhodes based his observations on an examination of over one thousand essays, some of which discussed evolution. These were sent to him from nearly every Catholic school in the state.[14]

Rhodes was skeptical about the formation of Adam's body through secondary causes. Messenger had not dissipated his skepticism. Rather than devoting considerable attention to the gradual accumulation of minor mutations, Messenger had focused on divine interventions giving rise to sudden miraculous changes. Attempting to explain the origin of Adam did not present the main problem. The formation of Eve's body seemed remote from any plausible scientific explanation.[15]

Genesis 2:21–22 stated: "the Lord God caused the man to fall into a deep sleep; and while he was sleeping, he took one of the man's ribs and closed up the place with flesh. Then the Lord God made a woman from the rib."[16] In writing about the formation of Eve, Messenger speculated that God might have somehow used parthenogenesis in the process.[17] Parthenogenesis is an asexual means of reproduction when an organism develops from an unfertilized egg. It occurs in some plants and in some primitive animals such as aphids and would be extremely unusual in mammals. Furthermore, if a human was to reproduce by parthenogenesis, it would have to be a female producing a female—not a male (Adam) producing a female (Eve).

Messenger's argument relied heavily on divine omnipotence, but it was hopelessly unscientific. Rhodes recognized this and formed the opinion that Messenger's hypothesis was likely to "scandalise the evolutionists without quite satisfying the theologians."[18] This was probably unduly negative, when cognizance is taken of theology. Messenger's opinions on human origins were tentative rather than assertive. He had put forward strong theological arguments that it was permissible for loyal Catholics to hypothesize about the creation of humanity through the medium of secondary causes—although he acknowledged that he did not know how the secondary causes acted.[19]

Rev. R. W. Meagher, professor of dogmatic theology at Ushaw College, originally reviewed Messenger's book in the March 1932 issue of *Ushaw Magazine*. He praised Messenger's book, but he pointed out that the question of God's *modus operandi* when creating the first humans was still very much in the realm of speculation. Messenger had argued at length that the teachings of the early church fathers about the origins of things were much more sympathetic toward evolution than the opinions of St. Thomas Aquinas and later theologians. However, he did not claim that the church fathers taught evolution in the modern sense. Reliance on the church fathers in support of any scientific hypothesis was regarded as erroneous by Meagher. Those theologians who had defended the geocentric theory on the basis of "unscientific" observations and a literal reading of scripture had been proved wrong by the advances of science. The idea of spontaneous generation as expressed by the church fathers was also wrong because the argument from appearances to reality was faulty. Therefore, Meagher argued, it was wrong to invoke the church fathers in support of a scientific theory when attempting to determine the precise meaning of scripture. He argued that it was also wrong to quote them in opposition to evolution—especially when they never suspected it. Furthermore, allowances had to be made for their lack of scientific knowledge.[20]

Meagher had argued that both the writings of theologians in the early centuries of the church and the Bible were neutral on the question of evolution. This left much room for debate. On this basis Catholics could judge the tenability of evolution on a scientific basis without reference to theology. John A. O'Brien, a professor at the Newman Foundation at the

University of Illinois, expressed his willingness to accept, without equivocation, the convergence of data from the various disciplines of the natural sciences that established evolution as a major theory in science. Evolution, he believed, was accepted by over 91 percent of scientists whose work impinged on it.[21] In the preface to his book *Evolution and Religion* (1932), he deplored the tendency of those who were motivated by religious considerations to oppose evolution. In his opinion, this unwarranted encroachment on science usually involved disputing and downgrading scientific evidence and exaggerating disagreements among scientists that were usually of little consequence to the general status of evolutionary theory.

O'Brien referred to *Providentissimus Deus* and to Dorlodot's *Darwinism and Catholic Thought* to reiterate the assertion that the Bible was not a textbook of science and was not to be treated as such. God created the universe, but details of the creative process were firmly in the domain of science (pp. 59–61). The failure by theologians to respect this principle, especially since the condemnation of the Copernican hypothesis, had led to "the army of theologians beating a retreat, to a safer and more remote terrain with the scientists in undisputed possession of the field" (p. 85). The condemnation of Galileo had arisen mainly because of a misunderstanding of the scope of the Bible. O'Brien vigorously argued that the church had blundered on this issue and that there was a need to admit frankly the mistakes of the past (pp. 85–89). He did not argue, of course, that Christians should accept without question every scientific conclusion (p. 38), but in some instances the findings of science were so well established that some scriptural narratives needed to be reinterpreted. For example, the antiquity of humans as calculated by the chronologies of Genesis was clearly untrue in the light of archaeological and palaeontological discoveries. From this he inferred that the chronology was "fragmentary" but that the Bible was not in error (p. 36).

Flexibility of reinterpretation was a highly effective defensive strategy. O'Brien was aware that it was clearly untenable to uphold a literal reading of the six days of creation. The most satisfactory approach here was to regard the story as figurative. It was simply intended to convey to the readership that God was the creator of the universe (p. 233). This statement came within the ambit of theology and philosophy—not science. This approach in turn effectively isolated the scriptural narrative from science and the difficulties presented by it. However, the option of selecting a figurative meaning was not always clearly available; especially concerning human evolution, which was associated with the dogma of original sin (this will receive further attention later in the text).

The extent to which evolution was accepted or rejected by Catholics is probably impossible to ascertain with a reasonable degree of accuracy. Sister Mary Frederick concluded from her survey of Catholic literature that there was "nothing that may be designated as the Catholic stand on the matter." Her book *Religion and Evolution since 1859* (1935) was published on the strength of studies for a doctoral degree at the University of Notre Dame. Frederick found that Catholic writing on the subject was "particularly abundant," and this indicated to her that it was "one of the most frequently discussed topics among Catholics . . . since the time of its earliest whisperings." All this, however, did not lead to a proportionate increase in understanding and open-mindedness. Frederick made a number of observations that help to explain why this was so:

1. From the time of John Henry Newman, very few Catholic students had studied science. There was a shortage of Catholic scientists with a sound understanding of philosophy.

2. Catholic apologists almost always wrote about evolution with their religion in mind.

3. Catholic antagonism toward evolutionary theory was provoked by philosophical ideas associated with it.

4. The Catholic philosophy of religion had not undergone any significant change since the theory of evolution was extensively publicized in the Victorian era. Ideas about God, the soul, original sin, human destiny, and "the first origin" remained the same. Evolutionary theory did not seem to pose a threat to the fundamentals of Catholic belief.

From the above findings it could be inferred that prejudice, motivated by religious considerations, in conjunction with a lack of advanced scientific and philosophical education, militated greatly against the acceptance of evolutionary theory. Frederick concluded tentatively that the majority of Catholics still declined to believe in evolution. On the basis of her findings, however, it seemed likely that in the future more and more Catholics would change their opinions about this grand generalization of science. Some Catholic scholars and students were changing their minds about the sustainability of "certain" interpretations of Genesis while, more generally, increasing numbers of Catholics were apparently viewing evolutionary theory in a more favorable light.[22]

The tendency of many Catholics to rule out the possibility of evolutionary theory, when it was upheld by the vast majority of scientists, left them vulnerable to the charge that their faith was incompatible with science. The Catholic author William M. Agar argued at length for an open-minded attitude. Influenced by Dorlodot's work, his purpose was not to prove that evolution was true but to show that it was permissible for Catholics to accept that such a natural process was directed by God. In *Catholicism and the Progress of Science* (1940), he observed that "the proof of man's animal ancestry is growing stronger and the Church stands ready to accept it when the final word is in." Agar believed it was important that the church was ready to act if overwhelming evidence was obtained. It would then be in a stronger position "to see that men do not twist a scientific fact into an evidence for materialism." The Catholic Church, like other Christian churches, needed to be proactive rather than reactionary. Christianity had been "fighting a rear-guard action for too long . . . forever beating off the invader and defending its fundamentals from the inroads made by materialistic principles." Agar's proposed remedy was for the church was to go beyond defensive action, to embark on an offensive strategy in order to diminish or eliminate the prospect of further gains by materialistic influences. Greater numbers of Catholic scientists and lay Catholic philosophers were necessary if the church was to "carry its own principles into the field of action."[23] His call to arms was made against the background of Pope Pius XI's promotion of Catholic Action—a lay movement working in cooperation with the hierarchy to promote the implementation of Catholic moral and social principles.[24]

It is evident from the published works of Agar and other Catholic apologists that Catholic attitudes, especially from about 1920 to 1940, had moved significantly closer to mainstream thinking in science. Dorlodot and Messenger were very influential in bringing this about. There is also evidence of progressive thinking in the upper echelons of the church, indicating that the ecclesiastical authorities wished to engage proactively with science. This will be discussed next.

The Pontifical Academy of Sciences

Pope Pius XI (Ambrogio Damiano Achille Ratti, reigned 1922–1939) was politically very active during his pontificate. He concluded concordats and other agreements with about twenty governments, including, most notoriously, the Nazi regime of Adolf Hitler. In 1929 he reached agreement with the Italian fascist dictator Benito Mussolini, which led to the signing of the Lateran Treaty. Under the terms of this treaty the papacy recognized Rome as the capital of the Italian state and renounced all claims to the former Papal States. Vatican City was established as a sovereign state, independent of Italy.

Pius, a former prefect of the Vatican Library and a scholar, was supportive of advanced learning and was relatively progressive in his attitude toward the sciences. He enlarged and modernized the Vatican Library and, in 1925, he founded the Pontifical Institute of Christian Archaeology. He relocated the Vatican Observatory to Castel Gandolfo with new modern equipment, and he presided over the installation of a radio station in Vatican City in 1931.

The reconciliation between the papacy and the Italian state led, indirectly, to changes in the structure and activities of the Pontifical Academy, renamed the Pontificia Accademia delle Scienze—Nuovi Lincei. On 12 January 1936 Pius announced the forthcoming renewal of the Academy. He regarded it as the senate of science of the Holy See, dedicated to serving the faith by searching for truth.[25] His *motu proprio*, "In multis solaciis," of 28 October 1936 renewed the Academy under the new title of Pontificia Academia Scientiarum (the Pontifical Academy of Sciences). The new institute was now dependent on the authority of the pope rather than on a "patron" cardinal. It was supported by the financial resources of the pope as bishop of Rome. On the same day as the establishment of the Academy Pius appointed seventy academicians, including such notable figures as the physicists Niels Bohr (1885–1962), Guglielmo Marconi (1874–1937), Max Planck (1858–1947), Ernest Rutherford (1871–1937), and Erwin Schrödinger (1887–1961). Of the seventy academicians, thirty-one were Italian. Those who were offered membership of the Academy were chosen on the basis of their scientific achievements and their "moral rectitude"—religion and race were not regarded as relevant.[26] In its early years the Academy experienced difficulties in organizing its activities on an international basis owing to political instability in Europe, which led to the outbreak of the Second World War in September 1939.

The Academy was not established to carry out scientific research. It was to promote science, to analyze and assess its findings, to plan new studies. It was to facilitate discussions through its plenary sessions, study weeks, and working groups on complex interdisciplinary topics. Meetings were held in Vatican City behind closed doors, where the participants could express their views free of public scrutiny. The conclusions of these meetings were publicized through the Academy's publications and from reports of the papal allocutions. The Academy's findings were communicated to the Catholic hierarchy so that it could more effectively fulfill its mission on a scientific basis. The Academy took as its core principle the belief that science must be directed to serve the best interests of humankind.[27]

Pius XI died on 10 February 1939 and was succeeded by his secretary of state, Cardinal Eugenio Pacelli, who took the name of Pius XII (reigned 1939–1958). The new pope was deeply interested in scientific issues and had contributed to the foundation of the Pontifical Academy of Sciences in his former position. In his address to the Academy on 3 December 1939 he expressed his vision of science as the study of God's creation, an activity that led humanity closer to God—except when the human intellect was "blurred" by "prejudice and error."[28] There was no conflict between faith and reason. Pius rejected the claim that the church was opposed to science. Mindful of the pronouncements of the First Vatican Council on faith and reason, he asserted that the church respected the autonomy of the sciences. However, he was critical of those authors who contradicted Catholic doctrine when they extended their work beyond their disciplinary boundaries.[29]

Pius XII addressed the Pontifical Academy of Sciences again on 30 November 1941 and spoke about the biblical account of creation. The pope indicated those statements in scripture that were beyond the limits of allegorical interpretation, and he made three assertions about the nature and origins of humans.

1. Humans are superior to animals because each of them, unlike animals, possesses an immortal soul.

2. The body of the first woman (Eve) was derived from the first man (Adam).

3. It is impossible that the father and progenitor of a man is not a man. In other words the first man could not have been the son of an animal. He could not have been "generated" by an animal in the "proper sense" of the term.[30]

These statements, like those of the Pontifical Biblical Commission, were not infallible pronouncements and were not even supported by the status of an encyclical. Nevertheless, the pope's influence was so great that many Catholics were guided by his expressed opinions. A literal reading of the pope's third assertion seemed to rule out Adam's animal ancestry. But, somewhat like the text of Genesis, there was doubt about whether or not the pope's statement should be taken literally. If a literal interpretation was correct, then either Adam was created directly by God or was the son of a man and woman already in existence. There was some doubt about what the term "proper sense" actually meant.[31]

Evidently, the pope was not pleased about the inclusion of humankind in the evolutionary process. Shortly after his speech on this matter another long-standing issue seemed to demand renewed attention. The year 1942 would be the three-hundredth anniversary of Galileo's death. To mark the occasion the Pontifical Academy of Sciences, under its first president, Fr. Agostino Gemelli (from 1936 to 1959), decided to sponsor the research and publication of a book about the scientist. Monsignor Pio Paschini (1878–1962), professor of history at the Pontifical Lateran University, was chosen for the task, although he had no experience in the history of science. He was highly respected as a scholar of church history and had extensive experience working in the Vatican libraries. His work was completed in 1944, and he submitted it to the Vatican authorities for approval—they did not grant it. The reasons for withholding approval were not made public, but it seems that the opposition to publication was based on the author's criticism of the Jesuits and of the church for condemning Galileo. Paschini refused to revise his manuscript, and he protested against the prohibitive decision. The authorities did not change their minds. Paschini took no further action and, as requested of him, maintained silence "for the good of the church."[32] The predominant ecclesiastical attitude of prioritizing the reputation of the church over considerations of truth and the admission of error precluded the publication of an impartial study during the pontificate of Pius XII.[33]

Pius was conservative in his outlook, perhaps even reactionary. But some of his theological initiatives were remarkably progressive. Through his encyclicals *Mystici Corporis* (29 June 1943) and *Mediator Dei* (20 November 1947) he introduced major changes that helped to prepare the church for the reforms of the Second Vatican Council. His encyclical *Divino Afflante Spiritu* ("Inspired by the Divine Spirit," 30 September 1943) drew attention to the great advances in archaeology and biblical studies since *Providentissimus Deus*.[34] After the publication of the encyclical there was an upsurge of interest in biblical studies, especially among the clergy.[35]

Those in positions of authority were urged to treat biblical scholars in accordance with justice and to "avoid that somewhat indiscreet zeal which considers everything new to be for that very reason a fit object for attack or suspicion."[36] The encyclical was regarded in some circles as a heavy blow against antimodernist repression. Published to celebrate the fiftieth anniversary of *Providentissimus Deus*, it encouraged Catholic scholars to use modern methods of historical and philological research in their exegetical work.

8

Pope Pius XII
and the New Theology

Nouvelle Théologie

A NEW, INVIGORATED THEOLOGY EMERGED IN POSTWAR EUROPE.
Catholic theologians wrote on a wide range of issues, including the
question of whether or not to use non-scholastic philosophies to address
theological matters of contention, relativism in the expression of revealed
truth, existentialism and mysticism, the subjectivity and objectivity of
dogma, and questions pertaining to Adam, original sin, polygenism, and
evolution. The Vatican did not appreciate their theological endeavors.
The *nouvelle théologie* ("new theology") became mistakenly associated with
the heresies of modernism because of its alleged diminution of the supernatural, and because of the assumption that it did not show due deference
to the teaching authority of the church. Pius XII, despite his earlier progressive theological initiatives, was very conservative and had become
increasingly apprehensive about the new scholarship he had encouraged.

As early as 1946 the pope decided to issue warnings against the new
theological trends. Jesuits and Dominicans had assembled in Rome to
elect new superior generals of their respective religious orders. In his
address to the Jesuits, Pius warned, "let no one undermine or try to change
what is changeless." He believed that there was a widespread failure to
grasp the implications of the new theology—"which goes on evolving
with the constantly evolving universe, so that it is always progressing
without ever arriving anywhere." Pius feared that if this evolutionary
process in theology was to proceed unchecked then the unity and stability of the faith would be endangered. Those who were straying from

orthodoxy had to be dealt with in a "friendly" but firm manner—there could be no compromise with error.[1]

Evidently, Pius feared that the evolutionary concept, which had proliferated beyond the natural sciences, would undermine the viability of changeless truths so essential to Catholic doctrine. In his later speech to the Dominicans he stated that the church's theology and philosophy were being called into question in discussions about science and faith. In making clear his opposition to this development he reaffirmed that the philosophy of St. Thomas Aquinas was still capable of defending the deposit of Catholic faith and that it served as a foundation for progress in theology and philosophy.[2]

It was all very well to speak about error and truth—as if these terms could be applied definitively to solve problems concerned with the interpretation of scripture. There were, for example, many conflicting opinions among biblical scholars—Catholic and non-Catholic—about the authorship and source material of the Pentateuch, and about the historicity of the first eleven chapters of Genesis. Pius was very much aware of the difficulties involved. When Cardinal Emmanuel Suhard, archbishop of Paris, made inquiries to the Vatican concerning these questions, Pius instructed the Pontifical Biblical Commission to draft a response. On 16 January 1948 the secretary of the commission, James Vosté, O.P., met the pope so that the commission's findings could be formally approved. Later that day Vosté wrote to Suhard, informing him that the commission did not intend, because of their present state of knowledge, to promulgate any new decrees on the questions that had been submitted to it. In reference to the first question, Vosté pointed out that the commission had already conceded that it was permissible to claim that Moses had used written or oral sources when composing his work. There was much uncertainty and various opinions about the nature and number of the documents that had been used. The uncertainty about the narratives of Genesis had increased in scope over time. In 1909 the Pontifical Biblical Commission addressed doubts about the factual accuracy of the first three chapters. Now the historicity of the first eleven chapters (from creation to the time of Abraham) was very much in doubt.

Rome was adamant that the scriptural narratives were historical, not mythical. But it was not history as the Greco-Latin authors would write it. Neither was it history as modern historians would write it. It was not history as we know it! The commission declared that the narratives conveyed "fundamental truths" necessary for salvation to "a less developed people." The literal style was simple and figurative in keeping with their limited intellectual capacities.[3]

Catholic biblical scholars were urged to undertake research in the literary styles, history, and culture of the "Oriental" peoples so that some progress could be achieved in ascertaining the true meaning of the scriptural narratives. However, this exhortation was overshadowed by considerations of dogma pertaining to original sin. Humphrey Johnson observed in his book *The Bible and the Early History of Mankind* (1943) that the Council of Trent had based the doctrine of original sin on the teaching of St. Paul.[4] There were linkages between the Old Testament and the New Testament that seemed to indicate that Adam really existed and that the Fall actually occurred. For example: "sin entered the world through one man, and death through sin, and in this way death came to all men, because all sinned . . . through the disobedience of the one man the many were made sinners" (Rom. 5:12, 19 NIV); and "as in Adam all die, so in Christ all will be made alive" (1 Cor. 15:22). In the second passage the Fall and redemption were inextricably associated with each other. If Genesis was discredited, then there was a danger that the whole theological edifice would collapse—and with it all hope of salvation.

Johnson, writing under the imprimatur of the bishop of Birmingham, acknowledged that there was a distinctly mythical dimension to the story of the Fall, with its talking serpent, its mysterious trees bearing fruit with the power to bestow knowledge and eternal life, and its cherubim with a flaming sword. Yet he argued that belief could be sustained because "the relation of facts under the form of parables was native to the Hebrew genius." The Garden of Eden could, for example, be regarded as a symbolization of the intimate contact between God and the first humans.[5] If history was veiled in metaphors, then there was still much uncertainty about what the "facts" really were. There was still much room for debate —and with it the risk of error.

Messenger's Sequel

Sometime in the late 1940s, Messenger anticipated that his *Evolution and Theology* was to be reissued, and, in view of this, he thought that the publication of an accompanying volume was opportune. In his second book, *Theology and Evolution* (1951), some of the reviews of his earlier work were republished, together with his comments and subsequent discussions between the reviewers and himself. The volume merits attention here because it indicates the continuing development of a more tolerant attitude toward evolution in the institutional church in the early postwar years.

Messenger observed that his book had not been censured. The "comparative silence" of Rome indicated to him that the teaching authority of the church was adopting a "wait and see" attitude toward evolutionary theory.[6] This did not surprise him because it seemed that Rome saw its function as one of preserving the faith rather than making theological advances. An indication of Rome's benign attitude was to be found in the amendments that were made in the third (1940) and fourth (1948) editions of the thesis *De Deo Creante*, taught in the Faculty of Theology at the Gregorian University in Rome by the Jesuit Père Boyer. Messenger believed that it was highly significant that Boyer had softened his attitude toward evolution and was now favorably disposed toward a "moderate form" of human evolution.[7] Ecclesiastical approval was negative rather than positive—that is, it was not explicit and was indicated by an absence of censure.

Messenger was of the opinion that the change in attitude at the Gregorian University far outweighed the adverse reviews his book had received. Thus, he was not concerned about the "decidedly intransigent" opinions expressed by a number of ultraconservative theologians, including a number of American Jesuits. This did not mean that he was complacent about the opposition. There was still some work to be done in persuading those who were resolutely opposed to the application of evolutionary theory to humans.[8]

Messenger argued that evolutionary theory was supported by converging lines of evidence from paleontology, the geographical distribution of plants and animals, comparative anatomy and physiology, comparative embryology, and ethology (the study of animal behavior, especially concerned with natural selection). If God created plants and animals through an evolutionary process, then, Messenger argued, it was likely that he used the same method to create the human body—he would make use of secondary causes as much as possible. Converging lines of evidence from comparative anatomy, physiology, vestigial organs, and paleontology provided strong evidence for human evolution. These strands of evidence, taken individually, were not conclusive and could be contested. This was the strategy of conservative theologians who wished to deny the possibility of evolution. But Messenger argued that this approach was a "Fallacy of Division," and he argued that a more reasonable attitude was to consider all the evidence collectively.[9]

Those who were resolutely opposed to the idea of human evolution contended that the "missing link" between humans and their ancestors

had not been discovered. Their position was becoming increasingly difficult to sustain with the accumulation of evidence in the form of hominoid
fossils. The discovery of Java Man in the late nineteenth century, and of
Peking Man in 1927, provided some evidence for man's animal ancestry.
These were both specimens of *Homo erectus* ("upright man"), a near ancestor of modern humans. Anthropologists expressed different opinions
about the human and ape-like features of these specimens. Messenger
observed that conservative theologians used this dissension to argue that
the fossils in question were not evidence for human evolution. This was,
he believed, an irrational response. He argued that when there was disagreement about whether fossils were those of humans or "anthropoid
apes" this strongly indicated an intermediate stage between the two—the
"missing link" that was not supposed to exist (p. 197).

Messenger observed that the conservative rejection of the evolution of
Adam was reinforced by the apparent impossibility of explaining the origin of Eve from Adam by natural means. It was argued that if Eve could
not have arisen by some natural process, then she must have been created
through a direct and immediate act of God. If this was accepted, then it
would be more appropriate to hold a similar opinion about the creation of
Adam. Messenger searched for an alternative explanation based on secondary causes. He reminded his readers about the hypothesis he put forward in *Evolution and Theology* that parthenogenesis was a possible
explanation for the origin of Eve. Messenger's quest for a natural explanation was hopelessly at variance with science, notwithstanding the point
that there were yet many surprising discoveries to be made about nature.
Even with this in mind he was forced to conclude that the natural process
of Eve's formation might never be ascertained. But he was not free to
express the view that the story of Adam and Eve was fictional, intended to
convey the simple message that humans occupied a special place in God's
creation.

The teaching authority of the church demanded assent to the theological "truth" that "somehow, and at some time, the first woman was formed
from the first man" (p. 207). Messenger contemplated the possibility that
the narrative of creation in Genesis was written with the intention of conveying moral principles and was not meant to be taken as literally true in
the historical sense. Such a liberal exegesis, however, seemed to be ruled
out by the second paragraph of the decree issued on 30 June 1909 by the
Pontifical Biblical Commission (p. 210).

Messenger observed that it was the primary duty of the Catholic
Church to teach the Catholic faith. But, in fulfilling its primary function,

it had to take cognizance of science because of the points of contact between Catholic doctrine and scientific theories. In this interdisciplinary area there was a natural conservatism among theologians, who were reluctant to modify or abandon long-established and cherished views. Messenger argued that this excessively cautious attitude needed to be overcome to avoid repeating the mistakes of the past. A tenacious adherence to such ideas as the literal interpretation of the six days of creation, the universality of the Flood, and the geocentric theory of the universe, had brought discredit on theology. Scientific progress had eventually forced theologians to abandon their archaic ideas. Messenger believed that the majority of theologians now accepted the evolution of plants and animals and that there was growing support for applying "some restricted form of evolution" to the human species. But there was still a strong tendency to adhere to a rigidly literal interpretation of the creation narrative about Eve. Messenger saw this as yet another lost cause. Theologians would be forced to abandon their positions, as their predecessors had done in the past (pp. 210–11).

As Messenger was making the final editorial changes to *Theology and Evolution*, he was aware of rumors, which had circulated from time to time, that Pope Pius XII was about to make an important pronouncement on the subject of evolution. This pronouncement was issued in the form of an encyclical, *Humani Generis* ("Of the Human Race"), on 12 August 1950. By that time *Theology and Evolution* was at the printer. Messenger hurriedly wrote a short addendum, expressing his "wholehearted submission" to the papal pronouncement (p. 215). He pointed out that he had included in the book criticism of his own views about evolution. Furthermore, he stated that he had deliberately refrained from giving unconditional assent to the theory of evolution. After a brief discussion of some statements in the encyclical, Messenger observed that the attitude of the church authorities toward the idea of human evolution was now "more benign" (p. 216). He was also of the opinion that the opposition of theologians had abated. Messenger had been cautious in not overstepping the bounds of orthodoxy. When he did speculate he did so tentatively. Not all Catholic theologians had been so prudent.

Humani Generis

Some scholars strayed from the straight and narrow path defined by the magisterium. Copies of a number of unpublished articles, some by "well-known" scholars, were circulated among seminarians and college students.[10] It was proposed that Adam was not an individual but rather an indefinite number of people from whom the entire human race descended. Original sin was regarded not as a true sin inherited by humans from their first ancestor but as a general turning away from God under the influence of sinful leaders. Furthermore, it was argued that philosophy and science were jointly exercising enormous pressure to apply the evolutionary concept to theological studies. Apparently, these papers were widely circulated.

The ideas that were expressed in privately circulated papers were also published in journals and books.[11] The pope decided to take decisive action—hence the encyclical *Humani Generis*. His offensive was particularly directed against French theologians. It was standard procedure for theological experts to draft, or to assist in the drafting of, encyclicals. In this instance the Catholic author (and nontheologian) C. Sejournas attributed authorship to "obscurantist Vatican bureaucrats."[12] The main drafter of the encyclical was one of Rome's most conservative theologians, the Dominican Reginald Garrigou-Lagrange—nicknamed "Reginald the Rigid."[13]

A remarkable feature of this authoritative papal document was that it explicitly mentioned the theory of evolution. This was unprecedented. The pope's main interest was not with scientific theory but with the extrapolation of evolutionary ideas beyond the realm of the natural sciences. Evolution was acknowledged as a valid but unproven scientific hypothesis. Pius condemned its use as an ideological device by communists to popularize dialectical materialism. Its uncritical acceptance, he believed, had paved the way for philosophical errors, including monism, pantheism, dialectical materialism, and existentialism.[14] Thomistic philosophy was presented as the preeminent and valid philosophy of the church. It could be improved, but one was not permitted to regard it as obsolete or to abandon it. Pius believed that some Catholic scholars, "desirous of novelty, and fearing to be considered ignorant of recent scientific findings," were in danger of departing from the teachings of the church and leading others into error (par. 10). Even some virtuous men, in their "imprudent zeal for souls," represented a serious danger to the church because they were willing to reform theological thinking beyond what was regarded as safe in an attempt to make the faith more adaptable to the demands of modern society (par. 11). Their good intentions were acknowledged, but there was to be no tolerance for those who sought compromise with error.

Pius deplored the tendency of some scholars to refer to the Biblical Commission's letter to Cardinal Suhard of Paris as a basis for an excessively liberal interpretation of the Old Testament books. He insisted that, although it could be conceded that the sacred writers used popular writings, they did so with the aid of divine inspiration and thus were protected from error in selecting and evaluating these documents. Therefore, despite the metaphorical expressions and the incorporation of myths, the scriptural narratives were not to be relegated to the status of myths and were still to be regarded as history "in a true sense" (par. 38). It was probably very difficult for some Catholic scholars, despite their loyalty, to resist the conclusion that the pope's position on this issue was self-contradictory.

A number of Catholic scholars had adopted an innovative exegetical approach to scripture, described as "symbolic" or "spiritual," in order to overcome the difficulties imposed by a literal interpretation (par. 23). Their endeavors, according to Pius, had "borne . . . deadly fruit in almost all branches of theology" and were deemed to be in violation of the principles and rules of interpretation laid down in the encyclicals *Providentissimus Deus*, *Spiritus Paraclitus*, and *Divino Afflante Spiritu* (parr. 24–25). Some specific theological errors were identified. These included:

1. It is doubtful if human reason, unaided by God's revelation and grace, can prove the existence of a personal God by inference from information about the universe.

2. The world did not have a beginning (par. 25).

3. It is not certain if there is any essential difference between matter and spirit.

4. Original sin, as defined by the Council of Trent, is in need of revision (par. 26).

5. The reasonable character and credibility of the Christian faith is in question (par. 27).

Catholics were obligated to believe that the human soul was created directly by God, but they were permitted to consider it possible that God created the human body through an evolutionary process. However, those Catholics who accepted the evolution of the human body as "completely certain and proved by the facts . . . as if there were nothing in the sources of Divine Revelation which demands the greatest moderation and caution" were deemed to have carelessly exceeded the liberty of thought and discussion open to loyal Catholics (par. 36). The implication here is that although evolution is a valid hypothesis it may be wrong. Pius's grudging concession to evolutionary theory was minimal and conditional. His encyclical did not concede enough to overcome the difficulties between Catholic theology and science.

The predominant view in science was that the human species (*Homo sapiens*) was descended from a single population rather than from a number of populations; that is, it was monophyletic rather than polyphyletic. A major difficulty arose for Catholics because evolutionary theory favored the origins of humankind from a population (polygenism) rather than from a single couple (monogenism).[15] The Catholic Church's position, as stated in *Humani Generis*, was both monogenist and monophyletic.[16] The traditional Catholic belief about human origins was that the species descended from one couple—Adam and Eve. Through the sin of Adam, all humans are sinners. All humans share the original sin of Adam because they are descended from him. Therefore, monogenism and the doctrine of original sin seemed to be inextricably connected. This created major problems for scholars who were working assiduously toward reconciling Catholic doctrine and science.

In *Humani Generis* Pius expressed concern about many authors who, mindful of polygenism, insisted on revising the doctrine of original sin (par. 35). The inheritance of original sin was to derive from a group rather than from one man. *Humani Generis* effectively ruled out such an explanation. Paragraph 37 of the encyclical states:

> When, however, there is a question of another conjectural opinion, namely polygenism, the children of the Church by no means enjoy such liberty. For the faithful cannot embrace that opinion which maintains either that after Adam there existed on this earth true men who did not take their origin through natural generation from him as from the first parent of all, or that Adam represents a certain number of first parents. Now it is in no way apparent how such an opinion can be reconciled with that which the sources of revealed truth and the documents of the Teaching Authority of the Church propose with regard to Original Sin, which proceeds from a sin actually committed by an individual Adam and which through generation is passed on to all . . . (Rom. 5:12–19).

Pius invoked the Principle of the Priority of Scripture (discussed above in chapter 1)—that is, if an apparent conflict arises between a biblical passage and a reasonable but unproven claim about nature, then the literal meaning of scripture should be held until sufficient evidence is discovered to demonstrate the scientific hypothesis. Pius's epistemological position was extremely demanding. Polygenism, like the broader question of human evolution, was not in the realm of "clearly proved facts"; it was one of a number of "conjectural opinions." Furthermore, it seems that Bellarmine's Principle of Limitation is also evident here—that is, there are limits to the interpretation of scripture when considering the implications of scientific observations and theories.[17] Pius asserted that if "such conjectural opinions are directly or indirectly opposed to the doctrine revealed by God, then the demand that they be recognised can in no way be admitted" (par. 35).

Catholics were not permitted to accept polygenism, nor, it seems, to pursue it as a hypothesis. The task of persuading well-informed Catholics to accept such a ruling, however, was quite formidable. Polygenism was accepted by the vast majority of scientists; it was supported by a large volume of research data; and it offered the best explanation of human origins. That Pius was to some extent aware of this counterargument is indicated by the words "it is in no way apparent" in paragraph 37 of his encyclical. This ambivalence suggested that the church's stance on the issue might change in the future. Therefore, it was prudent for the pope to leave some degree of flexibility in a directive that was otherwise excessively rigid and vulnerable to diminishing credibility as scientific evidence accumulated in favor of a theory that was already consolidated.

When Pius XII issued *Humani Generis*, he was not exercising his teaching authority to the fullest extent; that is, the controversial part of the document did not have the status of an infallible pronouncement. Nevertheless, he made it clear to theologians that they were forbidden to regard the subject as open to free debate when he declared in paragraph 20:

> if the Supreme Pontiffs in their official documents purposely pass judgement on a matter up to that time under dispute, it is obvious that that matter, according to the mind and will of the same Pontiffs, cannot be any longer considered a question open to discussion among theologians.

The reactionary stance of Pius XII dissipated suspicions that the papacy had softened its attitude against modernism.[18]

The Aftermath of *Humani Generis*

Catholic scholarship was severely curtailed in the latter half of Pius's pontificate. Some theologians were forbidden by Vatican authorities to teach or publish on the basis of guidelines such as those laid down in *Humani*

Generis. Those who were censured for their views, or who were very restricted in expressing their views, included, most notably, the French Dominicans Yves Congar and Marie-Dominique Chenu, and the Jesuits Henri de Lubac, Karl Rahner, Pierre Teilhard de Chardin, Jean Daniélou, and John Courtney Murray. These scholars and others were subjected to very close scrutiny, perhaps to the point of persecution, by the Holy Office (the Inquisition) headed by Cardinal Alfredo Ottaviani. There was some fear among theologians that the heresy hunts that had taken place under Pope Pius X would be renewed, but this did not occur. Pius XII understood the curia much better than Pius X, and he was not prepared to grant the heresy-hunters freedom of action.[19] Furthermore, the works of Congar, Chenu, de Lubac, and others had been very carefully constructed within the framework of Catholic traditional teaching. They had not left themselves vulnerable to charges of heresy. Therefore, it would have been imprudent for Pius XII to have denounced them explicitly in his encyclical. Nevertheless, he wielded enormous power in the church, and those theologians who were deemed to have strayed too far from the straight and narrow path of orthodoxy submitted to his judgment.[20]

The exercise of papal power, formidable as it was, contributed little to the harmonization of Roman Catholic interpretations of scripture with modern science. It would have been eminently sensible, for example, to regard the story of the creation of Eve as allegorical, but this was not permitted because the Pontifical Biblical Commission and Pius XII had pronounced against it. To expect that progress in science and in exegesis might somehow make possible a sensible scientific explanation of Eve's creation was unrealistic in the extreme. Catholic exegetes were confronted with the impossible task of reconciling rigid orthodoxy with the rational demands of science.

Pope Pius had dismissed polygenism as a mere "conjectural opinion." A contributor to the *Catholic Biblical Quarterly*, Michael J. Gruenthaner, argued that even if the scientific and philosophical tenability of polygenism was acknowledged by the church, it would still be irreconcilable with scripture. For example, Genesis 3:20 declares that Eve was to become the mother of all humanity. Acts 17:26 states that all nations on earth were descended from one man. St. Paul's First Epistle to the Corinthians was quoted in support of this (1 Cor. 15:45–49). For additional support against polygenism Gruenthaner referred to St. Paul's Epistle to the Romans (Rom. 5:12–21). Here Adam and Jesus Christ were contrasted in terms of sin, death, righteousness, and redemption. Jesus Christ was spoken of as "one man"; therefore, Gruenthaner argued, Adam must also have been an individual. From his perspective scripture and polygenism were "hopelessly at variance," and this conclusion was confirmed by *Humani Generis*.[21]

Gruenthaner's argument was formidable. When Pius XII spoke out against polygenism in paragraph 37 of his encyclical, he referred to Romans 5:12–19. All the scriptural passages that refer to the first humans seem to take it for granted that there was one man and one woman. The basis of the pope's objection, however, seems to have been mainly theological rather than scriptural, centered on the incompatibility between the doctrine of original sin and polygenism. The associate professor of anthropology at Fordham University in New York, J. Franklin Ewing, S.J., observed that the story of Adam and Eve as the first parents of all humans had not been defined by the church. Nevertheless, he added that ecclesiastical pronouncements on the subject of human origins seemed to assume that all humans were descended from Adam and Eve. Notable examples were the Council of Carthage (418), the Council of Orange (529), and the Council of Trent (1546), where reference was made to Adam as an individual when elaborating on original sin. Furthermore, the Pontifical Biblical Commission had decreed in 1909 that "the unity of the human race" was one of the fundamental doctrines of the church.[22] In view of the above there seemed to be little scope for progressive thinking in theology.

Conformity to orthodoxy was the dominant consideration for many theologians. The Jesuit author Gustave Weigel carried out a detailed study of the reaction to *Humani Generis*. About eighteen months after the encyclical was issued his survey of ninety-six articles was published in *Theological Studies*. Weigel conceded that there was some opposition but he dismissed it as of little significance. The malcontents, allegedly incapable of objective assessment, were either non-Catholic critics such as Georges Barrois or Catholic nontheologians such as C. Sejournas. The conformity of the majority was pleasing to Weigel, but he was well aware of the counterargument—that is, what else could be expected from Catholic theologians when confronted by the formidable authority of a papal encyclical?[23] From a non-Catholic perspective it seemed that some Catholic theologians, in affirming their submission, were "speaking with their tongues in their cheeks."[24]

The Jesuit author Cyril Vollert did not merely affirm his acceptance of the papal directive; he welcomed it "with joy."[25] Vollert argued that Catholic theologians would not have any difficulty in adhering to the directives of *Humani Generis*. The opinions of a Catholic theologian were merely human opinions and had no value unless approved of by the teaching authority of the church. Liberty of thought would be as wide as the domain of truth—and the arbiter of truth was the papal magisterium. Vollert was confident that theologians would be guided by an awareness of their true position. From a non-Catholic perspective this was regarded as an abdication of the intellect[26]—a charge that was probably not uncommon.[27]

Intellectual satisfaction was not of paramount importance to Catholic theologians. Bruno de Solages, rector of the Catholic Institute of Toulouse, explained why when he wrote,

> Without doubt the revelation of the gift of God to men, the eternal message of Heaven to Earth, is so overwhelmingly more important than the problems of natural science, that anything that science could discover would appear almost of indifferent value, from the point of view of Revelation, to the believer.[28]

Revelation clearly took priority over science, but this did not offer a dispensation to theologians to simply ignore the troublesome implications of scientific facts and theories. Faith had to be consistent with reason. There were precedents where syntheses of revelation and science had been constructed—a most notable example was the *Summa Theologica* of St. Thomas Aquinas. De Solages argued that the need for synthesis was ongoing. Reconciling the Genesis narrative of human origins with evolutionary theory was "a task of the greatest delicacy," and many theologians had erred on the side of caution by rejecting the evolutionary idea. However, de Solages believed that their position was becoming increasingly untenable. He asserted that, following the example of St. Thomas Aquinas, Christians had to rise to the challenge of harmonizing science and revelation. In a twentieth-century context this meant interpreting the facts of revelation against the background of a universal evolutionary process.[29]

De Solages, in common with other Catholic authors, observed that evolution, especially in the nineteenth century, had frequently been presented in an anti-Christian light and that this in turn had stiffened the resistance of many Catholics to the idea. In the 1950s there was still abundant evidence of the association of evolutionary theory with anti-Christian philosophies—especially communism. Jacques de Bivort de la Saudée, editor of *God, Man and the Universe* (1954), claimed that communism and materialism shared some basic principles—a "virtually" godless universe, evolution as a substitute for religion, and a blind determinism in psychology and in nature. Communism, regarded as irreconcilable with Roman Catholicism, frequently served to inculcate materialistic philosophy. De la Saudée noted that communism was not strong in English-speaking countries, but he was still concerned about their vulnerability to it. With the exception of Ireland he believed that the popular philosophy of these countries was materialistic. Marxist-Leninism did not pose an immediate and direct threat, but de la Saudée was concerned that, in the long term, "superficial 'scientianism'" would greatly weaken the West's resistance to communism.[30]

De la Saudée presented *God, Man and the Universe* as a "constructive exposition" of Catholic doctrine on a wide range of issues, not merely as a response to Marxist-Leninism. The subject matter extended across the social and natural sciences to cover such topics as materialistic philosophy and the existence of God, the origins of life, human evolution, the immortal soul, the origin of religion, Christology, church history, Catholic social teaching, and the problem of evil. Of particular interest here is "The Origin of Man in the Book of Genesis" by Ernest C. Messenger. He maintained that it had been clear for some time that the Genesis story of creation was not meant to be taken literally. Theologians in general were willing to accept a nonliteral interpretation of scripture pertaining to inorganic and organic evolution, but some of them still insisted on excluding Adam and Eve from the evolutionary process. Messenger argued against this inconsistency and quoted P. Bea, S.J., for support. Bea, a former rector of the Pontifical Biblical Institute in Rome, declared in his *Questioni Bibliche* (1950):

> As for the formation of the body (of the first man), there is no difference between the man and the animals. He who grants that the animal kingdom has evolved cannot make use of Genesis ii 7 in order to deny evolution in the case of man, so far as his body is concerned.[31]

Messenger argued that if the formation of Adam's body was part of the evolutionary process, then there was little reason to interpret the formation of Eve in a literal or quasi-literal sense. He believed that it was reasonable to regard the creation of Adam and Eve in the second chapter of Genesis as "a figurative and anthropomorphic account." But what about the formation of the first woman from the first man as a "fundamental" truth of the church as declared by the Pontifical Biblical Commission? Messenger swept this objection aside when he stated that the church's declaration did "not mean that there is no room for a certain latitude in interpreting the details of the scriptural account." On the specific issue of polygenism he observed that *Humani Generis* ruled it out until a way could be found to reconcile it with the doctrine of original sin—but he realized that this might never be achieved. Catholic theologians were in an unenviable position, caught between the strictures of orthodoxy and the intellectual demands of modern scientific theory. The way forward advocated by Messenger was for theologians to reexamine the question of original sin. Polygenism was still a topic for debate, because *Humani Generis* was not "a final and irreformable decision, or a dogmatic definition on the point in question by the Holy See. . . ."[32]

Messenger's chapter was published posthumously, and it was contrary to paragraph 20 of *Humani Generis*, which prohibited further debate by theologians on a controversial topic after the pope had passed judgment on it. Messenger's knowledge and understanding of science were weak, but, unlike his conservative colleagues, he did appreciate that aspects of scientific theory that created problems for theology could not be simply dismissed as unfounded speculation.

A flexibility of exegesis greater than the papacy was willing to concede was necessary if science and Catholicism were to be reconciled. An attitude of respectful dissent was called for. In an editorial note to Messenger's chapter it was acknowledged that the "great authority" of the decrees of the Pontifical Biblical Commission demanded "inward assent, not mere outward regard or respectful silence." However, these decrees were not infallible or unchangeable. It was "lawful to suspend judgement if we have really adequate motives for doubt, and it is even lawful to withhold this assent if the decree appears to be certainly false." Furthermore, in rare cases, an expert, with a "thorough knowledge" of the subject under discussion, could even come to a conclusion in opposition to the decree.[33] One such expert was Pierre Teilhard de Chardin—priest, paleontologist, and philosopher. His views on evolution and on original sin had caused some alarm in the church. He was forbidden to teach at the Institute Catholique in Paris because some of his opinions were considered unorthodox.[34] When Pius XII condemned opinions that he considered dangerous to the foundations of Catholic doctrine in *Humani Generis*, he referred implicitly to the theological views of Teilhard de Chardin. Teilhard believed that the encyclical expressed an extremely narrow view of humanity. He perceived that the Thomistic theologians in Rome had profoundly influenced the pope. In his opinion they failed to understand that the theory of cosmogony that he was proposing was much greater in its explanatory potential than Aristotelian Thomism when addressing theological subjects, such as creation, redemption, incarnation, and the communion. The private correspondence of Teilhard reveals how intensely he resented the stifling orthodoxy imposed by Rome. He speculated that a good psychoanalyst might see "the clear traces of a specific religious perversion" in *Humani Generis*—"the masochism and sadism of orthodoxy; the pleasure of swallowing, and making others swallow, the truth under its crudest and stupidest forms."[35]

Teilhard de Chardin saw the universe as God's handiwork, creatively endowed with energy to form increasingly complex structures. His vision represented a remarkable convergence of Christian theology and evolutionary theory. Molecules interacted to form life. Life evolved upward toward consciousness. Consciousness developed to attain self-consciousness and higher thought in humans. God then communicated with humankind through Jesus Christ, who became human. This enabled humans to become united in Christ to form the Mystical Body of Christ with the potential to constitute a new and supernatural organism. Animated by the virtue of grace, through this organism, humans in the future will become capable of a higher form of knowledge and will move toward supernatural consciousness. The evolutionary process will continue until higher states of collective human consciousness are reached, culminating in the Omega point.[36] Thus, through a divinely impelled evolutionary process, salvation will be attained.

Teilhard de Chardin had recast theology on an evolutionary basis. Matter, life, mind and spirit, the evolution of the universe, the person and work of Jesus Christ, the redemption of mankind—all were explained in the context of a progressive evolutionary process directing the universe toward the Omega point or unity with God. Although Teilhard's synthesis of Christianity and science won considerable approval in theological circles, it did not meet with the approval of the teaching authority of the Roman Catholic Church. Teilhard was forbidden by the Vatican to teach or publish his beliefs. Shortly after his death, his book *Le Phénomène Humain* (1955) was published in France (followed in 1959 by its English translation, *The Phenomenon of Man*). The posthumous publication stimulated much debate and influenced the outlook of many Catholics—despite the fact that very few of them fully understood his very abstruse work.

Cosmology and God

In his address to the Pontifical Academy of Sciences on 30 November 1941, Pope Pius XII declared that God is "the unique commander and legislator of the universe."[37] From this perspective he saw design, order, and purpose. In his allocutions to the Academy, on 21 February 1943 and 8 February 1948, he repudiated the notion that the universe had somehow come about by mere chance. The evidence of the Creator from the creation was a theme that Pius returned to in his speech to the Academy on 22 November 1951. In addressing this issue it is clear that physics, especially astrophysics, resonated with his theological outlook. The theory of biological evolution, in contrast, had troubled him because it was difficult to reconcile with the Catholic doctrine of original sin.

Before discussing the pope's views as elaborated in his 1951 speech, it is necessary to give some attention to the claim that an understanding of physics could be used to prove the existence of God. One way of proving God's existence was to disprove the atheistic hypothesis that there is no God. Atheists maintained that the universe had no beginning and was uncreated—therefore there was no need for God. Theists argued that such a hypothesis was flagrantly unscientific, and they invoked the laws of thermodynamics for support. Thermodynamics is that branch of physics which studies the laws that determine the conversion of energy from one form to another, the direction in which heat will flow, and the availability of energy to do work. The first law of thermodynamics—the law of conservation of energy—states that energy can neither be created nor destroyed (with the exception of nuclear reactions where matter and energy are interchangeable), but can be changed from one form to another. The second law of thermodynamics—the law of increasing entropy—states that, while the total amount of energy in the universe remains constant, it is being continuously dissipated. Energy flows from areas of high concentration, to areas of low concentration and this general trend is irreversible. Heat passes from hot bodies to cold bodies—not in the opposite direction.

Since the nineteenth century, scientists, notably the German physicist Rudolf Clausius (1822–1888) and Lord Kelvin, had considered the implications of a general dissipation of energy in the universe. The quantity of energy available for doing work is constantly decreasing. Ultimately, energy will become so dispersed that none of it will be available to do work—the universe will then be inert. But how was all this relevant to the existence of God? It was maintained that if the universe was infinitely old then all physical activity would have ended long ago because there was an unlimited amount of time for a complete dispersal of energy to occur. Thus, it was concluded that the second law of thermodynamics proved that the universe had a beginning and must also end. If the universe had a beginning, it must have been created—it was not reasonable to suppose that it originated from nothing.[38] Some scientists, however, disagreed with the above conclusion on the basis that the universe might be able to regenerate itself through some unknown mechanism. This was dismissed as an unjustified hypothesis,[39] and Catholic writers frequently cited increasing entropy as proof of God's existence, sometimes arguing that entropy was incompatible with the theory of evolution.

Entropy is a mathematical measurement of disorder—the higher the entropy the greater the disorder. All changes in a closed system contribute to entropy and therefore higher disorder. If the universe is a closed system, it follows that its entropy is increasing and its available energy for doing work is decreasing. Evolution, however, was the development of the complex from the relatively simple; it was the emergence of highly organized matter from matter that was far less organized. Evolution then, it was claimed, lacked credibility because it blatantly contradicted an established law of science.[40] This was completely false, because thermodynamics applied only to closed systems. It did not rule out a local decrease in entropy in, for example, the development of biological systems if this was dependent on a greater increase of entropy somewhere else (such as the Sun radiating solar energy). All this had been known for decades.[41]

Entropy continued to play an important role in Catholic apologetics when claims for the proof of God were being put forward. When Pope Pius XII addressed the Pontifical Academy of Sciences on 22 November 1951, he declared that entropy "eloquently postulates the existence of a necessary Being."[42] Entropy, of course, was not regarded as the only modern proof. It seemed that God was "standing, vigilant and waiting, behind every door which science opens" (p. 73). In the course of his speech, Pius referred to modern advances in cosmology that seemed to indicate the existence of a Creator. At this point it is opportune to summarize these developments.

In 1929 the American astronomer Edwin Powell Hubble (1889–1953) announced his discovery that galaxies were receding rapidly from each other at speeds that were increasing with distance. The importance of his discovery was not generally understood at the time, but Georges Henri Lemaître (1894–1966) did grasp its significance. If the universe is expanding, then it had to have been smaller in the past. This implied that the universe was at its smallest possible size at some point in the past, billions of years ago. Lemaître, a Belgian Jesuit priest working in the Vatican Observatory, was trying to construct a model of the universe consistent with Einstein's theories, but it was widely believed that he was attempting to find evidence for the creation of the universe. If it could be shown that the universe had a beginning, then this could be put forward as proof of creation. Lemaître relied heavily on Einstein's mathematical equations, but he did not accept a cosmological constant arbitrarily introduced by the famous scientist. Lemaître had already published his views about the expanding universe. He now elaborated further on this model, and he proposed the idea of the "primeval atom." Einstein was reluctant to abandon the view that the universe was eternal and unchanging, but Lemaître's meticulous presentation of his theory convinced him that the universe had indeed a definite beginning in time.

The phenomenon of the expanding universe formed the basis of modern cosmology. In 1946, George Gamow's Big Bang theory followed Lemaître's "primeval atom." In 1948 a joint paper (mainly the work of Gamow but also naming Ralph Alpher and Hans Bethe as co-authors) was published which gave a highly elaborate account of the Big Bang theory. It was envisaged that all the galaxies of the universe were contained in a single point in space and time billions of years ago. Matter existed in a state of incredibly high density, and its temperature was enormously high. Under these conditions the ordinary laws of physics did not operate. A gigantic explosion initiated the expansion of the universe. The universe, therefore, was of finite age. All this resonated well with creation theology. Pope Pius XII regarded the Big Bang as the mighty act of creative omnipotence. This primordial explosion also represented the outer frontier of science. The pope thought it futile for scientists to ask what preceded it. It was at this point that he invoked "philosophical speculation" to "penetrate the problem more profoundly" (p. 82).

Evidently, Pius was fascinated by the findings of scientists, but he realized that the natural sciences, in their present state of development, did not offer a reliable foundation for proofs of God's existence. For "absolute proof" of God he relied on metaphysics and revelation (p. 82). He was aware of conflicting opinions on this fundamental issue. Furthermore, he was conscious of the fact that scientific theories were not absolutely immutable or secure. In an earlier address to the Academy (8 February 1948), he had spoken about scientific theories that had "reached the apex of undisputed doctrines" that were later relegated to the status of hypotheses, or in some cases were discarded (pp. 67–68).

Generally, scientific thought rejected the notion that matter came from nothing. This, however, did not lead inevitably to the conclusion that matter was created by a supernatural being. Pius acknowledged the counterargument: "Matter exists. Nothing proceeds from nothing: in consequence matter is eternal. We cannot admit the creation of matter" (p. 83). The Big Bang theory did not overcome this argument. The universe could still have existed before the Big Bang—a possibility conceded by the British mathematical physicist and Pontifical academician Sir Edmund Whittaker (1873–1956), whom Pius quoted for support. If it could be proved that the universe began with the Big Bang, then Pius believed that he would have a powerful synthesis of philosophy and science in his favor and could confidently state: "Creation, therefore, in time, and therefore, a Creator; and consequently, God!" Pius was aware that such a claim was untenable in this context. Therefore he immediately added: "This is the statement, even though not explicit or complete, that We demand of science" (p. 84).

Several eminent scientists, especially those who were resolutely atheistic, repudiated the Big Bang theory. In 1948, Fred Hoyle, Hermann Bondi, and Thomas Gold proposed an alternative explanation. Their steady state theory envisaged that the universe was unchanged throughout time and was uniform in space. Matter was being spontaneously and continuously generated to fill the extra space caused by cosmic expansion. In the 1950s and early 1960s steady state theory offered a robust challenge to the idea of the Big Bang.[43] Its appeal to atheistic cosmologists was that it avoided a creation event—with all its concomitant religious implications.[44]

The inability of science to offer conclusive proof of God's existence did not mean, from Pius's point of view, that God had to be accepted on faith alone. He was convinced that metaphysics and revelation offered reliable proofs of the supreme Creator. The "five ways" of St. Thomas Aquinas offered "the sure and expeditious itinerary" to "the mind of God."[45] Science alone did not. The natural sciences fulfilled the important function of greatly strengthening the empirical foundation of the philosophical arguments for God's existence.[46] This was a strange synthesis of thirteenth-century philosophy and twentieth-century science.

In the twentieth century there was an element of superficial plausibility about Aquinas's five arguments for the existence of God. Aquinas observed, in his first argument, that nature is not static—it is dynamic. Objects do not move by themselves. Everything that moves is moved by something else, which is moved by something else and so on until a final cause of motion is encountered. Unless there is an infinite series of causes, Aquinas contended that there must be a single cause at the origin of the great chain of causality. This ultimate cause—the Prime Unmoved

Mover—was none other than God. The second argument was concerned with the existence of causes and effects in nature. There is a series of cause-and-effect relationships. Everything was caused by something that existed before it. Nothing can exist without a cause. It was argued that a sequence of cause and effect relationships could be traced backwards in time but that it was not infinite. There had to be a first cause of everything. God is the single original cause or First Cause. A similar type of reasoning was used in the third and fourth arguments, in which causal sequences were traced back to God.[47] Aquinas's fifth argument was logically dissimilar to the first four. He maintained that natural objects exhibited intelligent design and purpose. Objects could not design themselves —hence the need for a designer, God.[48]

Pius conveniently ignored what Enlightenment philosophy had to say about the matter. Major weaknesses in the traditional proofs of God's existence were exposed as far back as the eighteenth century. The argument from design was challenged by the German philosopher Immanuel Kant (1724–1804) and by the Scottish philosopher and historian David Hume (1711–1776). Both criticized the argument on the basis that it assumed the existence of a creator, the very point it was supposed to prove. St. Thomas had assumed, quite reasonably, that everything must have a cause or explanation, but then he introduced God, who did not have a cause or explanation. If an uncaused God is proposed, then why not an uncaused universe? Furthermore, the philosophical basis of the design argument is unsound. Hume questioned the validity of the analogy with machines. It is clear that machines, such as watches, were designed. But the universe could just as easily be compared to a living organism such as a plant, the design of which was in question.[49]

In philosophical matters Pius was clearly biased, taking from the discipline what suited him for purposes of apologetics. He adopted the same attitude toward the natural sciences. He had acknowledged that the universe had evolved over billions of years. He found the process of inorganic evolution, illuminated by the disciplines of physics and chemistry, very congenial to his outlook. But he avoided any discussion of the life sciences, probably because of the thorny issue of polygenism, which he had condemned nearly sixteen months earlier. Yet the evolution of species was on a much sounder foundation than the Big Bang theory at the time.

In 1952 Pius exaggerated the significance of the Big Bang in the context of God's act of creation when he stated:

> contemporary science . . . has succeeded in bearing witness to the august instant of the primordial Fiat Lux, when along with matter there burst forth

from nothing a sea of light and radiation. . . . Thus, with that concreteness which is characteristic of physical proofs, modern science has confirmed the contingency of the Universe and also the well-founded deduction to the epoch when the world came forth from the hands of the Creator.[50]

The pope's views were very different to those of Lemaître, who served as president of the Pontifical Academy of Sciences from 1960 to his death in 1966.[51] Lemaître viewed religion and science as distinct sectors of knowledge. He insisted that his theory of the primeval atom

must not be mixed up with metaphysical or religious questions. It leaves the materialist free to deny any supreme Being. . . . It does not include any familiarity with God on the part of the believer, which matches Isaiah's words when he spoke of the "hidden God" even from the beginning of creation.[52]

Lemaître consistently maintained the distinction between science and faith, and in his published work in science he never discussed, or made reference to, issues pertaining to faith. It is understandable, therefore, that Lemaître experienced difficulties with the views of Pius XII. In 1952 it seems that circumstances persuaded him to communicate his concerns to the pope. The Eighth General Assembly of the International Astronomical Union was due to be held in September of that year in Rome. Pius was to address the meeting, and, as the text of his speech was in preparation, Lemaître traveled to Rome to influence the proceedings. It seems that his mission was successful. When Pius spoke at the conference on 7 September he referred to a number of advances in the astronomical sciences, but he made no specific reference to scientific results concerning the Big Bang. Throughout the remainder of his pontificate he did not draw any philosophical or religious conclusions from Big Bang theory.[53]

The pope's interest in science was quite evident from his public statements. But such an interest was not matched by a degree of flexibility and tolerance that would have given Catholic scholars the necessary latitude in reconciling theology with science within the constraints imposed by the dogmas of the church. Pope Pius XII died on 9 October 1958 and was succeeded by Angelo Roncalli, the patriarch of Venice. Roncalli took the name of John XXIII. He had not completely escaped the misguided fervor of the antimodernist crusade, and this influenced him to be far more tolerant and liberal than his predecessors.[54] His pontificate (1958–1963) ushered in a new era in the history of the Roman Catholic Church.

Although the censorship of Teilhard de Chardin and other Catholic scholars had suppressed progressive thinking in the church, the theologi-

cal renewal quickly reemerged and was of central importance to the proceedings of the Second Vatican Council. Teilhard de Chardin's influence,
for example, has been discerned in *Gaudium et Spes*, the council's Pastoral
Constitution on the Church in the Modern World (1965), which states
that "the human race has passed from a rather static concept of reality to
a more dynamic, evolutionary one."[55] Some eminent proponents of the
"new theology" gradually won the approval of the institutional church
and gave expert advice to the Second Vatican Council. Some were
appointed to the Theological Commission set up by Pope Paul VI, and a
number of them served in positions of influence in seminaries and universities, as members of editorial boards of theological journals, and as
consultants to a variety of church bodies ranging from diocesan level to
the international. Three of the theologians who had suffered on account
of the excesses of the Vatican's authority were made cardinals—Jean
Daniélou by Pope Paul VI, Yves Congar and Henri de Lubac by Pope
John Paul II. The antimodernist era had ended.

9

Science, Faith, and the
Second Vatican Council

Evolution and Genesis

THE YEAR 1959 MARKED THE CENTENARY YEAR OF THE *ORIGIN of Species* and stimulated an upsurge of interest in Darwin and the evolutionary process. Catholic theologians were aware of the difficulties evolutionary theory posed for their discipline. The vast majority of them were probably also aware that evolutionary theory permeated modern thinking and was of central importance to scientific theory. Some theologians, therefore, made concessions to science with great reluctance.[1] However, although they expressed reservations about human evolution, there was a marked tendency to refrain from outright condemnation.[2] Robert W. Gleason, writing under the imprimatur of Archbishop Joseph E. Ritter of St. Louis, made the following observations in *Darwin's Vision and Christian Perspectives* (1960).

1. The first account of creation, especially the narrative concerning the creation of Adam and Eve, "probably" does not date back as far as Moses. It is "rather a sort of theological résumé of Mosaic tradition."

2. There is consensus among theologians that there is some historical basis to the assertions of Genesis, but it is a "peculiar type of history whose rules are still partly unknown to us" (this was based on a decree of the Pontifical Biblical Commission in 1909).

3. Scientific ideas expressed by the author of Genesis are possibly erroneous, derived as they were from contemporary notions about the natural world. However, it is not the intention of scripture to teach science.

4. It is not "popular" now to consider everything in the first chapter of Genesis to be dictation from God.

5. The creation of the human species through an evolutionary process does not now seem "improbable."[3]

Gleason observed that many theologians no longer felt it necessary to maintain that God created the first human immediately and directly from inorganic material. There was still great uncertainty about how God created humankind. Whether or not Adam and Eve represented one couple or a number of couples was still very much in doubt. Although it was still "perfectly acceptable" to Gleason to claim that God created Adam's body directly from inorganic material, this explanation was not quite satisfactory (p. 108). But he had to be careful in expressing his opinions on this matter because of his awareness that the teaching authority of the church was still very sensitive about the question of human origins (p. 105). Therefore he stated that some theologians "with much more knowledge of paleontological discoveries" believed that it was also permissible to hold the view that God created the first human body from an animal and transformed it to receive the human soul (p. 108). The inference here was clear: the more scientifically enlightened view among theologians favored the evolutionary process.

It was speculated that the transformation of the pre-human body (almost human) was brought about by "a series of sudden mutations," so that it would be suitable for the infusion of a divinely created soul. But concessions to science would have to be expressed equivocally to limit the dangerous potential of evolutionary theory. Therefore Gleason maintained that the emergence of Adam, body and soul, was due to the "special intervention" of God (p. 109). Humans are still essentially different from other animal species. But what about Eve? Gleason stated that it was "perhaps possible" to claim that scripture implied the formation of Eve from a part of Adam's body, or that Adam was the "exemplary cause" of Eve—that is, her body and nature were "fashioned" after his. There was still uncertainty about how her body was formed (pp. 111–12).

The Catholic biologist Philip G. Fothergill addressed the question of Eve's physical origin in his book *Evolution and Christians* (1961).[4] He too was mindful of the constraints imposed by the teaching authority of the church. The Pontifical Biblical Commission had decreed that the first woman was formed from man. Fothergill, unlike a number of Catholic apologists who struggled with this difficulty, had a sound understanding of biology. He received advice on the interpretation of scripture from Fr. Leonard Johnston of Ushaw College.

From a scientific perspective the parthenogenesis hypothesis of Messenger was clearly untenable. Fothergill searched for a scientifically credible explanation that would be compatible with Catholic doctrine. Genesis 2:23 indicated a very close relationship between Adam and Eve. She was bone of his bones, flesh of his flesh. Perhaps Eve was formed through the natural method of sexual reproduction? Fothergill proposed two possibilities: first, that Eve was the daughter of Adam; second, that Adam and Eve were fraternal twins whose parents were genetically on the threshold of humanity (pp. 327–28). Inbreeding in the first few generations would have been necessary to propagate the new species. Fothergill was aware that his hypothesis was repugnant because of the incestuous nature of the relationships. He defended it, however, on the basis that modern ideas and attitudes would not be helpful in our attempts to understand the attitudes and proclivities of the earliest humans (p. 329). Fothergill's hypothesis was scientifically plausible. But it was also somewhat scientifically deficient in that it was not possible to confirm or falsify such a claim—in that sense it was unscientific. Fothergill was aware of Teilhard de Chardin's observation that monogenism, by its very nature, was outside the realm of science.[5]

Fothergill examined in detail the official views of the church on human evolution and referred to paragraph 36 of Pius XII's *Humani Generis*, which rebuked those Catholics who believed that human evolution was "completely certain and proved by the facts." But how much evidence was necessary before a theory could be elevated to the level of "clearly proved facts"?[6] Or, more specifically, what degree of certainty was required for a scientific theory that impacted on Catholic doctrine to make it necessary to undertake revisions in theology? Fothergill maintained that if the majority of theologians, past and present, were in agreement about a particular issue in their discipline then it would be rash for ordinary Catholics to question it (p. 300). Biologists were entitled to the same deference concerning issues in their discipline. There was a very large volume of evidence for evolution from the biological sciences, and the vast majority of biologists accepted the general evolutionary hypothesis. Fothergill argued that if nonbiologists denied or expressed skepticism about evolution, then the heavy burden of disproof was on their shoulders (pp. 300–302).

If deference to professional consensus was to be the guiding principle, what were Catholics to believe when they perceived contradictions between theology and biology? Fothergill observed that few biologists would maintain that evolution could be asserted with absolute certainty. In a philosophical sense there is very little that can be maintained with complete certainty. But evolution could not be simply ignored by philosophers and theologians on the basis of this argument. There was very strong evidence in its favor. The evolution of plants and animals—excluding humankind—was widely accepted by theologians. Humans are animals, in a biological sense, and therefore there was, a priori, a good reason to believe that humans had evolved (p. 303). On what scientific basis could an exception be made for humans? Fothergill put forward two conflicting opinions. Human evolution, although at least "highly probable," had not been proved "with absolute moral certitude." It was not as firmly established as the general theory; therefore there was room for "legitimate doubt" (p. 303). The counterargument was that the evidence for human evolution was so strong that it justified the stance that if it was to be rejected then there was an obligation on those who dissented to propose an alternative explanation—equally reasonable and scientific—to account for observations to date. Fothergill seemed to agree with this position, but, if he did he changed his mind, confronted as he was by the pope's censure in paragraph 36 of *Humani Generis*. Loyal Catholics were still not permitted to take human evolution for granted, as if it had certainly happened.

Evolutionary theory explained the development of species on the basis of populations—there was no scientific reason to make an exception for humans. In the early 1960s there was still a strong tendency among Roman Catholic theologians, interpreting Genesis in the light of St. Paul and the Council of Trent, to explain the physical origins of the human species by referring to one couple. But by the early 1970s it seems that another major shift in theological thinking had occurred that leaned much further toward an allegorical reading of Genesis. Many biblical scholars, on the basis of a revised contextual analysis, had come to see the texts of St. Paul and the Council of Trent in a new light. It now seemed that these texts were "neutral" on the question of evolution. Adam was taken as representative of all humankind, and original sin was not merely a sin committed at the dawn of human history but a perverse and constant trait of human behavior where new sins are conditioned to a great extent by preceding sins. Many scholars believed that the Fall was a parable to illustrate the sinful nature of humankind.[7] However, their opinions did not reflect the authoritative teaching of the church. A clear divergence between

Roman Catholicism and science still existed, which created tension between the two domains of thought. The decrees of the Second Vatican Council, which will be discussed next, shed little light on the question of how to reconcile the Genesis narratives with evolutionary theory.

Aggiornamento

On 25 January 1959 Pope John XXIII announced that a general council was to be convened. It was not to be a continuation of the First Vatican Council, nor a docile assembly inspired by the *Syllabus of Errors*, opposed to modernity and reconciliation with the other Christian churches. Although John did not live to see the conclusion of the Second Vatican Council, he did profoundly influence the outcome of its proceedings.[8] It was due to his insistence that the church set itself the task of adapting itself to the needs of the world. Conservative curial officials who wished to reiterate the condemnations contained in *Pascendi Dominici Gregis* and *Humani Generis* found themselves in a minority, and the documents they submitted were rejected in favor of those more responsive to the needs and realities of modern society. The conservatives failed in their attempts to influence the church to reiterate its rejection of polygenism with greater force and to elevate the doctrinal status of monogenism.[9]

The decline of antimodernism in the church was indicated in a number of the Second Vatican Council's key documents, for example, in *Lumen Gentium* (Dogmatic Constitution on the Church), issued on 21 November 1964. In paragraph 25 the council reiterated the assertion of *Humani Generis* (par. 20) concerning obedience to noninfallible teachings. *Lumen Gentium* stated that Catholics were under moral obligation to give "loyal submission of the will and intellect" to the teaching authority of the pope—even when the pope was not speaking *ex cathedra*. But, significantly, the council did not repeat the statement in *Humani Generis* that prohibited public discussion of issues pronounced upon by the pope, despite the presence of such an assertion in the preliminary draft of 10 November 1962.[10]

Another indication of the weakening of antimodernism was when the Council issued *Gaudium et Spes*, which was published on 7 December 1965. This document addressed many issues of concern to the church, including its attitude toward science. In paragraphs 36 and 59 the "rightful autonomy" of the sciences were acknowledged. This indicated that article 57 of the *Syllabus of Errors*, which had asserted ecclesiastical authority over the natural sciences and philosophy, was no longer tenable.[11]

The council, in considering and clarifying the role of the church in the modern world, could not ignore the impact of science. It declared that research, when carried out in a "truly scientific manner" and in conformity with moral laws, could never come into conflict with faith. The ideal scientist would be led "by the hand of God in spite of himself."[12] It was all very well to reiterate the long-standing theological principle of harmony between Catholic faith and science, but the council could not ignore the Galileo case without detracting from the credibility of its pronouncements.

In late March 1964, a petition was addressed to Pope Paul VI requesting "a solemn rehabilitation of Galileo." It was signed by the Dominican priest Dominique Dubarle, an ecclesiastical councillor of the Union des Scientifiques Français, and by many scientists and university lecturers.[13] These scientists, in their submission to the bishops of the Vatican Council, declared that the condemnation of Galileo had "always been deeply resented by the whole of the scientific world as one of the most evident proofs of the suspicion with which the church has regarded and still regards the intellectual undertakings of science." They claimed that there was no subsequent indication of respect or goodwill to dispel the opinion that Catholicism was intrinsically adverse to science. The observations of George J. Béné, professor of physics at the University of Geneva, are particularly illuminating on this matter. As an influential apologist for the church (he was to serve as a consultant to the Roman Secretariat for Non-Believers) Béné believed that the polemics of the nineteenth century had highlighted the church's poor judgment on Copernicanism that led to the trial of Galileo. A consequence of this was that the majority of Catholic scientists suffered from a "guilt complex," which in turn influenced their appeals to the institutions of the church to remedy the matter. Apparently, Béné believed that such appeals were unjustified because the scientists who signed such petitions did not seem to be aware of "the reactions" of the Vatican in this matter since the eighteenth century—as if such measures were somehow adequate. And why were not scientists aware of the church's "reactions"? Béné's answer was that the church had "quietly, but clearly, retracted earlier decisions."[14] Evidently, the church had proceeded too quietly for its own good.

It will be recalled from chapter 7 that Pio Paschini had not been granted permission to publish his work on Galileo in the mid 1940s. He died in 1962, and his literary heir, M. Maccarrone, presented his manuscript on Galileo to a public library in Udine (northern Italy). Paschini's manuscript was of particular interest to the council in its deliberations. In

1964 (the four-hundredth anniversary of Galileo's birth) the Pontifical Academy of Sciences published it after changes were made by the textual scholar and Jesuit priest Edmond Lamalle. In his introductory note Lamalle stated that his changes to the text were minor. However, in 1979 a comparison of Paschini's original draft with the published version revealed that the changes that were made were so substantial that the text was now more favorable to the Jesuits and to the church, and more critical of Galileo—almost certainly contrary to what the author would have intended.[15]

The Second Vatican Council had turned its attention to this document when drafting *Gaudium et Spes*. The vast majority of the participants were almost certainly unaware of the amendments to Paschini's text. Some bishops, most notably Arthur Elchinger (the auxiliary bishop of Strasbourg) wished to acknowledge explicitly that Galileo had been unjustly treated by the church authorities.[16] They met with strong opposition from many of their fellow bishops. In the compromise that was subsequently worked out, only general statements about science were included in the main text of *Gaudium et Spes*. Therefore, the council indicated obliquely that the church had committed a serious error in censoring Galileo. It declared: "We cannot but deplore certain attitudes (not unknown among Christians) deriving from a shortsighted view of the rightful autonomy of science; they have occasioned conflict and controversy and have misled many into opposing faith and science" (*Gaudium et Spes* par. 36). The reference to Galileo was relegated to a footnote, which was placed after the above statement. It simply read: "Cf. Pius Paschini, *Vita e opere di Galileo Galilei*, 2 vol., Vatic., 1964."[17]

The cardinals and bishops, presided over by the pope, had acknowledged that the rightful autonomy of science was violated by misguided Christians. This was a significant step in coming to terms with the unjustified censorship, distress, and humiliation their predecessors had inflicted on Galileo. However, the indirect reference to Galileo was not in itself an adequate response to the realization that the church had punished a man who should not have been suspected of heresy. The institutional church's explicit admission of guilt had to await the initiatives of Pope John Paul II —this will be examined later.

In the three centuries after Galileo, it became increasingly difficult to adhere to a rigidly literal reading of scripture. This development per se did not create serious doubts about the veracity of the biblical narratives. It was reasonable to allow some scope for the use of nonliteral means of expression. This exegetical principle, however, was not unlimited in its potential to explain away the ever-increasing number of incompatibilities between scripture and the findings of scientists and historians. In the 1950s and 1960s it seemed that the doctrine of biblical inerrancy was unsustainable. Even in matters of a purely religious and moral nature— such as the afterlife and retribution, marriage, and the personality of God —there seemed to be contradictions in scripture. One method of dealing with this was to regard the Bible as a record of doctrinal and moral development. God did not explicitly, clearly, and unequivocally teach error. He tolerated the inclusion of errors for some time, especially those of ancient Israel, and then corrected them when it was appropriate to do so.[18]

Sometimes fiction was regarded as a better means of communicating a given religious truth than the minimal enunciation of the truth in question. It was not essential for the sacred writers to adhere strictly to "truths" of the natural sciences, which were "in no way profitable for salvation." A different approach was necessary for historical studies because God had revealed himself in the history of ancient Israel, and therefore the truth of revelation was heavily dependent on that history. But not all the details of the history of the Israelites were important, and, consequently, they were not covered by inerrancy. Therefore, Catholic exegetes could engage in literary and historical criticism "without impugning the divine veracity" of scripture. The criterion of inerrancy was not simply based on the ascertainment of fact. The intention of the author had to be determined. Exegetes were urged to "enter the very mind of the sacred writer" by examining the writer's sources, contemporary literary styles, and "the mentality of his audience."[19]

The importance attached to the concept of literary genres in *Divino Afflante Spiritu* enabled Catholic biblical scholars to acknowledge the presence of "so called approximations," hyperbole, poetry, mathematical inaccuracies, "fictitious and parabolic narratives," and even "false assertions"—all for the purpose of conveying some abstruse and higher supernatural truth. This exegetical idea served the church well, enabling apologists to reject many arguments against the inerrancy of scripture.[20]

The church's dogma of biblical inerrancy was maintained but was not "solemnly defined."[21] It suited the church to maintain this position. The magisterium was intransigent on many points of doctrine. Nevertheless it had to retain some degree of flexibility to contend with progress in the disciplines of history and science.

The Second Vatican Council addressed issues of biblical inspiration and inerrancy in *Dei Verbum*, the Dogmatic Constitution on Divine Revelation (18 November 1965). In doing so it was guided by a range of documents, including the decrees of Vatican I, the Pontifical Biblical Commission, *Providentissimus Deus*, *Spiritus Paraclitus*, and *Divino Afflante Spiritu*. The church maintained that God had chosen the sacred writers of the scriptures and had acted through them. Therefore, they wrote whatever God wanted, no more, no less—but it was not a matter of straightforward divine dictation. These authors were influenced by the cultural milieu of their time.[22] Since the nineteenth century it had become clear that Old Testament texts were influenced by the sacred books of other cultures, such as Egyptian, Sumerian, and Assyrian. If errors seemed to arise from human sources, then these could be explained away by complex arguments concerning the intention of the author in question and the typical patterns of perception, speech, and narrative of his time.

It seemed that Rome had maintained its position on the inerrancy of scripture. But had it? Paragraph 11 of *Dei Verbum* declared:

> Since, therefore, all that the inspired authors, or sacred writers, affirm should be regarded as affirmed by the Holy Spirit, we must acknowledge that the books of Scripture, firmly, faithfully and without error, teach that truth which God, for the sake of our salvation, wished to see confided to the sacred Scriptures.

There was much debate about this statement in the proceedings of the council. Those who were conservative agreed to it on the understanding that it reaffirmed scriptural inerrancy. But afterward many Catholic scholars tended to see the statement in a different light. Teaching the "truth" without error here was in the context of what is required for salvation. Since many "truths" of history and science are irrelevant to the quest for salvation then the inerrant statements of scripture are greatly reduced— or so it seems. The Second Vatican Council failed to clarify this issue, and its documents were quoted by those who wished to restrict the concept of scriptural inerrancy and by those who sought to extend it. Attempts were made to maintain at least the appearance of unity, but in reality deep divisions persisted on this issue.[23]

If biblical inerrancy was restricted to those scriptural texts deemed essential to the propagation and preservation of faith and morals, it would have rescued theologians from the perennial impasse created by the dissonance between modern science and scripture. Although the evolution of humankind was of central importance in this context, the church's interest in science extended far beyond this issue. Science was discussed by the Second Vatican Council in the broad context of human culture. In *Gaudium et Spes* the word "culture" was used to mean those things that contributed "to the refining and developing of man's diverse mental and physical endowments" (par. 53). The natural sciences were seen as a vital part of the rapid increase and specialization of human knowledge. It was deemed vital that everyone share in the benefits of cultural progress. This required that the development of the human person as a whole should be promoted, and that Christians especially should be helped to fulfill the tasks assigned to them (par. 56).

The positive contribution of scientific values to human culture was acknowledged—the search for truth, teamwork in technological development, cooperation at the international level, and improvements in the standard of living (par. 57). After acknowledging the benefits of science the Vatican Council then identified the dangers and misapplications of science and technology. The misuse of scientific knowledge and technical expertise in developing weapons of mass destruction was disabling the offensive against poverty. The use of modern military technology was facilitating savagery on a scale far exceeding the barbarities of previous wars. Most frightening of all was the continuous threat of total war between the superpowers, which had the potential to cause the deaths of entire populations (parr. 79–81).

A grave danger associated with modern scientific progress was agnosticism. It was believed by the authors of *Gaudium et Spes* that the practice of science, which by itself was unable to discover "the deepest nature of things," led to agnosticism when it was regarded as the "supreme norm" for investigating reality. Furthermore, it was feared that advances in science could give rise to an overconfidence that would lead many to abandon spiritual values (par. 57). Some authors whose outlook was contrary to the Catholic creed had insisted that it was not possible to know anything about God while others denied God's existence. There was also a tendency for those in the "positive sciences" to traverse the boundaries of their discipline, claiming that reason alone could explain everything (par. 19).

The Roman Catholic Church had good reasons to be apprehensive about the social effects of science. Technical progress and the constant stream of new ideas generated by science had a considerable destabilizing effect on traditional and religious beliefs.[24] Science was a powerful force for change, and this was acknowledged by the Second Vatican Council when it declared:

> The spiritual uneasiness of today and the changing structure of life are part of a broader upheaval, whose symptoms are the increasing part played on the intellectual level by the mathematical and natural sciences (not exclud-

ing the sciences dealing with man himself) and on the practical level by their repercussions on technology. The scientific mentality has wrought a change in the cultural sphere and on habits of thought, and the progress of technology is now reshaping the face of the earth and has its sights set on the conquest of space. (*Gaudium et Spes* par. 5)

Science was eroding faith in two ways. First, at an intellectual level, it offered alternative explanations of the origins and functioning of the universe. Second, the technical applications of scientific knowledge transformed lifestyles and attitudes so that there was less reliance on benevolent supernatural intervention to alleviate or eliminate human distress. This second effect was subtle and probably far more potent than the first.[25] The Catholic hierarchy was deeply worried about the adverse impact of science on the faith of the masses. On 28 October 1967 the Synod of Bishops expressed concern about "dangerous opinions" and the threat of atheism:

> Very many Fathers spoke of the difficulties which today are disturbing, or can disturb, the faith of the People of God. They also mentioned that these difficulties arise in great part from the modern crises of civilisation and of human culture themselves. The Second Vatican Council expressly treated of this crisis, especially in the Pastoral Constitution on the Church in the modern world . . . some noted that in secular life there is an evolution of structures and of the very way of thinking, and doubt is being cast on the traditional image of man and of the world. This happens partly, at least, because of the remarkable progress of science and of secular civilisation, by reason of which men are completely caught up in the demands of their work; partly, also, because of an ever-increasing awareness of the evolution of the universe and of man's own life and history.[26]

It was thought that these trends led to "a kind of anthropology" and overconfidence that caused people to neglect their relationship with God. Thus, many were led to atheism, "either practical or theoretical," and regarded the church as an obstacle to human progress.[27]

Religion versus Science?

The fears of the church were not assuaged by the tendencies of some eminent scientists to publicize their atheistic and agnostic beliefs when discussing scientific topics of general interest. Sir Julian Huxley (1887–1975), grandson of Thomas H. Huxley, had written about a universe without God and had put his faith in "human possibilities" instead.[28]

Jacques Monod (1910–1976) declared in his book *Chance and Necessity* (1970) that humankind was alone in a vast universe out of which it had emerged by chance.[29] In his very popular book *The First Three Minutes* (1977), Steven Weinberg concluded that the more the universe seems comprehensible, the more it seems devoid of purpose.[30] A number of scientists went further than this, attacking directly the very foundation of religious belief—the vital element of faith. The British zoologist Richard Dawkins was one of the most aggressive. In his international bestseller *The Selfish Gene*, he was quite vigorous in his offensive. For him faith was "blind trust, in the absence of evidence, even in the teeth of evidence." The only apostle he admired was Thomas, the man who dared to seek proof. He argued that if religious beliefs could be substantiated, then faith would be unnecessary because the evidence alone would compel us to believe.[31] But why did Dawkins, a scientist, concern himself with religion? Obviously, he felt compelled to move beyond science, to consider human nature in its totality. In doing so he focused very much on the pernicious effects of religion.

Faith was not simply regarded as a benign influence on human behaviour. It was viewed as the antithesis of rational inquiry, and it was held to be a major cause of intolerance, violence, and war. Dawkins constructed a grim picture of faith.

> Blind faith can justify anything. If a man believes in a different god, or even if he uses a different ritual for worshipping the same god, blind faith can decree that he should die—on the cross, at the stake, skewered on a Crusader's sword, shot in a Beirut street, or blown up in a bar in Belfast.[32]

He elaborated further on this point.

> [I]t is capable of driving people to such dangerous folly that faith seems to me to qualify as a kind of mental illness. It leads people to believe in whatever it is so strongly that in extreme cases they are prepared to kill and to die for it without the need for further justification. . . . Faith is powerful enough to immunize people against all appeals to pity, to forgiveness, to decent human feelings. It even immunizes them against fear. . . . What a weapon![33]

The polemical tendency in science, so reminiscent of Thomas H. Huxley and John Tyndall, was still alive and well.[34] It is not clear, however, to what extent Dawkins and other iconoclastic scientists influenced public opinion, but their cumulative impact was probably significant. The published works of Francis Crick, Richard Dawkins, Stephen Hawking, Carl Sagan, and Edward O. Wilson captured the attention of millions. Stephen Hawking's *Brief History of Time* sold over five million copies. The opinions of these scientists were discussed in newspapers and on television and reached a wide audience.[35]

A major problem for the church was that scientists continually demonstrated a strong tendency to stray beyond the boundaries of their discipline. Paul Davies, professor of natural philosophy at the University of Adelaide, claimed that "science offers a surer path to God than religion."[36] The English theoretical physicist Stephen Hawking speculated about the possibility of one unified theory—one set of rules and equations that could form the basis of a comprehensive explanation of the evolution and nature of the universe. He anticipated that if such a theory was discovered then it would, somehow, make an enormous contribution to answering why the universe exists. If we could understand why we and the universe exist, then "it would be the ultimate triumph of human reason—for then we would know the mind of God."[37] This conclusion, apparently for dramatic effect, should not be taken seriously. The notion that we could ever hope to "know" God's mind, contrary to the unbounded optimism of Hawking, is a gross exaggeration of our intellectual potential. Furthermore, it greatly underestimates the complexities and pitfalls of applying scientific knowledge to the "why" questions of philosophy and religion. Hawking seemed to realize this when he stated:

> Even if there is only one possible unified theory, it is just a set of rules and equations. What is it that breathes fire into the equations and makes a universe for them to describe? The usual approach of science of constructing a mathematical model cannot answer the questions of why there should be a universe for the model to describe.[38]

It is even doubtful if Hawking believed in anything resembling the God of Christianity. His speculation about the universe, "completely self-contained," without a boundary or edge, without beginning or end, left no place for a Creator.[39]

A number of eminent scientists suggested that science could explain the meaning of life. An extremely bleak analysis was that life has no meaning. Dawkins asserted that blind physical laws shaped the development of the universe. It was neither good nor evil; there was no justice, no design, no purpose—"nothing but blind, pitiless indifference." We were but creatures of our DNA—and "DNA neither cares nor knows. DNA just is. And we dance to its music."[40] It is in statements like this that Dawkins, Monod, Wilson, Sagan, and other scientific materialists dogmatically presented philosophical assumptions as if they were somehow overpowering scientific arguments for a godless universe.[41]

The views of Dawkins and other scientists of a similar persuasion could not, of course, be taken to represent the general outlook of their profession. Some scientists regarded it as a waste of time to enter into a debate about whether or not God exists, because, they asserted, science had nothing to say about such an issue.[42] Catholic apologists did not remain silent about the strident claims of atheistic scientists. They argued that scientists, no matter how eminent in their profession, were not competent to deal with questions that were within the realm of philosophy and theology.[43] Those scientists who insisted that science could explain everything were accused of indulging in fantasies. Their arguments, it was claimed, were based not on objective truth and rational debate but on a sterile ideology that failed to satisfy the fundamental human need for some kind of meaning to life.[44] The theory of evolution was incomplete, and it did not rule out the role of a supernatural Creator. It was regarded as important that scientists acknowledge that there are still many fundamental questions to be answered. They were urged to abstain from indulging in anti-religious polemics and scientific triumphalism. A policy of intellectual modesty was called for.[45]

Catholic apologists, in their efforts to defend their faith against the immoderate claims of science, continued to highlight the weaknesses and limitations of science. They still focused on the theory of evolution, which they asserted was only a theory,[46] but they did not confine their criticism to this aspect of scientific thought. They highlighted, for example, that the natural sciences in general were permeated by uncertainties and by subjectivity. Interpretation, judgment, guesswork, and imagination, in addition to factual information, played a large role in scientific research.[47] All our knowledge, including the scientific kind, was derived from information channeled through the senses and from reasoning based on this. The realm of the supernatural was not detectable through the senses; therefore it had to be founded on the second category of information. But human reasoning was often defective and lacking in objectivity. Furthermore, its empirical foundation was also suspect because our senses did not always provide us with reliable information about physical reality.[48]

The deficiencies of science, however, were greatly exaggerated. When Thomas Kuhn's book *The Structure of Scientific Revolution* was published in 1962, theologians "were already rejoicing that something akin to personal faith seemed to be emerging as a prerequisite for scientific research."[49] A number of scientists responded to critical assessments of science with a stinging counteroffensive. Richard Dawkins, in refuting the notion that Western science is as remote from truth as tribal mythology argued with characteristic aggressiveness.

> Western science, acting on good evidence that the moon orbits the Earth a quarter of a million miles away, using Western-designed computers and rockets, has succeeded in placing people on its surface. Tribal science, believing that the moon is just above the treetops, will never touch it outside of dreams.[50]

He treated tribal mythology and religion as synonymous *vis-à-vis* scientific truth.

> Science shares with religion the claim that it answers deep questions about origins, the nature of life, and the cosmos. But there the resemblance ends. Scientific beliefs are supported by evidence, and they get results. Myths and faith are not and do not.[51]

Paul Davies argued that religions, in contrast to science, are burdened with dogmatic principles and so-called immutable truths and therefore find it extremely difficult to adapt to new trends in modern thought. Science is much more amenable to change. When new discoveries, arising from observation and experimentation, are made, this can lead to existing hypotheses or theories being discarded, refined, or extended. New hypotheses are put forward to explain natural phenomena.[52] The testing and rejecting of hypotheses is of central importance to science. If a theory or hypothesis cannot be tested in principle, then it is not within the realm of science.

The vast majority of scientists, although acknowledging that evolution is a theory, were not prepared to countenance it being dismissed as a work of science fiction. Opinions varied about its veracity, from absolute certainty,[53] to near certainty, to regarding it as the only sensible explanation possible in view of what has been ascertained by scientific research.[54] If evolutionary theory was to be abandoned then an alternative explanation would have to be developed. However, some Catholic writers who were extremely critical of evolutionary theory, had not offered a credible alternative. Creationist claims based on a literal interpretation of Genesis did not command any significant degree of support among scientists. Evolutionary theory, despite the fact that it has to contend with many difficult questions, was firmly established and was most unlikely to be abandoned by scientists. Furthermore, the prestige and pervasiveness of science and technology were so great that its theories and hypotheses could not be conveniently rejected by theologians if they were to argue credibly that faith and science are compatible. Having stressed evolution's inherent limitations at every opportunity, Catholic apologists were still left with the difficulties of dealing with a highly potent source of knowledge, mostly because of the constraints imposed by Roman Catholic orthodoxy. Thus, they continued with a dual strategy—attacking the claims of scientists when these were seen as threatening to the faith while simultaneously asserting that Catholic doctrine had nothing to fear from the substantiated findings of science.

Science, Sex, and Theology

When Pope John XXIII addressed the Pontifical Academy of Sciences on 30 October 1961, he asserted that the Roman Catholic Church, wherever it had flourished, had always contributed to the development of intellectual culture. This was part of its pastoral mission and its role as educator —hence the setting up of the Academy.[55] In a later address to the Academy, on 5 October 1962, the pope expressed the hope that ideas about the opposition between faith and reason would decline. He was optimistic about the possibility of this development because, in his opinion, the discoveries and achievements of the previous six decades had strengthened rather than weakened the pronouncements of the First Vatican Council on this relationship. He believed that the advancement of science permitted a far greater understanding of creation, which in turn brought people closer to God (p. 107). The limited competence of science could, according to his successor, bring about a similar, if not identical, result. Pope Paul VI (reigned 1963–1978), in his address to the Pontifical Academy of Sciences on 3 October 1964, told his audience that when scientists were excessively confident of their abilities, they either distrusted or held in contempt spiritual and religious values. Now that scientists had come to appreciate the complexities of the world they felt "a sort of insecurity and fear" about where science might lead if completely left to its own devices. He believed that overconfidence had given way to "a salutary unease," which in turn led to a greater openness to religious values and to an enhanced sense of the spiritual world among scientists (p. 117).

It seemed that if science could strengthen religious faith, then it could also weaken it. On 23 April 1966 Pope Paul expressed concern about the dangers of excessive specialization, which, he believed, counteracted spiritual tendencies. In reference to *Gaudium et Spes* (par. 57) he observed that, in a scientifically advanced society, there might develop a tendency to rely so much on technology that "man . . . may even think that he is sufficient unto himself and no longer seek any higher realities" (pp. 120–21). He returned to this theme again on 27 April 1968. Scientific research, he believed, could be so intellectually absorbing and satisfying that it could displace a desire to seek knowledge of God, leading eventually to atheism (pp. 126–27). In his discourse of 18 April 1970, however, he asserted that "true science" acts as a "springboard" that enables Christians to "rise" toward God. If people were led by science to atheism, or to agnosticism, it was because of their failure to grasp a broader reality, that unity of knowledge which brought together faith and reason (pp. 130, 132).

Paul VI told members of the Pontifical Academy of Sciences that the setting up of the institute was proof of the church's deep respect for and love of the scientific community. The Academy was established not only to promote intellectual and spiritual development but also to assist in the application of science to a multitude of practical problems. The Academy had a long-standing interest in the application of science to assist the socioeconomic development of poor nations. This interest increased after the publication of Paul VI's *Populorum Progressio* ("On the Progress of Peoples," 26 March 1967). In this social encyclical the pope deplored the glaring maldistribution of wealth between rich and poor nations. He declared that God intended the resources of the earth to be used for the benefit of everyone.

The church acknowledges the complex multidimensional nature of humanity and its corresponding needs—spiritual, intellectual, psychological, social, economic, and physical. The Academy, through its study weeks and working groups, reflected the church's broad range of interests in seven main areas as follows:

1. Basic science is subdivided into six main areas: cosmology and astrophysics, neurosciences, the structure of matter, the origin of life and evolution, the biochemical bases of biological processes, and econometric analysis (making plans for economic development on a scientific basis).[56]

2. The application of science and technology to global problems is studied in the following areas: humans and the environment, geophysics, and the utilization of satellite technology.[57]

3. The application of science to promote development and overcome problems in the Third World: the areas of interest are agricultural production, tropical diseases, energy resources, and the use of satellite technology.[58]

4. Scientific policy: this area covers a broad range of topics and overlaps with subjects listed in some of the other areas of activity. Issues covered include the need for scientific resources to be used in initiatives to solve global problems, the responsibility of scientists con-

cerning the abuse of science—especially in the armaments industries, the moral implications of scientific research, the origins and significance of the antiscientific movement, and the need to transfer science and technology resources to meet the growing needs of the Third World.[59]

5. Bioethics: the subject matter included genetic engineering, the exposure of humans to ionizing radiation, the artificial prolongation of life, and *in vitro* fertilization techniques to treat human infertility.[60]

6. The history of science—there are two areas of interest. First, Renaissance science: the works of Federico Cesi, who founded the Lincei Academy (Rome); Galileian studies; and the publication of documents in the Vatican Secret Archives and in the Apostolic Library. Second, the works of scientists who served as members of the Pontifical Academy of Sciences, including Marconi, Lemaître, and Heisenberg.[61]

7. Science for peace: In the spring of 1980 a working group of Academicians started scientific research on the effects of nuclear war. Their findings were used by Pope John Paul II in his address to the United Nations Educational, Scientific and Cultural Organisation (UNESCO) in June 1980 and at Hiroshima in February 1981. In October 1981 a working group of Academicians completed a report on the devastating impact of nuclear weapons. The Academy, at the request of the pope, sent five delegations to the United Nations headquarters in New York, Washington, Moscow, London, and Paris. Their purpose was to explain the Academy's report on the adverse effects of nuclear weapons. The Academy continued its work in promoting awareness about the threat of nuclear weapons. In September 1982, after discussions with representatives of thirty-five scientific academies and a number of international scientific organizations, it published a "Declaration on the Prevention of Nuclear War." Representatives of scientific organizations from East and West signed the document. In his appeals for peace Pope John Paul II referred to information derived from the Academy's studies.[62]

As the papacy endeavored to establish a harmonious relationship between the church and the natural sciences under a number of headings, it encountered the highly controversial issue of artificial birth control. In 1930 Pope Pius XI had declared in his encyclical *Casti Connubii* that artificial contraception was a "sin against nature . . . shameful and intrinsically vicious."[63] For Roman Catholics who wished to adhere rigidly to directives emanating from the Vatican, this ruled out the use of diaphragms, spermicidal jellies, douches, and condoms. The contraceptive pill, which was first marketed in the United States of America in 1960, was not quite in the same category. It appeared to imitate some aspects of female reproductive physiology and, therefore, seemed to be in harmony with "natural" contraceptive methods—such as the rhythm method—approved of by Pope Pius XII in 1951. Furthermore, Pius XII expressed support for scientific research that would enhance the efficacy of the rhythm method. For many Catholics the contraceptive pill represented an advance in science no different, in a moral sense, from the research in the 1930s that had enabled calculations to be made about the frequency and length of infertile periods in the menstrual cycle of women. They believed that there was no ethical distinction to be made between the use of hormones in controlling the menstrual cycle and the use of mucous tests in ascertaining periods of infertility.[64] The Vatican was urged from within the church to review its stance on the contraceptive issue. Pope John XXIII responded in 1963 by setting up a small commission to study the problem. Pope Paul VI reappointed the commission and increased its membership. The Pontifical Commission on Population, Family and Birth (frequently referred to as the "Papal Birth Control Commission") was very unusual, in terms of church commissions, because the laity, including married women, were included to give advice on Catholic doctrine.

In June 1966 Pope Paul received a report representing the dominant view among the members, advising that it was morally permissible for married couples to use artificial means of contraception. After agonizing over the issue for two years, he decided effectively to reject the advice of his commission by accepting a minority view which advocated an adherence to the traditional position of the church. Cardinal Alfredo Ottaviani, secretary of the Holy Office, played a central role in influencing the pope to reach this decision. Karol Wojtyla, archbishop of Kraków and the future Pope John Paul II, also played a key role.[65]

Artificial contraception was not accepted as a morally appropriate alternative to the rhythm method. On 25 July 1968 Paul issued the encyclical *Humanae Vitae*. He wrote about the regulation of the human birth rate against a background of rapid population growth. He noted humanity's "stupendous progress" in regulating nature, which included the human mind and body.[66] His intention was to speak authoritatively on the Catholic principles governing marriage, sexuality, and reproduction. The Roman Catholic Church was entrusted by Jesus Christ with the task of being guardian and interpreter of the entire moral law, which included not only the law of the gospel but also the "natural law." Paul asserted that the natural law, illuminated by divine revelation, "declares the will of God, and its faithful observance is necessary for men's eternal salvation." He did not give any latitude for freedom of conscience when he proclaimed: "Let no Catholic be heard to assert that the interpretation of the natural moral law is outside the competence of the Church's Magisterium. It is in fact indisputable" (par. 4).

Catholic doctrine dictated that there was a compelling connection, established by God, between the love-giving (unitive) and life-giving (procreative) aspects of sexual intercourse between husband and wife; that is, there could be no separation between the sexual and reproductive aspects of the marriage act (par. 12). On the basis of natural law, sexual activity in marriage was not to be subjected to an impairment of its natural potential to procreate human life (par. 11). Abortion and artificial means of contraception were condemned as immoral methods of birth control. Marital sexual intercourse, when it was "deliberately contraceptive," was deemed to be "intrinsically wrong" (par. 14). Catholic couples were, however, permitted to exercise birth control by taking advantage of the infertile days of the menstrual cycle because they could "rightly use a facility provided them by nature," as distinct from "means which directly exclude conception" and "obstruct the natural development of the generative process" (par. 16). It made no difference that in both cases married couples clearly intended to avoid having children and had good reasons for doing so.

The rhythm method, sometimes referred to as "Vatican roulette," was notoriously unreliable.[67] Therefore Pope Paul appealed to scientists for help, informing them that: "It is supremely desirable . . . that medical science should by the study of natural rhythms succeed in determining a sufficiently secure as well as a moral basis for the regulation of birth" (par. 24). Scientific research so conducted would enable the church to assert that there was no contradiction between two divine laws—one governing human reproduction and the other concerned with the fostering of marital love. Scientists, however, were not overwhelmed by a desire to please the pope and proceeded to undertake research, the results of which would make it more difficult for the Catholic Church to reconcile itself with the new "reproductive" technologies (this will be discussed later).

In *Humanae Vitae* (par. 20) Pope Paul anticipated that many people would view the church's teaching as "not merely difficult but even impossible to observe." Even men and women who exercised "great endurance" could not succeed without the assistance of divine grace. Many Catholics were not predisposed to exercise the level of self-denial called for by the pope and probably placed more faith in the contraceptive pill than in divine grace when struggling to limit the size of their families. Surveys of Catholic opinion showed, consistently, that over eighty percent of Catholic couples ignored the exhortations of *Humanae Vitae*.[68]

Humanae Vitae provoked a storm of protest around the world, especially in Europe and North America. In an atmosphere of optimism created by the progressive reforms of the Second Vatican Council, there was widespread anticipation that the pope would change the church's teaching on artificial contraception. Many Catholics were deeply disappointed and shocked when he did not do so. The church was profoundly damaged by the controversy that followed. The subject of artificial contraception was not confined to precepts of sexual morality and the natural law. Much broader issues—such as distinctions between infallible and fallible pronouncements, the nature of dogma, the development of doctrine, and obedience to ecclesiastical authority—impinged on the debate. It was difficult for the Catholic hierarchy to change its long-standing position on contraception because of the considerable risk of losing credibility, not just on this topic but generally. Obedience to authority, rather than a reasoned consideration of the arguments for and against different methods of birth control, seemed to be the central issue.[69] Punitive measures were taken against priests and theologians who openly opposed the encyclical. But the vast majority of Catholics who dissented did so quietly. There was no longer the same degree of confidence in the teaching authority of the church. Pope Paul was so traumatized by the reaction to *Humanae Vitae* that he never issued another encyclical.

The papal directive on birth control was based on the theological concept of the natural law or the law of nature. It was believed that such a law was amenable to discovery by the faculties of reason and, supposedly, provided the foundation of some moral principles. In reality, natural law was a religious belief masquerading as a philosophical theory.[70] From a traditionalist Catholic perspective, the morally appropriate decision would be made on the basis of an adherence to religious faith and an unswerving obedience to ecclesiastical authority—it would not be an outcome of rational discourse. It was not as if there were no valid concerns about the contraceptive pill in the 1960s. The pill was a synthetic form of the female hormone, progesterone, and acted to suppress ovulation. If it made the womb unsuitable for implantation of the fertilized ova cell, then it could be regarded as an abortifacient and could be condemned by reference to the commandment not to commit murder. A number of adverse side effects were associated with the pill, including nausea, vomiting, headaches, and increased weight; and it gave rise to some neurological problems. Furthermore, there was little or no scientific evidence to indicate what its long-term side effects would be. Concerns were further heightened by awareness that the tranquilizer drug Thalidomide had caused abnormalities in children whose mothers had taken it in the first trimester of their pregnancies.[71] A tentative opposition to the use of the pill on the basis of medical science would have been more credible than a dogmatic denunciation grounded on abstruse theological ideas.

In the late 1960s the accelerating pace of scientific progress gave rise to some unease among those who reflected on the ethical implications of new discoveries about nature. At the time it was very unclear what moral dilemmas might arise from developments in the life sciences, especially human genetics and reproduction. One of the most eminent Catholic theologians of the twentieth century, Karl Rahner, addressed this subject in a seminal essay entitled "The Problem of Genetic Manipulation" (1967). The prospect of the "genetic self-manipulation" of humankind placed Catholic moral theologians in an extremely difficult position. No direct answers could be obtained from the Bible, and decisions could not be left to individual consciences. This placed a heavy burden of responsibility on the shoulders of theologians, who could not simply ignore the life sciences. But if they were to pass sound judgments on scientific issues, then they would first have to make great efforts to understand specialized scientific data. There was a need to move beyond the deductive methods of theology. A static nonevolutionary view of humankind was unsatisfactory. If "the nature of man" was to be discussed in any meaningful sense, then cognizance would have to be taken of the biological and social sciences. The genetic manipulation of humans, in an abstract sense, could not be shown to be immoral per se. The central question was not whether or not to use genetic techniques but to decide which ones were morally acceptable and which ones were not. Techniques that were immoral were those that threatened to bring about changes contrary to "the nature of man" (whatever that might be). For example, any initiative would be reprehensible if it damaged the ability of humans to communicate with one another. Personal dignity and the welfare of society needed to be safeguarded.[72]

In the upper echelons of the church there was considerable apprehension about developments in science and technology. The Sacred Congregation for the Doctrine of the Faith expressed concern in November 1974 that developments in technology would make it easier for women to procure abortions and would make it possible to "manipulate human life in every possible direction."[73] Evidently there was much concern about the future. But there was also concern about that part of the past which would not stay in the past. In the late twentieth century, the Roman Catholic Church proclaimed to the world, through *Gaudium et Spes*, several papal addresses, and the activities of the Pontifical Academy of Sciences, that it was supportive of science when scientific initiatives were used to serve the best interests of humankind. An essential objective was the pursuit of truth, but the church itself had to come to terms with an unpleasant truth —the bitter legacy of its persecution of Galileo. A clear expression of repentance was long overdue.

10

Pope John Paul II's Philosophy of Science and Faith

The Reopening of the Galileo Case

O N 16 OCTOBER 1978 CARDINAL KAROL WOJTYLA, ARCHBISHOP of Kraków, was elected pope and took the name of John Paul II. He was the first Slavic pope and the first non-Italian since Hadrian VI (1522–1523). Under his pontificate the Roman Catholic Church maintained its conservative stance on a wide range of issues such as contraception, divorce, and the ordination of women priests. Disciplinary action was taken against a number of theologians throughout the church for various reasons. Jacques Pohier (French) was compelled to seek specific authorization to preach, give lectures, or to submit his work for publication. Hans Küng (Swiss), a well-known lecturer at the University of Tübingen, was deprived of his academic position and was no longer regarded as a Catholic theologian. Leonardo Boff (Brazilian), who was forbidden to teach or write for one year, eventually left the Franciscan order and the priesthood in protest against the Vatican's disciplinary action. Edward Schillebeeckx, a Dutch Dominican, had to endure oppressive scrutiny from the Vatican. The American moral theologian Charles Curran was forced to leave the faculty of theology at the Catholic University of America.[1] Despite all of the above, however, it would be excessively critical to describe John Paul's outlook as entirely conservative and reactionary. His social encyclicals, for example, are widely regarded as progressive. His views about the relationship between science and Catholicism are not so well known. This aspect of his thinking will now be explored in some detail.

Science did not feature significantly in John Paul's theological or philosophical writings before his election to papal office.[2] Nevertheless, he was probably well acquainted with developments in science when he was archbishop of Kraków. This is indicated in his address to the European Physics Society on 30 March 1979. He told his audience that when he was in Kraków he frequently requested meetings with specialists in the natural sciences (especially physics). These communications were "fruitful." He referred to paragraph 59 of *Gaudium et Spes*, which acknowledged the rightful autonomy of science. This paragraph, he declared, was of special importance to him, but with freedom came responsibilities. John Paul referred to his first encyclical, *Redemptor Hominis*, which had been published earlier that month. He stressed the need for the application of moral principles so that science would serve the needs of everybody. Technology, based on scientific discoveries, had great potential for solving a wide range of serious problems, especially concerned with food production, energy, and the struggle against diseases. But for progress to occur, humankind had to learn to live in harmony with the natural environment.

John Paul declared that science and faith were connected with each other, and he quoted Galileo's *Letter to Castelli* to make the point that the Bible and the natural world originated from the same God. Therefore there could be no conflict between faith and science when the different methods and principles pertaining to both were properly understood.[3] But conflict had occurred because the Catholic Church failed to respect the rightful autonomy of the natural sciences. A rift developed between Roman Catholicism and science, which to some extent was still in place because the church had not fully acknowledged its error of forcing Galileo Galilei to abjure the Copernican hypothesis in 1633. If reconciliation was to be achieved then some unfinished business needed to be addressed.

Whatever mistakes Galileo had made in dealing with his clerical contemporaries, there was no escaping the conclusion that a court of theologians had condemned a man who was a loyal Catholic, a great scientist, and much closer to the truth than those who judged him. This provided those who were hostile to Roman Catholicism with a splendid opportunity for denouncing it as backward and incompatible with science. In the late twentieth century renewed efforts were made, at the highest level, to address this problem. On 10 November 1979 Pope John Paul II addressed a plenary session of the Pontifical Academy of Sciences, which was convened to commemorate the centenary of the birth of Albert Einstein. However, the pope said very little about Einstein and focused instead on

Galileo. Mindful of paragraph 36 of *Gaudium et Spes*, he proposed that the church reexamine the case of Galileo. He stated: "The greatness of Galileo is known to everyone, like that of Einstein; but unlike the latter . . . the former had to suffer a great deal—we cannot conceal the fact—at the hands of men and organisms of the Church." He then referred to paragraph 36 of *Gaudium et Spes*, where the Second Vatican Council acknowledged, indirectly, its error in forcing Galileo to abjure the Copernican hypothesis. John Paul indicated his desire for the Catholic Church to advance beyond the council's admission when he declared:

> I hope that theologians, scholars and historians, animated by a spirit of sincere collaboration, will study the Galileo case more deeply and, in loyal recognition of wrongs from whatever side they come, will dispel the mistrust that still opposes, in many minds, a fruitful concord between science and faith, between the Church and the world. I give all my support to this task, which will be able to honor the truth of faith and of science and open the door to future collaboration.[4]

John Paul was determined to create harmony where conflict had so frequently been perceived. He claimed that the agreements between science and religion were greater and more numerous than the "incomprehensions" which had been the source of conflict and acrimonious controversy over the centuries following Galileo. To support this claim he made three points about Galileo and the church. First, he cited Galileo's letter to Benedetto Castelli (21 December 1613), in which the astronomer expressed his conviction that the truths of faith and the truths of science could never contradict each other. Second, he quoted the *Sidereus Nuncius* to make the point that Galileo believed his scientific discoveries were inspired by God. He linked these statements with paragraph 36 of *Gaudium et Spes*. Third, he conceded that Galileo "formulated important norms of an epistemological character, which are indispensable to reconcile Holy Scripture and science." In this context reference was made to Galileo's *Letter to the Grand Duchess Christina*, in which Galileo argued that a literal interpretation of scripture does not always reveal its true meaning. The teaching authority of the Catholic Church accepted this exegetical principle; it accepted that there is a "plurality" of rules for the interpretation of scripture. John Paul, in making this point, referred to Pope Pius XII's encyclical *Divino Afflante Spiritu*, which recognized the existence of various literary styles in the books of scripture. John Paul had put forward some plausible arguments in support of his thesis of harmony but these were not sufficient to overcome the legacy of the past. He realized this and was, therefore, determined to initiate a process that would lead to an "honourable solution" to the Galileo controversy and put an end to "old oppositions."[5]

On 3 July 1981 the Pontifical Academy of Sciences set up an interdisciplinary commission for this purpose. Bishop (later Cardinal) Paul Poupard served as chairman.[6] Poupard is reported to have stated that the pope's initiative was in response to claims, inspired by Enlightenment and leftist ideologies, that the church was oppressive. The cardinal allegedly viewed it as a public relations problem.[7] From this perspective the moral imperative of addressing a long-standing wrong was of secondary importance.

At the onset of the commission's investigations, it was realized that it would be difficult to avoid the conclusion that the church authorities responsible for censuring Galileo were guilty of a serious error of judgment. In 1984, about eight years before the commission completed its work, the Vatican issued a statement which conceded that "Church officials had erred in condemning Galileo."[8] The pope was determined that the church would address the mistakes of the past so that it could, in the future, constructively interact with the natural sciences.

John Paul's Philosophy of Science

In 1980 John Paul, through the medium of a number of public speeches, explained his views about science in a broad social context, and in relation to Catholic doctrine. On 1 April he addressed approximately six thousand students from forty-three countries who had been participating in the international congress "Univ 80," organized by the Institute for University Cooperation. The views he expressed indicated an outlook that was holistic and interdisciplinary. He was conscious of the rapid growth in knowledge in both social and natural sciences and he saw a major problem arising from this. The quantity of data had become so vast that it had led to an increase in specialization that in turn had led to a fragmentation of knowledge. But humans are by nature interdisciplinary, and therefore there was an urgent need to cultivate a counterbalancing integrative approach to study and research. This was necessary to discover and safeguard the "grandiose interior unity of man" so that man would not lose sight of his nature, purpose, and destiny.[9] Science, in this context, was not an end in itself, it was not an exclusively intellectual activity. It was subject to the moral order and, as an indispensable part of a renewed Christian culture, it had an important role to play in assisting humankind to achieve its spiritual duty and destiny.

In his address to representatives of the United Nations Educational, Scientific and Cultural Organisation (UNESCO), at their headquarters in Paris on 2 June, the pope spoke about the misuse of science, especially in the production of nuclear, chemical, and biological weapons. Science was frequently being used for purposes of destruction and death rather than for the enhancement of human life. John Paul deemed it necessary that ethics should play a central role in technology and that science should form "an alliance" with conscience. The isolation of Catholic ethics from science and technology was not an option.[10]

John Paul was deeply concerned about scientific research and the applications of science in biology and especially in medicine. On 27 October he expressed these concerns to about three thousand participants at two medical congresses; the eighty-first Congress of the Italian Society of Internal Medicine, and the eighty-second Congress of the Italian Society of General Surgery. There was a pressing need for proper ethical guidelines in, for example, birth control and fertility treatments, genetic engineering, and organ transplants. The pope asserted that a new research technique should not be considered lawful simply because it increased scientific knowledge. Science was not to take priority over all other values. The individual's personal rights—to life, to psychological and physical integrity—were to be of paramount importance.[11]

From a Catholic moral perspective, science should be limited in what it could do. It was also limited in what it could accomplish. John Paul made his views known about the finite potential of science on 15 November when he addressed an audience of lecturers and university students at Cologne Cathedral. He asserted that reason, the mental faculty that underpins science, is finite. Reason cannot do everything alone. Science is a great driving force of cultural progress but it alone cannot give complete answers to questions of meanings and values. It cannot shed light on the purpose of life—that has to be found outside of science. Therefore, there is a need for dialogue between the church and science so that they can become allies in the search for truth. Scientific knowledge enhances both intellectual and economic development, but the principles of faith are necessary to guide its applications. Otherwise science would be alienated from the truth and vulnerable to wayward ideologies which in turn would lead to its misuse, much to the detriment of humanity.[12]

On 21 June 1985 John Paul addressed an international gathering of scientists at the Marcel Grossman Meeting on Relativistic Astrophysics. Before an audience representing more than thirty nationalities, he stressed the need for every nation to contribute to scientific research.

Science was rapidly extending the frontiers of knowledge, about humankind and the universe. The pope welcomed this, but he was concerned that other disciplinary or professional activities were relatively static or even regressive. He feared that a lack of constructive interaction between the natural sciences and the practical and theoretical endeavors of politics, economics, philosophy, ethics, and theology could lead to catastrophe unprecedented in magnitude. He returned to the theme that science was not omnipotent; it was not a substitute for religious faith, moral principles, political science, or art. But in their search for truth scientists could inspire these other human activities by providing them with a richer physical context. Thus, science could "finally lead humanity to bow before the Creator of the universe."[13]

The search for truth required that dialogue take place between theologians and scientists. Philosophers had an important role in mediating the interaction. The pope, through the offices of the Vatican Secretariat of State, requested the director of the Vatican Observatory, Rev. Dr. George V. Coyne, S.J., to convene an international research conference on physics, philosophy, and theology. The conference was held on 21–26 September 1987, and it commemorated the three hundredth anniversary of the publication of Isaac Newton's *Philosophiae Naturalis Principia Mathematica*. A number of essays, based mainly on the conference proceedings, were published under the title of *Physics, Philosophy and Theology: A Common Quest for Understanding* (1988), edited by Robert J. Russell, William R. Stoeger, S.J., and George V. Coyne. When the essays were being prepared for publication, Pope John Paul wrote to Coyne, thanking him and, through him, all those who had contributed to what he regarded as an important enterprise.

The pope's letter to Coyne, dated 1 June 1988, reiterated some of the points that he had made in previous speeches, for example, the need for ethics in science, the unity of truth, and the need for dialogue between religion and science. However, this letter gives a deeper insight into the pope's vision of how theology and science should interact with each other and is deserving of a more extensive examination than his previous communications. Coyne believed that the pope's message was so important that it deserved a very detailed commentary from experts in religious studies, science, and philosophy—hence the publication of the multiauthored volume *John Paul II on Science and Religion: Reflections on the new view from Rome* (1990), also edited by Russell, Stoeger, and Coyne.[14]

John Paul expressed concern about a world scarred by conflict, a world fragmented by racial and religious animosities and disjointed by a gross maldistribution of wealth. This fragmentation of culture existed also in the academic world, but the pope perceived that there was a movement toward intellectual coherence and collaboration. Convergence was happening in science, where, for example, physicists were attempting to construct a grand unified field theory that would explain the four physical forces of electromagnetism, gravitation, the strong nuclear forces, and the weak nuclear forces.

John Paul visualized "the unity of all things and all peoples in Christ."[15] It was in this context that he wrote about the fragile but definite movement toward dialogue between religion and science. A more in-depth discussion between scientists and theologians would serve the purpose of establishing a greater understanding between the disciplines, ascertaining their competencies, limitations, and areas of common interest. However, the pope made it clear that he was not envisioning a disciplinary unity between religion and science when he stated:

> the unity that we seek . . . is not identity. The Church does not propose that science should become religion or religion science. On the contrary, unity always presupposes the diversity and the integrity of its elements. . . . both religion and science must preserve their autonomy and their distinctiveness. Religion is not founded on science nor is science an extension of religion. Each should possess its own principles, its pattern of procedures, its diversities of interpretation and its own conclusions. (M8–M9)

What he hoped for was that the "fragmented vision of the world" would be overcome so that partial perspectives could be expanded to form "a new unified vision" for the good of humankind. Each discipline was to be open to the insights and discoveries of the other.

Isolation was not an option. The pope realized that it was inevitable that Catholics would be influenced by science. This perception prompted him to ask whether or not they would reflect on scientific ideas about the world "with depth and nuance or with a shallowness that debases the Gospel" (M13). Evidently the pope was aware that Christians could not speak with credibility about God's creation if they neglected to inform themselves about scientific theories concerning its development and functional mechanisms.

The church and the scientific community were both morally obliged to collaborate. But what had science to gain from such collaboration? John Paul argued that the best interests of science were served when its findings were integrated into the broader human culture. Therefore scientists were duty bound to engage with the concerns of philosophers and theologians on a wide range of issues. An integration of scientific and religious perspectives was particularly beneficial, because "[s]cience can purify religion from error and superstition; religion can purify science from idolatry and false absolutes" (M13). The pope observed that twentieth-century history testified to the massive destructive potential of science when it was not guided by the moral principles that theology had to offer.

John Paul believed that science, as a search for truth, had much to offer theology. But what theological issues would benefit from an in-depth knowledge of science? The pope gave a number of examples. He pointed out that the cosmologies of ancient Near Eastern culture had been "purified" and incorporated into the story of creation in Genesis. This suggested that reflections about creation might benefit from recent discoveries in cosmology. He asked if the evolutionary concept could be used to address questions pertaining to theological anthropology, the human person made in the image of God, and Christology. Could evolution even be applied to the development of doctrine? To what extent should theological methodology be influenced by the philosophy of science and by scientific methodology? (M11).

The pope was aware of the complexities and risks associated with the use of scientific and philosophical concepts in theology. There was a danger that theology could become too closely associated with a scientific theory that might be extensively changed or overturned by new discoveries. Scientific theories were, by their very nature, provisional. For example, "classical physics" was superseded by the new theories of quantum mechanics and relativity. If theology became too heavily reliant on scientific theories, then it was likely to become as provisional as science. Therefore, theologians would have to be very careful when evaluating a new theory before applying it to their subject matter. As an example, John Paul cited the "Big Bang" theory in cosmology (M11–M12). This implied some degree of criticism of his predecessor, Pius XII, who had not been sufficiently cautious in his address to the Pontifical Academy of Sciences in 1951 when he spoke about the Big Bang in the context of arguments for the existence of God.[16]

Any process of dialogue would be encumbered by difficulties; but the pope insisted that theologians could not simply ignore scientific theories that might be of relevance to theology. The most suitably qualified experts for promoting such dialogue were those who had acquired professional qualifications in both disciplines. They were to work for the advancement of theology with insights from the most firmly established theories. The pope believed that their expertise would help them to avoid making imprudent use of contemporary theories when writing apologetically.

The application of science and philosophy to theology raised a very difficult question. If a scientific or philosophical concept is used in theology, does it then become an authoritative or immutable feature of a theological doctrine? When Thomistic philosophy was being revived in the late nineteenth century, one of the arguments advanced to support it was that it had been used to formulate defined dogma. For example, when the Council of Trent defined the doctrine of the Eucharist, it was profoundly influenced by Aristotelian natural philosophy,[17] which had been adopted by Scholastic philosophers, especially by St. Thomas Aquinas. Did this mean that the church adjudicated on the truth or falsity of Aristotelian hylomorphism, which had been used to gain a greater understanding of the Eucharist? John Paul declared that it had not. This implied that the church was not competent to decide on the truth or falsity of a claim outside the realm of theology.

John Paul observed that Aristotelian philosophy in thirteenth-century Western Europe had created difficulties for theology. But a number of medieval theologians, most notably St. Thomas Aquinas, rose to the challenge and used Aristotelian philosophy as an intellectual resource to enrich theology. The pope believed that contemporary developments in science posed a far greater challenge to theologians. It seems that he was not at all impressed by the work of twentieth-century theologians when he declared that they should ask themselves if they had accomplished as much as their medieval predecessors in making the best use of what was on offer from the natural sciences, philosophy, and other academic disciplines.[18]

Critical Responses
to the New View from Rome

The response to the pope's message by the nineteen authors who contributed to the volume *John Paul II on Science and Religion* was quite varied. Some of the opinions were favorable. For example, John B. Cobb, a retired professor of theology and not a Roman Catholic, expressed "deep gratitude" for the pope's message and believed that it was the finest statement he knew of on the subject of theology and the natural sciences.[19] George F. R. Ellis, a professor of mathematics and the author of many papers on cosmology and relativity theory, praised the general content of

John Paul's letter.[20] However, criticisms were expressed that reflected more on the Vatican, the broader institutional church, and the nature of theology, than on the pope himself.

Rosemary Radford Ruether, a professor of applied theology, observed that there was a lack of interest in dialogue in both the scientific and religious disciplines. The majority of specialists were satisfied to remain in their own intellectual domains. If this was to change, there would have to be a profound change of attitude in the church and in the scientific community.[21] Karl Schmitz-Moormann, professor of philosophical anthropology and ethics, observed that such a change had occurred in the Catholic Church as indicated by *Gaudium et Spes*. But dialogue did not occur because of a lack of institutional support. In European Catholicism theological institutes did not give adequate attention to issues of common interest to theology and science. Schmitz-Moormann believed that the lack of initiative in promoting science–theology dialogue was not due to restrictions imposed by the papacy, although he observed that conditions had been very different before the Second Vatican Council.[22]

Richard J. Blackwell, a philosopher of science, supported and expanded on Schmitz-Moormann's point about the lack of institutional support for dialogue. He observed that the scientific education of Catholic clergy and theologians was very poor. To develop this point he referred to the Catholic colleges and universities of the United States of America. Most of the education and research activities in the natural sciences in these institutions were directed toward preparing students for professional careers in science and technology. There was very little interaction between the faculties of the natural sciences, philosophy, and theology. Very few scholars obtained professional qualifications in science and philosophy and/or theology. The University of Notre Dame was the only Catholic university in the United States with an advanced graduate program in the history and philosophy of science. There was a scarcity of individuals in Catholic institutes of higher education who had become eminent experts in both theology and science. Furthermore, there was a very marked underrepresentation of Catholic scholars at national meetings of the Philosophy of Science Association and the History of Science Society.[23]

The interest in dialogue was weak also among scientists. It is worthwhile exploring the probable underlying attitudes for this by referring to the perceptions of a number of authors in *John Paul II on Science and Religion*. Blackwell observed that, historically, the interaction between science and religion was not a dialogue between equals. He argued that, when dialogue was urgent in the seventeenth century, religion was the dominant cultural force in society. This dominance eventually led to a rift between religion and science, especially as a result of the trial and censorship of Galileo. In the late twentieth century the roles had been reversed: science and technology were now the dominant cultural forces in the Western world, and religion was at a disadvantage. Genuine dialogue between those who were unequal would be obstructed by the dominant party claiming to have a monopoly on truth, or at least the best method of acquiring it.[24] Another obstacle to progress identified by Blackwell was the church's adherence to Thomism. This philosophy was associated with Aristotelian science, which modern science had rejected. Blackwell argued that Aristotelian philosophy was incompatible with modern science; therefore, it had to be discarded. He was not sure if Thomism could survive such a radical change.

Lindon Eaves, an Anglican priest and professor of genetics, claimed that, from a scientific point of view, there was a strong tendency in theology to "baptize" science when it was "convenient" and to emphasize disciplinary autonomy when a number of scientific questions became "too threatening." Physics and cosmology, in contrast to the biological sciences, did not generally present any moral or theological dilemmas for the Catholic Church. Eaves believed that the church's friendly attitude toward physics and cosmology did not extend to the biological sciences; especially concerning issues such as genetic manipulation. He asserted that biologists needed to be reassured that their discipline would be given the same respect and understanding that the pope's message extended to physics. Was the church prepared to enter dialogue with the life sciences where it was likely to hurt the most? Evidently, Eaves believed that it was important for the church to do so; otherwise "theoretical and cultural stagnation" would occur. Science would continue to make progress regardless of whether or not theology chose to engage positively with it.[25]

The pope claimed that science would gain from dialogue with theology. Many scientists and philosophers of science were probably not convinced about this. Carl Mitcham, a philosopher of science, acknowledged that Christianity had provided "some cultural basis" for the origins of scientific enterprise. But it was not clear that Christianity had any beneficial effect on science since the Enlightenment. Since then many Christians had called for a constructive interaction between science and religion. Mitcham's rhetorical question was: Who would benefit from such a dialogue? The inference from history was that scientists had nothing to gain. In support of this Mitcham claimed that no scientific organization had ever felt the need to appeal for harmonization with Christianity.[26]

The German theologian Wolfhart Pannenberg agreed with the pope when he wrote about the autonomy and distinctiveness of religion and science. But he observed that their mutual autonomy was not "symmetrical." Science was not dependent on theology to make it complete—although the same could not be claimed for its relationship with philosophy. Theology, on the other hand, was relatively disadvantaged; it had to take cognizance of the natural sciences. Pannenberg referred to the pope's "evolutionary perspective" and agreed with him that theological doctrines need to be reexamined in the light of developments in science, especially in relation to evolutionary theory in biology. This had profound implications for theological anthropology, especially pertaining to monogenism and the doctrine of original sin.

A large portion of theological doctrine had been formulated on the basis of assumptions that had been later called into question, modified, or overturned. Pannenberg maintained that it was a matter of urgency to distinguish the essential core of traditional doctrine from its nonessential appendages. In this context the papal message seemed to indicate that the church was "remarkably open" to dialogue.[27] But dialogue, even assuming a strong and sustained commitment from scientists and theologians, would be extremely difficult to pursue at a deep level. The scientist Malu wa Kalenga was skeptical about the possibilities for constructive interaction envisaged by the pope. Theology and the natural sciences were associated with different values, methodologies, and interests. To overcome these major differences a new interdisciplinary paradigm would have to be devised, and consensus "at a suitable hierarchical level" on both sides of the disciplinary divide would have to be achieved. Malu wa Kalenga concluded that an interdisciplinary paradigm was feasible but extremely difficult.[28]

Perhaps the greatest obstacle to dialogue was the dogmatic nature of theology. George F. R. Ellis argued that an essential condition for discussion was that each person abandon the claim of having exclusive access to a particular truth or to the whole truth. The value of any theory or concept is how well it helps to explain reality—insofar as reality can be tested. Ellis believed that this principle applies equally to concepts in the natural sciences, philosophy, and theology. Theology and science would be in a better condition to engage constructively with each other if they examined and acknowledged their own "foundational" and internal difficulties, which would bring them to recognize their own "fallibilities and limitations."[29]

It was most unlikely that the Roman Catholic Church would acknowledge the fallibilities and limitations of its own theology, constrained as it was by the assertion of infallibility and by the imperatives of dogma. Blackwell's opinion was that if substantial dialogue was to occur, the effects on both theology and science would be unpredictable. He asked if the Catholic Church was willing to expose itself to the risks involved. Would the guardians of the faith permit, or even encourage, discussions between theologians and scientists in accordance with Pope John Paul II's expressed wishes, or would they choose the safer option of condemning new ideas? Blackwell was not optimistic about this. An awareness of church history and a consideration of Catholic intellectual culture did not inspire confidence.[30]

The Catholic theologian Elizabeth A. Johnson queried if it would be "safe" for theologians to explore issues where science and religion came into contact. A historical perspective of the relationship between hierarchical authorities and theologians indicated that it would be a risky undertaking. Johnson praised the papal message for its "genuine excellence," but she believed that it would be more credible and more influential if its principles were applied to discussions arising from new ideas within the community of faith as well as to dialogue external to it.[31]

The process of dialogue envisaged by John Paul II required the granting of a much greater degree of intellectual freedom to theologians. Hierarchical controls needed to be loosened if progress was to take place. This did not occur. As noted earlier, hierarchical authority during the pontificate of John Paul became even more of a constraint on theological initiatives. This was clearly evident in, for example, the decision by the American Catholic bishops in June 2001 to implement rules making it necessary for Catholic theologians to obtain authorization from their local bishops for the purpose of teaching at Catholic colleges and universities. To obtain a bishop's authorization—referred to as a *mandatum*—a theologian had to undertake to teach only "authentic Catholic doctrine." This was in accordance with the papal document issued in 1990, *Ex Corde Ecclesiae* ("From the Heart of the Church"). Some theologians were angered by the obligation to seek a *mandatum*, regarding it as an indication of distrust by the Vatican. It was seen in the educational sector as a threat to academic freedom.[32]

The pope's message, despite the progressive views expressed in the document, did not dispel suspicions and cynicism toward the Catholic Church. The physicist Tullio Regge pointed to a tense and troubled relationship between the Catholic Church and some sectors of the scientific community where "memories of the stormy past" were still "lingering." He sounded a note of urgency when he called on the Catholic Church to state clearly its position concerning Galileo.[33] Work was already in progress on this matter.

Galileo and Darwin Reviewed

On 31 October 1992 the interdisciplinary commission that had been set up in July 1981 by the Pontifical Academy of Sciences concluded its work when it presented its findings to the pope in the Sala Regia of the Apostolic Palace. Cardinal Paul Poupard gave a short account of the commission's findings. It addressed three questions. What happened? How did it happen? Why did it happen? The commission's response to the first question added little to what was already known. The more interesting questions of how and why were answered simply by Poupard: Galileo was unable to prove the heliocentric hypothesis, and therefore it was not necessary for theologians to revise their interpretations of scripture.

John Paul II thanked the members of the commission for their work, and, in his address to the Pontifical Academy of Sciences, he spoke about the relationship between faith and science. He acknowledged that the theologians who judged Galileo had failed to understand the nonliteral meaning of the biblical text when it described the physical world. The majority of theologians did not perceive the formal distinction between scripture and its interpretation, and this "led them unduly to transpose into the realm of the doctrine of the faith a question which in fact pertained to scientific investigation." They, like Galileo, had failed to discern the boundaries between theology, philosophy, and science. However, Galileo was adjudged to be more perceptive than the theologians. The lesson to be learned from this experience was that it is vitally important for professional groups to define their disciplines, their fields of study, their methods, and the implications of their findings. Theologians were urged to keep themselves regularly informed about advances in science and to determine whether or not changes in teaching were warranted by new developments. Otherwise another "sad misunderstanding," similar in effect to the Galileo affair, might occur in the future.

John Paul was generous in his praise of Galileo, but he also made a point of quoting, with approval, Bellarmine's letter to Foscarini when the cardinal stated that, if the earth's orbit around the sun was proved, one would have to reinterpret very cautiously those scriptural passages which appeared contrary to such a finding. This would call for an admission that the verses in question were not properly understood, rather than a denial of sound scientific evidence. In reference to Poupard's speech, the pope stated that the sentence of 1633 was "not irreformable, and that the debate, which had not ceased to evolve thereafter, was closed in 1820 with the *imprimatur* given to the work of Canon Settele." This segment of his speech was, evidently, designed to soften the painful admission of institutional guilt. It was hardly credible to claim that the debate ended in 1820 when Galileo's *Dialogue* was retained on the Vatican's Index of Forbidden Books for another fifteen years and especially considering the church's failure to explicitly admit its error until the late twentieth century.

The Copernican controversy in the seventeenth century was not entirely concerned with intellectual matters. John Paul maintained that there was also a pastoral dimension to be considered. How was the church to judge a scientific hypothesis that seemed to contradict the Bible? The appropriate response was to avoid the "double trap of a hesitant attitude and of hasty judgement," both of which have the potential to do much harm to the faith of Catholics. In this context the pope had the Copernican controversy in mind. But he also referred to the modernist crisis, which was concerned mainly with the historical sciences. Advances here had "made it possible to acquire a new understanding of the Bible. . . ." At a time when the rationalist presentation of new discoveries seemed to pose a threat to Christian belief, "certain people" reacted by rejecting well-founded historical conclusions. The pope described this rejection as "a hasty and unhappy decision."[34] He was careful not to mention who those "certain people" were, for example, one of his predecessors, Pope Pius X. Nor, in the context of the Galileo affair, did he criticize his more distant predecessors Paul V and Urban VIII.

The confession of error, in general terms, by the church was probably a liberating experience for most of those Catholics who were aware of the burden of history. However, it presented newspaper cartoonists, not very concerned with the virtue of accurate and charitable commentary, with an opportunity not to be missed. The front-page headline of the *New York Times* read, "After 350 years, Vatican says Galileo was right: it moves." The leading article in the *Los Angeles Times* declared "It's Official! The Earth Revolves Around the Sun, Even for the Vatican."[35] The response of Galilean scholars was, of course, nuanced and based on in-depth analysis. Some of them were disappointed and critical of the conclusions reached by the Vatican's reexamination of the Galileo case.[36] Maurice A. Finocchiaro, philosopher at the University of Nevada-Las Vegas, was critical of

Cardinal Poupard's chairmanship of the Vatican's interdisciplinary commission. He was scathing in his comments about *Galileo Galilei: Toward a Resolution of 350 Years of Debate—1633–1983* (1983), edited by Poupard.[37] Finocchiaro was convinced that most of the essays lacked originality and were permeated by untenable assertions, oversimplifications, superficialities, ambiguities, and distortions. The book had reiterated the traditional Catholic apologetic stance—that although Galileo was right, his scientific arguments for Copernicanism were inadequate. Finocchiaro maintained that Poupard had relied very much on a summary of the 1983 book when speaking to the pope and to the Pontifical Academy of Sciences about the commission's work. John Paul's "original liberal and refreshing intentions," expressed in 1979, had been stymied by conservative and reactionary elements in the institutional church. Cardinal Poupard was identified as the "main villain."[38]

Michael Segre was critical of the commission's emphasis on Galileo's lack of proof for the Copernican hypothesis. First, he argued, there is the issue of intellectual freedom. Galileo had the right to express his opinions, even if there were some errors in his scientific work. Second, the issue of proving a scientific hypothesis is not as simple as Poupard seemed to believe. Aristotelian cosmology was not regarded as entirely satisfactory— even Bellarmine questioned it on the basis of scriptural texts. The main thrust of Segre's argument here is that an impossible burden of proof was placed on Galileo's shoulders to provide an excuse for the enforcement of Bellarmine's views and, more generally, for bringing science firmly under the control of theology.[39]

Stellar parallax and Foucault's pendulum experiment are now accepted as proofs of heliocentricism.[40] These proofs were not ascertained until the nineteenth century. Yet, in 1757, long before such evidence was available, the Congregation of the Index decided to omit the decree that prohibited the circulation of all books teaching the mobility of the earth and the immobility of the sun. Although Poupard spoke about the Congregation's decision of 1757, the publication of Canon Settele's work, and other important events, he did not clarify the reasons behind the church's decisions. Why, asked Michael Sharratt, did the church officially permit heliocentricism to be regarded as true before conclusive evidence was discovered? Perhaps the discovery of the aberration of starlight by James Bradley in 1728 was the decisive factor. Poupard's report also failed to shed light on the position of theologians in the century following Galileo's trial.[41]

It was all very well to blame the theologians for the church's mistake, but their role was very restricted after the Congregation of the Index pub-

lished its decree in 1616. Furthermore, by blaming the majority of theologians, Pope John Paul had spread responsibility for the church's error
very wide and diluted the role of the ecclesiastical authorities. Pope Urban
VIII had played a central role in the church's persecution of Galileo.[42] Yet
no official statements were issued, either by the commission or by the
pope, that were critical of Urban's behavior or the excesses of the inquisi-
tors. The same attitude prevailed concerning Pope Paul V. This was consistent with the long-standing policy of popes not referring to their
predecessors except in instances where they wished to emphasize the continuous development of doctrine. James Reston, a biographer of Galileo,
found the omission of Urban VIII unsatisfactory and, in April 1993, he
questioned Cardinal Poupard about it. Poupard replied that the commission's study was not concerned with individuals; its inquiries were about
events. Reston, understandably, was still not satisfied.[43] Poupard regarded
the Galileo case as closed.[44] The church had nothing more to say on the
matter. But some dissatisfaction still lingered—even from within the institutional church. Fr. George V. Coyne criticized the failure to address the
errors of judgment of the Roman Inquisition, the Congregation of the
Index, Pope Paul V, Pope Urban VIII, and Cardinal Robert Bellarmine.
He took issue with both Poupard's and the pope's discourses which placed
the church's burden of guilt so excessively on theologians.[45]

On 22 October 1996 John Paul addressed another scientific issue of
great relevance to Catholic theology when he sent a message to the Pontifical Academy of Sciences indicating the church's position on evolutionary theory. There was a tendency in the media to exaggerate and
misrepresent what he had said.[46] In the scientific journal *Nature*, the papal
message was briefly discussed under the misleading headline "Papal confession: Darwin was right about evolution."[47] The pope did concede a little toward evolution, but his views remained firmly anchored in *Humani
Generis*, which states that there is no contradiction between evolution and
Catholic doctrine provided due cognizance is taken of certain articles of
faith. If loyal Roman Catholics accept evolutionary theory, then they are
duty bound to comply with two conditions in accordance with the
requirements prescribed in *Humani Generis*. First, evolution is not to be
accepted as "a certain, proven doctrine." Second, the acceptance of evolution has to take into account certain theological questions that it raises.
Humani Generis was invoked to stress the essential point that if humans
are descended from primitive life forms this in no way conflicts with the
dogma that the spiritual soul was "immediately" created by God. The
Galileo case had impressed upon John Paul the importance of a high stan-

dard of hermeneutics. If scripture was to be correctly interpreted, then exegetes and theologians were obligated to keep themselves informed about developments in the natural sciences.

The pope maintained that, strictly speaking, there were several theories of evolution rather than one. This plurality arose, first, at the scientific level, where different mechanisms were postulated for the evolutionary process, and, second, in philosophy, where various approaches—spiritualist, reductionist, and materialist—were associated with it. The spiritual status of humankind was very much in question; therefore the church's magisterium was "directly concerned" with the question of evolution.

The theory of evolution was "worthy of investigation and in-depth study equal to that of the opposing hypothesis." Forty-six years of scientific research and progress since the publication of Pius XII's encyclical called for a diminished skepticism about evolution. John Paul recognized this when he stated

> Today, almost half a century after the publication of the Encyclical new knowledge has led us to realize that the theory of evolution is no longer a mere hypothesis. It is indeed remarkable that this theory has been progressively accepted by researchers, following a series of discoveries in various fields of knowledge. The convergence, neither sought nor fabricated, of the results of work that was conducted independently is in itself a significant argument in favor of this theory.[48]

Taking into account the circumstances of his time, John Paul II, like Pius XII, conceded the minimum to evolutionary theory. Furthermore, he failed to address the issue of polygenism. The pope had, notwithstanding some outstanding difficulties, made peace with Galileo, but he did not completely come to terms with Darwin.

Intelligent Design or Contingency?

John Paul's concerns about the theological implications of evolution were probably not shared by the majority of those Catholics who were well informed about science and theology. Leading Catholic scholars, including Pierre Teilhard de Chardin, Ernan McMullin, Karl Rahner, Karl Schmitz-Moormann, and Rosemary Radford Ruether, all had written about Christian faith without any sense of unease about the theological implications of evolutionary theory.[49] By stating that evolution was not "certain" or "proven," John Paul seemed to say that it had not been proven beyond reasonable doubt. If this is a correct interpretation, then very few scientists would have agreed with the pope on this point. Francisco Ayala, professor of biological sciences at the University of California (Irvine), argued that biological evolution was as well established as such scientific findings as a spherical earth and the orbiting of planets around the sun. The evidence for evolution was so strong that it was appropriate to refer to it as a "fact."[50] Ayala, whose religious affiliation is thought to be Roman Catholic, argued that everything in nature, including all species of life, can be explained on the basis of natural processes, regulated by the laws of nature. This did not pose a problem for religious belief. Even Darwin's theory of evolution was neutral on the question of divine action in nature.[51]

Ayala maintained that "design," so apparent in organisms, could be accounted for by natural selection working in tandem with random mutations.[52] He was writing against a background where the notion of "intelligent design" was gaining acceptance, especially in the United States of America, where it has proved particularly controversial. Proponents of intelligent design argue that it should be included in the science curricula of schools so that it offers an alternative explanation to Darwinian (or more correctly neo-Darwinian) evolution—which is believed, in some quarters, to foster atheism. Scientists, and teachers of science, declare their opposition to intelligent design, not generally on atheistic or agnostic grounds, but because they see it as an ideological, metaphysical, or theistic concept. For them it represents an unwarranted intrusion into the domain of science.[53] The battle over intelligent design was, and still is, being fought mainly in the public domain and in the courts. It is not, to any significant extent, contested within the disciplines of the natural sciences because it is widely regarded by scientists as irrelevant to their work. The majority of scientists are reluctant to engage in debate with design theorists because they fear that to do so will give a measure of credibility to the claim that there is a meaningful debate about the veracity of neo-Darwinian evolution within science.

There is a widespread perception of design in nature, as if various features were designed with a particular purpose in mind. Even trenchant defenders of Darwin are not averse to acknowledging the appearance of design. But such design is held to be illusory—the outcome of mindless natural selection—hence, for example, the Blind Watchmaker of Richard Dawkins.[54] Those who advocate intelligent design argue that intelligent causes, instead of undirected natural causes, offer better explanations of how many complex features of nature came to exist. Design theorists emphasize their differences with creationists. Generally, they do not believe in a "young" earth, nor do they refer to the Bible in support of their views about nature. They claim that there is an actual scientific basis for intelligent design—and that it is "empirically detectable."[55] Some proponents of intelligent design maintain that it does not refer directly to God. This raises the question: If intelligent design is not pointing to a creator God, then what is it pointing to? In his *Deeper than Darwin* (2003), John F. Haught, professor of theology at Georgetown University, observed that the great majority of intelligent design theorists are Christians, and he expresses skepticism about the claim that they are not motivated by theological considerations.[56] His opinion is almost certainly widely held. However, it is important for design theorists to keep God out of the argument for legal reasons. In 1987 the Supreme Court of the United States ruled against the teaching of "creation science" alongside evolution in public schools on the grounds that it is in violation of the First Amendment to the Constitution, which prescribes the separation of church and state. It was shortly after this ruling that the intelligent design movement began to emerge in the United States. Its origins can be traced back to Phillip E. Johnson's *Darwin on Trial* (1991).

The intelligent design movement gained considerable organizational coherence in 1996 with the setting up of the Center for the Renewal of Science and Culture (later known as the Center for Science and Culture), supported by the Discovery Institute in Seattle. Leading proponents of intelligent design include the biochemist Michael J. Behe, the mathematician and philosopher William A. Dembski, the molecular and cell biologist Jonathan Wells, and the philosopher of science Stephen C. Meyer—director of the Center for Science and Culture. Those who are prominent in the opposition include the biologist Kenneth R. Miller, the biologist and philosopher Robert T. Pennock, and the physical anthropologist Eugenie C. Scott—executive director of the National Center for Science Education and president of the American Association of Physical Anthropologists. Behe and Miller are Roman Catholics.

In 1996 Behe argued against the plausibility of Darwinian evolution in his book *Darwin's Black Box: The Biochemical Challenge to Evolution*. He argued that biochemical pathways in organisms are so complex and interconnected that they could not be explained by numerous small incremental changes from simpler precursors. All the components of living cells had to be in place simultaneously and had to work in a highly integrated way. This was at variance with the Darwinian scheme, which envisaged cellular components falling into place one by one. Darwinism could not explain the cell, much less higher orders of complexity in multicellular organisms. Biochemical processes in nature were subject to "irreducible complexity"—that is, these processes simply could not occur if even one single component was removed. Behe discussed the immune system, blood clotting, and intracellular transport to bolster his contention. He asserted triumphantly that the observation of intelligent design in cellular biochemistry "must be ranked as one of the greatest achievements in the history of science," rivaling the works of such great scientists as Newton, Lavoisier, Pasteur, Darwin, Schrödinger, and Einstein.[57] And yet intelligent design is not widely accepted by scientists.[58] Even Behe conceded that the majority of scientists accept Darwinism as true.[59] Furthermore, it is doubtful if a majority of those Catholics who cultivate an interest in science would find intelligent design a satisfactory alternative to what is generally taken for granted by scientists.

At the higher levels of Catholic scholarship there seemed to be very little enthusiasm for invoking intelligent design in scientific explanations of nature. George V. Coyne proposed that God acts through the process of evolution. Creation is, therefore, continuous. In the context of promoting dialogue between theology and science, Coyne argued that the concept of continuous creation could be best understood in the light of the highest standards in science. Furthermore, Coyne contended that God does not intervene arbitrarily in nature but allows creation to develop with considerable freedom and spontaneity. God's intervention, insofar as it does occur, is motivated by love.[60] In view of the immense suffering in nature —of which humankind is a part—it might be wondered how this could be consistent with the activity, or inactivity, of a loving, benevolent deity. The idea of an omnipotent and omniscient God did not seem compatible with the randomness, suffering, and "waste" of the evolutionary process.[61] Some theologians, such as John F. Haught, turned to "process" theology to address this problem. Process theology was influenced very much by the philosophy of Alfred North Whitehead (1861–1947). It encompasses a wide range of ideas, including those of Pierre Teilhard de Chardin. God is seen as continuously active in the created order, which is in a constant state of development—consistent with an evolutionary worldview.

If God is all powerful why did he not eliminate or greatly reduce suffering? An answer to this question calls for some speculation about divine characteristics. Haught tentatively proposed a God of process theology who is not a divine despot, who restrains his power. This God acts persuasively and efficaciously. His acts are the acts of a loving God, suffering with his creation, allowing it sufficient freedom to develop. If God chooses otherwise, if he uses power excessively, then creation would not develop to its full potential. Creation would be but a sterile appendage of its creator. Hence, contingency and suffering are presented as necessary features of an ongoing creative process.

Haught did not claim that process theology is without difficulties, and he observes that it is not accepted by all theologians. He gave three reasons for such reluctance. First, process theology needs further development if it is to be consistent with traditional teachings about creation. Second, there is a resistance to what seems to be an excessive diminution of God's power to create and redeem. Third, theologians do not give due attention to evolution, and to the natural world generally.[62]

Haught's ideas about how theology could be enriched by Darwinian theory are expressed at length in his *God after Darwin: A Theology of Evolution* (2000). With authors such as Richard Dawkins and Daniel Dennett in mind, Haught maintains that Darwinism did not offer a full explanation of life. He distinguishes between Darwinism purely as a scientific theory and as a scientific theory associated with an atheistic or materialistic philosophy of life. Haught does not accept Behe's hypothesis of intelligent design as an adequate response to atheistic evolution. Intelligent design does not explain the "disorderly" and "undirected" features of evolution that are so evident in life. Furthermore, it sidesteps the "darker hues" of Darwinism, which are difficult to reconcile with theology. Although mindful of its shortcomings, Haught accepted the "general integrity" of Darwinism, in deference to the judgment of the majority of biologists.[63] Darwinism, as a scientific theory, has far more to offer theology than intelligent design. It offers prospects for the emergence of things "truly new."[64] It is, arguably, the only way of creating "the best of all possible worlds."[65]

Theologians and prelates alike spent much time in reflection about evolution and how it could be used to deepen their understanding of the doctrine of the *imago Dei*—that is, humans created in the image of God. The Vatican's International Theological Commission set up a subcommission to study the theme of "man created in the image of God."[66] The subcommission's findings were discussed at several plenary sessions of the International Theological Commission in Rome from 2000 to 2002. In July 2004 the commission, presided over by Cardinal Joseph Ratzinger, published the outcome of its deliberations under the title of *Communion and Stewardship: Human Persons Created in the Image of God.* When discussing evolution, the commission did not limit the scope of its study to the emergence of life and its subsequent diversification. Some attention was devoted to the Big Bang theory when examining the doctrine of *creatio ex nihilo* ("creation from nothing"). The commission contended that belief in an absolute beginning was not in opposition to science. The Big Bang could be regarded as an absolute beginning, but this was not certain. Therefore, this momentous event seemed to give "merely indirect support" for the doctrine of creation which could only be known through faith.[67]

The commission observed that although scientists were divided on the mechanisms and details of biological evolution there was no reasonable doubt that it had actually occurred—it was "virtually certain." Furthermore, there was "a convincing case" that humans had evolved from a hominoid population in Africa about 150,000 years ago (par. 63). The commission referred to Pope John Paul's message to the Pontifical Academy of Sciences in 1996 to make the point that there were "several theories of evolution" associated with "materialist, reductionist and spiritualist" ideas that were incompatible with Catholic doctrine (par. 64).

The commission was aware of the controversy about intelligent design in nature. In paragraph 69 of *Communion and Stewardship* it observed that many neo-Darwinian scientists, and some of their critics, shared in common the belief that an evolutionary process generated by random genetic variation and natural selection excluded a role for divine causality. Some scientists reacted by arguing that there was evidence for design that could not be explained entirely on the basis of neo-Darwinism. The commission maintained that it was not within the professional competence of theologians to judge whether or not the scientific evidence to date favored inferences of chance or design. Nor was it critically important to pronounce definitively on this matter when cognizance was taken of Catholic teaching about divine causality. It was possible to accept that true contingency in nature was a feature of God's creative process. Divine causality was present whether the process was contingent or guided in the natural realm. The commission maintained that those neo-Darwinians who claimed that evolution was absolutely unguided were making claims that were beyond the domain of science (par. 69). From this perspective the church had nothing to fear from neo-Darwinism. The special creation of the human soul, which set humans apart from the rest of creation, was beyond the reach of science (par. 70).

The International Theological Commission's *Communion and Stewardship* received some attention in scientific circles. Dr. Lawrence M. Krauss, professor of physics and astronomy at Case Western Reserve University in Cleveland, Ohio, commented on the significance of its findings in the *New York Times* on 17 May 2005. He was mindful of the decision by the

Kansas Board of Education to eliminate references to evolution in its school science standards in August 1999. Krauss is not a Roman Catholic, but he is well informed about the church's position on evolution. He maintained that the church was at ease with evolutionary theory. One could invoke evolution in support of atheism or theism. The fact that such opposite views could be associated with the same scientific theory demonstrates that the arguments are essentially nonscientific. Biologists, whether religious or not, can agree entirely on how life evolved. The introduction of intelligent design into school science curricula creates confusion about what is scientific and what is not. It is an unwarranted imposition of theological speculation on a scientific theory. Krauss was critical of the Discovery Institute's slogan that schools should "Teach the Controversy." There is, he asserted, no scientific controversy.[68]

In view of the assurances given by the International Theological Commission, it seemed that controversy might give way to quiescence among Catholics. This was not to be. Cardinal Christoph Schönborn of Vienna stirred the embers with his "Finding Design in Nature." This essay was published in the *New York Times* on 7 July 2005. Schönborn stated that the church acknowledged that scientists were free to work out the details of evolution. Nevertheless the church proclaimed that

> by the light of reason the human intellect can readily and clearly discern purpose and design in the natural world, including the world of living things. Evolution in the sense of common ancestry might be true, but evolution in the neo-Darwinian sense—an unguided, unplanned process of random variation and natural selection—is not. Any system of thought that denies or seeks to explain away the overwhelming evidence for design in biology is ideology, not science.[69]

Schönborn dismissed John Paul's 1996 message to the Pontifical Academy of Sciences as "rather vague and unimportant," pointing instead to the pope's statements made before a general audience in 1985, which were more "robust" about nature. On that occasion the pope saw "finality" in nature, which was taken by Schönborn to mean "final cause, purpose or design."

Pope John Paul II died on 2 April 2005 and was succeeded by Cardinal Joseph Ratzinger, who took the name of Benedict XVI. Schönborn objected to what he saw as an attempt by neo-Darwinists to depict the new pope as "a satisfied evolutionist." They had referred to the International Theological Commission's *Communion and Stewardship* in support of their claim, observing that, at the time, Benedict was president of the commission. Schönborn, however, maintained that the document reaffirmed the church's teaching about design in nature and was critical of "the widespread abuse" of John Paul's 1996 message on evolution. Furthermore, he referred to the declaration by the First Vatican Council that "by the use of reason alone mankind could come to know the reality of the Uncaused Cause, the First Mover, the God of the philosophers." The cardinal believed that the multiverse hypothesis in cosmology, and neo-Darwinism, were "invented to avoid the overwhelming evidence for purpose and design found in modern science." He concluded by stating that "scientific theories that try to explain away the appearance of design as the result of 'chance and necessity' are not scientific at all, but, as John Paul put it, an abdication of human intelligence."[70]

Schönborn's essay raised concerns that the Catholic Church was changing its stance on evolution, which would damage its reputation. John F. Haught was critical of Schönborn's essay, referring to the cardinal's opinions as fearful and defensive, in contrast to John Paul's pronouncements, which he saw as confident and supportive of science. Professor Michael Hoonhout, a theologian at the Catholic University of America, speculated that Schönborn's comments were directed mainly against those who saw evolutionary theory as a credible basis for atheism.[71]

On 12 July 2005 Lawrence Krauss, Francisco Ayala, and Kenneth Miller wrote an open letter to Pope Benedict XVI about the issues raised by Schönborn. Copies were also addressed to Schönborn and to Archbishop William J. Levada, the new prefect of the Congregation for the Doctrine of the Faith. The letter was also copied for a wider circulation and posted on the Internet. Krauss, Ayala, and Miller were well-known scientists and their views received widespread attention in the mass media.[72] In contrast to Schönborn, they referred to John Paul's 1996 letter as "magnificent." Reference was made to the fact that Benedict, formerly Cardinal Ratzinger, had presided over the International Theological Commission which concluded that there was nothing intrinsically incompatible between Catholic theology and the scientific concept of an evolutionary process driven by random genetic variation and natural selection. The three scientists expressed concern that Schönborn's article might be preparing the ground for a regressive shift in the church's attitude toward evolution. They sought clarification of the church's position from Pope Benedict. Clarification in this context meant a reaffirmation of the "remarkable statements" of John Paul II and of the International Theological Commission. It would then be clear that Schönborn's opinions did not represent those of the Holy See.[73]

Schönborn was highly influential in the church hierarchy. He was known to be close to Pope Benedict and served on the Vatican's Congregation for Catholic Education. In some quarters it seemed that the church might make another serious error of judgment concerning science. On 9 July Schönborn's opinions received further attention in the *New York Times*. In an article written by Cornelia Dean and Laurie Goodstein, Schönborn was reported to have said that his essay did not receive approval from the Vatican. He had spoken to Benedict, then a fellow cardinal, two weeks before the outcome of the conclave in April, expressing a desire to make the church's position more explicit about evolution. Benedict encouraged him to proceed;[74] however, all this fell far short of a redefinition of the church's position.[75] Professor Phillip Reid Sloan, a philosopher and historian of science at the University of Notre Dame, observed that Schönborn's rejection of neo-Darwinism had no basis in Catholic doctrine.[76]

Apparently, Schönborn was encouraged to write his essay by Mark Ryland, a vice president of the Discovery Institute in Seattle, who also assisted the cardinal in publishing his views through the *New York Times*. Schönborn and Ryland knew each other through their work at an international theological institute in Gaming, Austria.[77] Evidently, Schönborn needed little encouragement from Ryland. He had been angry for some time about what he perceived to be frequent misrepresentations of the church's attitude toward evolution. He strongly objected to claims, many of them by Catholic authors, that the church endorsed evolutionary theory when prominence was given to random events. Nevertheless, he stated that the Congregation for Catholic Education did not intend to publish new guidelines about evolution for teachers in Catholic schools.[78]

The Roman Catholic Church was unlikely to pronounce in favor of intelligent design as proposed by Michael Behe, William Dembski, and others. There would have been strong opposition to such a move from many leading Catholic scientists and theologians. On 18 July, John L. Allen, Rome correspondent with the *National Catholic Reporter*, interviewed Professor Nicola Cabibbo, President of the Pontifical Academy of Sciences. Cabibbo disagreed with Schönborn's assessment of John Paul's 1996 message on evolution, although he allowed for the possibility that a poor translation from the original German text might have given rise to a misunderstanding of the cardinal's opinion. Cabibbo maintained that purpose and design in nature could not be clearly identified at a scientific level. There was no proof of God's existence from scientific studies.[79] Any inferences about design were external to science itself.

Allen spoke to a number of Catholic scientists and theologians about Schönborn's essay. There was consensus that if his claims about design and purpose were read in a theological sense then he was on solid ground. However, if his statements were interpreted as claims about science itself, then there was the considerable risk of creating a rift between the church and science.[80] Allen sought clarification from Schönborn himself. The cardinal stated that he agreed completely with paragraph 69 of *Communion and Stewardship*. His central contention was that neo-Darwinians who claimed that natural selection and random genetic variation were convincing evidence of an absolutely unguided evolutionary process were venturing beyond the realm of science. Evolutionary theory did not provide a holistic explanation of life. Allen concluded, therefore, that Schönborn's argument was philosophical, not scientific.[81] Schönborn had tacitly retreated from his hard-line anti-Darwinian stance.

At this point the Vatican's chief astronomer, Rev. George V. Coyne, had taken steps to express open dissatisfaction with the cardinal's essay. His critique of Schönborn was published in *The Tablet* on 6 August 2005. Coyne referred to the Galileo Commission, which had attempted to dispel misunderstandings and myths about an unshakable hostility between the Roman Catholic Church and science. He observed that almost all historians and philosophers of science who expressed an opinion on the matter were critical of the commission's work and that it fell short of realizing the pope's expectations. He saw the work of the International Theological Commission, under the presidency of Cardinal Ratzinger, as yet another initiative to improve the relationship between the church and science. Progress had been made with the commission's declaration that there was no contradiction between the acceptance of an underlying divine causality and "a truly contingent" mechanism in nature driving the evolutionary process.

It was against this background of painstaking progress that Coyne viewed Schönborn's essay. The cardinal had muddied the waters by claiming that neo-Darwinian evolution clashed with the church's teaching about God's design and purpose in creation. Coyne observed that there was a "nagging fear" in the church that evolution, with its vast time scale, contingency, and natural selection, effectively pushed God out of the universe. However, he maintained that such a fear was groundless because science was "completely neutral with respect to philosophical or theological implications that may be drawn from its conclusions." Coyne argued that the notion of God as dictator, and designer—a Newtonian God—was no longer in harmony with modern science, nor was it compatible with the best of biblical scholarship. He concluded by arguing that there was no basis for the fear that God would no longer seem real if people accepted the best that science had to offer.[82]

Schönborn reiterated his intention to clarify the church's teaching on creation. Through the "Official Educational Communiqué" of the Vienna archdiocese he stated that evolutionary theory is not in opposition to a belief in God provided that scientists do not extrapolate beyond their disciplinary boundaries so that "the role of chance is not expanded to such an extent that everything—from the Big Bang to Beethoven's Ninth Symphony . . . is principally, exclusively and irrevocably seen as a product of chance." If evolution is discussed only as a scientific theory, then there is no cause for concern.[83] Schönborn probably took cognizance of the criticisms of his eminent co-religionists and realized that his anti-Darwinian pro–intelligent design ideas were difficult to defend. He had overstepped the mark, seeking to impose on science ideas that could be construed as theological. If intelligent design theorists in the United States hoped for wholehearted support from the Roman Catholic Church, then they were disappointed.

Statements by President George W. Bush added fuel to the debate. On 1 August 2005 Bush seemed to express support for the idea that intelligent design should be taught in public schools. He stated that people should be exposed to different ideas in the educational system. His comments were criticized by scientists and by those who were adamant about the separation of church and state.[84] Concern was expressed that the president's statements about "a pseudoscience issue" diverted attention away from the far more important matter of sustaining the competitive edge of American science.[85] However, opinion polls indicated that the president was in tune with popular opinion on the issue.[86]

The political and religious culture of the United States of America and its constitutional prohibition against the teaching of religion in public schools strongly indicate that intense debates and court cases concerning evolution and intelligent design are likely to recur for quite some time. The notion that God has left divine fingerprints in nature offers comforting reassurances to those who seek a supernatural presence. In this context it is interesting to recall Schönborn's assertion, based on a declaration by the First Vatican Council, that "by the use of reason alone mankind could come to know the reality of the Uncaused Cause." If intelligent design is not held to be discernible in nature, how then are Catholics to look for evidence of God's existence? Do the natural sciences have a role in answering this question? Or is it even deemed necessary to provide some rational basis for belief in God? The theology and philosophy of Pope John Paul II will now be examined with these questions in mind.

A Hidden God

Truly you are a God who hides himself, O God and Savior of Israel.
—Isaiah 45:15

Pope John Paul II believed that science could assist humankind in drawing closer to God.[87] Through the medium of a number of public speeches, he explained how science could be of assistance to humankind's spiritual quest. Advances in cosmology have impressed upon us our physical insignificance in an incredibly vast universe. We can now view our planetary home from the somewhat startling perspective of outer space. The more we know about the universe, the more we can appreciate the mystery of God, and our understanding of our own origins and destiny will be greatly enhanced. But, although we are rooted in the material world, certain aspects of our lives transcend the physical dimension and are beyond the reach of science.[88] The justification for Christianity is within itself, and Christians should not expect science to provide them with the primary reason for their faith.[89]

Belief in God is primarily based on faith—but not on faith alone. On 10 July 1985 John Paul told a general audience at St. Peter's Square that there are proofs of God's existence. He asserted, however, that these proofs are not to be found in science.

> In speaking of the existence of God we should underline that we are not speaking of proofs in the sense implied by the experimental sciences. Scientific proofs in the modern sense of the word are valid only for things perceptible to the senses since it is only on such things that scientific instruments of investigation can be used.

Scientific proof of God is not only impossible; it is undesirable.

> To desire a scientific proof of God would be equivalent to lowering God to the level of the beings of our world, and we would therefore be mistaken methodologically in regard to what God is. Science must recognize its lim-

its and its inability to reach the existence of God: it can neither affirm nor deny his existence.[90]

Scientific theories neither prove nor disprove the doctrine of creation. Neither does science affirm or deny the presence of a spiritual soul in humans.[91] Although many scientists believe in God, the Roman Catholic Church maintains that it is not prepared to accept affirmations of God from sources that are not rigorously rational in their approach to the question.[92] Where then does it seek proof? The church, according to John Paul II, seeks proof from the logical deductions of philosophers,[93] giving preeminence to the philosophy of St. Thomas Aquinas.[94] The pope claimed that arguments for God's existence can be simplified so that they are accessible to those who seek to understand the meaning of the world around them.[95] In his encyclical *Fides et Ratio* (14 September 1998) he maintained that "if human beings with their intelligence fail to recognize God as Creator of all, it is not because they lack the means to do so, but because their free will and their sinfulness place an impediment in the way" (par. 19). A similar point of view was expressed by Pius XII in *Humani Generis*.[96]

Elementary philosophical principles such as causality, finality, and sufficient reason—rather than the experimental scientific method—were invoked as a means of affirming religious belief.[97] In applying this philosophy, however, John Paul took cognizance of advances in modern science. In *Fides et Ratio* he declared:

> in reasoning about nature, the human being can rise to God: "From the greatness and beauty of created things comes a corresponding perception of their Creator" (Wis 13:5). This is to recognize as a first stage of divine Revelation the marvellous "book of nature," which, when read with the proper tools of human reason, can lead to knowledge of the Creator. (*Fides et Ratio* par. 19)

The expansion of the universe was explained in the context of Big Bang theory, but this theory does not necessarily imply an absolute beginning in time or the existence of a Creator.[98] John Paul was aware of this. In his speech to the Pontifical Academy of Sciences on 3 October 1981, he told his audience that the hypothesis of the "primitive atom," from which the entire universe developed, did not actually explain the beginning of the universe. Science was incapable of providing an answer to the question of the universe's origin.[99] He saw an intended finality in the complexity of matter, especially in the development of life. To attribute all this to chance would be the same as accepting effects without a cause, which in turn would be irrational. Thus he concluded: "the proofs for the existence of God are many and convergent."[100] This was not at all clear. There was no consensus among philosophers supportive of the pope's conclusion. Furthermore, natural theology was now more modest in its claims. It no longer asserted that it could prove the existence of God. There was a tendency to regard it as a provider of "a coherent and deeply intellectually satisfying understanding of the total way things are."[101]

It has been observed that if God exists he remains hidden. Richard Elliott Friedman discussed this topic at great length in his book *The Disappearance of God: A Divine Mystery* (1995).[102] There are many references in the Bible to a hidden God (see, e.g., Deut. 31:17–18; 32:20 NIV). In the Book of Psalms God is portrayed several times as hidden and remote from humanity (Pss. 10:1, 11; 13:1; 44:24; 30:7; etc.). The philosopher John Leslie argued that a universe very obviously created by God would tend to be one of puppetry rather than of freedom. On the other hand, God would not be so devious as to obscure every sign of his existence in nature. Therefore, Leslie, observing that the universe has the appearance of design, attached equal strength to the arguments for and against God's existence.[103] Pope John Paul addressed the idea of a hidden God in his book *Crossing the Threshold of Hope* (1994). "Why isn't there more concrete proof of God's existence? Why does He seem to hide Himself, almost playing with His creation? Shouldn't it all be much simpler? Shouldn't his existence be obvious?" The pope placed these questions in the "the repertory of contemporary agnosticism."[104] He pointed out that God revealed himself to humans through the human incarnation of Jesus Christ, and in doing so God went as far as possible. Humanity, the pope argued, could not tolerate closer contact and rebelled against it. This protest was manifested through the synagogues of the Jews and the mosques of Islam—neither could accept a God who was so human. It is here that John Paul relied on faith rather than attempting to proceed with objective argument. This approach did not present a problem for Catholics whose faith was strong. However, it is highly probable that those outside Roman Catholicism, and those inside whose faith was wavering, were not persuaded by the words of John Paul.

11

Bioethics

Donum Vitae

IN THE LATE TWENTIETH CENTURY THERE WAS A GROWING AWARE-
ness of a broad range of environmental problems arising from the misuse and excessive exploitation of the world's natural resources. A great
diversity of problems, including global warming, depletion of the ozone
layer, acid rain, the dangers of nuclear power, the unpredictable effects of
genetically modified crops, desertification, the widespread destruction of
rainforests, and the extinction of many animal and plant species, have all
received much attention from the mass media. In the 1960s there was relatively little awareness or appreciation of the destructive impact of human
activities on various ecosystems throughout the world. In *Lumen Gentium*
and *Gaudium et Spes*, the Second Vatican Council expressed its views
about nature from a strong anthropocentric perspective. Nature was
viewed as God's creation, hierarchically structured with humanity at the
apex. Humans had the right to dominate and exploit the earth and all its
creatures. But this was not approval for individualistic greed. The
resources of the earth were to be used to serve the needs of all humankind.
It is here that the theology of creation was brought into close contact with
the social teaching of the church, particularly the central idea of serving
the common good.[1] Environmental issues were not directly addressed at
the time.

Since the 1960s the Roman Catholic Church, like other Christian
churches, has become increasingly concerned about the protection of natural environments. This is reflected in the published works of Catholic
authors such as Leonardo Boff, Marcelo de Barros, José Luis Caravias,
and Ivone Gebara; in documents based on the proceedings of regional and
national conferences of bishops, and in papal pronouncements. Pastoral

letters include, for example, the "Pastoral Letter on the Relationship of Human Beings to Nature" (1987) issued by the bishops of the Dominican Republic; and "Renewing the Earth: An Invitation to Reflection and Action in Light of Catholic Social Teaching" (1991) issued by the bishops of the United States of America. As Catholic bishops around the world found themselves confronted by the related issues of environmental degradation and economic injustice they issued pastoral documents against the unique backgrounds of their own regional and national circumstances. Their source material extended beyond the Bible and Vatican texts to include the opinions of a wide range of authors and organizations.[2]

Vatican opinions about environmental issues were expressed through the medium of a number of documents and speeches, including Pope John Paul II's "World Day of Peace" statement "The Ecological Crisis: A Common Responsibility" (1 January 1990), and his encyclical *Centesimus Annus* (1991); Archbishop Renato R. Martino's address to the United Nations Conference on the Environment and Development (the "Earth Summit") held in Rio de Janeiro in June 1992; and the *Catechism of the Catholic Church* (1994). Anthropocentrism is still a central feature of Catholic environmental theology, but there is now some acknowledgment of the need to protect the environment, not just in terms of human needs but for its own sake. Despite the advances in Catholic environmental thinking from the 1970s to the dawn of the twenty-first century, the church's teaching on environmental issues is still very underdeveloped. It has been argued that if intellectual innovation and a widespread radical change of attitude are to occur this will require, *inter alia*, a constructive exchange of ideas between theology and science.[3]

In the late twentieth century, the Roman Catholic Church expressed an interest in, and pronounced solemn judgments on, many aspects of science and technology. However, it was mainly concerned about developments in the biological sciences. Within this major sphere of scientific activity the church's main preoccupation was with the human body. Thus a Catholic code of bioethics evolved, addressing such topics as contraception, abortion, *in vitro* fertilization, gene therapy, experimentation on embryos, organ transplantation, withdrawal of medical treatment, diagnosis of death, and euthanasia. Moral questions pertaining to the use of the contraceptive pill and other contraceptive devices were not resolved, at least not to the satisfaction of the majority of Roman Catholics. But the teaching authority of the church maintained its position. In 1987 Pope

John Paul II asserted that the church's official stance on the matter was not open to free discussion among theologians. This elicited a critical response—from 163 theologians from Germany, Austria, Switzerland, and the Netherlands. Their protest, *The Cologne Declaration*, received support from 130 French, 63 Italian, and 60 Spanish theologians; and from 431 members of the Catholic Theological Society of America.[4] It is highly probable that the majority of Catholic priests and theologians were dissatisfied with the traditionalist stance of the Vatican on contraception but chose to stay silent out of deference to or fear of ecclesiastical authority.

From a liberal Catholic perspective the issue of contraception is relatively simple and straightforward to address. In marked contrast to this are the extremely complex moral questions arising from developments in the biological sciences since the late 1970s. The birth of Louise Brown—the world's first "test tube" baby—in July 1978 was made possible by the medical research of two doctors, Patrick Steptoe and Robert Edwards. For nearly a decade they had worked on the development of *in vitro* ("in glass") fertilization (IVF). In this process ova (egg cells) are taken from a woman's body and fertilized by spermatozoa (sperm cells) in a culture dish. The fertilized cells are then replaced in the mother's reproductive system. *In vitro* fertilization offers some couples the prospect of having children when medical problems would otherwise prevent it.

At first the Roman Catholic hierarchy seemed favorably disposed toward IVF. Pope John Paul I (Albino Luciani) praised the scientific achievement and extended good wishes to the parents of Louise Brown. The bishops of England and Wales stated that they could find no moral basis for objecting to the procedure. But John Paul I reigned from only 26 August to September 28 in 1978, and the bishops of England and Wales later changed their opinions on the matter because IVF involved the intentional destruction of early-stage embryos and separated procreation from sexual intercourse.[5] The practice of IVF gave rise to a number of complex moral and legal questions pertaining to the moral status of the embryo and the rights of the child, surrogacy and the nature of parenthood. Surrogacy serves as a good illustration of the difficulties that had to be addressed. There are two categories of surrogacy. A surrogate mother could give birth to a child genetically unrelated to her because the ovum was donated by another woman. In the second category the surrogate mother is the source of the ovum, and it is fertilized, through insemination, with the spermatozoon of a man who is not married to her. In both cases the woman agrees to hand over the child to the party who commissioned the pregnancy. But what course does the law take if the surrogate mother changes her mind and claims the child as her own? Is parentage on the mother's side determined more by the womb than by the ovum?

A question of central importance is, When does human life truly begin? Does a zygote (a fertilized ovum) merit the status of a person with human rights? Fr. Richard A. McCormick, S.J., addressed this in the context of *in vitro* fertilization, in which more than one ovum is fertilized. The elimination of excess early-stage embryos was condemned as abortion by those who regarded the embryos as persons in a moral sense. An opposing view regarded such embryos as merely human tissue and saw no moral problem in their creation and elimination, especially when it was known that many zygotes are lost from *in vivo* attempts at pregnancy. McCormick argued against both of these extreme opinions. He observed that many reputable theologians and philosophers do not accept the idea of a zygote as a person. The zygote is neither a person nor a mere thing. It deserves "respect and awe." The respect due to nascent human life precludes its creation for research purposes, but not for the purpose of achieving a pregnancy. McCormick was cautious in framing his argument and left some scope for retreat by indicating the tentative nature of his reflections.[6]

Charles E. Curran argued against the idea of full human rights for embryos in early stages of development mainly on the basis of the concept of individuality. Individual human life is not established until about two weeks after conception. The zygote, morula, and blastocyst are important but not important enough to be accorded full human rights. It is thus morally permissible to discard excess zygotes and embryos in the early stages of development (pre-embryos), or to put them at risk to facilitate *in vitro* fertilization and embryo transfer.[7] Curran and McCormick were both eminent Catholic theologians, but their views did not represent the official teaching of the church.[8]

In the 1980s it was widely perceived that rapid strides in the biomedical sciences had left medical ethics far behind. The Congregation for the Doctrine of the Faith, presided over by the conservative Cardinal Joseph Ratzinger, received inquiries about the moral implications of biomedical techniques from episcopal conferences, individual bishops, theologians, scientists, and medical doctors. It responded with *Donum Vitae* (*Instruction on Respect for Human Life and Its Origin and on the Dignity of Procreation*, 22 February 1987). A number of other important church documents were also published by the Catholic hierarchy to address a range of ethical dilemmas presented by developments in the biomedical sciences. These included the *Ethical and Religious Directives for Catholic Health Services* (1994) of the U.S. National Conference of Catholic Bishops; and Pope John Paul II's encyclical, *Evangelium Vitae* (25 March 1995).[9]

In the introduction of *Donum Vitae* the Congregation for the Doctrine of the Faith stated the underlying principles for its findings.

1. There is a moral imperative to place science and technology at the service of the human person.

2. Science and technology are not morally neutral. What is technically possible is not necessarily morally permissible.

3. The human body cannot be treated as if it is only a highly organized structure of tissues and organs; it is to be regarded as fundamentally different from other animal bodies.

4. Human procreation is subject to unique moral criteria that distinguish it from reproduction in all other forms of life. Therefore, it is not always morally permissible to "use means and follow methods which could be licit in the transmission of the life of plants and animals." Human procreation has to take place in marriage "through the specific and exclusive acts of husband and wife."

5. Human life is to be "respected in an absolute way" from the moment of conception to death.[10]

The Congregation for the Doctrine of the Faith stated that a human life begins when the nucleus of a spermatozoon and the nucleus of an ovum fuse to become one. The zygote is then regarded, in a moral sense, as a person with full human rights (p. 4). The Congregation then proceeded to address some specific issues relating to the biomedical sciences. Prenatal diagnosis was morally permissible when it was motivated by concerns to protect and treat pathological conditions in embryos and fetuses. It was immoral when it was carried out with the intention of inducing an abortion in the event of an abnormality or hereditary illness being diagnosed. The Congregation did not object to medical research being carried out on live embryos provided that certain conditions are met. First, there is to be a "moral certainty" of not harming the mother and child, and, second, the parents have to give their free and informed consent for the procedure to be undertaken (p. 5).

The Congregation observed that in IVF procedures some of the resultant embryos are not transferred to the mother's body but are destroyed. There is a tendency to generate "spare" embryos to ensure against the failure to fertilize. In terms of immoral practices it compared the destruction of these embryos to induced abortion. The Congregation acknowledged that embryos created *in vitro*, sometimes through splitting ("twin fission"), can benefit medical research. Nevertheless, it objected to this practice on the basis that these tiny embryos are human beings with rights, not material resources for the benefit of others (p. 6). IVF techniques were also condemned because of the fear that these could create opportunities for the unethical manipulation of human beings, such as fertilization between human and animal gametes (spermatozoa and ova), and the gestation of human embryos in the wombs of animals. This concern was expressed against the background of developments in recombinant DNA technology, which enables scientists to transfer genes (functional units of the genetic code) from one organism to another; sometimes between distantly related species.

Procreation by asexual methods (i.e., without sex), through "twin fission," cloning or parthenogenesis, is unacceptable because these methods are considered inimical to human dignity and contrary to the moral law. There was also a moral prohibition against the freezing of embryos, because it is thought to present a risk of injury or death. Low temperature preservation was deemed to be unacceptable because it deprives embryos of maternal shelter and gestation, and this in turn exposes them to further malpractice. The authors of *Donum Vitae* urged that human dignity be safeguarded against the excesses of scientific practices. Those attempts at genetic engineering that are not therapeutic, carried out to procreate humans with selected gender or other predetermined qualities, are regarded as contrary to the integrity and identity of the human person (p. 6). It is ethical to remedy something that is defective but not to enhance something that is in a good functional condition.

The Congregation for the Doctrine of the Faith did not object to medical intervention to regulate human procreation on the basis that such methods are artificial (p. 3). However, it asserted that a child has a right to be conceived, nurtured in the womb, born, and brought up within marriage. In every marriage the husband and wife could become parents only through each other. Adherence to these moral principles was deemed essential for the welfare of family life and for the good of society (p. 7). It was mainly for these reasons that heterologous artificial fertilization, in which spermatozoa or ova are donated by a third party, was judged to be contrary to the moral law. It was believed that this procedure created problems for relationships within the family, leading to problems of personal identity for the child and creating a divide between the different aspects of parenthood—genetic, gestational, and the responsibility for upbringing. It poses a threat to the unity of family life. Surrogate motherhood was condemned for similar reasons (p. 8).

If heterologous artificial fertilization is to be rejected on the basis that a third-party donor of either spermatozoa or ova is morally unacceptable, then what is the ethical status of homologous artificial fertilization that does not involve a third-party donor? There are two methods to evaluate: IVF and embryo transfer, and artificial insemination. It was here that the Congregation invoked the theological argument that led the church to condemn artificial means of contraception. Contraception—deliberately depriving the conjugal act of its procreative potential—and homologous artificial fertilization, failing to conform to the unitive aspect, were both ruled out because of the church's insistence that both dimensions have to be complied with. The Congregation clung tenaciously to the teaching of *Humanae Vitae* (par. 12) that there is an "inseparable connection, willed by God and unable to be broken by man on his own initiative, between the two meanings of the conjugal act: the unitive meaning and the procreative meaning" (p. 8).

The Congregation acknowledged that it is natural for married couples to desire children and that in some cases IVF techniques can help them to achieve this. However, its response was that the end does not justify the means. Only God has the right to create life and to end it (p. 6). It is morally permissible for married couples to avail themselves of medical techniques to assist the conjugal act for purposes of procreation, but it is morally illicit for the medical procedure to replace the conjugal act for such a purpose (p. 10). Furthermore, the Congregation maintained that marriage does not give spouses the right to have a child, but only the right to "perform those natural acts" which are designed for procreation. The Congregation acknowledged that childlessness is "a difficult trial" for many married couples and suggested that adoption, charitable work, and educational service to the community are alternative ways of seeking fulfillment in life (p. 11). This is cold comfort for those who are experiencing fertility problems.

The church viewed medical science as an immoral intruder when homologous IVF and embryo transfer techniques are used to overcome infertility, because a vital part of the reproductive process is carried out external to the bodies of the couple. The Congregation argued:

> The one conceived must be the fruit of his parents' love. He cannot be desired or conceived as the product of an intervention of medical or biological techniques; that would be equivalent to reducing him to an object of scientific technology. . . . Such fertilization entrusts the life and identity of

the embryo into the power of doctors and biologists and establishes the domination of technology over the origin and destiny of the human person. Such a relationship of domination is in itself contrary to the dignity and equality that must be common to parents and children. (pp. 9–10)

This attitude persisted and found expression the *Catechism of the Catholic Church* several years later.[11]

Catholic doctors and nurses, and those who are in charge of Catholic hospitals and clinics, are urged to fulfill their moral obligations in conformity with their church's guidelines. However, relying on the conscience of individuals and depending on the self-regulation of researchers is not deemed to be sufficient, and the Congregation therefore appealed to the legislature to regulate the applications of biomedical science in order to safeguard and promote the welfare of society.[12]

Alternatives to IVF procedures were developed with the objective of complying with the directives of the Congregation's *Donum Vitae*. These methods are known as gamete intra-fallopian transfer (GIFT), tubal ovum transfer (TOT), and lower tubal ovum transfer (LTOT), which is similar to TOT. All three methods facilitate the fertilization of ova within the mother's body (*in vivo*), after sexual intercourse, instead of in a glass dish under laboratory conditions. The perceived merit of fertilization *in vivo*, from a Catholic moral point of view, is that there is less artificial interference, and it does not present opportunities for the manipulation or discarding of embryos.[13] However, some Catholic married couples who need medical assistance if they are to become parents prefer to avail themselves of IVF techniques and take little cognizance of abstract theological principles. The church's insistence that the procreative and unitive dimensions must be present in every act of sexual intercourse makes little sense to them when infertility is a persistent problem. It is highly probable that many Catholics are unable to understand why their church should object to IVF on a moral basis when it values parenthood so much.[14] Furthermore, it seems preposterous to suggest that a child conceived through medical intervention might somehow be regarded as "an object" or product of technology. It is most unlikely that married couples who turn to IVF techniques to overcome infertility resent the "domination" of technology, which sometimes can serve them so well. Dissenting attitudes do not exist just among the laity. A "substantial majority" of eminent Catholic theologians are not opposed to the use of biomedical technology to achieve conception when nature fails to do so, provided that: (1) spermatozoa and ova originate from husband and wife; (2) all the embryos produced can be safely implanted in the mother's uterus; (3) abortion is not considered an option if abnormality occurs.[15]

The church will continuously need to develop and revise its doctrines, subject to the constraints of dogma, if it is to respond adequately to a constant succession of changes brought about by advances in the natural sciences. The theological enterprise—"faith seeking understanding"—plays a critical role here. Innovative theologians will tend to push out the boundaries of doctrine so that church teaching will resonate with what are regarded as desirable features of modern culture. The hierarchical teaching authority of the church, on the other hand, is primarily concerned with proclaiming and safeguarding the faith. In carrying out these functions it will tend to restrain theological hypothesizing. Thus, there will always be tension between theologians and the magisterium, especially when there is an excessive use of ecclesiastical authority. During the pontificate of Pope John Paul II some theologians expressed criticism of "creeping infallibility"—the marked tendency of the magisterium to place noninfallible teachings beyond criticism.[16]

In view of the above it should not be surprising that some theologians do not accept all the precepts of *Donum Vitae*. The assertion that a zygote, or a pre-embryo,[17] deserves full rights due to a person is contested by a number of authors. It is clear from *Donum Vitae* that the Congregation for the Doctrine of the Faith had taken cognizance of scientific data from genetics and embryology. However, the Congregation had assumed, mistakenly, that the unique genetic code of the zygote established individuality.[18] In 1988 the Australian priest Fr. Norman F. Ford challenged the claim that a zygote is an actual human individual in his widely read book *When Did I Begin?* Twelve years later he maintained that the status of the human pre-embryo was still not settled in Catholic theology.[19]

If ethicists are to address this complex issue then it is necessary for them to study carefully the most recent scientific data from genetics and embryology. However, there is still much to be discovered from research in these disciplines that will in turn call for ongoing revisions of ethical perspectives. Furthermore, there is also a philosophical dimension. Scientific data alone cannot address questions that are essentially philosophical. How are scientific data to be interpreted? Facts cannot be interpreted in a philosophical vacuum. There has to be a philosophical framework encompassing notions of meaning and importance. How is personhood to be defined? What are the minimum requirements for being a person? Although Roman Catholic authors frequently refer to *Donum Vitae* to make the point that the Congregation for the Doctrine of the Faith has not pronounced definitively on when a "person" begins, they nevertheless argue that human life is to be given the benefit of the doubt and granted full protection from conception onwards.[20]

The origins of an individual human being are more complex than allowed for by the Congregation. Lisa Sowle Cahill, professor of theology at Boston College, observed that those authors who decline to accept that pre-embryos should be given the moral status of persons tend to do so for two reasons. First, about 60 percent of fertilized ova do not survive beyond the blastocyst stage of development. Second, individuality is not established in zygotes or in pre-embryos.[21] A single zygote can give rise to identical twins. Therefore, a unique genetic code does not guarantee individuality. In very rare cases two pre-embryos of different genetic origin can fuse to become one individual. Thus, individuality is not established until about the fourteenth day after fertilization. Twinning is almost certainly precluded after the formation of a structure known as the primitive streak.[22] All this has profound theological and ethical implications.

Traditional Catholic accounts of the distinctive nature of human persons rest on two assumptions. First, one's personhood cannot be shared with others. Second, God cannot infuse a single soul into two or more bodies. Fr. Norman Ford maintained that the primitive streak has to be formed before the infusion of a soul. He argued that irreversible individuation is an essential precondition for personal human life. Ford's position is supported by a number of other Catholic ethicists, including Thomas Shannon, Allan Wolter, and Richard McCormick, and also from the published works of two Catholic scientists—Carlos Bedate and Robert Cefalo. The notion of a pre-embryo as a person does not seem plausible. This strengthened the position of those who argue that absolute protection for the pre-embryo is not warranted. If the pre-embryo is not actually a person, then there is no absolute moral obligation to grant it human rights.[23]

Mark Johnson, professor of moral theology at Marquette University, argued in opposition to the above view. He believed that the "biological unity" evident in the zygote and in the pre-embryo indicates the probable existence of a human being—notwithstanding the fact that it is "difficult to find certitude in biology, and even more difficult to apply biology with certitude to theology."[24] He observed that identical (monozygotic) twins occurs very rarely. Therefore, it is difficult to justify viewing such births as normal occurrences when evaluating the importance of biological data.[25] Jean Porter, of the University of Notre Dame, did not find Johnson's philosophical interpretation of biological findings persuasive. From a statistical perspective, however, biology seems to favor Johnson's position. If the vast majority of pre-embryos do not divide to become twins, then it cannot be easily denied that they are "identical" with the persons that they will eventually become. On this basis, therefore, all zygotes and pre-embryos should be given the benefit of the doubt and be treated as persons with all the rights that that entails. Porter conceded that this is an arguable position but disagreed with it. She believed that the potential for twinning, rather than its frequency, is the basis of the argument against the personhood of the zygote or pre-embryo. But she did express doubts about her opinion that some human organisms are not human persons. This line of reasoning enabled her to move closer to the teaching of the magisterium and to regard zygotes and pre-embryos as if they were persons, in terms of rights.[26]

Thomas A. Shannon, professor of religion and social ethics at Worcester Polytechnic Institute, adopted a position similar to Porter's, maintaining that an organism's genotype does not automatically bestow individuality, which is an essential prerequisite for personhood.[27] The differences of opinion between Shannon and Johnson arose mainly from their contrasting philosophical perspectives. Johnson emphasized normal development in embryogenesis; Shannon focused on the exceptions.[28] Another argument used by Shannon was the distinction between potentiality and actuality. An acorn is potentially an oak tree but is not yet an oak tree. Similarly, a blastocyst is potentially a person but is not actually a person. In view of "the less than personal status" of the pre-embryo, some research to ascertain the efficacy of embryonic stem cell therapy is justifiable in principle. Shannon declared his respect for the teachings of the magisterium on the moral status of human pre-embryos, but he was, nevertheless, not able to accept that they should be regarded as persons.[29]

Catholic ethicists expressed a range of opinions on a number of biomedical issues. Even those authors who firmly accept the precepts of *Donum Vitae* do not always reach consensus. Some ethical questions remain unanswered. For example, Is it morally licit for a woman to act as a surrogate mother for the purpose of "rescuing" a frozen embryo from certain death when it has been deemed surplus to requirements? A number of authors, all in agreement with the teachings of *Donum Vitae*, were divided on how to interpret this document in answering the above question. These included Bishop Elio Sgreccia, vice president of the Pontifical Academy for Life; Dr. William E. May, William B. Smith, Germain Grisez, Geoffrey Surtees, Mary Geach, and Helen Watt.[30]

It is likely that Catholic ethicists feel somewhat overwhelmed, at least occasionally, by multiple reports of progress emanating from the twin domains of science and technology.[31] Concerns about the role of science in the creation, manipulation, and termination of human life are not, of course, exclusive to the domain of Roman Catholicism. Objections to the inappropriate uses of science and technology are expressed by those of varying religious beliefs and none, including scientists. In view of the broad scope and complexity of bioethics, however, orthodox Roman Catholic views will continue to be the main focus of attention.

New Frontiers

From a papal perspective, Western civilization was in the grip of a "culture of death." IVF, which seemed to be "at the service of life," was in reality creating "new threats against life."[32] In April 1991 the College of Cardinals convened to discuss the lack of due regard for the dignity of human life in contemporary Western society. At the end of the meeting the cardinals called upon Pope John Paul II to speak out authoritatively on the issue. After four years of consultation and drafting, the pope responded with his eleventh encyclical, *Evangelium Vitae* ("The Gospel of Life").[33] The encyclical is a complex document, relating Catholic moral doctrine to the freedoms of modern democratic states. Only those aspects of the encyclical pertaining to science will be discussed here.

John Paul condemned contraception, induced abortion, the destruction of embryos arising from IVF, and euthanasia. The misuse of science, he believed, was playing a key role in the increasing incidence of abortion. Massive investments in the development of pharmaceutical products were making it possible to terminate the life of the fetus in the mother's womb without relying on medical intervention. The pope grossly exaggerated the magnitude of the problem when he expressed the opinion that scientific research seemed to be "almost exclusively preoccupied" with developing new and more effective abortifacients, which would in turn place the practice of induced abortion beyond "any kind of control or social responsibility" (par. 13). Liberal democracies, permeated by the promotion of individualism, permitted, or were giving consideration to, practices that would violate the human rights of its weakest citizens (par. 20). These included unborn children, the severely handicapped, the elderly—especially those who were not economically self-sufficient, and those who were terminally ill (par. 15). In this socio-political milieu the threats against life were growing stronger and these threats were "scientifically and systematically programmed" (par. 17). God was forgotten and marginalized. A "certain technical and scientific way of thinking" had developed in contemporary culture that was "prevalent" and, apparently, had led to a rejection of God and his plan for life. Human life was relegated from the status of the sacred to the lowly level of a mere "thing," to be owned, controlled, and, if deemed appropriate, to be rejected (par. 22). Near the end of the lengthy encyclical John Paul returned yet again to the subject of contraception. He believed, despite his awareness of widespread opposition to the idea, that natural methods of controlling fertility were becoming increasingly effective. Therefore, it would be easier for married couples to make choices that were compatible with the moral teaching of the church (par. 97).

In the liberal Western democracies, which the pope seems to have had particularly in mind, *Evangelium Vitae* made little impact on public opinion.[34] Furthermore, developments in the biological sciences continue to generate a considerable degree of controversy. In February 1997 the birth of Dolly the sheep, the first successfully cloned mammal, aroused widespread public interest in the potential applications of cloning and related techniques. Jan Wilmut and K. H. S. Campbell and their team of scientists at the Roslin Institute, Edinburgh, removed the nucleus from an ovum, leaving only its mitochondrial DNA—which is less than one percent of the total cellular DNA in mammals. They then transferred the nucleus of an adult somatic cell (not a reproductive cell) into the ovum. Therefore, the transferred nucleus contained a copy of almost all the genetic inheritance of the donor. The ovum with its new nucleus was then manipulated so that it behaved as though it were fertilized and proceeded to divide and multiply in the normal way. In previous years it had been thought that somatic cells in higher animal species, which had become functionally specialized (differentiated) with the growth and development of the organism, could not be manipulated to become totipotent—that is, could not be induced to reacquire their former potential to develop into any type of cell.

It was clear that if a mammal, such as a sheep, could be cloned by somatic cell nuclear transfer (SCNT), then there was no reason, at least theoretically, why a similar procedure could not be used to reproduce humans. Most states reacted strongly against such an idea; however, a number of states, such as Britain and Ireland, did not legislate explicitly to prohibit it.[35] The Vatican responded through the medium of its Pontifical Academy for Life, comprised of moral philosophers, theologians, and scientists. In its document *Reflections on Cloning* (1997), the Academy observed that the duplication of body structure did not "necessarily imply a perfectly identical person in his ontological and psychological reality." There is a limit to what science can achieve. The spiritual soul—an essential element of every human being—can be created only directly by God. It cannot be created by the parents, or by cloning, or by means of artificial fertilization. Furthermore, psychological development and environmental conditions invariably lead to the formation of unique personalities. This is clearly the case with identical twins, who inherit the same genetic blueprint.

The Academy associated the aspiration for human cloning with eugenics and condemned it for this reason among others. The prospect of human cloning was seen to have much in common with a number of activities linked to industrial production, such as market research, the refinement of experimentation, and the incessant creation of new products. Women were seen as victims of an immoral exploitative process, reduced to the level of biological resources, suppliers of wombs and ovaries for the fabrication of humans in laboratories. In this imaginary environment, basic human relationships, such as parenthood, were "perverted." Thus, a woman could be "the twin sister of her mother, lack a biological father and be the daughter of her grandfather." It was argued that IVF had already led to "the confusion of parentage." Cloning would bring about an extreme escalation of this problem.

The Academy envisaged that even if the practice of reproductive cloning was limited in its frequency, it would still have a disproportionately adverse effect because it would tend to encourage an attitude that viewed humans in terms of biological characteristics rather than as individuals with distinct personalities. In this cultural milieu, the dignity of the clone would be deeply affected. The clone, although only a biological copy of another human being, would suffer a crisis of identity arising from an awareness of its counterpart.

The threat of human cloning was seen to arise from a number of related developments, such as the moral malaise of Western civilization, the abandonment of belief in God, and the emergence of scientific practices unrestrained by ethical principles. However, the Academy did not limit its argument to moral principles based entirely on religion. It invoked two principles of human rights: the principle of equality and the principle of nondiscrimination. Violation of the principle of equality was thought to occur because some individuals would have total domination over their fellow human beings. Discrimination was discerned in the selective-eugenic aspect of cloning, by which biological traits were selected and manipulated on the basis of arbitrary or utilitarian criteria. The Academy observed that a resolution of the European Parliament on 12 March 1997 clearly stated that human cloning was contrary to the above two principles, and it called for a prohibition of such a procedure to uphold the dignity of human beings. The Academy stated near the end of its *Reflections* that it did not reject the idea of human cloning on the basis that it was an extremely artificial means of procreation. Rather, human cloning was rejected because it was thought contrary to the dignity of procreation and to the dignity of the person who was subjected to the procedure.[36]

Reproduction of the organism is not usually the objective in cloning projects. Cloning techniques generally are applied to animals to produce pre-embryos as sources of stem cells. These cells are extracted from the inner cell mass of a five- to six-day-old pre-embryo, which is destroyed in the process. At present most of the existing human embryonic stem cell lines are those derived from unused blastocysts created for couples undergoing IVF therapy. These stem cells are used for scientific research, and it is hoped that, sometime in the future, stem cells will be produced by SCNT to be used for the replacement of diseased or deficient tissues because of their potential to generate any type of tissue. SCNT permits the use of the patient's own genetic material. This in turn overcomes the problem of an immune rejection response from the patient's body because the genetically identical cells are not recognized as foreign tissue. However, there is much scientific research yet to be done before therapeutic cloning becomes possible. In February 2004 Woo Suk Hwang and his team of scientists at the Seoul National University in South Korea claimed to have obtained stem cells from one of thirty human blastocysts that they created through SCNT. The results indicated the enormous technical difficulties in creating stem cells from pre-embryos in this way. Nevertheless, it now seemed that therapeutic cloning would be possible in humans.[37] However, such a possibility receded further into the future in January 2006 when an investigative committee at Seoul National University concluded that two published research papers by Hwang and his coauthors contained fabricated data.

Obtaining stem cells is only the first step in generating new tissues and organs. Cultured neurons, for example, would be useful only if they were placed in the nervous system and manipulated to make the appropriate connections to other neurons. The differentiation process will have to be regulated to produce the appropriate kind of cell and to avoid undesirable tissue types and cancerous tumors.

It is important to observe that stem cells can be obtained from sources other than pre-embryos—from the umbilical cord of newly born babies and from some tissues in adults such as bone marrow. However, it is thought by many scientists that adult stem cells are differentiated to some extent and do not have the same variable potential as embryonic stem cells. Furthermore, there are formidable technical obstacles to the identification, retrieval, and propagation of these cells.[38] In September 2002 the Vatican informed the United Nations that it supported scientific research on stem cells of postnatal origin as an ethical and promising way of furthering possibilities for transplantation and cell therapies in the medical sciences. On the same occasion it took the opportunity to reiterate its condemnation of human reproductive cloning and the intended use of human embryonic stem cells for research.[39]

Embryonic stem cells are the most promising, but moral objections arise from the fact that pre-embryos have to be sacrificed to obtain them. If it could be shown that some cloned human pre-embryos were not viable, then would it be morally acceptable to sacrifice them for the advancement of biomedical science? Some ethicists and scientists answer in the affirmative. Some lower forms of life, such as insects and reptiles can reproduce through parthenogenesis ("virgin births"). In mammals parthenogenesis can be induced under laboratory conditions when ova are manipulated to retain two sets of chromosomes instead of the normal single set, and stimulated to divide as if they had been fertilized. The resultant embryos do not have the capacity to develop into human beings. Parthenogenetic human pre-embryos have been created and developed as far as the blastocyst stage by a research team led by David Wininger at the biotech company Stemron in the United States. Stem cells extracted from one of the pre-embryos survived for a few days. But stem cells derived from parthenogenetic human pre-embryos have limited potential because they will be able to provide matching stem cells only for a limited range of patients, excluding men and post-menopausal women. Much research has yet to be done to see if stem cells produced in this way can give rise to normal tissues.[40] From an orthodox Roman Catholic perspective this area of scientific research is immoral because, as noted earlier, it violates the prohibition, expressed in *Donum Vitae*, against creating human embryos by asexual means.

The outcome of scientific research in recent years has created some bizarre possibilities—even if some of these are remote possibilities owing to a range of formidable technical obstacles, ethical objections, and legal prohibitions. Scientists in Japan and the United States succeeded in their efforts to transform mouse embryonic stem cells into ova and spermatozoa. This suggests that all forms of infertility might be amenable to treatment in the future. It even indicates that two men could become genetic parents of the same child with the aid of a surrogate mother, if samples of their body cells are manipulated to eventually become gametes.[41] In April 2004 a similar line of research led to the strange announcement that Kaguya, the Japanese "homoparental" mouse, was created when Tomohiro Kono and his scientific team at the Tokyo University of Agriculture fused two ova and manipulated their DNA so that the new cell behaved like a fertilized ovum. The mouse, therefore, had two mothers and no father. In theory it demonstrated the future possibility that a child could be born of a lesbian couple without recourse to a sperm donor.[42] Other highly controversial and ethically questionable lines of scientific research include interspecies cloning leading to the production of rabbit-human stem cells and the creation of sheep-human chimeras as sources of organs for transplantation to humans.[43]

The Roman Catholic Church, in principle, is not opposed to xenotransplantation, which is the transplantation of organs, tissues, and cells from one species to another. From a theological perspective humankind is placed at the summit of creation. In view of the fact that animals are treated as sources of food and clothing and harnessed for work, there is no ethical objection to the proposal that scientific research may present opportunities for the introduction of an additional kind of service. Animals could be used as sources of organs and tissues, which would be of great medical value in view of the very limited number of human donors.

The Pontifical Academy for Life observed that there is very little empirical data concerning the transplantation of animal tissues or organs to humans. It is, therefore, extremely difficult to assess the risks. It is possible that micro-organisms that are not harmful to animals could become pathogenic in human recipients and that such diseases could become contagious. The Academy recommended that patients be quarantined and that those in close contact with them be monitored. Other risk factors, such as the likelihood of infections arising from immunosuppressive therapies, are better understood, although there is need of further research here also. Patients are to be informed about the risks involved and about alternative therapies if these are available.[44]

It is critically important that the implantation of animal tissue not psychologically traumatize the patient. Counseling services have to be provided. The identity of the person has to be safeguarded. Some tissues and organs contribute more than others to the personal identity of the patient. The Academy observed that some tissues and organs are of crucial importance to the identity of the person, such as the encephalon (the brain) and the gonads, when, in the latter case, these glands are supplied for the purpose of supplying spermatozoa and ova rather than merely as sources of hormones. The transplantation of these organs could never be morally permissible.[45] The Academy's moral strictures based on these examples seem superfluous when cognizance is taken of the central importance of the brain, the implications of xenotransplantation, and—especially in the case of the brain—the present state of medical science.

The Academy insisted that the stress, pain, and sacrifice of animals for human benefit should be kept to a minimum. This was especially true of transgenic animals. These are animals whose genotypes are modified by the insertion of one or more genes of a different species, sometimes of human origin. These changes will be passed on to the offspring. The Academy believed that this type of genetic engineering is acceptable when a number of ethical guidelines are adhered to, such as an assessment and control of any adverse effects of human gene expression in animals. Transgenic animals are to be maintained under conditions of high security to prevent them from escaping into the natural environment.

A central feature of the Academy's guidelines is the emphasis on constructing a cost–benefit analysis, relating to the patient and to the economic aspect of the health services. The Academy took cognizance of the argument that xenotransplantation therapy might consume such a large quantity of resources from the health services that it would lead to diminished support for other kinds of therapeutic treatment. Nevertheless, it argued that if the cautious acquisition of new knowledge shifted xenotransplantation mainly from the experimental phase to an advanced level of clinical treatment, then the heavy use of resources would be justified on the basis that lives would be saved when otherwise there was no hope of survival.

At present there seems to be much greater concern about the prospect of human reproductive cloning than about xenotransplantation. Catholics and non-Catholics alike anticipate that some scientists will undertake research without due regard for the dignity of human life. These scientists are probably in a very small minority. In September 2003 the scientific academies of sixty-three countries submitted a joint declaration to the United Nations demanding a worldwide ban on reproductive cloning. They argued that no ban should be imposed on therapeutic cloning because of its great potential benefit to the biomedical sciences.[46]

How likely is it that a cloned baby will be born in the next few years? According to Clonaid, a company set up by the Raelian cult, human cloning has already been achieved. At a press conference in early January

2003 Clonaid announced that the first cloned child—Eve—was born on 26 December 2002, at an undisclosed location. Statements made by the controversial Italian medical scientist Severino Antinori, and by his colleague Panayiotis Zavos, indicate that Clonaid is not alone in its endeavors. But no case of human reproductive cloning has yet been verified. That may soon change. The essential resources are not so great to rule it out. These include an estimated minimum of one million American dollars, a small team of scientists, and a large number of ova—which, in the case of a religious cult, could be supplied by a more than adequate number of volunteers. Other key resources are a micromanipulator and a skilled technician to operate it so that nuclei can be extracted from ova and be replaced by adult cell nuclei.[47] Experimental data derived from research in therapeutic cloning will probably be of great assistance to aspiring reproductive cloners.

It has been argued that a lack of consensus at the United Nations makes it easier for someone in search of fame or financial reward to be the first to clone a human being. The Vatican and the United States played leading roles in attempts to introduce a global ban on both reproductive and therapeutic cloning. They were supported by a number of states, many of which were mainly Roman Catholic, and some of which were Islamic.[48] There was broad agreement on reproductive cloning, but proposals for a total ban met with stiff opposition. Some national governments, including those of Britain, South Korea, Singapore, China, and Japan, saw great potential benefit in embryonic stem cell research and granted generous financial assistance to promote it.[49] It would have been possible to overcome the impasse by banning reproductive cloning and agreeing to negotiate on therapeutic cloning at a later date. But Spain and a number of other countries objected to this proposal because they maintained that there was no moral or legal distinction between the two procedures.[50]

Confusion prevailed, in the UN and elsewhere. In the United States no federal legislation was in place.[51] This seemed strange in view of the fact that the administration of President George W. Bush was unambiguously opposed to cloning. Many politicians were dissatisfied with a partial ban, anticipating that those scientists who were not constrained by ethical principles could transfer a cloned embryo, created for stem cell research, to a woman's uterus instead.[52] On the other side of the Atlantic, the European Parliament failed to gain consensus, with the result that member states were left to decide for themselves. In 2004 the United Nations was still deadlocked on the issue of whether to opt for a total ban or not. Even if consensus is achieved, it might have very little impact. An international treaty prohibiting human reproductive cloning would be operative only in the signatory states. Non-signatory states could still allow such cloning to occur in their jurisdictions. Each country that signed up would have to enact legislation to effect the treaty's provisions, which could take years. Furthermore, UN treaties are often breached without fear of punitive action because, frequently, enforcement mechanisms are not in place.[53]

The arguments against human reproductive cloning are particularly strong. First, research data from experimentation on animals indicates that, in humans, there would be an extremely high failure rate, which is a formidable problem, given the very limited supply of human ova. Dolly the sheep was the only animal born from a total of 277 oocyte-donor nucleus fusions at the Roslin Institute. Second, the cloning process is far from perfect, and the majority of those cloned animals born to date have suffered from a wide range of deformities, some so severe that the animals had to be put down. Dolly developed arthritis, which was not typical for a sheep of her age and died prematurely in February 2003. Third, cloned animals and their placentas can be much larger than normal, thus greatly endangering the health and life of the surrogate mothers and resulting in higher than normal fatality rates. Given the present state of scientific knowledge, human reproductive cloning would contribute greatly to human suffering and death. These findings provide compelling moral arguments against human reproductive cloning, and, for these reasons at least, the Roman Catholic Church will not be alone in vigorously opposing such a practice.

The church will find much less support for its opposition to therapeutic cloning. In terms of bioethics, reproductive cloning and therapeutic cloning are in very different locations in the moral spectrum, ranging from what is deemed to be repugnant to what is considered tolerable, desirable, or even compelling.[54] It has already been observed that there is a range of ethical and technical problems associated with the generation of stem cells from individually cloned pre-embryos. Research on mouse pre-embryos by Bob Lanza and his colleagues at Advanced Cell Technology in Worcester, Massachusetts, indicates that it may be possible in the near future to extract stem cells from human pre-embryos without destroying the embryos.[55] It may be, however, that treating patients with embryonic stem cells is inherently impracticable, especially because of the shortage of human ova.[56] There are also formidable obstacles to be overcome if xenotransplantation is to be used to replace human organs and tissues. It is possible that these procedures may lose their net beneficial potential if scientists gain an understanding of how cells can be induced to change from a differentiated state to an unspecialized condition so that they can be further manipulated to produce personalized tissues without recourse to egg or embryo, and without risk of mutation or cancer. It is likely that clinical treatment arising from such progress is decades away.

Research in the biomedical sciences is driven by investment from both the public sector and private companies. The Roman Catholic Church does not object to companies in the private sector making profits on their investments. Indeed it would be conspicuously irrational for the church to do so, since the profit motive is of central importance in stimulating enterprise. Investment in the broader arena of the biosciences promises to yield generous dividends. Pharmaceutical companies have gained enormously from advances in genetic engineering. Recombinant DNA technology has enabled the transfer of genes from one species to another, giving rise to transgenic organisms that can be used for a variety of purposes. For example, bacteria can be genetically modified by the insertion of the appropriate human gene to synthesize insulin for the treatment of diabetes. In the agricultural sector genetically modified varieties of cotton, maize, soya, and tomato have been cultivated with certain advantageous characteristics in mind. In tomatoes, for example, a gene that speeds up the process of decay was removed, thus prolonging the shelf life of the product. Other crops have been genetically modified to withstand the toxic effects of herbicides so that weeds can be controlled with greater efficiency.

Those who support the cultivation of genetically modified (GM) crops claim that the new technology will play a key role in boosting world food supplies. Those who are opposed, skeptical, or cautious, point to a number of contraindications that need to be taken into account. There is uncertainty about the long-term effects of GM crops on human health and on the environment. GM crops may lead to a reduction of biodiversity and may impact adversely on the agricultural systems of economically disadvantaged nations. The transfer of genes from one species to another also poses risks to animal welfare. Transgenic animals, such as pigs, have suffered from a range of health problems, including arthritis and blindness, arising from the expression of human genes. More scientific research needs to be done, and more stringent safety procedures need to be developed and applied in response to the above problems. Those who support inter-species gene transfer argue that risk factors are invariably associated with any new technology. This raises a number of questions. Do the benefits outweigh the risks? Who is most likely to gain? Who is likely to lose?[57] Those Roman Catholics who are aware of the issues will form judgments on the basis of promoting the common good, safeguarding the environment, and ensuring that animals are not subjected to unnecessary suffering. In these matters they will have much in common with those outside the church.

The social teaching of the Catholic Church does not condemn capitalism, but it does condemn the excesses of the system that are contrary to the common good. On 25 March 2002 Pope John Paul II condemned inappropriate scientific research programs funded by pharmaceutical companies that are driven by the profit motive to cater for "the medicine of desires." Research projects consistent with ethics and justice, which required greater investment, more time, and yielded lower profits, are neglected because the overriding concern of the pharmaceutical industry is for maximum financial gain. John Paul condemned scientific research programs that gave rise to contraceptive products. In contrast to this, he claimed, there is little support for research to prevent and treat infertility. Profits take precedence over ethics. The pope saw the same tendency at work when he observed that embryonic stem cell research is attracting large investors while the "ethically acceptable and scientifically valid programs" using adult stem cells draw very little support because projected profit margins are less. Pharmacological consumerism reigns supreme. In economically advanced states vast amounts of money are spent on the development and production of medicines for "hedonistic purposes," while in the poorer states there is little or no access to the most basic of medical products.

The Roman Catholic Church has frequently been castigated for infringing on the rightful freedom of science. Possibly with this in mind the pope now pointed to a growing trend that restricts the freedom of scientists to pursue the primary aim of science—to discover "the truth." Those who lobby for the practice of science free of ethical constraints are unwittingly promoting the subservience of science to economic interests. The primacy of ethics has to be established, but the pope did not express confidence in pharmaceutical companies to create an economic environment driven by virtuous motivation. Instead he looked to public authorities, whose primary role is to uphold the common good. This means that scientific research will have to be carried out under conditions where the pursuit of commercial profit is reconciled with the good of society. This entails the imposition of restrictions on unethical research and the allocation of public funding for research worthy of support but neglected by the private sector. Government sponsored projects are to take cognizance of poverty-stricken nations, which lack the necessary resources to conduct scientific research for their economic development.[58]

Governments, of course, do not always serve the common good and frequently work against it in pursuance of their own political interests.[59] And public sector companies cannot be relied upon to prioritize ethics over profit. Therefore, the autonomy of science will continue to be substantially compromised by its economic dependency on the public and private sectors, where support is usually given conditionally.

The Roman Catholic Church has genuine grounds for concern about where biomedical technology may be leading. But it has damaged its credibility to a large extent by opposing techniques and products that do function in the service of humankind. As observed earlier, a very large majority of Roman Catholics have disagreed, and continue to disagree, with the official teaching of the church on contraception. Many married couples, intending to act as responsible parents, limit the size of their families by using artificial contraceptive methods instead of the less reliable rhythm method advocated by the church. Others turn to IVF treatment as a means of last resort to overcome infertility. Contrary to magisterial opinions from on high, many Roman Catholics will follow their own consciences and will not be unduly influenced by abstract theological principles that are not clearly necessary for a Christian way of life.

12

Reflections

In Search of God

IN CHRISTIAN DOCTRINE THE ORIGINS OF EVERYTHING CAN BE traced back to God—"in the beginning God created the heavens and the earth" (Gen. 1:1). John 1:3 declares that the universe was created *ex nihilo*—"through him all things were made; without him nothing was made that has been made." The Roman Catholic profession of faith, inspired by scripture, begins with an expression of belief in "one God, the Father, the Almighty, maker of heaven and earth, of all that is, seen and unseen."[1] Without God, Roman Catholic theology, in common with Christian belief generally, is utterly meaningless. Even life itself can seem grim and futile. The idea that humankind owes its existence to some blind, purposeless evolutionary process does not satisfy human psychological needs. Many believe that there is little sense or purpose to human existence if God is excluded from the explanation.

Human needs run deeper than a desire for intellectually satisfying answers to the fundamental questions of life. For believers, God offers security, protection, and consolation, especially in times of persecution, distress, and tragedy. Belief in God can satisfy deep-seated psychological needs. Conversely, the prospect of a godless universe can be a source of intense despair. The French philosopher and scientist Blaise Pascal (1623–1662) vividly described his feelings about humankind, God, and the universe in his *Pensées*.

> When I see the blind and wretched state of man, when I survey the whole universe in its dumbness and man left to himself with no light, as though lost in this corner of the universe, without knowing who put him there, what he has come to do, what will become of him when he dies, incapable

of knowing anything, I am moved to terror. . . . I marvel that so wretched a state does not drive people to despair.[2]

Pascal was intensely aware of human limitations and of his relative insignificance in a vast universe. He sought comfort from God, who was "nothing less than our redeemer from wretchedness." He believed that it was possible to "know" God through Jesus Christ, whose divine status in turn could be ascertained by the fulfillment of biblical prophecies. Otherwise, it was impossible to obtain absolute proof that God exists.[3] His God, therefore, was not the God of philosophers and scientists.

Many Catholic philosophers and theologians disagreed with the opinions expressed by Pascal. For centuries the Five Ways of St. Thomas Aquinas seemed to offer robust arguments for belief in God. By the late twentieth century, however, many Catholics had lost confidence in the Five Ways.[4] Other traditional arguments had also been weakened. Paley's watchmaker analogy was a convincing one for theists, but for those who were not it fell far short of solid proof. Persisting with the old discredited arguments could only damage the credibility of belief in God. But relying on faith alone was not satisfactory from a rational perspective. In the absence of sound arguments, belief in God would not be intellectually respectable and could be dismissed as a mere superstition. It seems that Catholic prelates and their theological advisors realized this in 1870, when the First Vatican Council declared that God could be known "with certainty from the consideration of created things, by the natural power of human reason." This pronouncement about God was reaffirmed by the Second Vatican Council in *Dei Verbum*, its Dogmatic Constitution on Divine Revelation (18 November 1965).[5] But does the study of nature lead inevitably to God? St. George Jackson Mivart thought not, arguing that "God will not allow himself to be caught at the bottom of any man's crucible, or yield Himself to the experiments of gross-minded and irreverent inquirers." In his opinion, evidence for the God of Christianity was not clearly established on the basis of reason alone. The "Christian system" is one which puts the strain on "every faculty of man's higher nature . . . A moral element enters into the acceptance of that system . . . it evidently has not been the intention of the Creator to make the evidence of His existence so plain that its non-recognition would be the mark of intellectual incapacity." Mivart believed that it was futile to search for divine action in nature "such that no one could sanely deny it."[6]

Many Christians, both Catholic and Protestant, have taken a different view. Some looked to science to bolster their beliefs.[7] In the twentieth century, for example, they saw the creative hand of God in the birth of the universe as postulated by the Big Bang theory. In the 1960s Arno Penzias and Robert Wilson discovered the existence of cosmic microwave background radiation—the residual heat from the great primordial explosion. This consolidated the position of the Big Bang as the most satisfactory scientific explanation of cosmic origins. As astrophysicists extended their knowledge and understanding of the cosmos they calculated that an incredibly small variation in any one of a number of physical constants would have resulted in the evolution of a totally different universe. Precise values of physical constants—such as the ratio of the mass of the proton to the electron, the charge of the electron, Planck's constant, gravitational force, the velocity of light—were all essential for the eventual emergence of life.[8] All this gave rise to the anthropic cosmological principle. This was a new version of the design argument, and a much improved account in that there was no need for divine intervention in the evolutionary process after the creation event. Humankind's privileged status in the universe, it seemed, had been restored. From an atheistic perspective there was a major difficulty in explaining away the enormous improbability of the universe that had supposedly evolved to its present condition by chance. It seemed as if it had been designed and fine-tuned with humans in mind.

Atheists responded in a number of ways to the anthropic cosmological principle, arguing that there were errors in the mathematical calculations and that life could have evolved under many different conditions. Many philosophers accept that the universe is finely tuned but do not accept the existence of an intelligent designer. How then do they explain the statistical improbability of the universe evolving as it did by chance? It is argued, for example, that physical laws and constants are not the same throughout the universe and, therefore, that statistical probabilities favor the emergence of life in some regions. However, all the evidence available supports the claim that laws and constants are the same everywhere in the universe. Furthermore, the science of astrophysics is based on the assumption that this is the case.

The anthropic principle was sometimes opposed on the basis that there was, or still is, more than one universe. Given numerous universes, it could then be argued that life could arise in at least one of them. There are two variants of this argument: (1) an oscillating universe giving rise to a series of universes; and (2) the notion of parallel universes. A formidable objection against both arguments is that there is very little if any evidence to support them. The oscillating hypothesis is groundless because it has not been established that the density of matter is sufficiently high to eventually overcome the outward thrust of the Big Bang to cause a Big Crunch. Even if such a contraction or implosion occurred, it is not clear that this would in turn lead to another Big Bang creating a new universe.

A minority of physicists favor the idea of parallel universes, but this idea is highly speculative. The concept of parallel universes is scientifically weak because it lacks evidence. It is philosophically unsound because it contravenes the respected philosophical principle: if two theories possess equal explanatory power then accept the simpler of the two. Ockham's razor dictates that entities are not to be increased beyond necessity.

Both science and philosophy then seem supportive of belief in some kind of creative supernatural force.[9] However, this does not mean that there is overwhelming evidence for the existence of an omnipotent supernatural being. Scientist and theologian Alister E. McGrath argued that, although the anthropic principle is "strongly consistent" with theism, it does not prove the existence of God.[10] A similar opinion was expressed by Ernan McMullin, Catholic philosopher of science at the University of Notre Dame. He observed that as early as 1981 the anthropic principle was already showing signs of weakness as "inflationary" explanations of early cosmic expansion were indicating that the remarkable coincidences of physical constants might not be so extremely improbable after all. The debate was in a very fluid state, and McMullin concluded that the best that can be hoped for is "consonance." From this perspective, belief in the Creator, in the Christian sense, is in harmony with contemporary cosmological theory. Although it is "much less than proof," it is "more than logical consistency."[11]

The observations of the American Catholic theologian James A. Wiseman were supportive of McMullin's position when he pointed to weaknesses in the anthropic principle in his book *Theology and Modern Science: Quest for Coherence* (2002). Some authors who are professedly religious are wary about using the anthropic principle in the service of theology because of their awareness that the progress of science may lead to the construction of scientific explanations that will show that there is nothing remarkably coincidental about physical constants. A fundamental theory of physics may be devised that will demonstrate that the constants could not have been different from their present values. The basis of the argument, therefore, is essentially an objection to the erroneous notion of a "God-of-the-gaps," where supernatural intervention is postulated when no scientific explanations are available.[12]

Physics and chemistry seem more supportive of belief in God than biology. This is probably because of the central importance of Darwin's theory in the life sciences. Two of its central features, random change and natural selection, can be invoked to reject the contention of intelligent design in nature. Theists have argued in response that the evolution and development of life are sustained and guided by God. This in turn has been challenged, especially by Richard Dawkins. In his book *The Blind Watchmaker* (1991), he expressed little patience with such an argument because, he observed, it is not possible to prove or disprove it, especially if God's intervention in nature produced the same results, or very similar effects, to what could be expected from natural selection working alone. Therefore, God is dismissed as "superfluous" on the basis that God does not offer a rational explanation for the organized complexity in nature.[13] This anti-teleological stance is difficult to refute in the biological sciences, but it leaves the anthropic principle untouched.

Biological evolution is postulated in a universe where the physical and chemical conditions are precisely set for the emergence and development of life. Yet it is easy to overestimate the power of science as an instrument to detect a divine presence in the universe. Science has its limitations, as theologians have frequently pointed out. Much of physical reality can be explained in terms of physical laws, but this does not penetrate to the core of reality, which is too "big" for science to explain.[14] Science, for example, cannot explain why the universe exists. Generally, scientists do not dispute this. Stephen Hawking, in his *Brief History of Time*, reflected on what was behind physical laws and why the universe existed. But he did not rely on religious faith when confronted with the inherent limitations of his discipline. Instead he referred to one of a series of arguments put forward by the philosopher David Hume against St. Thomas Aquinas's proofs for the existence of God. Hawking posed the question: if God created the universe, who created God?[15] If we accept that everything has a cause, why make an exception for God? To make such an exception is seen as undermining the very foundation of the argument.[16] The standard theological response to Hume and Hawking is that the cause of God is within God and that God has always existed. However, for those who do not embrace religious faith, this point of view is dismissed on the basis that it is dogmatic rather than rational. From an agnostic perspective, the eternity of God is as difficult to understand as the idea of an infinitely old universe. Even more perplexing is the notion that a finitely old universe could have somehow caused itself.[17]

Catholic theologians are cautious about relying on science to counter assertions of agnosticism and atheism. For centuries they felt the need to protect themselves against theories emanating from science, and they became quite adept at exposing its limits and weaknesses. Therefore, in some theological quarters, it was felt that the natural sciences had little to contribute to a consolidation of religious faith. A god proved by science would be at the mercy of science. There was always the danger that a creator proved on the basis of a scientific theory would be abandoned if the theory was later overturned. This is particularly true of physics. This discipline lacks logical consistency because no satisfactory theory was devised that unites quantum mechanics with general relativity.[18]

At the dawn of the twenty-first century cosmological theories were in a state of flux. It seemed that the emergence of the universe from a singularity—infinitely small, infinitely hot and dense—might not have occurred. Some mathematical calculations suggested that the Big Bang occurred without the singularity and that it was not the origin of the universe. String theory, which has gained widespread acceptance among physicists, predicts the existence of new particles and forces, and six or seven spatial dimensions additional to the three already observed. It suggests an infinitely old universe enduring forever. Future scientific research may even reveal some information about the pre–Big Bang epoch. Such information may be acquired through observations of the polarization of cosmic background microwave radiation brought about by variations in the gravitational field. It is thought that this gravitational radiation may have survived from an era predating the Big Bang.[19] All of the above calls into question the idea of a universe of finite age and serves to exemplify how unreliable science can be in the service of theism. Nevertheless, it is difficult for Catholic theologians to relinquish the claim that it is possible to know that God exists—the declarations of the first and second Vatican councils, as already observed, dictated against such an opinion. What then is the role of science in arguments for the existence of God? The Catholic Church does not teach that science can prove the existence of God; rather it teaches that philosophy, assisted by science, is capable of providing such proof.

In Catholic thought an important distinction is made between questions and methods of inquiry appropriate to the natural sciences and those within the realm of philosophy. The Catholic philosopher Étienne Gilson maintained that science describes what natural things are and how they interact with each other. It does not concern itself with the ultimate cause or causes of their existence. Why does the universe exist? Why do physical things behave in regular and predictable ways? Gilson, writing in 1941, placed these questions in the domain of metaphysics—beyond the competence of the natural sciences. Science, therefore, does not cover the entire field of rational inquiry.[20]

Pope Paul VI, in his allocution to the Pontifical Academy of Sciences on 23 April 1966, placed much emphasis on the limited competency of science. It does not "exhaust the whole of reality." The scientific "truths" of today are unreliable—"dethroned tomorrow by some new discovery." Science, he believed, could not give underlying reasons for the things it discovered. The pope stated, for example, that scientific research can lead one to a greater knowledge and understanding of human anatomy and physiology, but it cannot tell us why humans exist. He asserted that scientific inquiry, if it is to stay within its proper limits, stops on the verge of the "decisive" questions. Who are we? Where did we come from? What is our future?[21]

The answers to the pope's questions depend very much on whether we were created by God as part of some cosmic plan or whether we are merely the creatures of the Blind Watchmaker as elaborated by Richard Dawkins. Those who strive to maintain intellectual integrity in addressing this issue will find little understanding for their difficulties in papal pronouncements. If the power of reason could lead to "a true and certain knowledge of the one personal God," why is it so difficult to know—rather than merely believe—that God exists? The response of Pope Pius XII in *Humani Generis* was dogmatic and harsh on this point. In the second paragraph he declared:

> The truths that have to do with God and the relations between God and men completely surpass the sensible order and demand self-surrender and self-abnegation in order to be put into practice and to influence practical life. Now the human intellect, in gaining the knowledge of such truths, is hampered both by the activity of the senses and the imagination, and by evil passions arising from original sin. Hence men easily persuade themselves in such matters that what they do not wish to believe is false or at least doubtful.

In the fourth paragraph Pius observed "the human intelligence sometimes experiences difficulties in forming a judgement about the credibility of the Catholic Faith" despite "the many wonderful external signs that God has given." The evidence was "sufficient to prove with certitude by the natural light of reason alone the divine origin of the Christian religion." But those who resisted or declined to accept "the evidence of the external proofs" did so because of "prejudice or passion or bad faith."[22] As observed in a previous chapter, Pope John Paul II supported this stance, although not quite so trenchantly. Furthermore, he stated that reason would only lead to the ascertainment of truth when it was "enlightened by faith."[23]

The papal position on the question of God's existence is not only offensive to those of a different persuasion who sincerely strive for truth; it is merely a profession of faith presenting itself as philosophy. The preliminary steps of "self-surrender," "self-abnegation," the denigration of the senses and the imagination, the suppression of "evil passions," the purging of "bad faith," the reprehension of "sinfulness," and the primacy of faith over reason, all imply a process of indoctrination rather than the pursuit of genuine philosophical discourse. If the "external signs" of God are so "many" and "wonderful," why did the Vatican councils and the popes fail to give us a few illuminating and persuasive examples?

The central weakness in the papal argument for the existence of God is that it simply assumes the existence of God—the very point at issue. The assertions of popes and Vatican councils on this matter are not the outcome of an unprejudiced debate. There is no consensus among philosophers that the arguments in favor of the existence of God are stronger than those against. Catholic theology is not an unbiased search for truth; it starts with the conclusion.[24] Therefore, given the current state of apologetics, the God of Roman Catholicism is still a hidden God, within the realm of faith.

Dissonance or Consonance?

Although the subject matter of science is neutral on the question of God's existence, it is not neutral toward all religious belief.[25] The natural sciences created problems for sustaining specific religious ideas or doctrines concerned with the interpretation of scripture. The Roman Catholic Church was slow to adapt its theology to modern scientific discoveries. In the case of Galileo it took the church about three and a half centuries to explicitly admit its error. The discoveries of science continued to create problems for Catholic theology, and these intensified in the nineteenth century. Many Catholics experienced great difficulties when they struggled to reconcile the narratives of Genesis with progressive developments in the historical, geological, and biological sciences. A favored tactic of Catholic apologists was to assert that the Bible is not intended to teach history or natural science. This was a prudent course of action when the weight of evidence in favor of science and history was very strong. Therefore, when archaeology and paleontology demonstrated that humans had emerged much earlier than allowed for by the chronologies of Genesis, Catholic apologists responded by refusing to admit that there are errors in scripture. They maintained that the chronology is not an error—it is merely "fragmentary."[26] Many critics probably found this argument implausible and disingenuous.

The Book of Genesis in particular needed to be freed from the burdensome implications of science. If God had intended to inform the readership about nature, what terminology would God have used? That of Galileo? Or Newton? Or Einstein? But all of these would become antiquated. The use of language in accordance with the "outward appearances of things" was considered to be the best method of producing a work that would "endure for ever."[27] If by these words it is meant that scripture was deliberately written in a style to make it accessible to all generations, from ancient Israel to the new Jerusalem, then it is remarkable how it became so abstruse that it engendered a multiplicity of conflicting interpretations, which in turn created and exacerbated pernicious divisions in the Christian world. Indeed, the true meanings of many verses in scripture are so difficult to ascertain that the Catholic Church, with its enormous intellectual resources, declined to issue definitive interpretations.[28] It is difficult to reconcile all this with the principle of accommodation.

Of course it was not reasonable to expect that the language of modern science would have been used in pre-Christian and early Christian times—but the protective value of this observation is limited. Mivart saw anomalies in scripture that could not be explained away by simply asserting that the inspired author's style was conditioned by the need to communicate essential spiritual truths to an unsophisticated people (the Israelites). He argued, for example, that it was unnecessary for God to inspire the use of "such misleading words" as "evening" and "morning" in the account of the days of creation.[29] The elimination of "evening" and "morning" would have facilitated an allegorical interpretation of the creation narrative—in this case the only one consistent with the established findings of modern science—without detracting from the essential message that God created everything. However, it seems that the author, influenced by the mythologies of the ancient Near East (especially Mesopotamia),[30] intended his account of creation to be understood literally.

Greater weight is added to Mivart's assertions of errors in scripture when cognizance is taken of the antievolutionary stance of one of his leading Catholic critics, Fr. Jeremiah Murphy. The Irish priest argued that if human evolution was in harmony with a true interpretation of the creation narrative in scripture then it was

> strange that no Catholic for 1800 years should have even a remote conception of this meaning. For all that time the Church taught the above revealed proposition, and for all that time the faithful believed it; and yet all along the Fathers and Theologians were ignorant of what she taught, and the faithful ignorant of what they believed – that is if Evolution be applicable to man![31]

The biblical account of the creation of humankind was so precise, he maintained, that if evolution had really occurred then the scriptural text could not have been better calculated to deceive its readers if this had been the intention of its inspired writers.[32]

The contention of scriptural error put forward by Mivart was contrary to Pope Leo XIII's *Providentissimus Deus*, which proclaimed an infallible Bible interpreted by an infallible church. Mivart was unable to reconcile himself to the principles expressed in the encyclical, declaring that, as a scientist, he should be free to reject errors in scripture such as those associated with the Fall, the Flood, and the Tower of Babel. His sense of reason was offended by some scriptural narratives. He thought it incredible that he should be obliged, as a Roman Catholic, to accept as true such incredible stories as Tobias repelling the unwelcome attentions of a demon with a fish's liver, or an angel seizing Habakkuk by his hair and flying him from Judah to Babylon for the express purpose of giving his bowl of pottage and bread to the prophet Daniel, who at the time was incarcerated with seven ravenous lions.[33] Other incredible tales included Jonah's sojourn in the belly of a whale and the solar legend of Joshua.[34] All this, he believed, stretched credibility beyond the breaking point. The passing of the twentieth century did not diminish the need for a suspension of critical faculties concerning these and some other narratives in the Bible. This, of course, is a problem for all Christians, not just Roman Catholics.

It can be argued that Mivart's foray into theology can be brushed aside on the basis that he was found to have expressed heretical views. But this does not address the substance of his critique of scripture and Catholic theology. The church authorities chose to respond by censure and excommunication rather than seriously attempting to engage in meaningful dialogue as Mivart so naively hoped they would. The infallibility of the church was a core principle of Catholicism, and its theology was based on the Bible. Mivart, in attacking both, should not have entertained any doubts about the inevitability of punitive action by the ecclesiastical authorities. If the Catholic Church conceded that there were errors in scripture this would have undermined its doctrines and its authority. Austere claims of infallibility enhanced its vulnerability. It was feared that error, once admitted, would spread like a highly contagious disease to destroy the very core of Catholic doctrine. It is likely that the ecclesiastical authorities were mindful of the anti-theological, and sometimes anti-Catholic, writings of Thomas Henry Huxley—Mivart's great antagonist. Huxley argued that if the first nine chapters of the Pentateuch were found to be unhistorical, then the historical accuracy of the remainder would be called into question. He saw religious faith in a protracted retreat before the advances of science and envisaged that eventually it would stand in isolation from "fact of any kind." Only in such a position would it be "for ever proudly inaccessible to the attacks of the infidel." In the meantime the "modern Reconcilers" would manipulate the meaning of scripture to create "some sort of non-contradiction of scientific truth."[35]

Catholic apologists were numbered among such reconcilers, and one of their most intense difficulties was harmonizing human evolution with the Genesis narrative. It was in the best interests of the church to encourage their initiatives when the constraints of dogma were respected. Instead, the ecclesiastical authorities in Rome frustrated their efforts. In the 1890s the ultraconservatives were in the ascendant. However, uncompromising opinions gradually lost ground to tolerant attitudes. This was due in no small measure to the works of Canon Henri de Dorlodot and Rev. Ernest C. Messenger in the early twentieth century. In *Humani Generis* (1950) the papacy explicitly acknowledged, for the first time, that evolutionary theory in general was a valid hypothesis. But it did not grant freedom to loyal Roman Catholics to embrace the concept of polygenism because of its apparent contradiction of the doctrine of original sin. In his "Credo of the People of God" (*Solemni hac liturgia*, 30 June 1968), Pope Paul VI declared that, in accordance with the Council of Trent, original sin, committed by Adam, is passed on from one generation to the next, "along with human nature, not by imitation but by propagation," to each individual person.[36] The official teaching of the church, it seems, still regarded Adam and Eve as a single couple. This effectively obstructed progress on the issue of reconciling polygenism with original sin.

In his message to the Pontifical Academy of Sciences on 22 October 1996, Pope John Paul II accepted evolution as highly probable, but he asserted that it should not be regarded as proven beyond doubt. But why the emphasis on absolute proof? A non-Catholic could argue that double standards are in evidence here—a higher standard of proof is arbitrarily applied to science. If such a demanding epistemological criterion was applied to Catholic doctrine, would it fare as well as evolutionary theory?

The pope's message indicates the dilemma faced by the church. To reject the theory (or theories) of biological evolution, including the evolutionary development of humankind, would be to adopt a doctrinal position conspicuously deficient in credibility. To accept evolution (as generally understood by scientists) as conclusively proven would render the doctrine of original sin (as taught by the church) untenable. It is highly significant that the pope, in referring to *Humani Generis*, did not mention polygenism. Perhaps he hoped that sometime in the future a theory of evolution based on monogenism would find substantial support among scientists—a remote possibility. In the meantime the persistent problem of incompatibility between original sin and polygenism will not be of great concern to the church—it will suspend judgment at its leisure. Given time, doctrine will evolve, perhaps imperceptibly, to overcome the problem. A retreat from an unsustainable position can then be presented as a development of knowledge. Dom Cuthbert Butler's introduction to Bishop Hedley's *Evolution and Faith with Other Essays* (1931) gives a succinct commentary on this point. He observed that many ideas concerning, for example, the Copernican hypothesis, the six days of creation, and the geographical nonuniversality of the Flood, were subjected to "the whole gamut of theological censure." Initially regarded as heretical, these ideas were then regarded as erroneous, rash, tolerable, and freely accepted—in that order.[37]

The church tended to stifle or avoid discussion as much as possible when conflict arose between faith and science. This reaction, grossly inadequate by itself, was supported by a number of defensive strategies. The strategy of isolation was sometimes adopted—that is, theology and science occupy different domains of knowledge and differ fundamentally in their methods, epistemological criteria, and objectives. Their points of contact are reduced to the minimum, so that the potential for conflict is correspondingly diminished.[38] Another tactic was to assume that "real" science cannot contradict a dogma of the church; that is, truth does not contradict truth. Catholic apologists then proceeded to argue that the text of Genesis is open to a number of interpretations and that the church has not bound itself to any particular reading of scripture. The imprecise nature of scriptural texts was used to great advantage. It was then argued that scientific theories are not conclusive and are continually changing. These defensive tactics, when used together, were particularly effective in neutralizing a perceived threat to a cherished belief of the church.[39]

In view of the pliancy of scripture, it would have been reasonable to expect tolerance for the published works of those Catholic scholars, such as Leroy, Zahm, and Teilhard de Chardin, who attempted to make progress in harmonizing the book of nature with the book of revelation. These authors were not so fortunate. Their ideas were too far in advance of most of those in authoritative positions. Furthermore, it was feared that the process of adapting religious beliefs to the advances of science might lead to a loss of faith. The church's primary mission was to preserve the faith of the multitudes, who could not be relied upon to distinguish the essential elements of belief from those that were deemed to be revisable. The church's response to disturbing ideas tended to be one of "prudential condemnation," followed by gradual assimilation. This "conservative principle" of the church is exemplified in the acceptance of Aristotle's philosophy—at first condemned, then gradually accepted owing especially to the synthesis of St. Thomas Aquinas.[40]

The conservatism of the church was facilitated to some extent by the slow progress of knowledge. This situation has changed, especially in relation to applied science. Since about 1980 Catholic moralists have become increasingly worried about the difficulties in keeping ethics up-to-date with momentous developments in biomedical science. There was a tendency to too readily condemn new scientific techniques that had the potential to improve the quality of life for many people. This was consistent with the church's record in responding to developments in science. Fr. Jerome J. Langford, in his book *Galileo, Science and the Church* (1992), succinctly described the traditional reaction of the Roman Catholic Church.

> The Church's reaction to scientific advance has seemed to follow the same pattern for centuries. The scientific discovery of theory is announced, and theologians react defensively. The scientific evidence gains acceptance, and theologians begin to investigate ways of incorporating the new insights either by changing their interpretation of Scripture or by doing a bit of reorganizing of their pet world-views. Usually by the time theologians get around to accepting a scientific discovery, they are years behind the times.[41]

Langford argued that organized religion, including Catholicism, was struggling for survival and could no longer afford to sustain such inadequacy. Although he exaggerated the dangers to the faith he did present a compelling argument for a more positive and proactive approach from theologians to anticipated scientific developments. In the sphere of science, unjustified condemnation would only serve to work against the welfare of the church, whose mission was to help humankind to advance in knowledge, justice, and love.[42]

It can be argued that Langford's concerns about the danger of conflict between Catholicism and science are not justified. The old cosmological and evolutionary controversies are dormant if not dead. The Roman Catholic Church, notwithstanding some unresolved problems, has made peace with Galileo and Darwin; therefore, the scope for conflict seems to be considerably narrowed. However, this assessment may be unduly optimistic. Richard Blackwell argued that there is a potential for future conflict and that it is to be found in the characteristics of two disparate cultures. Religious authority, at least in Catholicism, is "monolithic, centralized, esoteric, resistant to change, and self-protective." In contrast, authority in science is "pluralistic, democratic, public, fallibilistic, and self-corrective."[43] Blackwell did not proceed to claim that conflict is inevitable, only that there is a possibility—and a small one at that—because science and technology are now so much stronger relative to religion as agents of change. However, he did conclude that illiberal influences and a lack of intellectual honesty in the Catholic Church may give rise to another incident similar to that of the Galileo affair. This statement was made against the background of the failure of the Vatican to clarify the circumstances behind the adulteration of Pio Paschini's *Vita e Opere di Galileo Galilei*.

The Italian professor Marcello Pera also saw a potential for future conflict between science and Catholicism. Pera argued that Galileo's principle of independence is incompatible with Bellarmine's principle of limitation because the "truths" of science may someday clash with the "truths" of faith. He maintained that some aspects of faith cannot be abandoned or revised such as the resurrection of Jesus Christ or the virginity of his mother, Mary. He claimed that these articles of faith, and others that are held on the basis of miracles, are contrary to science. This of course is reasonable if one assumes an atheistic position. It would be consistent with agnosticism not to believe in miracles on the basis that there is no proof but not to go so far as to reject, absolutely, the possibility that such events never occurred. Christians will maintain that the resurrection of Christ and the Immaculate Conception are not amenable to scientific investigation. If one accepts the existence of a supernatural order then it is logical to accept that events dependent on supernatural action do occur which by definition are beyond the competence of science—because science can only explain what is natural. If miracles are to be denied on the basis of science, then it would be logical to deny the creation of the universe *ex nihilo*—arguably a miracle of unsurpassed magnitude.

Pera speculated about four possible scientific claims in the future that may clash with essential Catholic beliefs. His possible "truths of science" (in reality scientific hypotheses or scientific theories) versus "truths of faith" are as follows:

1. The universe is infinite in time versus God created the universe.

2. Life in the universe stems from inorganic matter versus God gave the gift of life.

3. Life originated in more than one place versus God gave the gift of life to one original couple.

4. Psychical life is reducible to biological and social conditions versus God gave the human a body and a soul independent of that body.

Pera's arguments are rather weak, and he seems to undermine them when he acknowledges that the above scientific claims would not be "empirically testable in a strict, direct sense" and would be more appropriately regarded as "metaphysical cores of research programs." In other words, such claims would be philosophical or theological rather than scientific.[44]

To claim that the universe is infinite would be philosophical rather than scientific. If scientists could somehow deduce from their research data that there was a previous universe, it could still be argued that there was only a finite series of universes, each of finite duration. Failure to detect or identify an absolute beginning in time does not lead one inevitably to the conclusion of a universe of infinite age.

Pera's second point can be refuted on the basis that there is no unavoidable contradiction between faith and science claims here. If Catholics accept the evolution of life as a "truth" of science, they can still claim that God created life through secondary causes. The third point, concerning one original couple, has created theological difficulties for the church, especially regarding original sin, but, as indicated earlier, the church will be able to adapt its doctrine. Alternatively, it may continue to argue that science is not capable of proving with absolute certainty that humankind descended from a population rather than from a single couple, thus preserving its doctrinal position. Such a position would have a veneer of philosophical authenticity about it, although it would fail to gain any significant support among scientists. The worst possible outcome, from a Catholic perspective, is that the church would feel compelled to admit such a profound change of doctrine that its claim to infallibility would be discredited or endangered. This development is extremely improbable, especially when cognizance is taken of church history.

Pera's fourth point seems to be the strongest. It seems possible that the human mind is potentially explicable in terms of neuronal networks, biochemistry, genetic predispositions, and environmental influences. But the claims of science here may be vulnerable to philosophical objections that may challenge any claim that the human mind could be completely accounted for by scientific and social conditions. For example, John Tyndall argued that if scientists could somehow associate specific physico-chemical processes in the brain with particular thoughts, this would not constitute an explanation in the deepest sense of the term. He argued that scientists, at best, could only correlate two disparate classes of phenomena; the underlying connections would still defy explanation.[45] Scientific progress is unlikely to overturn belief in the immortal soul, which is likely to find sanctuary in the deepest recesses of the great unknown.

If conflict does arise between Roman Catholicism and science in the near future, it is likely to occur more for reasons identified by Blackwell rather than for those by Pera. The institutional church no longer seems to be deeply concerned about theological difficulties arising from cosmological and evolutionary theories. Its main concern in the twenty-first century is with the immoral applications of scientific knowledge. Science in the service of humankind requires, *inter alia*, the allocation of resources away from the production of weapons of mass destruction (especially nuclear weapons) and toward the support of socioeconomic policies concerned with the alleviation of poverty and the enhancement of the natural environment. The church is morally bound to use its influence, and its resources, in support of such causes. However, its energies may become too narrowly focused on bioethical issues pertaining to human sexuality and reproduction.

Finally, it is now appropriate to conclude by reference to the past. The history of the relationship between Roman Catholicism and science is extremely complex, having within it elements of harmony and conflict, dialogue, collaboration, and isolation. All too frequently the critics and defenders of Catholicism have tended to focus on either the conflicting or harmonious aspects respectively, because of bias and self-interest. Their polemical efforts have led to widespread misunderstanding, generating more heat than light in the process. It is hoped that this book will contribute significantly to a greater understanding of the multifaceted relationship that exists between the faith of Roman Catholicism and the rational but fallible nature of the natural sciences.

Notes

Introduction

1. These include: Jacob W. Gruber, *A Conscience in Conflict: The Life of St. George Jackson Mivart* (Westport, Conn.: Greenwood Press, 1960); Harry W. Paul, *The Edge of Contingency: French Catholic Reaction to Scientific Change from Darwin to Duhem* (Gainesville, Fla.: University Presses of Florida, 1979); G. B. Marini-Bettòlo, *Outlines of the Activity of the Pontifical Academy of Sciences 1936–1986* (Vatican City: Pontificia Academia Scientiarum, 1986); and Noor Giovanni Mazhar, *Catholic Attitudes to Evolution in Nineteenth-Century Italian Literature* (Venice: Istituto Veneto di Scienze, Lettere ed Arti, 1995).

2. See Emanuel Rádl, *The History of Biological Theories*, trans. E. J. Hatfield (London: Oxford University Press, 1930), 91–92.

3. If the earth was to be relegated to the lowly status of a planet, then this suggested that other planets might also be inhabited. If this was true then the special status of humankind was very much in question. The notion of intelligent extraterrestrial life had profound implications for Christian belief, especially concerning Jesus Christ's incarnation and redemption. Some scholars, concerned about the compatibility of these core doctrines with heliocentricism, distanced themselves from Copernicus's novel hypothesis. Michael J. Crowe, "Astronomy and Religion (1780–1915): Four Case Studies Involving Ideas of Extraterrestrial Life," in *Science in Theistic Contexts: Cognitive Dimensions*, ed. John Hedley Brooke, Margaret J. Osler, and Jitse M. van der Meer, *Osiris* 16 (2001): 210.

4. For example, Joshua 10:12–13, which states that the sun stopped moving across the sky at midday while the Israelites fought, and triumphed over, the Amorites. Other examples are: "The sun rises and the sun sets, and hurries back to where it rises" (Eccl. 1:5); and "the world is firmly established; it cannot be moved" (Ps. 93:1). Insofar as the church fathers had made reference to astronomical phenomena, there was no unanimity of interpretation. Nonliteral interpretations of scripture had also been proposed, for example, in reference to Joshua 10:12–13 (cited earlier) and Isaiah 38:8. In some instances there was even a theo-

logical imperative to interpret scripture in the nonliteral sense. Human features, for example, were ascribed to God in some biblical passages. The notion of God having eyes and ears was, of course, heretical. Galileo was aware of this argument. But even if a literal reading was the preferred choice in the context of astronomical observations, then, in his opinion, the Copernican rather than the Ptolemaic system was closer to the teachings of the Bible. Galileo maintained that the sun, in its central position, rotates on its axis. This rotation generates a force that causes its orbiting planets also to rotate. If the sun and its planets were to cease moving, then the day on earth would be increased in length. Therefore, the words of Joshua could be interpreted literally because the sun did become stationary, which in turn caused the planets to cease moving. Kenneth J. Howell, *God's Two Books: Copernican Cosmology and Biblical Interpretation in Early Modern Science* (Notre Dame, Ind.: University of Notre Dame Press, 2002), 191–93.

5. The Reformation provoked the Roman Catholic Church to adopt a defensive position, and it became increasingly determined to maintain its authority. Therefore it was not simply an issue of determining whether or not a particular interpretation of scripture was correct. There was also the issue of whether the person proposing the interpretation was authorized to do so. Furthermore, because of the defensive stance of the church, biblical exegesis had become increasingly literalistic in the second half of the sixteenth century. Richard Blackwell, "Could There Be Another Galileo Case?" in *The Cambridge Companion to Galileo*, ed. Peter Machamer (Cambridge: Cambridge University Press, 1998), 352–53.

6. Robert S. Westman, "The Copernicans and the Churches," in *God and Nature: Historical Essays on the Encounter between Christianity and Science*, ed. David C. Lindberg and Ronald L. Numbers (Berkeley: University of California Press, 1986), 78, 80.

7. David C. Lindberg, "Galileo, the Church, and the Cosmos," in *When Science and Christianity Meet*, ed. David C. Lindberg and Ronald L. Numbers (Chicago: University of Chicago Press, 2003), 48–49.

8. Maurice A. Finocchiaro, "Science, Religion, and the Historiography of the Galileo Affair: On the Undesirability of Oversimplification," in *Science in Theistic Contexts*, ed. Brooke, Osler, and van der Meer, 116, 128.

9. John Brooke and Geoffrey Cantor, *Reconstructing Nature: The Engagement of Science and Religion* (Edinburgh: T&T Clark, 1998), 118; and Lindberg, "Galileo, the Church, and the Cosmos," in *When Science and Christianity Meet*, ed. Lindberg and Numbers, 58–60.

10. Jean Dietz Moss, "Galileo's Letter to Christina: Some Rhetorical Considerations," *Renaissance Quarterly* 36, no. 4 (Winter 1983): 554–55, 564–65; and Ernan McMullin, "Galileo on science and Scripture," in *Cambridge Companion to Galileo*, ed. Machamer, 289–90.

11. He argued that all the planets except the earth revolved around the sun, and that the sun, with its orbiting planets, revolved around a stationary earth. As

the Ptolemaic system became less tenable Tycho Brahe's hypothesis became more prominent. Therefore, it was not a simple choice between a discredited theory and a modern one founded on irrefutable evidence. Tycho Brahe's system was not contradicted by a single telescopic observation. Brooke and Cantor, *Reconstructing Nature*, 115–17.

12. William R. Shea, "Galileo and the Church," in *God and Nature*, ed. Lindberg and Numbers, 127.

13. Mary Jo Nye, "The Moral Freedom of Man and the Determinism of Nature: The Catholic Synthesis of Science and History in the *Revue des Questions Scientifiques*," *The British Journal for the History of Science* 9, no. 33 (November 1976): 276.

14. In the introduction to the first volume of his book White expressed admiration for Draper's work but disagreed with him on one very important point. Draper regarded the conflict as one between science and religion; White saw it as a struggle between science and dogmatic theology. Andrew D. White, *A History of the Warfare of Science with Theology in Christendom* (1896; reprint, 2 vols. in 1, New York: George Braziller, 1955), 1:ix.

15. John William Draper, *History of the Conflict between Religion and Science*, 10th ed. (London: Henry S. King & Co., 1877), x–xi, 328, 363.

16. Claude Welch, "Dispelling Some Myths about the Split between Theology and Science in the Nineteenth Century," in *Religion and Science: History, Method, Dialogue*, ed. W. Mark Richardson and Wesley J. Wildman (New York: Routledge, 1996), 29–30.

17. Brooke and Cantor, *Reconstructing Nature*, 122.

18. "Introduction," in *God and Nature*, ed. Lindberg and Numbers, 6.

19. Brooke and Cantor, *Reconstructing Nature*, xi. In his earlier work, *Science and Religion: Some Historical Perspectives* (Cambridge: Cambridge University Press, 1991) John Hedley Brooke states that "serious scholarship in the history of science has revealed so extraordinarily rich and complex a relationship between science and religion in the past that general theses are difficult to sustain" (p. 5).

20. Ian G. Barbour, *Religion and Science: Historical and Contemporary Issues* (London: SCM Press, 1998), chapter 4. Barbour sees four elements in the relationship —conflict, independence, dialogue, and integration.

21. Finocchiaro, "Science, Religion and the Historiography of the Galileo Affair," in *Science in Theistic Contexts*, ed. Brooke, Osler, and van der Meer, 114–32.

22. The Irish Catholic experience, for example, is yet to be explored and elucidated. See Dorinda Outram, "The History of Natural History: Grand Narrative or Local Lore?" in *Nature in Ireland: A Scientific and Cultural History*, ed. John Wilson Foster and Helena C. G. Chesney (Dublin: Lilliput Press, 1997), 468; and John Wilson Foster, "Natural History in Modern Irish Culture," in *Science and Society in Ireland: The Social Context of Science and Technology in Ireland, 1800–1950*, ed. Peter J. Bowler and Nicholas Whyte (Belfast: Institute of Irish Studies, The Queen's University of Belfast, 1997), 127.

23. David N. Livingstone, "Science, Region, and Religion: The Reception of Darwinism in Princeton, Belfast, and Edinburgh," in *Disseminating Darwinism: The Role of Place, Race, Religion and Gender*, ed. Ronald L. Numbers and John Stenhouse (Cambridge: Cambridge University Press, 1999), 7–38.

24. Ronald L. Numbers and John Stenhouse, "Introduction," in *Disseminating Darwinism*, ed. Numbers and Stenhouse, 2.

25. These include the *Syllabus of Errors* (1864), the Dogmatic Constitution on the Catholic Faith, *Constitutio Dogmatica de Fide Catholica* (1870), *Providentissimus Deus* (1893), "The Church and Liberal Catholicism: A Joint Pastoral Letter," by the Cardinal Archbishop and the Bishops of the Province of Westminster (1900), *Lamentabili Sane Exitu* (1907), *Pascendi Dominici Gregis* (1907), the decrees of the Pontifical Biblical Commission (1905, 1909), the antimodernist oath *Sacrorum Antistitum* (1910), *Divino Afflante Spiritu* (1943), *Humani Generis* (1950), the Pastoral Constitution on the Church in the Modern World, *Gaudium et Spes* (1965), "On Dangerous Opinions and on Atheism," *Ratione habita*, by the Synod of Bishops (1967), and *Fides et Ratio* (1998). In addition to the above documents numerous papal speeches are referred to, especially those of Pope John Paul II.

26. Patrick Granfield, *The Limits of the Papacy: Authority and Autonomy in the Church* (London: Darton, Longman and Todd, 1987), 125–27.

27. Tad Szulc, *Pope John Paul II: The Biography* (New York: Scribner, 1995), 316–18; Jonathan Kwitny, *Man of the Century: The Life and Times of Pope John Paul II* (New York: Warner Books, 1998), 188–89.

28. In Ireland, for example, very few Roman Catholics have attempted to promote the practical application of Catholic social principles. See Don O'Leary, *Vocationalism and Social Catholicism in Twentieth-Century Ireland: The Search for a Christian Social Order* (Dublin: Irish Academic Press, 2000); The Irish Episcopal Conference, *Work Is the Key: Towards an Economy That Needs Everyone* (Dublin: Veritas, 1992), par. 66; The Irish Catholic Bishops' Conference, *Prosperity with a Purpose: Christian Faith and Values in a Time of Rapid Economic Growth* (Dublin: Veritas, 1999), see parr. 9, 98, 167, and 171; and Justice Commission, Conference of Religious of Ireland, *Resources and Choices: Towards a Fairer Future* (n.p.: CORI, November 1999), 21–24. There is no evidence to indicate that Catholics in Ireland are exceptional in not taking the social teaching of their church seriously. For similar observations about social Catholicism in Britain and the United States of America respectively, see Michael Phelan, "Is It the Business of the Church?" *Priests & People* 12, no. 5 (1998): 176–80, and Edward P. DeBerri, James E. Hug, Peter J. Henriot, and Michael J. Schultheis, eds., *Catholic Social Teaching: Our Best Kept Secret*, 4th ed. (Maryknoll, N.Y.: Orbis Books; Washington, D.C.: Center of Concern, 2003), 3–4.

29. Lara V. Marks, *Sexual Chemistry: A History of the Contraceptive Pill* (New Haven: Yale University Press, 2001), chapter 9; especially pp. 217, 219, 229–34.

30. In this study the following works are of particular importance: Galileo's *Letter to the Grand Duchess Christina* (1615), Gerald Molloy's *Geology and Revelation*

(1870), St. George Jackson Mivart's *Genesis of Species* (1871), Fr. John A. Zahm's *Evolution and Dogma* (1896), Canon Henri de Dorlodot's *Darwinism and Catholic Thought* (1921 and 1925); and Rev. Ernest C. Messenger's *Evolution and Theology* (1931), *Theology and Evolution* (1951), and his article "The Origin of Man in the Book of Genesis," in *God, Man and the Universe*, ed. Jacques de Bivort de la Saudée (1954).

31. See Owen Chadwick, *The Secularization of the European Mind in the Nineteenth Century* (Cambridge: Cambridge University Press, 1975), 164, 168–69, 172–73.

32. Martin Conway, *Catholic Politics in Europe 1918–1945* (London: Routledge, 1997), 12.

33. Alvar Ellegård, *Darwin and the General Reader: The Reception of Darwin's Theory of Evolution in the British Periodical Press, 1859–1872* (Chicago: University of Chicago Press, 1990), 20–23.

34. Ibid., 5, 23.

35. Owen Chadwick, "Christianity Since 1800: Great Britain and Europe," in *The Oxford Illustrated History of Christianity*, ed. John McManners (Oxford: Oxford University Press, 1992), 344.

1. From Galileo to Darwin

1. Galileo's exegetical principles were not novel. It would not have served his best interests if he had written a highly original work of hermeneutics, especially considering the Tridentine emphasis on the unanimity of the church fathers and the strong tendency of many clergymen to adhere to well-established precedents. Kenneth J. Howell, *God's Two Books: Copernican Cosmology and Biblical Interpretation in Early Modern Science* (Notre Dame, Ind.: University of Notre Dame Press, 2002), 187. The principles of Prudence, Independence, and Accommodation were probably familiar to educated and thoughtful laymen, and it is likely that Galileo read about Accommodation and Independence in the preface to Johannes Kepler's *Astronomia Nova* (1609). Ernan McMullin, "Galileo on science and Scripture," in *The Cambridge Companion to Galileo*, ed. Peter Machamer (Cambridge: Cambridge University Press, 1998), 302.

2. These five exegetical principles are discussed at length in McMullin, "Galileo on science and Scripture," 271–347. See Marcello Pera, "The god of theologians and the god of astronomers: An apology of Bellarmine," 367–87. Both of the above in *The Cambridge Companion to Galileo*, ed. Machamer. The Principle of Independence is called the Principle of Limitation by McMullin.

3. McMullin, "Galileo on science," 308; see also 314–19.

4. Ibid., 316–19.

5. Cardinal Bellarmine to Foscarini, 12 April 1615, in *The Galileo Affair: A Documentary History*, ed. and trans. Maurice A. Finocchiaro (Berkeley: University of California Press, 1989), 67.

6. Pera, "God of theologians," in *Cambridge Companion to Galileo*, ed. Machamer, 373–74.

7. Cardinal Bellarmine to Foscarini, 12 April 1615, in *Galileo Affair*, ed. Finocchiaro, 68.

8. *Galileo's Abjuration*, 22 June 1633, in *Galileo Affair*, ed. Finocchiaro, 292.

9. W. E. Knowles Middleton, "Science in Rome, 1675–1700, and the Accademia Fisicomatematica of Giovanni Giustino Ciampini," *British Journal for the History of Science* 8, no. 29 (July 1975): 138.

10. Protestants who made important contributions to the discipline of chemistry included Robert Boyle (1627–1691), Jean Beguin, Nicaise Le Febvre, Nicolas Lémery (1645–1715), Andreas Libavius (c. 1560–1616), and Daniel Sennert. There was no Catholic chemist of distinction except Johannes Baptista van Helmont (1579–1644). Most of his work was published posthumously, probably because of opposition from the Catholic Church. William B. Ashworth, Jr., "Catholicism and Early Modern Science," in *God and Nature: Historical Essays on the Encounter between Christianity and Science*, ed. David C. Lindberg and Ronald L. Numbers (Berkeley: University of California Press, 1986), 150–51.

11. Ibid., 151–53.

12. See Lewis Pyenson and Susan Sheets-Pyenson, *Servants of Nature: A History of Scientific Institutions, Enterprises and Sensibilities* (London: Fontana Press, 1999), 217; John Hedley Brooke, *Science and Religion: Some Historical Perspectives* (Cambridge: Cambridge University Press, 1991), 100; and Peter J. Bowler and Iwan Rhys Morus, *Making Modern Science: A Historical Survey* (Chicago: University of Chicago Press, 2005), 346.

13. Brooke, *Science and Religion*, 108.

14. See Ashworth, "Catholicism and Early Modern Science," 153–54; and Jane T. Tolbert, "Peiresc and Censorship: The Inquisition and the New Science, 1610–1637," *Catholic Historical Review* 89, no. 1 (January 2003): 24–38.

15. See Massimo Mazzotti, "For science and for the Pope-King: Writing the history of the exact sciences in nineteenth-century Rome," *British Journal for the History of Science* 33 (2000): 276.

16. Annibale Fantoli, *Galileo: For Copernicanism and for the Church*, 2nd ed., trans. George V. Coyne (Vatican City State: Vatican Observatory Publications, 1996), 493–96; and John L. Heilbron, "Censorship of Astronomy in Italy after Galileo," in *The Church and Galileo*, ed. Ernan McMullin (Notre Dame, Ind.: University of Notre Dame Press, 2005), 279–322.

17. The first volume of *Elements of Optics and Astronomy* was published in 1818, and its subject matter was optics. The second volume was to be about astronomy.

18. Fantoli, *Galileo*, 520 n. 24.

19. Jerome J. Langford, *Galileo, Science and the Church*, 3rd ed. (Ann Arbor: Ann Arbor Paperbacks, University of Michigan Press, 1992), 134.

20. For an extensive study of polemical discourses about the Galileo affair see Maurice A. Finocchiaro, "Galileo as a 'bad theologian': A formative myth about

Galileo's trial," *Studies in History and Philosophy of Science* 33A, no. 4 (December 2002): 753–91.

21. Calculations of capacity on the basis of either Hebrew or Egyptian cubits made no significant difference to the problem at hand. The ark was approximately 140 meters long, 23 meters wide, and 13.5 meters high when calculations are made on the basis of Hebrew cubits (footnote to Gen. 6:15 NIV).

22. John A. O'Brien, *Evolution and Religion: A Study of the Bearing of Evolution upon the Philosophy of Religion* (New York: Century Co., 1932), 96–98; William M. Agar, *Catholicism and the Progress of Science* (New York: Macmillan, 1940), 49; and David Young, *The Discovery of Evolution* (Cambridge: Cambridge University Press, 1992), 47–50.

23. See Rhoda Rappaport, "Geology and Orthodoxy: The Case of Noah's Flood in Eighteenth-Century Thought," *British Journal for the History of Science* 11, no. 37 (March 1978): 13–14.

24. Janet Browne, "Noah's Flood, the Ark, and the Shaping of Early Modern Natural History," in *When Science and Christianity Meet*, ed. Lindberg and Numbers, 137.

25. Humphrey J. T. Johnson, *The Bible and the Early History of Mankind* (London: Burns Oates, 1943), 60.

26. J. A. Zahm, *Bible, Science, and Faith* (Baltimore: John Murphy & Co., 1894), 140 (page references in subsequent paragraphs refer to this work).

27. Ernan McMullin, "Introduction: Evolution and Creation," in *Evolution and Creation*, ed. Ernan McMullin (Notre Dame, Ind.: University of Notre Dame Press, 1985), 33.

28. Martin J. S. Rudwick, "The Shape and Meaning of Earth History," in *God and Nature*, ed. Lindberg and Numbers, 313.

29. Mott T. Greene, "Genesis and Geology Revisited: The Order of Nature and the Nature of Order in Nineteenth-Century Britain," in *When Science and Christianity Meet*, ed. Lindberg and Numbers, 158–59.

30. William J. Astore, "Gentle Skeptics? American Catholic Encounters with Polygenism, Geology, and Evolutionary Theories from 1845 to 1875," *Catholic Historical Review* 82 (January 1996): 52–53. The full title of Sorignet's book published in English in 1862 is *Sacred Cosmogony; or, Primitive Revelation Demonstrated by the Harmony of the Facts of the Mosaic History of the Creation, with the Principles of General Science* (St. Louis, 1862).

31. The full title and bibliographical details of Walworth's book are as follows: *The Gentle Skeptic; or, Essays and Conversations of a Country Justice on the Authenticity and Truthfulness of the Old Testament Records*, by a Country Justice, ed. Rev. C. Walworth (New York, 1863).

32. [Molloy, Gerald], "Geology and Revelation," parts 1–9, *Irish Ecclesiastical Record* 3 (1867): 121–34, 241–61, 358–74, 448–67; 4 (1868): 49–66, 169–87, 326–41, 373–85; 5 (1869): 49–73, 193–223.

33. Gerald Molloy, *Geology and Revelation: or The Ancient History of the Earth considered in the light of geological facts and revealed religion* (London: Longmans, Green, Reader, and Dyer; Dublin: McGlashan and Gill, and W. B. Kelly, 1870), preface.

34. Molloy, "Geology and Revelation," part 8, *Irish Ecclesiastical Record* 5 (1869): 56–57; and idem, *Geology and Revelation*, 323–25. On p. 325 of *Geology and Revelation* Molloy mentions only Pianciani as a supporter of the day-age hypothesis. In his journal article (p. 56) he mentions both Pianciani and Miller.

35. Molloy, *Geology and Revelation*, 401. For another discussion of Molloy's *Geology and Revelation*, see Thomas Duddy, *A History of Irish Thought* (London: Routledge, 2002), 257–59.

36. "Pius IX and Rev. Dr. Molloy's Work on Geology and Revelation," *Irish Ecclesiastical Record* 6 (1870): 636–37.

37. [Gerald] Molloy, "The Historical Character of the First Chapter of Genesis," *Record of the Maynooth Union* (1895–1896): 31.

38. Walter McDonald, *Reminiscences of a Maynooth Professor*, edited with a memoir by Denis Gwynn (Cork, Ireland: Mercier Press, 1967), 75.

39. Perry Curtis, *Apes and Angels: The Irishman in Victorian Caricature*, rev. ed. (Washington: Smithsonian Institution Press, 1997), 102–3. See also Josef L. Altholz, *The Churches in the Nineteenth Century* (Indianapolis: Bobbs-Merrill, 1967), 127–29.

40. G. Blair Nelson, "Men before Adam! American Debates over the Unity and Antiquity of Humanity," in *When Science and Christianity Meet*, ed. Lindberg and Numbers, 178.

41. Charles Darwin, *The Origin of Species by Means of Natural Selection or The Preservation of Favoured Races in the Struggle for Life* (1859; reprint, edited with an introduction by J. W. Burrow, London: Penguin Books, 1985), 458.

42. See Michael Denton, *Evolution: A Theory in Crisis* (London: Burnett Books, 1985), 66–67.

43. Alvar Ellegård, *Darwin and the General Reader: The Reception of Darwin's Theory of Evolution in the British Periodical Press, 1859–1872* (1958; reprint, with a foreword by David L. Hull, Chicago: University of Chicago Press, 1990), 95–97.

44. Francis Darwin, ed., *The Autobiography of Charles Darwin and Selected Letters* (New York: Dover Publications, 1958), 59–69. The reasons for Darwin's loss of faith were not just scientific but arose from events in his personal life and from "extra-scientific" reflections. See John Hedley Brooke, "Revisiting Darwin on Order and Design," in *Design and Disorder: Perspectives from Science and Theology*, ed. Niels Henrik Gregersen and Ulf Görman (London: T&T Clark, 2002), 39–41.

45. Tess Cosslett, "Introductory Essay," in *Science and Religion in the Nineteenth Century*, ed. Tess Cosslett (Cambridge: Cambridge University Press, 1984), 4, 7–8.

46. John C. Greene, *Darwin and the Modern World View* (Baton Rouge:

Louisiana State University Press, 1961), 62–63. Darwin used random variation and natural selection to explain the adaptation of structure to function in organisms. Christian apologists regarded this explanation as incomplete. From a liberal Christian perspective it could be conceded that processes of variation could lead to changes in plants and animals and that environmental conditions might favor some varieties over others. But variations did not create; they only modified something already existing that needed to be explained. Nor did Darwin's theory explain the origin of life, or the origin of the underlying physical and chemical laws that gave rise to life.

47. John Henry Newman, *The Idea of a University*, edited, with introduction and notes by I. T. Ker (London: Oxford University Press, 1976), quotations from 190, 361, 348. Newman argued that "from religious investigations, as such, physics must be excluded, and from physical, as such, religion; and if we mix them, we shall spoil both" (p. 189).

48. Ibid., 354.

49. A. Dwight Culler, *The Imperial Intellect* (New Haven: Yale University Press, 1955), 267, quoted in John Lyon, "Immediate Reactions to Darwin: The English Catholic Press' First Reviews of the 'Origin of Species,'" *Church History* 41 (March 1972): 78.

50. Ellegård, *Darwin and the General Reader*; see 195, 332–37.

51. Peter J. Bowler, *Charles Darwin: The Man and His Influence* (Cambridge: Cambridge University Press, 1996), 139, 156.

52. The *Origin of Species* (1859) does not address the question concerning the origin of life. Darwin, aware of his lack of knowledge on the subject, prudently chose to ignore it. Michael Ruse, "The Changing Face of Darwinism," *Victorian Studies* 45, no. 2 (Winter 2003): 313.

2. Religion and Science in Victorian Britain

1. See Frank M. Turner, "John Tyndall and Victorian Scientific Naturalism," in *John Tyndall: Essays on a Natural Philosopher*, ed. W. H. Brock, N. D. McMillan, and R. C. Mollan (Dublin: Royal Dublin Society, 1981), 169.

2. See John Durant, "Darwinism and Divinity: A Century of Debate," in *Darwinism and Divinity: Essays on Evolution and Religious Belief*, ed. John Durant (Oxford: Basil Blackwell, 1985), 32–33.

3. Turner, "John Tyndall," 173–74.

4. Cyril Bibby, ed., *The Essence of T.H. Huxley: Selections from his writings* (London: Macmillan; New York: St. Martin's Press, 1967), 26; see also 115.

5. Frank Turner, *Contesting Cultural Authority: Essays in Victorian Intellectual Life* (Cambridge: Cambridge University Press, 1993), 157–58.

6. Cyril Bibby, ed., *T.H. Huxley on Education: A selection from his writings* (Cambridge: Cambridge University Press, 1971), 43.

7. J. V. Jensen, "The X Club: Fraternity of Victorian Scientists," *British Journal for the History of Science* 5, no. 17 (1970): 63.

8. Ruth Barton, "'An Influential Set of Chaps': The X-Club and Royal Society Politics 1864–1885," *British Journal for the History of Science* 23, no. 76 (March 1990): 57.

9. Harry W. Paul, "The Crucifix and the Crucible: Catholic Scientists in the Third Republic," *Catholic Historical Review* 58 (April 1972–January 1973): 195–219.

10. David Friedrich Strauss, *Der Alte und der neue Glaube* (The Old Belief and the New, 1872), quoted in Emanuel Rádl, *The History of Biological Theories*, trans. E. J. Hatfield (London: Oxford University Press, 1930), 94–95.

11. See John Hedley Brooke, *Science and Religion: Some Historical Perspectives* (Cambridge: Cambridge University Press, 1991), 302–3.

12. Walter L. Arnstein, *Protestant versus Catholic in Mid-Victorian England: Mr. Newdegate and the Nuns* (Columbia: University of Missouri Press, 1982), 50.

13. Walter L. Arnstein, "Victorian Prejudice Reexamined," *Victorian Studies* 12 (June 1969): 452.

14. By the beginning of the twentieth century approximately 80 percent of Catholics in Britain were Irish immigrants. Patrick Allitt, *Catholic Converts: British and American Intellectuals Turn to Rome* (Ithaca, N.Y.: Cornell University Press, 1997), 161.

15. J. P. Parry, *Democracy and Religion: Gladstone and the Liberal Party, 1867–1875* (Cambridge: Cambridge University Press, 1986), 195–96, 314–15, 344, 371–72; Turner, *Contesting Cultural Authority*, 26; and Jeffrey Paul von Arx, *Progress and Pessimism: Religion, Politics and History in Late Nineteenth Century Britain* (Cambridge, Mass.: Harvard University Press, 1985), especially 8, 203–5.

16. See A. R. Vidler, *A Century of Social Catholicism 1820–1920* (London: S.P.C.K., 1964), 114; and Roger Aubert, "Internal Catholic Controversies in Connection with Liberalism" in *History of the Church*, vol. 8, *The Church in the Age of Liberalism*, ed. Hubert Jedin and John Dolan (London: Burns and Oates, 1981), 296–99.

17. Parry, *Democracy and Religion*, 43.

18. Lord John Acton resided in Rome to give Dr. Ignatz von Döllinger, his former tutor, information about the proceedings of the First Vatican Council. On 1 January 1870 he wrote to Gladstone, informing him that three papers were being circulated among the bishops at the First Vatican Council. The first document proposed giving the pope the power of issuing decrees and defining dogmas, leaving the bishops and cardinals the mere function of rubber-stamping papal pronouncements. The second document proposed that the new church constitution would reiterate "the excommunications directed against the spirit of civilised governments." The third document condemned "secular science," and it declared that science could not be independent of revelation because it had no foundation apart from the institutions of the church. In theory this meant that the church could

"lawfully" issue censures against "any disturbing conclusions of historical or physical science." Acton feared that all three documents might be accepted by the council and would lead to papal absolutism, which would be hostile to the rights of church, of the state, and of the intellect. On the latter point he was concerned that "an organised conspiracy" was in progress that would so enhance the power of the papacy that it would become "the most formidable enemy of liberty as well as of science throughout the world." Acton to Gladstone, 1 January 1870, in John Neville Figgis and Reginald Vere Laurence, eds., *Selections from the Correspondence of the First Lord Acton*, vol. 1, *Correspondence with Cardinal Newman, Lady Blennerhassett, W.E. Gladstone and Others* (London: Longmans, Green and Co., 1917), 89–91.

19. E. R. Norman, *Anti-Catholicism in Victorian England* (London: George Allen and Unwin, 1968), 216.

20. Jeffrey Paul von Arx, "Interpreting the Council: Archbishop Manning and the Vatican Decrees Controversy," *Recusant History* 26, no. 1 (2002): 230–31.

21. Arnstein, *Protestant versus Catholic*, 190–92.

22. Josef L. Altholz, "The Vatican Decrees Controversy, 1874–1875," *Catholic Historical Review* 57, no. 4 (January 1972): 593–605.

23. Frank Turner, "The Victorian Crisis of Faith and the Faith That Was Lost," in *Victorian Faith in Crisis: Essays on Continuity and Change in Nineteenth-Century Religious Belief*, ed. Richard J. Helmstadter and Bernard Lightman (Stanford, Calif.: Stanford University Press, 1990), 18.

24. Wilfrid Ward, *Problems and Persons* (London: Longmans, Green and Co., 1903), 234–35.

25. Frank M. Turner, "Science and Religious Freedom," in *Freedom and Religion in the Nineteenth Century*, ed. Richard Helmstadter (Stanford, Calif.: Stanford University Press, 1997), 75–76.

26. Turner, *Contesting Cultural Authority*, 83–84.

27. Ibid., 195.

28. Ibid., 196.

29. See Alvar Ellegård, *Darwin and the General Reader: The Reception of Darwin's Theory of Evolution in the British Periodical Press, 1859–1872* (1958; reprint, with a foreword by David L. Hull, Chicago: University of Chicago Press, 1990), 102–8.

30. Quotation from Garrett Pierse, "Evolution and Creation: A New Argument for the Latter," *Irish Theological Quarterly* 15 (1920): 228.

31. J. Vernon Jensen, "Return to the Wilberforce-Huxley Debate," *British Journal for the History of Science* 21, no. 69 (June 1988): 161–79.

32. See Bernard Lightman, "Victorian Sciences and Religions: Discordant Harmonies," in *Science in Theistic Contexts: Cognitive Dimensions*, ed. John Hedley Brooke, Margaret J. Osler, and Jitse M. van der Meer, *Osiris* 16 (2001): 343–66; and James R. Moore, *The Post-Darwinian Controversies* (Cambridge: Cambridge University Press, 1979), 82–85.

33. See Claude Welch, "Dispelling Some Myths about the Split between The-

ology and Science in the Nineteenth Century," in *Religion and Science: History, Method, Dialogue*, ed. W. Mark Richardson and Wesley J. Wildman (New York: Routledge, 1996), 31.

34. Turner, "John Tyndall," 174.

35. Bibby, *Essence of T.H. Huxley*, 111.

36. Gavin de Beer, "Introduction," in *Autobiographies: Charles Darwin, Thomas Henry Huxley*, ed. Gavin de Beer (London: Oxford University Press, 1974), xvii.

37. Bibby, *Essence of T.H. Huxley*, 115; see also Adrian Desmond, *Huxley: From Devil's Disciple to Evolution's High Priest* (London: Penguin Books, 1998), 287.

38. Bibby, *Huxley on Education*, 24, 113–15.

39. Bibby, *Essence of T.H. Huxley*, 117–19.

40. Bibby, *Huxley on Education*, 38.

41. Ibid., 53.

42. John Tyndall, *Fragments of Science: A Series of Detached Essays, Addresses, and Reviews*, vol. 1, 6th ed. (London: Longmans, Green & Co., 1879), 343–49, 354–55.

43. Bernard Lightman, *The Origins of Agnosticism: Victorian Unbelief and the Limits of Knowledge* (Baltimore: Johns Hopkins University Press, 1987), 15, 180.

44. Tyndall, *Fragments of Science*, 503–4.

45. See John Tyndall, *Fragments of Science: A Series of Detached Essays, Addresses, and Reviews*, vol. 2 (New York: D. Appleton & Co., 1896), 6.

46. Turner, "John Tyndall," 174–79.

47. Tyndall, *Fragments of Science* (1896), especially 32–35; page references in the following paragraphs refer to this work.

48. Tess Cosslett, editorial note to "John Tyndall, 'The Belfast Address,' Nature, 20 August 1874," in *Science and Religion in the Nineteenth Century*, ed. Tess Cosslett (Cambridge: Cambridge University Press, 1984), 172. Huxley's objective in his debate with Wilberforce was relatively modest. He was trying persuade those clergymen and scientists who opposed evolution to give it a fair hearing. Tyndall, as will be seen from an examination of his speech, put forward radical claims for science.

49. Tyndall, *Fragments of Science* (1896), 211.

50. "Science at the Irish Catholic University," *The Times*, 2 December 1873, p. 7.

51. Ibid.

52. Tyndall, *Fragments of Science* (1896), 146–47.

53. Turner, "John Tyndall," 171.

54. Tyndall, *Fragments of Science* (1896), 197.

55. Ibid., 140–44, 147, 176–77; quotation from 143.

56. A. S. Eve and C. H. Creasey, *Life and Work of John Tyndall* (London: Macmillan, 1945), 186–87.

57. N. D. McMillan and J. Meehan, *John Tyndall: 'X'emplar of scientific and technological education* (Dublin: N.C.E.A., 1980), 146 n. 56.

58. *Pastoral Letters and Other Writings of Cardinal Cullen*, ed. Patrick Francis

Moran, vol. 3 (Dublin: Browne & Nolan, 1882), 587. Page numbers in the next paragraphs refer to this work.

59. In the seventeenth century the disciplines of religion and science became increasingly differentiated, although the study of nature was still frequently seen as the study of God's creative handiwork. The English philosopher and statesman Sir Francis Bacon (1561–1626) set forth his concept of the "two books" in 1605. The "book" of nature could help biblical scholars to ascertain the true meaning of the scriptures, but it was unwise, in his opinion, to reverse this relationship. The Baconian idea was a compromise, offering advantages to both religion and science. In addition to assisting biblical exegesis it would serve to illustrate the almighty power of God. Science would benefit because those who studied nature could do so without curtailment from interpreters of scripture. Eminent scientists such as Robert Boyle and Isaac Newton followed the Baconian concept, which, bolstered by Galileo's *Letter to the Grand Duchess Christina*, became conventional in English-language scholarship for more than two centuries. James R. Moore, "Geologists and Interpreters of Genesis in the Nineteenth Century," in *God and Nature: Historical Essays on the Encounter between Christianity and Science*, ed. David C. Lindberg and Ronald L. Numbers (Berkeley: University of California Press, 1986), 323. Bacon stressed the need to use the inductive method. He emphasized the importance of experiments in conjunction with meticulous observations.

60. *Pastoral Letters*, ed. Moran, 595, 598–99.

61. *The Times*, 31 October 1874.

62. See David N. Livingstone, "Darwin in Belfast: The Evolution Debate," in *Nature in Ireland: A Scientific and Cultural History*, ed. John Wilson Foster and Helena C. G. Chesney (Dublin: Lilliput Press, 1997), 387–408.

63. *Pastoral Letters*, ed. Moran, 604.

64. Tyndall, *Fragments of Science* (1896), 204.

65. "Pastoral Address of the Archbishops and Bishops of Ireland," 20 September 1875, published in *Irish Ecclesiastical Record* n.s. 12 (1876): 5.

66. Norman McMillan, "Tyndall the philosopher: John Tyndall (1820?–1893)," *Carloviana* [County Carlow, Ireland], no. 40 (1992–93): 25–29.

67. Norman McMillan and Martin Nevin, "Tyndall of Leighlin," in *John Tyndall: Essays*, ed. Brock, McMillan, and Mollan, 30–34.

68. Emmet Larkin, *The Historical Dimensions of Irish Catholicism* (Washington, D.C.: Catholic University of America Press; Dublin: Four Courts Press, 1984), 9–10.

69. John Stenhouse, "Catholicism, Science, and Modernity: The Case of William Miles Maskell," *Journal of Religious History* 22, no. 1 (February 1998): 65; see also 67 and 81.

70. Ibid., 80.

71. John Lyon, "Immediate Reactions to Darwin: The English Catholic Press' First Reviews of the 'Origin of Species,'" *Church History* 41 (March 1972): 93.

72. Jacob W. Gruber, *A Conscience in Conflict: The Life of St. George Jackson Mivart* (Westport, Conn.: Greenwood Press, 1960), 156.

73. See John D. Root, "English Catholic Modernism and Science: The Case of George Tyrrell," *Heythrop Journal* 18 (July 1977): 274.

74. J. Derek Holmes, "Newman and Mivart—Two Attitudes to a Nineteenth-Century Problem," *Clergy Review* n.s. 50, no. 11 (November 1965): 861–62.

75. See William J. Astore, "Gentle Skeptics? American Catholic Encounters with Polygenism, Geology, and Evolutionary Theories from 1845 to 1875," *Catholic Historical Review* 82 (January 1996): 40, 45–46; and John Rickards Betts, "Darwinism, Evolution, and American Catholic Thought, 1860–1900," *Catholic Historical Review* 45 (April 1959–January 1960): 162.

76. See Betts, "American Catholic Thought," 181.

77. Astore, "Gentle Skeptics?" 71–73.

78. R. Scott Appleby, "Exposing Darwin's 'hidden agenda': Roman Catholic responses to evolution, 1875–1925," in *Disseminating Darwinism: The Role of Place, Race, Religion and Gender*, ed. Ronald L. Numbers and John Stenhouse (Cambridge: Cambridge University Press, 1999), 175–78.

79. See Betts, "American Catholic Thought," 170, also 180. William Ebenstein (Department of Political Science, University of Wisconsin) claimed that, in the United States, Protestant writers, although critical of Darwin's theory, were to some extent conciliatory and were prepared to accept it if additional incontestable scientific evidence was advanced to support it. He contrasted the conciliatory attitude of Protestant authors to the intolerance of Catholic authors, who "were crying for nothing less than the blood of the heretics." This assessment, however, is a gross exaggeration and an oversimplification. Ebenstein's evidence for the attitudes of Catholics is too weak to make such a generalization. His opinion is based on only five articles; two in the *Catholic World* and three in the *American Catholic Quarterly Review*, from 1873 to 1879. William Ebenstein, "The Early Reception of the Doctrine of Evolution in the United States," *Annals of Science* 4 (1939): 315–17.

80. Appleby, "Exposing Darwin's 'hidden agenda,'" in *Disseminating Darwinism*, ed. Numbers and Stenhouse, 178–79.

81. John L. Morrison, "William Seton—A Catholic Darwinist," *Review of Politics* 21, no. 3 (1959): 578, 582–83.

82. Lightman, *Origins of Agnosticism*, 179–81.

83. Turner, *Contesting Cultural Authority*, 75–80.

84. Notable examples include Fyodor Dostoevsky's *Brothers Karamazov* (1880), Henrik Ibsen's *Ghosts* (1881), Mrs. Humphry Ward's *Robert Elsemere* (1888), Émile Zola's "Three Cities" trilogy (1890s), and Thomas Hardy's *Tess of the d'Urbervilles* (1891) and *Jude the Obscure* (1895). Hugh McLeod, *Secularisation in Western Europe, 1848–1914* (Basingstoke [United Kingdom]: Macmillan Press; New York: St. Martin's Press, 2000), 147–48.

85. See Welch, "Dispelling Some Myths," 34–35.

86. Ibid., 34; and J. M. Roberts, *The Penguin History of the World*, 3rd ed. (London: Penguin Books, 1995), 844.

87. Roberts, *History of the World*, 844–49; idem, *A History of Europe* (Oxford: Helicon, 1996), 342–45; McLeod, *Secularisation in Western Europe*, 113–16; and Ellegård, *Darwin and the General Reader*, 172–73.

88. Peter J. Bowler, *Evolution: The History of an Idea*, 3rd ed. (Berkeley: University of California Press, 2003), 216–17.

89. Peter J. Bowler and Iwan Rhys Morus, *Making Modern Science: A Historical Survey* (Chicago: University of Chicago Press, 2005), 355–58.

3. A Church under Siege

1. K. Theodore Hoppen, "The First Vatican Council," *History Today* 19, no. 10 (1969): 714.

2. Richard L. Camp, *The Papal Ideology of Social Reform* (Leiden: E. J. Brill, 1969), 5–10.

3. Tess Cosslett, "Introductory Essay," in *Science and Religion in the Nineteenth Century*, ed. Tess Cosslett (Cambridge: Cambridge University Press, 1984), 12–14. The eminent English Catholic author Lord John Acton, writing in late 1861, expressed the opinion that the greatest threats to Roman Catholicism, and to religion in general, came from the social sciences rather than from the natural sciences. In his opinion, natural science by itself—that is, not in association with social science—rarely presented serious difficulties for religious belief. Lord Acton, *Lord Acton and his Circle: Letters of Lord Acton*, ed. Abbot Gasquet (London: George Allen, Burns & Oates, 1906), 192–93, 223.

4. See J. M. Roberts, *The Penguin History of the World*, 3rd ed. (London: Penguin Books, 1995), 843–45.

5. See Harry W. Paul, "Religion and Darwinism: Varieties of Catholic Reaction," in *The Comparative Reception of Darwinism*, ed. Thomas F. Glick (Chicago: University of Chicago Press, 1988), 406.

6. Ernest C. Messenger, *Evolution and Theology: The Problem of Man's Origin* (London: Burns, Oates & Washbourne, 1931), 226.

7. Ibid., 226–27.

8. The establishment of the Pontificia Accademia dei Nuovi Lincei was inspired by the awareness of an earlier institute, the Accademia dei Lincei, which had been set up in Rome in 1603 by Federico Cesi. Galileo was one of its most distinguished members. Cesi died in 1630, and soon afterwards the Academy lapsed into dormancy. G. B. Marini-Bettòlo, *Outlines of the Activity of the Pontifical Academy of Sciences 1936–1986* (Vatican City: Pontificia Academia Scientiarum, 1986), xv.

9. "Pius IX and the Civilta Cattolica," *Dublin Review* n.s. 7, no. 14, (1866): 414–15.

10. Victor Conzemius, "Acton: The Lay Theologian," *Cristianesimo Nella Storia* 21, no. 3 (2000): 577.

11. Wilfrid Ward, *The Life of John Henry Cardinal Newman: Based on His Private Journals and Correspondence*, 2 vols. (London: Longmans, Green and Co., 1921), 1:641.

12. It was inevitable that Galileo's intrusion into theological debate would be deeply resented by the theologians. He was warned by his friends in Rome not to venture into theological arguments. He was assured that if he spoke strictly as a scientist and proposed the Copernican system as a hypothesis, then he was on safe ground. It can be argued that Galileo did not have a choice when he entered theological debate. The theologians were not staying within their disciplinary domain and were interfering in science. Galileo would not agree to accept Copernicanism as a mere hypothesis. In a letter to his friend Piero Dini, he explained his predicament arising from this stance. If he held Copernicanism to be true then he would be told that it was contrary to Catholic doctrine. If he challenged such an assertion, then he would be told to stay out of the sacristy. Michael Sharratt, *Galileo: Decisive Innovator* (Cambridge: Cambridge University Press, 1996), 126.

13. Acton wrote in a private journal in 1858 that scientific research should be undertaken for its own sake and must be allowed to reach its own findings independent of external interference. In the *Rambler* (11 [1859]: 73–90) he maintained that science "was hostile to Catholics only when they rejected it and permitted it to be usurped by their enemies." Gertrude Himmelfarb, *Lord Acton: A Study in Conscience and Politics* (San Francisco: Institute for Contemporary Studies, 1993), 41.

14. E. E. Y. Hales, *Pio Nono: A study in European politics and religion in the nineteenth century* (London: Eyre & Spottiswoode, 1954), 270–71. See also Wayne M. O'Sullivan, "Henry Nutcombe Oxenham: *Enfant Terrible* of the Liberal Catholic Movement in Mid-Victorian England," *Catholic Historical Review* 82 (1996): 657.

15. The origins of the *Syllabus of Errors* are quite complex and can be traced back to the proceedings of the Council of Spoleto in 1849. The council was presided over by Gioacchino Pecci, the bishop of Perugia and future successor of Pope Pius IX. He proposed that the council should request the pope to condemn the most pernicious errors of modern society concerning the authority and property rights of the church. Pecci's idea was favored by the Jesuits, and it was discussed in *Civiltà Cattolica* in 1851. Cardinal R. Fornari was instructed by the pope to carry out some preparatory work on the list of errors in 1852, and the task was later handed over to the commission that had prepared the bull on the Immaculate Conception. The first draft of the *Syllabus* was completed in the spring of 1860, but in the autumn of that year a lengthy pastoral instruction by Bishop Philippe Gerbet of Perpignan (France), containing a list of eighty-five erroneous propositions, was brought to the attention of the pope. A larger commission was set up which made Gerbet's list the basis of its deliberations. In 1862 this body drafted a list of sixty-one theses with attached theological censures. In June of the same year, Pius IX, with the approval of a council of bishops, condemned these theses in the allocution *Maxima quidem*. However, the text of the list was leaked

to a Turin newspaper, *Il Mediatore*, and provoked a storm of protest from both liberal Catholics and anticlericals. The pope was persuaded to delay and modify his plans. He appointed a new commission under the chairmanship of Luigi Bilio, which prepared the final list of eighty errors, including thirty of the former sixty-one. For more details, see J. B. Bury, *History of the Papacy in the 19th Century (1864–1878)* (London: Macmillan, 1930), 2–4; Raymond Corrigan, *The Church and the Nineteenth Century* (Milwaukee: Bruce Publishing Company, 1938), 177; and Roger Aubert, "Internal Catholic Controversies in Connection with Liberalism," in *History of the Church*, vol. 8, *The Church in the Age of Liberalism*, ed. Hubert Jedin and John Dolan (London: Burns and Oates, 1981), 294–95.

16. Emiliana P. Noether, "Vatican Council I: Its Political and Religious Setting," *Journal of Modern History* 40, no. 1 (March 1968): 220–23.

17. The pope did not sign the *Syllabus*, but he was responsible for its publication. It is not an independent document. The propositions referred to were already condemned in a number of allocutions, encyclicals, and other papal documents, and these were indicated in the text of the *Syllabus*. The propositions, therefore, were separated from their context.

18. *Syllabus of Errors*, in *The Popes against Modern Errors: 16 Papal Documents*, edited and arranged by Anthony J. Mioni (Rockford, Ill.: Tan Books, 1999), 39.

19. Josef L. Altholz, *The Churches in the Nineteenth Century* (Indianapolis: Bobbs-Merrill, 1967), 83–84.

20. For details of the background and reaction to the *Syllabus of Errors*, see Hales, *Pio Nono*, 255–62; Dom Cuthbert Butler, *The Vatican Council: The story told from inside in Bishop Ullathorne's letters*, 2 vols. (London: Longmans, Green and Co., 1930), 1:69–72; and David Mathew, *Lord Acton and His Times* (London: Eyre & Spottiswoode, 1968), 160–66.

21. *Popes against Modern Errors*, ed. Mioni, 29.

22. Ibid., 28.

23. Ibid., 29

24. Ibid., 36.

25. "Pius IX and the Civilta Cattolica," 414–18.

26. The controversy was provoked by Herzen's lecture "Sulla parentela fra l'uomo e le scimmie" given at the Museo di storia naturale in Florence on 21 March 1869. See Noor Giovanni Mazhar, *Catholic Attitudes to Evolution in Nineteenth-Century Italian Literature* (Venice: Istituto Veneto di Scienze, Lettere ed Arti, 1995), chapters 1 and 4.

27. See Paul, "Religion and Darwinism," in *Comparative Reception of Darwinism*, ed. Glick, 404.

28. Ibid., 408.

29. Thomas F. Glick, "Spain," in *Comparative Reception of Darwinism*, ed. Glick, 327–29. The condemned treatise, in 3 volumes, was *Estudios históricos, climatológicos y patológicos de las Islas Canarias* (Las Palmas: La Atlántida, 1876–1891) by Gregorio Chil y Naranjo.

30. Roger Aubert, "The Backwardness of Religious Studies and the Controversy about the 'German Theologians,'" in *History of the Church*, ed. Jedin and Dolan, 228–35.

31. Mary Jo Nye, "The Moral Freedom of Man and the Determinism of Nature: The Catholic Synthesis of Science and History in the *Revue des Questions Scientifiques*," *British Journal for the History of Science* 9, no. 33 (November 1976): 275. Major progress in the reform of French Catholic education was achieved in 1875 with the enactment of legislation providing for the setting up of five Catholic institutes of higher education. An eminent French cleric, Maurice d'Hulst, advocated, in a number of speeches and in *Le rôle scientifique des facultés catholiques* (1883), that an essential function of the new Catholic institutes was to provide scientific training for those who were loyal to the faith (ibid.).

32. Dom Cuthbert Butler, who supported the infallibilists, conceded that there was some truth in the claim that the real purpose of the council was to define the status of the pope, especially pertaining to his infallibility (*Vatican Council*, 2:239).

33. Himmelfarb, *Lord Acton*, 100–104.

34. Roger Aubert, "The Vatican Council," in *History of the Church*, ed. Jedin and Dolan, 315.

35. Norman P. Tanner, ed., *Decrees of the Ecumenical Councils*, vol. 2, *Trent to Vatican II* (London: Sheed & Ward; Washington, D.C.: Georgetown University Press, 1990), 806.

36. See Alan Richardson and John Bowden, eds., *A New Dictionary of Christian Theology* (London: SCM Press, 1989), 393.

37. Kenneth Scott Latourette, *Christianity in a Revolutionary Age: A History of Christianity in the Nineteenth and Twentieth Centuries*, vol. 1, *The Nineteenth Century in Europe: Background and the Roman Catholic Phase* (London: Eyre & Spottiswoode, 1959), 376.

38. Tanner, *Decrees*, 2:808–9.

39. Ibid., 811

40. Ibid., 663, 664, 806.

41. Ibid., 809.

42. Mazhar, *Catholic Attitudes to Evolution*, 72.

43. Robert E. Stebbins, "France," in *Comparative Reception of Darwinism*, ed. Glick, 157.

44. The response of Italian society to the theory of evolution is examined here in reference to Mazhar, *Catholic Attitudes to Evolution*, 56–69.

45. Massimo Mazzotti, "For science and for the Pope-King: Writing the history of the exact sciences in nineteenth-century Rome," *British Journal for the History of Science* 33 (2000): 278.

46. Karl Otmar von Aretin, *The Papacy and the Modern World* (London: Weidenfeld and Nicolson, 1970), 103–4.

47. Eamon Duffy, *Saints and Sinners: A History of the Popes* (New Haven: Yale University Press and S4C, 1997), 243–44.

48. Hugh McLeod, *Religion and the People of Western Europe 1789–1970* (Oxford: Oxford University Press, 1981), 36, 47–51, 130.

49. Von Aretin, *Papacy*, 138.

50. Pope Leo XIII, *Quod Apostolici Muneris* ("Concerning Modern Errors: Socialism, Communism, Nihilism"; 28 December 1878), in *The Pope and the People: Select Letters and Addresses on Social Questions by Pope Leo XIII*, rev. ed. (London: Catholic Truth Society, 1920), 30.

51. See Bill McSweeney, *Roman Catholicism: The Search for Relevance* (Oxford: Basil Blackwell, 1980), 69, 71.

52. Ibid., 74.

53. See J. W. Burrow, *The Crisis of Reason: European Thought, 1848–1914* (New Haven: Yale University Press, 2000), 36–41, 51–56; Owen Chadwick, *The Secularization of the European Mind in the Nineteenth Century* (Cambridge: Cambridge University Press, 1975), chapter 7; and Sander Gliboff, "Evolution, Revolution, and Reform in Vienna: Franz Unger's Ideas on Descent and Their Post-1848 Reception," *Journal of the History of Biology* 31 (1998): 204–5. For an account of the connections between evolutionary anthropology, radical politics, philosophical materialism, and anticlericalism in nineteenth-century France, see Michael Hammond, "Anthropology as a Weapon of Social Combat in Late-Nineteenth-Century France," *Journal of the History of the Behavioural Sciences* 16 (1980): 118–32.

54. Hugh McLeod, *Secularisation in Western Europe, 1848–1914* (Basingstoke [United Kingdom]: Macmillan Press; New York: St. Martin's Press, 2000), 120–21, 149–57.

55. Mazzotti, "For science and for the Pope-King," 273–74, 279–80.

56. Pope Leo XIII, *Sapientiae Christianae* ("The Chief Duties of Christians as Citizens"), in *Pope and the People*, 154.

57. George V. Coyne, "Evolution and the Human Person: The Pope in Dialogue," in *Evolutionary and Molecular Biology: Scientific Perspectives on Divine Action*, ed. Robert John Russell, William R. Stoeger, and Francisco J. Ayala (Vatican City State: Vatican Observatory Publications; Berkeley, Calif.: Center for Theology and the Natural Sciences, 1998), 12. The source of the quotation in the above work is from Pope Leo XIII, *Motu Proprio, Ut Mysticam*, published in Sabino Maffeo, *In the Service of Nine Popes: One Hundred Years of the Vatican Observatory*, trans. G. V. Coyne (Vatican City State: Vatican Observatory Publications, 1991), 205. See also George V. Coyne, "The Church in Dialogue with Science: The Wojtyla Years," in *New Catholic Encyclopedia; Jubilee Volume: The Wojtyla Years* (Detroit, Mich.: Gale Group, 2001), 101.

58. William Clifford, "The Days of the Week, and the Works of Creation," *Dublin Review* 3rd ser. 5 (April 1881): 311–32; quotation from 314.

59. Some readers questioned his orthodoxy, but Clifford, confident of his position, did not concern himself about this. Instead, he responded to readers who objected that his theory was not supported by sufficient proof. See William Clifford, "The Days of Creation: A Reply," *Dublin Review* 3rd ser. 6 (October 1881): 498–507.

60. Sources given by Vaughan include an anonymous French bishop, quoted in a note from the editor of *Annales de Philosophie Chrétienne* [Paris] (December 1881/January 1882); P. de Foville, *Review des Questions Scientifiques* [Brussels] (January 1882): section 9, 78; Arthur Richard, *Revue Générale* (Fevrier 1882): 247, 248; and Pfarrer Westermeher, "Natur und Offenbarung" (Siebenundzwanzigsten Bandes zwölftes, Heft., Münster, 1881): circa 735.

61. John S. Vaughan, "Bishop Clifford's Theory of the Days of Creation," *Dublin Review* 3rd ser. 9, no. 1 (January 1883): 32–47; quotations from 33, 47, 39–40.

62. William Clifford, "The Days of Creation: Some Further Observations," *Dublin Review* 3rd ser. 9 (1883): 397–417; quotation from 416.

63. John H. Cardinal Newman, "On the Inspiration of Scripture," *Nineteenth Century* 15, no. 84 (February 1884): 187.

64. Ibid., 191.

65. Ibid., 190.

66. Ibid., 189, 190.

67. Ibid., 190.

68. Ibid., 197–98.

69. John Healy, "Cardinal Newman on the Inspiration of Scripture," *Irish Ecclesiastical Record* 3rd ser. 5 (March 1884): 137–49.

70. *What Is of Obligation for a Catholic to Believe concerning the Inspiration of the Canonical Scriptures: Being a Postscript to an article in the February No. of the 'Nineteenth Century Review' in answer to Professor Healy* (London: Burns & Oates, 1884), 7, quoted in James Tunstead Burtchaell, *Catholic Theories of Biblical Inspiration since 1810: A Review and Critique* (London: Cambridge University Press, 1969), 76–77.

71. H. J. T. Johnson, "Leo XIII, Cardinal Newman and the Inerrancy of Scripture," *Downside Review* 69 (1951): 420.

72. John Cuthbert Hedley, "Can the Scriptures Err?" *Dublin Review* 3rd ser. 20 (1888): 145.

73. Ibid., 154.

74. Ibid., 145, 148–50, 158.

75. Ibid., 158–60, 155.

76. Ibid., 161.

77. Harvey Hill, "Leo XIII, Loisy, and the 'Broad School': An Early Round of the Modernist Crisis," *Catholic Historical Review* 89, no. 1 (January 2003): 41–42.

78. Alec R. Vidler, *The Modernist Movement in the Roman Church: Its Origins & Outcome* (London: Cambridge University Press, 1934), 82–85.

79. Pope Leo XIII, *Providentissimus Deus*, in *The Great Encyclical Letters of Pope Leo XIII* (New York: Benziger Brothers, 1903), 292–93.

80. Ibid., 282.

81. Ibid., 282, 293.

82. Ernan McMullin, "Galileo on science and Scripture," in *The Cambridge Companion to Galileo*, ed. Peter Machamer (Cambridge: Cambridge University Press, 1998), 343–44 n. 141.

83. Michael Segre, "Critiques and Contentions: Light on the Galileo Case?" *Isis* 88 (1997): 485; and Paul Poupard, "Introduction: Galileo Galilei: 350 Years of Subsequent History," in *Galileo Galilei: Toward a Resolution of 350 Years of Debate—1633–1983*, ed. Paul Poupard (Pittsburgh, Pa.: Duquesne University Press, 1987), xviii.

84. Annibale Fantoli, *Galileo: For Copernicanism and for the Church*, trans. George V. Coyne, 2nd ed. (Vatican City State: Vatican Observatory Publications, 1996), 502–3.

85. Leo XIII, *Providentissimus Deus*, 296. Parenthetical references to *Providentissimus Deus* refer to page numbers in *Great Encyclical Letters of Pope Leo XIII* (n. 79 above).

86. The points raised by Galileo concerning the Copernican hypothesis could also be made in defense of evolutionary theory. Galileo believed that the conclusions of the church fathers concerning propositions about nature derived from scripture should be accepted only on matters that were debated "with great diligence" and on which opinion was unanimous. But this was not the case concerning the sun's stationary position and the earth's motion. There was no reflection, no controversy, no conclusion, therefore nothing could be inferred from the silence of the fathers on this issue. *Letter to the Grand Duchess Christina*, in *The Galileo Affair: A Documentary History*, ed. and trans. Maurice A. Finocchiaro, (Berkeley: University of California Press, 1989), 108. Furthermore, cognizance had to be taken of the Principle of Accommodation: even if the heliocentric and geokinetic ideas had been conclusively demonstrated, it would still have been necessary to state the opposite in order to "maintain credibility" with the vast majority of people (ibid., 106). Therefore, if the consensus of the fathers was established, it would not testify to the truth; rather it would only point to a means of expression designed to accommodate popular understanding. But what about the decree on scripture issued by the Council of Trent? Galileo argued that the church did not oblige its members to regard conclusions about natural phenomena as articles of faith when these arose from the unanimous interpretation of scripture by the fathers. The decree in question pertained only to "those propositions which are articles of faith or involve morals" (ibid., 108–9). Galileo maintained that the "holiest Fathers" were very prudent and that they "knew how harmful and how contrary to the primary function of the Catholic church it would be to want to use scriptural passages to establish conclusions about nature, when by means of observation and necessary demonstrations one could at some point demonstrate the contrary of what the words literally say" (ibid., 110).

87. Leo XIII, *Providentissimus Deus*, 295.

88. Paschal Scotti, "Wilfrid Ward: A Religious Fabius Maximus," *Catholic Historical Review* 88, no. 1 (January 2002): 53.

89. J. Derek Holmes, "Some Notes on Liberal Catholicism and Catholic Modernism," *Irish Theological Quarterly* n.s. 38, no. 4 (October 1971): 352.

90. Leo XIII, *Providentissimus Deus*, 290.

4. Defensive Strategies

1. See Harry W. Paul, "Religion and Darwinism: Varieties of Catholic Reaction," 405–6; and Robert E. Stebbins, "France," 157, both in *The Comparative Reception of Darwinism*, ed. Thomas F. Glick (Chicago: University of Chicago Press, 1988).

2. Harry W. Paul, *The Edge of Contingency: French Catholic Reaction to Scientific Change from Darwin to Duhem* (Gainesville: University Presses of Florida, 1979), 24.

3. Peter J. Bowler, *Charles Darwin: The Man and His Influence* (Cambridge: Cambridge University Press, 1996), 133–34, 154–55, 163–64; and idem, *The Eclipse of Darwinism: Anti-Darwinian Evolution Theories in the Decades around 1900* (Baltimore: Johns Hopkins University Press, 1983), 22–26 and 229 n. 8; David N. Livingstone, *Darwin's Forgotten Defenders: The Encounter between Evangelical Theology and Evolutionary Thought* (Grand Rapids: William B. Eerdmans; Edinburgh: Scottish Academic Press, 1987), 52–53.

4. Charles Darwin, *The Origin of Species by Means of Natural Selection or The Preservation of Favoured Races in the Struggle for Life* (1859; reprint, edited with an introduction by J. W. Burrow, London: Penguin Books, 1985), 205; parenthetical page references in this section are to this edition.

5. Natural selection did not give rise to "absolute perfection." Even the "most perfect organ"—the eye—was flawed. The sting of a bee was far from perfect; it could not be withdrawn without causing the death of the insect (Darwin, *Origin*, 229–30).

6. John Tyler Bonner and Robert M. May, introduction to *The Descent of Man and Selection in Relation to Sex*, by Charles Darwin (1871; reprint, Princeton, N.J.: Princeton University Press, 1981), xvii–xx.

7. J.G.C., "Darwinism," *Irish Ecclesiastical Record* n.s. 9 (1873): 339.

8. Stephen G. Brush, "The Nebular Hypothesis and the Evolutionary Worldview," *History of Science* 25, no. 3 (1987): 263–64.

9. Alvar Ellegård, *Darwin and the General Reader: The Reception of Darwin's Theory of Evolution in the British Periodical Press, 1859–1872* (1958; reprint, with a foreword by David L. Hull, Chicago: University of Chicago Press, 1990), 174–75, 189–90.

10. John Hedley Brooke, *Science and Religion: Some Historical Perspectives* (Cambridge: Cambridge University Press, 1991), 286–87.

11. Ellegård, *Darwin and the General Reader*, 194.

12. Bowler, *Charles Darwin*, 166.

13. Lewis Pyenson and Susan Sheets-Pyenson, *Servants of Nature: A History of Scientific Institutions, Enterprises and Sensibilities* (London: Fontana Press, 1999), 404.

14. Darwin, *Descent of Man*, 2:389; see also chapter 1, vol. 1.

15. J.G.C., "Darwinism," 361.

16. Patrick Allitt, *Catholic Converts: British and American Intellectuals Turn to Rome* (Ithaca, N.Y.: Cornell University Press, 1997), ix.

17. Jacob W. Gruber, *A Conscience in Conflict: The Life of St. George Jackson Mivart* (Westport, Conn.: Greenwood Press, 1960), 224.

18. William J. Schoenl, *The Intellectual Crisis in English Catholicism: Liberal Catholics, Modernists, and the Vatican in the Late Nineteenth and Early Twentieth Centuries* (New York: Garland Publishing, 1982), 18.

19. James Tunstead Burtchaell, "The Biblical Question and the English Liberal Catholics," *Review of Politics* 31, no. 1 (January 1969): 109–10.

20. See Edward Norman, *The English Catholic Church in the Nineteenth Century* (Oxford: Clarendon Press, 1984), 343.

21. Huxley, after joining the Metaphysical Society (London), came into regular contact with a number of well-known Catholics, including Cardinal Henry Edward Manning, William George Ward, and Fr. John Dobree Dalgairns. The members of the society embraced a diversity of beliefs—Roman Catholicism, Anglicanism, Unitarianism, positivism, pantheism, and agnosticism. Huxley's relationship with the Catholic members of the society was "most friendly." Cordiality, it seems, proved inimical to debate, and in Huxley's words "the society died of too much love." Wilfrid Ward, *Problems and Persons* (London: Longmans, Green and Co., 1903), 234–35.

22. Gruber, *Conscience in Conflict*, 36–37. Subsequent parenthetical references in this section are to the pages in this volume.

23. St. George Mivart, *The Genesis of Species*, 2nd ed. (London: Macmillan, 1871), 317.

24. Ibid., 302–5.

25. Ibid., 319.

26. George Ward was regarded as "more papal than the Pope." He frequently referred to various ecclesiastical decrees when engaging in debate and tended to exaggerate the meaning of these documents. His criticism of Cardinal Newman was "unsparing and without reticence." Percy Fitzgerald, *Fifty Years of Catholic Life and Social Progress: Under Cardinals Wiseman, Manning, Vaughan, and Newman*, 2 vols. (London: T. Fisher Unwin, 1901), 1:138.

27. Gruber, *Conscience in Conflict*, 70–74.

28. Ibid., 77.

29. John Brooke and Geoffrey Cantor, *Reconstructing Nature: The Engagement of Science and Religion* (Edinburgh: T&T Clark, 1998), 257.

30. Gruber, *Conscience in Conflict*, 87.

31. Ibid.

32. Ibid., 92. See also Ruth Barton, "Evolution: The Whitworth Gun in Huxley's War for the Liberation of Science from Theology," in *The Wider Domain of Evolutionary Thought*, ed. David Oldroyd and Ian Langham (Dordrecht, Holland: D. Reidel Publishing Company, 1983), 267, 271.

33. Bertram C. A. Windle, *A Century of Scientific Thought & Other Essays* (London: Burns & Oates, 1915), 3.

34. Gruber, *Conscience in Conflict*, 97.

35. Ibid., 222–23.

36. Ellegård, *Darwin and the General Reader*, 182.

37. N. D. McMillan, "Convergent Opposites: The Correspondence of the Irishmen George Gabriel Stokes and John Tyndall," *Carloviana* [County Carlow, Ireland] no. 48 (December 2000): 41.

38. Frank M. Turner, *Contesting Cultural Authority: Essays in Victorian Intellectual Life* (Cambridge: Cambridge University Press, 1993), 190–95.

39. James R. Moore, *The Post-Darwinian Controversies: A study of the Protestant struggle to come to terms with Darwin in Great Britain and America 1870–1900* (Cambridge: Cambridge University Press, 1979), 120.

40. J. Murphy, "The Case of Galileo," *Nineteenth Century* 19 (May 1886): 722.

41. J. Murphy, "Evolution and Faith," *Irish Ecclesiastical Record* 3rd ser. 5 (1884): 756–67; idem, "Faith and Evolution," *Irish Ecclesiastical Record* 3rd ser. 6 (1885): 481–96, 723–36; John S. Vaughan, "Faith and Evolution: A Further Consideration of the Question," *Irish Ecclesiastical Record* 3rd ser. 6 (1885): 413–24; idem, "Faith and Evolution: A Reply," *Irish Ecclesiastical Record* 3rd ser. 6 (1885): 651–64.

42. Gruber, *Conscience in Conflict*, 166.

43. John D. Root, "The Final Apostasy of St. George Jackson Mivart," *Catholic Historical Review* 71, no. 1 (January 1985): 5.

44. St. George Mivart, "Modern Catholics and Scientific Freedom," *Nineteenth Century* 18 (July 1885): 39.

45. Ibid., 40–41.

46. Ibid., 43.

47. Murphy, "Evolution and Faith" (1884), 761. Mivart quoted him in "Modern Catholics and Scientific Freedom," 43.

48. Murphy, "Evolution and Faith," 765–66.

49. Ibid., 760; Mivart, "Modern Catholics," 45.

50. Mivart, "Modern Catholics," 46.

51. Adrian Desmond, *Huxley: From Devil's Disciple to Evolution's High Priest* (London: Penguin Books, 1998), 538.

52. Huxley to Mivart, 12 November 1885, in St. George Mivart, "Some Reminiscences of Thomas Henry Huxley," *Nineteenth Century* 42 (December 1897): 998.

53. Gruber, *Conscience in Conflict*, 168–69.

54. Murphy, "Case of Galileo," 736.

55. *Inter Gravissimas* declared that "all philosophers who wish to be sons of the Church, and philosophy itself likewise, are bound in duty never to say anything contrary to the Church's teaching, and to retract those things about which she may have admonished them." This statement applied with equal effect to scientists. *Tuas Libenter* stated that "although the natural sciences depend on their own

principles known from reason, yet Catholic students of these sciences must keep their eyes on revelation as a guiding star, that they may avoid the labyrinths of error." Pope Pius IX then proceeded to state that Catholic scientists were bound to accept not only defined articles of faith but also the teaching of the ordinary magisterium of the church (ibid., 737). The church granted the autonomy of science with one hand and withdrew it with the other.

56. St. George Mivart, "The Catholic Church and Biblical Criticism," *Nineteenth Century* 22 (July 1887), 32, 36. Page numbers in parentheses in the next few paragraphs refer to this article.

57. J. F. Stephen, "Mr. Mivart's Modern Catholicism," *Nineteenth Century* 22 (October 1887), 586. Page numbers in parentheses refer to this article.

58. St. George Mivart, "Catholicity and Reason," *Nineteenth Century* 22 (December 1887), 852–53. Page numbers in parentheses in the following paragraphs refer to this article.

59. For a similar opinion see James Tunstead Burtchaell, *Catholic Theories of Biblical Inspiration since 1810: A Review and Critique* (London: Cambridge University Press, 1969), 82–83.

60. J. Anselm Wilson, *The Life of Bishop Hedley* (London: Burns, Oates & Washbourne, 1930): 208–10.

61. St. George Mivart, "Letter from Dr. Mivart on the Bishop of Newport's Article in Our Last Number," *Dublin Review* 3rd ser. 19 (January–April 1888): 180–87.

62. J.C.H., "The Bishop of Newport's Rejoinder," *Dublin Review* 3rd ser. 19 (January–April 1888): 188–89.

63. John Cuthbert Hedley, "Can the Scriptures Err?" *Dublin Review* 3rd ser. 20 (1888), 164–65.

64. Mivart understood that he was permitted to retain his opinions about hell but that he was forbidden to disseminate them because of the fear that they would give rise to "misapprehensions." See Gruber, *Conscience in Conflict,* 184–85.

5. The Suppression of the Mivartian Hypothesis

1. Harry W. Paul, "Religion and Darwinism: Varieties of Catholic Reaction," in *The Comparative Reception of Darwinism,* ed. Thomas F. Glick (Chicago: University of Chicago Press, 1988), 426–27.

2. Harry W. Paul, "Science and the Catholic Institutes in Nineteenth-Century France," *Societas—A Review of Social History* 1, no. 4 (1971): 272–73.

3. Paul, "Religion and Darwinism," 430.

4. John A. O'Brien, *Evolution and Religion: A Study of the Bearing of Evolution upon the Philosophy of Religion* (New York: Century Co., 1932), 110. In the debate mentioned earlier between Fr. Jeremiah Murphy and Fr. John S. Vaughan, the latter priest declared that it would put the obedience and faith of his co-religionists

to a cruel test if they were told by their church that human evolution was irreconcilable with church doctrine. See John S. Vaughan, "Faith and Evolution: A Reply," *Irish Ecclesiastical Record* 3rd ser. 6 (1885): 652.

5. Early Christian theologians such as St. Gregory of Nyssa (A.D. 331–396) and St. Augustine of Hippo (A.D. 354–430) were influenced by Greek philosophy when attempting to ascertain the true sense of scripture. The Alexandrine fathers supported the notion that the universe originated from a single divine act and that the six days of creation were to be understood in an allegorical sense. Gregory argued that what was created at the beginning had properties that would permit the development of all that was to emerge later. Augustine hypothesized about *rationes seminales*—the "seed principles"—which served the function of reconciling two apparently conflicting claims: first, that God made all kinds of things at the beginning of time; and, second, that different kinds of things came into existence gradually throughout the course of time. To what extent Augustine's view of nature can be regarded as evolutionary is a matter of debate. The most important aspect of his work concerning this subject is that it showed how ideas about evolution and creation could be harmonized. In bringing various kinds of things into existence God could intervene directly and miraculously in each case or establish secondary causes in nature to bring about a gradual emergence of new kinds. Augustine believed that scripture could be interpreted with either of these two ideas in mind. Ernan McMullin, "Introduction: Evolution and Creation," in *Evolution and Creation*, ed. Ernan McMullin (Notre Dame, Ind.: University of Notre Dame Press, 1985), 11–17.

6. Harry W. Paul, *The Edge of Contingency: French Catholic Reaction to Scientific Change from Darwin to Duhem* (Gainesville: University Presses of Florida, 1979), 74; see also 71–72.

7. Ernest C. Messenger, *Evolution and Theology: The Problem of Man's Origin* (London: Burns, Oates & Washbourne, 1931), 232–33.

8. Barry Brundell, "Catholic Church politics and evolution theory, 1894–1902," *British Journal for the History of Science* 34 (2001): 87–88.

9. J. A. Zahm, *Bible, Science, and Faith* (Baltimore: John Murphy & Co., 1894), 38–42.

10. Thomas J. Schlereth, new introduction to *Evolution and Dogma*, by John Augustine Zahm (1898; reprint, New York: Arno Press, 1978), 4–5.

11. Zahm, *Evolution and Dogma*, xii–xiv, xvi. Page numbers in parentheses in the following paragraphs refer to this work.

12. Schlereth, new introduction to *Evolution and Dogma*, by Zahm, 8.

13. Ralph E. Weber, *Notre Dame's John Zahm: American Catholic Apologist and Educator* (Notre Dame, Ind.: University of Notre Dame Press, 1961), 99, 106–7.

14. R. Scott Appleby, "Exposing Darwin's 'hidden agenda': Roman Catholic responses to evolution, 1875–1925," in *Disseminating Darwinism: The Role of Place, Race, Religion and Gender*, ed. Ronald L. Numbers and John Stenhouse (Cambridge: Cambridge University Press, 1999), 193.

15. Brundell, "Catholic Church politics," 88–92.

16. Words in quotation marks from Messenger, *Evolution and Theology*, 233.

17. Weber, *Notre Dame's John Zahm*, 123–24.

18. Messenger, *Evolution and Theology*, 234.

19. Brundell, "Catholic Church politics," 91.

20. Giuliano Pancaldi, *Darwin in Italy: Science across Cultural Frontiers*, trans. Ruey Brodine Morelli (Bloomington: Indiana University Press, 1991), 164.

21. Bishop Hedley, *Evolution and Faith with Other Essays* (London: Sheed & Ward, 1931), 54; from an article previously published in the *Dublin Review* (July 1871).

22. John Cuthbert Hedley, "Physical Science and Faith," *Dublin Review* 4th ser., no. 28 (October 1898): 258.

23. J. Anselm Wilson, *The Life of Bishop Hedley* (London: Burns, Oates & Washbourne, 1930), 169–70.

24. Brundell, "Catholic Church politics," 93.

25. Schlereth, new introduction to *Evolution and Dogma*, by Zahm, 9.

26. Alec R. Vidler, *The Modernist Movement in the Roman Church: Its Origins & Outcome* (London: Cambridge University Press, 1934), 60–65.

27. Barry Brundell emphasized that the Jesuits in Rome were untypical of their order. The Jesuits in France in the 1890s, for example, were much less reactionary. For evidence of this Brundell points to their journal *Etudes* (83 n. 5).

28. Ibid., 93–94.

29. Dom Paschal Scotti, "Happiness in Hell: The Case of Dr. Mivart," *Downside Review* 119, part 416 (2001): 187.

30. Jacob W. Gruber, *A Conscience in Conflict: The Life of St. George Jackson Mivart* (Westport, Conn.: Greenwood Press, 1960), 191.

31. St. George Mivart, "Roman Congregations and Modern Thought," *North American Review* 170 (April 1900): 571.

32. St. George Mivart, "Some Recent Catholic Apologists," *Fortnightly Review* 67 (1900): 34, 36.

33. Maurice A. Finocchiaro, "Galileo as a 'bad theologian': A formative myth about Galileo's trial," *Studies in History and Philosophy of Science* 33A, no. 4 (December 2002): 776–77.

34. St. George Mivart, "The Continuity of Catholicism," *Nineteenth Century* 47 (January 1900): 61–62.

35. Mivart, "Some Recent Catholic Apologists," 38.

36. Mivart, "Continuity of Catholicism," 72 n. 32. Cardinal Francesco Satolli, the first permanent apostolic delegate to the United States and a declared opponent of evolution, was excluded from this group of prelates. Mivart, "Some Recent Catholic Apologists," 37.

37. Mivart, "Continuity of Catholicism," 56, 72.

38. It was not credible, in the light of scientific discoveries, to argue that the work of creation occurred over a period of six days (each day corresponding to an

axial rotation of the earth). Therefore Christian apologists tended to argue that the six days were not to be taken literally, despite the emphasis on the words "morning" and "evening" in the biblical text. Furthermore, these days did not necessarily correspond to geological epochs. Such a conveniently nebulous interpretation of "day" facilitated the defense of scripture against the troublesome implications of scientific theories. For an example of this approach to reconciling the Bible and science, see John Smyth, *Genesis and Science: Inspiration of the Mosaic Ideas of Creative Work* (London: Burns & Oates, 1898).

39. Mivart, "Some Recent Catholic Apologists," 43; idem, "Continuity of Catholicism," 59.

40. R. F. Clarke, "Dr. Mivart on the Continuity of Catholicism," *Nineteenth Century* 47 (February 1900): 254–55. The eminent Catholic apologist Wilfrid Ward also expressed the opinon that Mivart was not a Catholic. Wilfrid Ward, "Liberalism and Intransigeance," *Nineteenth Century* 47 (June 1900): 961 n. 1.

41. Gruber, *Conscience in Conflict*, 198.

42. David G. Schultenover, *A View from Rome: On the Eve of the Modernist Crisis* (New York: Fordham University Press, 1993), 132–33.

43. St. George Mivart and Herbert Vaughan, *Under the Ban: A Correspondence between Dr. St. George Mivart and Herbert Cardinal Vaughan* (New York: Tucker Publishing Co., 1900), 4.

44. Ibid., 10–13. Mivart demanded "reparation" in one of the following ways: (1) a letter from Vaughan expressing regret for the offensive statements made against him in the *Tablet*; (2) the publication in the *Tablet* of a retraction and an apology; (3) a letter from the author of the article withdrawing the offensive statements and requesting forgiveness.

45. Mivart's assessment of *Providentissimus Deus* was particularly harsh. It is interesting to note that Andrew D. White, a self-declared opponent of dogmatic theology, was benign in his attitude toward both Leo XIII and his encyclical. See White, *A History of the Warfare of Science with Theology in Christendom*, 2 vols. (1896; reprint, 2 vols. in 1, New York: George Braziller, 1955), 2:364–66.

46. Mivart, "Roman Congregations and Modern Thought," 574.

47. St. George Mivart, "Scripture and Roman Catholicism," *Nineteenth Century* 47 (March 1900): 425–42.

48. Robert Edward Dell, "A Liberal Catholic View of the Case of Dr. Mivart," *Nineteenth Century* 47, no. 278 (April 1900): 669.

49. Schultenover, *View from Rome*, 90; see also pp. 124–25 for background information on these Catholic writers. Fr. William Barry and Mivart were "on most friendly terms" from about 1886, but Barry, a liberal Catholic, did not share Mivart's unorthodox views. William Barry, *Memories and Opinions* (London: G. P. Putnam's Sons, 1926), 220–22, and Appendix (pp. 295–300).

50. William J. Schoenl, *The Intellectual Crisis in English Catholicism: Liberal Catholics, Modernists, and the Vatican in the Late Nineteenth and Early Twentieth Centuries* (New York: Garland Publishing, 1982), 90–91.

51. In 1901 the Catholic apologist Percy Fitzgerald wrote that liberal Catholics could no longer express criticism of their church with impunity. After the excommunication of Mivart it was now more likely that they would be confronted with the stark choice of retracting their views or suffering the ultimate sanction of expulsion. Percy Fitzgerald, *Fifty Years of Catholic Life and Social Progress: Under Cardinals Wiseman, Manning, Vaughan, and Newman*, 2 vols. (London: T. Fisher Unwin, 1901), 2:421.

52. Schultenover, *View from Rome*, 138–43, 148–51.

53. Edward Norman, *The English Catholic Church in the Nineteenth Century* (Oxford: Clarendon Press, 1984), 334.

54. Text of the Joint Pastoral Letter, by the Cardinal Archbishop and the Bishops of the Province of Westminster, Appendix B in *Letters from a "Modernist": The Letters of George Tyrrell to Wilfrid Ward 1893–1908*, introduced and annotated by Mary Jo Weaver (Shepherdstown, W.V.: Patmos Press; London: Sheed & Ward, 1981), 132. Page numbers in parentheses in subsequent paragraphs refer to this book.

55. Paschal Scotti, "Wilfrid Ward: A Religious Fabius Maximus," *Catholic Historical Review* 88, no. 1 (January 2002): 62; in reference to "The Recent Anglo-Roman Pastoral," *Nineteenth Century* 49 (May 1901): 736–54.

56. Wilson, *Bishop Hedley*, 171.

57. Brundell, "Catholic Church politics," 92.

58. Schultenover, *A View from Rome*, 150–51, 158 n. 78.

6. Antimodernism

1. Roger Aubert, "The Modernist Crisis," in *History of the Church*, vol. 9, *The Church in the Industrial Age*, ed. Hubert Jedin and John Dolan (London: Burns and Oates, 1981), 420.

2. Josef L. Altholz, *The Churches in the Nineteenth Century* (Indianapolis: Bobbs-Merrill, 1967), 161.

3. Alec R. Vidler, *The Modernist Movement in the Roman Church: Its Origins & Outcome* (London: Cambridge University Press, 1934), 53–59.

4. H. Daniel-Rops, *A Fight for God: 1870–1939* (London: J. M. Dent; New York: E. P. Dutton, 1966), 208.

5. Peter J. Bowler, *Reconciling Science and Religion: The Debate in Early Twentieth-Century Britain* (Chicago: University of Chicago Press, 2001), 208.

6. See Harry W. Paul, *The Edge of Contingency: French Catholic Reaction to Scientific Change from Darwin to Duhem* (Gainesville: University Presses of Florida, 1979), 189.

7. See Edward P. Arbez, "Genesis I–XI and Prehistory," part 1, *American Ecclesiastical Review* 123 (1950), 83.

8. Oskar Köhler, "The Question of the Bible," in *History of the Church*, vol. 9, ed. Jedin and Dolan, 329.

9. Kenneth Scott Latourette, *Christianity in a Revolutionary Age: A History of Christianity in the Nineteenth and Twentieth Centuries*, vol. 1, *The Nineteenth Century in Europe: Background and the Roman Catholic Phase* (London: Eyre & Spottiswoode, 1959), 395.

10 In the first decade of the twentieth century the greatest progress in Catholic theological studies was occurring in France, Germany, Belgium, Britain, and Italy. There was very little theological creativity in America, Spain, Poland, and other countries with Catholic communities. See James Tunstead Burtchaell, *Catholic Theories of Biblical Inspiration since 1810: A Review and Critique* (London: Cambridge University Press, 1969), 3–4.

11. Harvey Hill, "Leo XIII, Loisy, and the 'Broad School': An Early Round of the Modernist Crisis," *Catholic Historical Review* 89, no. 1 (January 2003): 58–59.

12. Alister E. McGrath, *Christian Theology: An Introduction*, 2nd ed. (Oxford: Blackwell Publishers, 1997), 105.

13. Latourette, *Christianity in a Revolutionary Age*, 317.

14. Martin Clark identified four different but interacting strands in modernism. First, some modernists called for modest revisions in traditional views of Christian origins. Modernists in this category avoided open conflict with the ecclesiastical authorities. They included the French prelate Archbishop Eudoxe-Irénée Mignot of Albi and the Italian priest Giovanni Semeria. Second, there was an explicit call for progress and change within the church, especially by the Irish Jesuit George Tyrrell. Third, there were attempts to construct a new understanding of Catholic dogma in order to harmonize it with the findings of modern scholarship. The most eminent exponent of this strand was Alfred Loisy. Fourth, there was a philosophical strand derived mainly from the works of Maurice Blondel (1861–1949). It attempted to create an understanding of Christian belief that would be more robust in a culture of skepticism. See Martin Clark, "The Theology of Catholic Modernism," *Church Quarterly Review* 164 (1963): 458–59. Clark's analysis elicited sharp criticism from Alexander Dru in his article "Modernism and the Present Position of the Church," *Downside Review* 82 (1964): 103–10.

15. See Edward R. Norman, *The English Catholic Church in the Nineteenth Century* (Oxford: Clarendon Press, 1984), 334.

16. The Congregation for the Doctrine of the Faith, *Lamentabili sane exitu*, 3 July 1907, in *The Popes against Modern Errors: 16 Papal Documents*, edited and arranged by Anthony J. Mioni (Rockford, Ill.: Tan Books, 1999), 178–79.

17. Pope Pius X, *Pascendi Dominici Gregis*, 8 September 1907, in *Popes against Modern Errors*, ed. Mioni, par. 6.

18. Pius X, *motu proprio, Praestantia Sacrae Scripturae*, 18 November 1907, in *Rome and the Study of Scripture: A Collection of Papal Enactments on the Study of Holy Scripture together with the Decisions of the Biblical Commission*, 7th ed. (St. Meinrad, Ind.: Abbey Press, 1964), 41.

19. Pope Pius X, "The Oath against Modernism," 1 September 1910, in *Popes against Modern Errors*, ed. Mioni, 270–72.

20. Richard P. McBrien, *Lives of the Popes: The Pontiffs from St. Peter to John Paul II* (New York: HarperCollins, 2000), 354.

21. Eamon Duffy, *Saints and Sinners: A History of the Popes* (New Haven: Yale University Press and S4C, 1997), 250–51.

22. Mark Schoof, *A Survey of Catholic Theology, 1800–1970* (Paramus, N.J.: Paulist Newman Press, 1970), 63.

23. There is some speculation about the authorship of *Pascendi Dominici Gregis*. Those who are said to have contributed include "a certain" Fr. L. Billot, Fr. Joseph Lemius—a Vatican theologian who died in 1923—and Cardinal Steinhüber; see Bernard M. G. Reardon, *Roman Catholic Modernism* (London: Adam and Charles Black, 1970), 63. Eamon Duffy states that Lemius drafted the encyclical. See Duffy, *Saints and Sinners*, 249. Roger Aubert attributes authorship to P. J. Lemius (he probably meant J. B. Lemius) and Cardinal Vives y Tutó; see Aubert, "Intervention of Ecclesiastical Authority and the Integralist Reaction," in *The Church in the Industrial Age*, ed. Jedin and Dolan, 458 n. 15.

24. J. B. Lemius, *A Catechism of Modernism* (1908; reprint, Rockford, Ill.: Tan Books, 1981), 5.

25. Stephen G. Lyng and Lester R. Kurtz, "Bureaucratic Insurgency: The Vatican and the Crisis of Modernism," *Social Forces* 63, no. 4 (June 1985): 901–22.

26. Altholz, *Churches in the Nineteenth Century*, 165–66.

27. Vidler, *Modernist Movement*, 216–24.

28. James J. Walsh, *The Popes and Science: The History of the Papal Relations to Science during the Middle Ages and down to Our Time* (New York: Fordham University Press, 1908), 17.

29. The controversy over *The Origin of Species* was not only between Darwinists and theologians but also between younger scientists who supported Darwin and older conservatives who opposed him—there were a number of notable exceptions in the latter group such as Sir Charles Lyell and John Stevens Henslow. In late 1860, Darwin wrote to Huxley, expressing the opinion that widespread acceptance of his theory depended on the younger rather than on the older scientists. J. Vernon Jensen, "Return to the Wilberforce-Huxley Debate," *British Journal for the History of Science* 21, no. 69 (June 1988): 174.

30. Walsh, *Popes and Science*, Appendix I: "Opposition to Scientific Progress," 391.

31. He argued this point in detail, giving as examples the experiences of Andreas Vesalius (1514–1564), William Harvey (1578–1657), Nicolaus Steno (also known as Niels Stensen, 1638–1686), Leopold Auenbrugger (1722–1809), Edward Jenner (1749–1823), René Laënnec (1781–1826), Thomas Young (1773–1829), Georg Simon Ohm (1787–1854), Ignaz Philipp Semmelweis (1818–1865), and Louis Pasteur (1822–1895).

32. Walsh, *Popes and Science*, 390–412.

33. Karl Alois Kneller, *Christianity and the Leaders of Modern Science: A Contribution to the History of Culture in the Nineteenth Century*, trans. T. M. Kettle (Lon-

don: B. Herder, 1911), 5–6. Page numbers in parentheses in the following paragraphs refer to this work.

34. Kneller gave many examples, including the following: the chemists Jöns Jacob Berzelius (1779–1848), Jean Baptiste André Dumas (1800–1884), and Justus von Liebig (1803–1873); the physicists Alessandro Giuseppe Volta (1745–1827), André Marie Ampère (1775–1836), and Michael Faraday (1791–1867); the astronomers Urbain Le Verrier (1811–1877) and Pierre Simon de Laplace (1749–1827); the physician René Laënnec (1781–1826); and the founder of modern bacteriology, Louis Pasteur (1822–1895). Kneller's list on p. 390 is more extensive; see also p. 392.

35. Darwin was impressed by the argument from design, but it did not convince him to accept the existence of a First Cause because there would still be a difficulty in explaining how it originated. *The Autobiography of Charles Darwin and Selected Letters*, ed. Francis Darwin (New York: Dover Publications, 1958), 61. Darwin observed many instances of imperfection, waste, and suffering in nature which made it difficult for him to believe in a benevolent deity. He could not persuade himself that "a beneficent and omnipotent God would have designedly created the Ichneumonidae with the express intention of their feeding within the live bodies of Caterpillars, or that a cat should play with mice." Quoted in Tess Cosslett, "Introductory Essay," in *Science and Religion in the Nineteenth Century*, ed. Tess Cosslett (Cambridge: Cambridge Universtiy Press, 1984), 8. Kneller, who read Francis Darwin's *Life and Letters of Charles Darwin*, vol. 1 (London: 1888), was probably aware of Darwin's views about the implications for religion arising from the imperfections and suffering in nature.

36. Kneller, *Leaders of Modern Science*, 373–86.

37. Bill McSweeney, *Roman Catholicism: The Search for Relevance* (Oxford: Basil Blackwell, 1980), 86.

38. Carroll Stuhlmueller, "Catholic Biblical Scholarship and College Theology," *The Thomist* 23, no. 4 (October 1960): 540–41. Stuhlmueller stated that "no Catholic scholar dared to touch such books as Genesis, Josue, Judges or Isaias" for twenty or thirty years after the beginning of antimodernism. He gave, as evidence for this observation, bibliographies of "modern" Catholic commentaries such as *A Catholic Commentary on Holy Scripture*, ed. B. Orchard (London: Nelson, 1953), and John M. T. Barton's "Recent Catholic Exegesis in English-Speaking Lands," in *Mémorial Lagrange* (Paris: Gabalda, 1940), 239–44.

39. The Pontifical Biblical Commission, "Concerning the Narratives in the Historical Books Which Have Only the Appearances of Being Historical," 23 June 1905, in *Rome and the Study of Scripture*, 117–18.

40. The Pontifical Biblical Commission, "On the Historical Character of the First Three Chapters of Genesis," 30 June 1909, in *Rome and the Study of Scripture*, 122–24.

41. John A. O'Brien, *Evolution and Religion: A Study of the Bearing of Evolution upon the Philosophy of Religion* (New York: Century Co., 1932), 25.

42. Canon Dorlodot, *Darwinism and Catholic Thought*, trans. Ernest Messenger (New York: Benziger Brothers, 1925), 2–3. Page numbers in parentheses refer to this work.

43. Paul, *Edge of Contingency*, 95.

44. Dorlodot, *Darwinism and Catholic Thought*, 62–63.

45. Galileo quoted St. Augustine's *De Genesi ad litteram* at length when warning against the dangers associated with the inappropriate application of scripture to conclusions about nature. Those who were in positions of authority were likely to damage the credibility of the Bible if they used it in support of "distorted and false opinions." This would ruin any prospect of converting knowledgeable non-Christians to the Catholic faith. Galileo quoted St. Augustine as follows: "For how can they believe our books in regard to the resurrection of the dead, the hope of eternal life, and the kingdom of heaven, when they catch a Christian committing an error about something they know very well, when they declare false his opinion taken from those books, and when they find these full of fallacies in regard to things they have already been able to observe or to establish by unquestionable argument?" *Letter to the Grand Duchess Christina*, in *The Galileo Affair: A Documentary History*, ed. and trans. Maurice A. Finocchiaro (Berkeley: University of California Press, 1989), 112.

46. See Bowler, *Reconciling Science and Religion*, 324.

47. See, for example, Paul, *Edge of Contingency*, 78–79.

48. Karl Frank, *The Theory of Evolution in the Light of Facts*, with a chapter on "Ant Guests and Termite Guests" by P. E. Wasmann (London: Kegan Paul, Trench, Trübner & Co.; St. Louis: B. Herder, 1913), 14, 235.

49. Karl Frank ruled out the possibility of spontaneous generation—the essential starting point for the evolution of life (*Theory of Evolution*, 84–108). Life, he asserted, could not be scientifically explained in terms of physics and chemistry.

50. Ibid., especially 159, 230.

51. Bertram C. A. Windle, *The Church and Science* (London: Catholic Truth Society, 1920), 386–87.

7. Catholicism and Science in the Interwar Years

1. John Butler Burke, "Mr. Wells and Modern Science," *Dublin Review* 169, no. 339 (October–December 1921): see especially 222–23, 235–36. J. Ashton, S.J., very much attuned to the philosophy of St. Thomas Aquinas, supported the idea of a teleological evolutionary process ("Evolution as a Theory of Ascent," *Dublin Review* 180 [1927]: 53–72).

2. C. C. Martindale, preface to *Anthropology and the Fall*, by H. J. T. Johnson (Oxford: Basil Blackwell, 1923), x. Page references in parentheses in subsequent paragraphs are to this work.

3. H. Muckermann, *Attitude of Catholics towards Darwinism and Evolution*, 4th ed. (St. Louis: B. Herder, 1924), 110; see also 6–7, 16–17, 22, and 99–100.

4. Harry W. Paul, *The Edge of Contingency: French Catholic Reaction to Scientific Change from Darwin to Duhem* (Gainesville: University Presses of Florida, 1979), 97.

5. See, for example, Hilaire Belloc, "A Few Words with Mr. Wells," *Dublin Review* 166, no. 333 (April–June 1920): 182–202.

6. See Gordon McOuat and Mary P. Winsor, "J.B.S. Haldane's Darwinism in its religious context," *British Journal for the History of Science* 28, no. 97 (June 1995): 227–31.

7. Peter J. Bowler, *Reconciling Science and Religion: The Debate in Early Twentieth-Century Britain* (Chicago: University of Chicago Press, 2001), 327–28, 395–98.

8. Paul, *Edge of Contingency*, 101–2.

9. Ibid., 104.

10. Ibid., 104–5; for background and details of the conference at Altamira, see also John C. Greene, *Darwin and the Modern World View* (Baton Rouge: Louisiana State University Press, 1961), 25–26.

11. E. C. Messenger, "Introduction," in *Theology and Evolution: A Sequel to Evolution and Theology*, ed. E. C. Messenger (London: Sands & Co., 1951), 1, 3.

12. Ernest C. Messenger, *Evolution and Theology: The Problem of Man's Origin* (London: Burns, Oates & Washbourne, 1931), 274. Page numbers in parentheses in subsequent paragraphs refer to this work.

13. The reviewers were from England, Scotland, Ireland, the United States of America, Belgium, and France. They were Rev. P. G. M. Rhodes, professor of dogmatic theology at Oscott College; Rev. R. W. Meagher, professor of dogmatic theology at Ushaw College; Dom Christopher Butler, O.S.B., later abbot of Downside; Rev. P. J. Flood, professor at St. Peter's College, Bearsden, Glasgow; Rev. J. O. Morgan, later canon of Liverpool; Rev. Michael Browne, professor of moral theology at Maynooth College, later bishop of Galway; Rev. William H. McClellan, S.J., professor at St. Mary's College, Woodstock, Maryland; Rev. E. F. Sutcliffe, professor of Scripture at Heythrop College; A. Janssens, College of the Scheut Fathers, Louvain; Professor J. Bittremieux, faculty of theology, Louvain University; Rev. Père A. Brisbois, S.J., Abbé J. Gross, master of conference at the faculty of Catholic theology, University of Strasbourg; Père Lagrange, O.P. The second part of the book was devoted to a study of animation theories by Messenger, Canon Henry de Dorlodot, and Bishop Michael Browne.

14. P. G. M. Rhodes, "The Problem of Man's Origin," in *Theology and Evolution*, ed. Messenger, 3–5.

15. Ibid., 7–9.

16. Messenger observed that the word "rib" was a translation of the Hebrew word *sela*, but *sela* had a broader meaning. Therefore, Eve could have been formed from any part of Adam's body. E. C. Messenger, "Evolution and Theology Today: A Re-examination of the Problems," in *Theology and Evolution*, ed. Messenger, 206–9.

17. Messenger, *Evolution and Theology*, 269–73.

18. Rhodes, "Problem of Man's Origin," 8.

19. Messenger, *Evolution and Theology*, 225.

20. R. W. Meagher, "Evolution and Theology," in *Theology and Evolution*, ed. Messenger, 12–18.

21. John A. O'Brien, *Evolution and Religion: A Study of the Bearing of Evolution upon the Philosophy of Religion* (New York: Century Co., 1932), viii. In support of his claim that the vast majority of scientists regarded evolution as a solidly established theory, O'Brien referred to a statement issued by the council of the American Association for the Advancement of Science at its seventy-sixth meeting in Boston (December 1922). Two thousand members attended out of a total of eleven thousand. No dissenting voice was raised against the assertion that evolution was far more than a "mere guess" (ibid., 20). Page references in subsequent paragraphs are to this work.

22. Sister Mary Frederick, *Religion and Evolution since 1859: Some Effects of the Theory of Evolution on the Philosophy of Religion* (Chicago: Loyola University Press, 1934), 168–71.

23. William M. Agar, *Catholicism and the Progress of Science* (New York: Macmillan, 1940), 95, 99–100. Agar's book was written under the imprimatur of the archbishop of New York, Francis J. Spellman.

24. Pope Pius XI's first encyclical, *Ubi Arcano Dei Consilio* (23 December 1922), was issued in the first year of his pontificate. Its promotion of Catholic Action envisaged the active involvement of the laity in the apostolate of the hierarchy.

25. Pope Pius XI, Discourse on 12 January 1936, in *Discourses of the Popes from Pius XI to John Paul II to the Pontifical Academy of Sciences 1936–1986*, ed. Paul Haffner (Vatican City: Pontificia Academia Scientiarum, 1986), 5–8.

26. G. B. Marini-Bettòlo, *Outlines of the Activity of the Pontifical Academy of Sciences 1936–1986* (Vatican City: Pontificia Academia Scientiarum, 1986), 4, 6. See also Walter Moore, *Shrödinger: Life and thought* (Cambridge: Cambridge University Press, 1992), 322.

27. Ibid., 85–86.

28. Pius XII emphasized more than once that scientific study and research helped people to draw closer to God. A greater understanding of creation assisted in the development of a closer relationship with the Creator. See *Discourses of the Popes*, ed. Haffner, 33–34, 64, 68–69, 73–84; quotation from 33.

29. Pope Pius XII, Discourse to the Pontifical Academy of Sciences, 3 December 1939, in *Discourses of the Popes*, ed. Haffner, 37.

30. P. Flick, S.J., "L' origine del corpo del primo uomo" in *Gregorianum* (1948): 402, quoted in Messenger, *Theology and Evolution*, 188.

31. It was speculated that if the sperm and ova cells that formed Adam's genotype acted in accordance with some kind of divine intervention, so that his body was suitable for the infusion of an immortal soul, then God could be regarded as the "father" of Adam. This point is discussed at greater length by Philip G. Fothergill, *Evolution and Christians* (London: Longmans, Green & Co., 1961), 318–19.

32. Richard Blackwell, "Could there be another Galileo case?" in *The Cambridge Companion to Galileo*, ed. Peter Machamer (Cambridge: Cambridge University Press, 1998), 363.

33. Annibale Fantoli, *Galileo: For Copernicanism and for the Church*, 2nd ed., trans. George V. Coyne (Vatican City State: Vatican Observatory Publications, 1996), 504–5.

34. *Divino Afflante Spiritu* was written by the Jesuit rector of the Pontifical Biblical Institute, Augustine Bea. He was later made cardinal and was highly influential in the proceedings of the Second Vatican Council. Hermann Sasse, "Rome and the Inspiration of Scripture," *Reformed Theological Review* 22, no. 2 (June 1963): 41.

35. Raymond E. Brown, "The Contribution of Historical Biblical Criticism to Ecumenical Church Discussion," in *Biblical Interpretation in Crisis: The Ratzinger Conference on Bible and Church*, ed. Richard John Neuhaus (Grand Rapids: William B. Eerdmans, 1989), 36.

36. Pius XII, *Divino Afflante Spiritu* (1943), par. 49 (London: Catholic Truth Society, 1945).

8. Pope Pius XII and the New Theology

1. Pius XII, formal address "Ad Patres Societatis Iesu in XXIX Congregatione generali electores," *Acta Apostolicae Sedis* 38 (1946): 384f., quoted in Cyril Vollert, "Humani Generis and the Limits of Theology," *Theological Studies* 12 (March 1951): 18.

2. Pius XII, address "Ad Patres delegatos ad Capitulum generale Ordinis Fratrum Praedicatorum," *Acta Apostolicae Sedis* 38 (1946): 387, quoted in Vollert, "Humani Generis," 19.

3. "A Response of the Biblical Commission" to Cardinal Emmanuel Suhard, Archbishop of Paris, 16 January 1948; in *Rome and the Study of Scripture: A Collection of Papal Enactments on the Study of Holy Scripture together with the Decisions of the Biblical Commission*, 7th ed. (St. Meinrad, Ind.: Abbey Press, 1964), 150–53.

4. Humphrey J. T. Johnson, *The Bible and the Early History of Mankind* (London: Burns Oates, 1943), 38.

5. Ibid., 40.

6. E. C. Messenger, ed., *Theology and Evolution: A Sequel to Evolution and Theology* (London: Sands & Co., 1951), 1, 172–73. *Evolution and Theology* had not been reviewed either in *Gregorianum* or in *Biblica*. It received a very cautious review by the Dominican Père Ceuppens in *Angelicum* (October–December 1932): 515–17.

7. Messenger, *Theology and Evolution*, 1, 86, 171.

8. Messenger gives examples of those who were resolutely opposed to the notion that humankind was part of the evolutionary process (*Theology and Evolution*, 173–75). Some of the details are as follows: Thesis 27 of P. Daffara, O.P., *Cursus manualis Theologiae Dogmaticae ad usum Seminariorum*, vol. 2 (Turin: Marietti, 1947), devoted to *De Deo Creatore*; Thesis 33 of the Jesuit P. Bozzola, in his treatise *De Deo Creante* (Naples, 1948); and Cardinal Ruffini's *La teoria dell 'evoluzione*

secondo la scienza e la fede (Rome, 1948). Those who were prepared to consider the possibility of human evolution included P. Victor Marcozzi, professor of biology and anthropology in the Faculty of Philosophy at the Gregorian University; P. Flick, S.J., professor of dogmatic theology; and Dr. Grenier, professor of philosophy at the University of Laval, Canada (see pp. 175–76).

9. Messenger, *Theology and Evolution*, 192–96, 198. Page references in subsequent paragraphs are to this work.

10. It is likely that one of these Catholic scholars was Pierre Teilhard de Chardin, as claimed by Michael John Anthony Fallona, "Polygenism and Theology: Humani Generis and Some Subsequent Developments" (M.A. thesis, Faculty of Theology, University of St. Michael's College, Toronto, Canada, 1967), 23 and 92 n. 8.

11. Vollert, "Humani Generis," 15–16. Vollert carefully avoids giving details about names, places, and exact dates of published and unpublished documents that were deemed to be inimical to the faith.

12. Gustave Weigel, "Current Theology: Gleanings from the Commentaries on Humani Generis," *Theological Studies* 12 (1951): 531.

13. See Jonathan Kwitny, *Man of the Century: The Life and Times of Pope John Paul II* (New York: Warner Books, 1998), 99.

14. Pius XII, *Humani Generis* (1950), parr. 5–6, in *The Popes against Modern Errors: 16 Papal Documents*, edited and arranged by Anthony J. Mioni (Rockford, Ill.: Tan Books, 1999).

15. In his survey of ninety-six articles about *Humani Generis*, Gustave Weigel states ("Commentaries on Humani Generis," 544) that there was "unanimous agreement" about the meaning of polygenism in the encyclical. Polygenism is defined as "the origin of the human race . . . not from a single couple but from an indefinite number of original pairs, unrelated among themselves and directly produced by evolution."

16. Martin Brennan, "Adam and the Biological Sciences," *Irish Theological Quarterly* 35, no. 2 (April 1968): 152–53.

17. The observation that Bellarmine's Principle of Limitation is expressed in *Humani Generis* is made by Marcello Pera, "The god of theologians and the god of astronomers: An apology of Bellarmine," in *The Cambridge Companion to Galileo*, ed. Peter Machamer (Cambridge: Cambridge University Press, 1998), 367, 382–84.

18. Bill McSweeney, *Roman Catholicism: The Search for Relevance* (Oxford: Basil Blackwell, 1980), 87.

19. Karl Otmar von Aretin, *The Papacy and the Modern World* (London: Weidenfeld and Nicolson, 1970), 226.

20. McSweeney, *Roman Catholicism*, 114–15.

21. Michael J. Gruenthaner, "Evolution and the Scriptures," *Catholic Biblical Quarterly* 13 (1951): 26–27.

22. J. Franklin Ewing, "The Present Catholic Attitude Towards Evolution,"

appendix to "Human Evolution–1956," *Anthropological Quarterly* 29 (1956): 137–38.

23. For an argument in support of this point, see Tord Simonsson, *Logical and Semantic Structures in Christian Discourses* (Oslo: Universitetsforlaget, 1971), 52.

24. Weigel, "Commentaries on Humani Generis," 526–27.

25. Vollert, "Humani Generis," 5.

26. Ibid., 5, 21–22.

27. Edward P. Arbez, "Genesis I–XI and Prehistory," part 1, *American Ecclesiastical Review* 123 (1950): 81.

28. Bruno de Solages, "Christianity and Evolution," *Cross Currents* 1 (1951): 26. For a similar opinion see Ewing, "Human Evolution–1956," 133.

29. De Solages, "Christianity and Evolution," 27–28.

30. Jacques de Bivort de la Saudée, ed., *God, Man and the Universe: A Christian answer to modern materialism* (London: Burns & Oates, 1954), vi.

31. E. C. Messenger, "The Origin of Man in the Book of Genesis," in *God, Man and the Universe*, ed. de Bivort de la Saudée, 161, quoting P. Bea, *Questioni Bibliche* (Rome: Pontifical Biblical Institute, 1950), 2:42.

32. Messenger, "Origin of Man," 163.

33. De Bivort de la Saudée, *God, Man and the Universe*, 147 n. 1.

34. Mark Schoof, *A Survey of Catholic Theology, 1800–1970* (Paramus, N.J.: Paulist Newman Press, 1970), 117; Stanley J. Grenz and Roger E. Olson, *Twentieth-Century Theology: God and the World in a Transitional Age* (Milton Keynes, U.K.: Paternoster Press, 1992), 132.

35. Robert Speaight, *Teilhard de Chardin: A Biography* (London: Collins, 1967), 298–99.

36. See Martin Brennan, "From Matter to Man: The Evolutionism of Teilhard de Chardin," *University Review* 5, no. 2 (Summer 1968): 223–33.

37. Pius XII, Discourse to the Pontifical Academy of Sciences, 30 November 1941, in *Discourses of the Popes from Pius XI to John Paul II to the Pontifical Academy of Sciences 1936–1986*, ed. Paul Haffner (Vatican City: Pontificia Academia Scientiarum, 1986), 47.

38. Francis J. McGarrigle, "Could the World Have Had No Beginning?" *Irish Ecclesiastical Record* 5th ser. 41 (January 1933): 1–12.

39. See R. Fullerton, "Basis of Monism—Evolution," *Irish Ecclesiastical Record* 4th ser. 28 (August 1910): 167–68.

40. Henry V. Gill, "Entropy, Life and Evolution," *Studies* 22 (March 1933): 134–38; and idem, *Fact and Fiction in Modern Science* (Dublin: M. H. Gill and Son, 1944), 92–98.

41. Stephen G. Brush, "The Nebular Hypothesis and the Evolutionary Worldview," *History of Science* 25, no. 3 (1987): 262–65.

42. *Discourses of the Popes*, ed. Haffner, 79.

43. Peter J. Bowler and Iwan Rhys Morus, *Making Modern Science: A Historical Survey* (Chicago: University of Chicago Press, 2005), 292–93.

44. David Filkin, *Stephen Hawking's Universe: The Cosmos Explained* (London: BBC Books, 1997), 92; and Trinh Xuan Thuan, *The Changing Universe: Big Bang and After* (London: Thames and Hudson, 1993), 65–66.

45. *Discourses of the Popes*, ed. Haffner, 73.

46. Ibid., 75, 83.

47. In his third argument Aquinas maintained that humans are contingent beings; their existence requires explanation. Everything must have an explanation external to itself. Nothing can provide an explanation for its own existence. In contrast, God is "a necessary being." Humans came to exist because something that already existed (i.e., God) brought them into being. God is the original explanation of our existence. In his fourth argument Aquinas asked, Where do human values, such as truth, nobility, and goodness, come from? His answer was that these qualities must come from something that is itself truthful, noble, and good. He claimed that God is the original source of these ideas.

48. Alister E. McGrath, *Christian Theology: An Introduction*, 2nd ed. (Oxford: Blackwell Publishers, 1997), 160–61.

49. See Alister E. McGrath's *Science and Religion: An Introduction* (Oxford: Blackwell Publishers, 1999), 102, for a summary of Hume's main criticisms of the argument from design.

50. Pope Pius XII, *Acta Apostolicae Sedis* 44 (Vatican City State: Tipografia Poliglotta Vaticana, 1952), 41–42, quoted in George V. Coyne, "Evolution and the Human Person: The Pope in Dialogue," in *Evolutionary and Molecular Biology: Scientific Perspectives on Divine Action*, ed. Robert John Russell, William R. Stoeger, and Francisco J. Ayala (Vatican City State: Vatican Observatory Publications; Berkeley, Calif.: Center for Theology and the Natural Sciences, 1998), 13.

51. George V. Coyne, "The Church in Dialogue with Science: The Wojtyla Years," in *New Catholic Encyclopedia; Jubilee Volume: The Wojtyla Years* (Detroit, Mich.: Gale Group, 2001), 102.

52. G. B. Marini-Bettòlo, *Outlines of the Activity of the Pontifical Academy of Sciences 1936–1986* (Vatican City: Pontificia Academia Scientiarum, 1986), 34.

53. Coyne, "Evolution and the Human Person," 13.

54. See Francis Xavier Murphy, *The Papacy Today* (London: Weidenfeld and Nicolson, 1981), 34–35.

55. Richard P. McBrien, *Catholicism*, new ed. (San Francisco: Harper, 1994), 139; and Anne M. Clifford, "Creation," in *Systematic Theology: Roman Catholic Perspectives*, ed. Francis Schüssler Fiorenza and John P. Galvin (Dublin: Gill and Macmillan, 1992), 229.

9. Science, Faith, and the Second Vatican Council

1. See, e.g., Rémy Collin, *Evolution: Hypotheses and Problems* (London: Burns & Oates, 1959), 116–17, 132–38.

2. J. Franklin Ewing, "Darwin Today," *America*, 21 March 1959, 711.

3. Robert W. Gleason, "A Note on Theology and Evolution," in *Darwin's Vision and Christian Perspectives*, ed. Walter J. Ong (New York: Macmillan, 1960), 105–6 (page numbers in subsequent paragraphs refer to this article). In the foreword of the book, Bishop John Wright of Pittsburg made it clear that he was not prepared to endorse the opinions that had been expressed by the five Catholic authors because such views were of necessity "tentative and cautious" (p. viii).

4. Philip G. Fothergill, *Evolution and Christians* (London: Longmans, Green and Co., 1961). Page references in the following paragraphs are to this work.

5. Ibid., 292; in reference to P. Teilhard de Chardin, *Phenomenon of Man* (1959).

6. For quotations, see *Humani Generis*, paragraphs 35 and 36, in *The Popes against Modern Errors: 16 Papal Documents*, ed. Anthony J. Mioni (Rockford, Ill.: Tan Books, 1999).

7. "Contextualizing Comments," and André-Marie Dubarle, "Original sin in the light of modern science and biblical studies," in *The Problem of Evolution: A study of the philosophical repercussions of evolutionary science*, by John N. Deely and Raymond J. Nogar (New York: Appleton-Century-Crofts, 1973), 313–16.

8. See Eamon Duffy, *Saints and Sinners: A History of the Popes* (New Haven: Yale University Press and S4C, 1997), 270–74.

9. É. Fouilloux, "The Antepreparatory Phase: The Slow Emergence from Inertia (January, 1959–October, 1962)," in *History of Vatican II*, vol. 1, *Announcing and Preparing Vatican Council II toward a New Era in Catholicism*, ed. Giuseppe Alberigo and Joseph A. Komonchak (Maryknoll, N.Y.: Orbis, 1995), 138; and J. A. Komonchak, "The Struggle for the Council during the Preparation of Vatican II (1960–1962)," 244, in ibid.

10. Richard P. McBrien, *Catholicism*, new ed. (San Francisco: Harper, 1994), 765.

11. Ted Peters, "Theology and the Natural Sciences," in *The Modern Theologians: An introduction to Christian theology in the twentieth century*, 2nd ed., ed. David F. Ford (Oxford: Blackwell Publishers, 1997), 651.

12. *Gaudium et Spes*, par. 36, in *Vatican Council II: The Conciliar and Post Conciliar Documents*, new rev. ed., ed. Austin Flannery (Dublin: Dominican Publications, 1992).

13. Annibale Fantoli, *Galileo: For Copernicanism and for the Church*, 2nd ed., trans. George V. Coyne (Vatican City State: Vatican Observatory Publications, 1996), 528 n. 42. See also James Reston, *Galileo: A Life* (London: Cassell, 1994), 140.

14. Georges J. Béné, "Galileo and Contemporary Scientists," in *Galileo Galilei: Toward a Resolution of 350 Years of Debate—1633–1983*, ed. Paul Poupard (Pittsburgh, Pa.: Duquesne University Press, 1987), 181, 189–90.

15. Richard Blackwell, "Could there be another Galileo Case?" in *The Cambridge Companion to Galileo*, ed. Peter Machamer (Cambridge: Cambridge University Press, 1998), 364.

16. Michael Sharratt, *Galileo: Decisive Innovator* (Cambridge: Cambridge University Press, 1996), 211; and Fantoli, *Galileo*, 528–29 nn. 42, 43.

17. *Vatican Council II*, ed. Flannery, 935.

18. John P. Weisengoff, "Inerrancy of the Old Testament in Religious Matters," *Catholic Biblical Quarterly* 17 (1955): 248–57.

19. J. T. Forestell, "The Limitation of Inerrancy," *Catholic Biblical Quarterly* 20 (1958): 9–18.

20. P. Zerafa, "The Limits of Biblical Inerrancy," *Angelicum* 39 (1962): 98–100, 112.

21. Jean de Fraine, *The Bible and the Origin of Man* (New York: Desclee Company, 1962), 7.

22. *Dei Verbum*, parr. 11–12, in *Vatican Council II*, ed. Flannery, 756–58.

23. David F. Wells, *Revolution in Rome* (Downers Grove, Ill.: Intervarsity Press, 1972), 29–34.

24. See J. M. Roberts, *The Penguin History of the World*, 3rd ed. (London: Penguin Books, 1995), 986–88; Richard Bessel, "European Society in the Twentieth Century," in *The Oxford Illustrated History of Modern Europe*, ed. T. C. W. Blanning (Oxford: Oxford University Press, 1998), 251; Bill McSweeney, *Roman Catholicism: The Search for Relevance* (Oxford: Basil Blackwell, 1980), 55; and Ernan McMullin, *Science and the Catholic Tradition* (New York: America Press, 1960), 8.

25. Steve Bruce, *Choice and Religion: A Critique of Rational Choice Theory* (Oxford: Oxford University Press, 1999), 14–17, 21; and idem, *God Save Ulster: The Religion and Politics of Paisleyism* (Oxford: Oxford University Press, 1986), 236–37.

26. Synod of Bishops, "On Dangerous Opinions and on Atheism" (*Ratione habita*), 28 October 1967, in *Vatican Council II: More Postconciliar Documents*, 1st ed., ed. Austin Flannery (Collegeville, Minn.: Liturgical Press, 1982), 663.

27. Ibid.

28. Julian Huxley's *New Bottles for New Wine* (1957), quoted in *Evolution Extended: Biological Debates on the Meaning of Life*, ed. Connie Barlow (Cambridge, Mass.: MIT Press, 1995), 175.

29. Jacques Monod, *Chance and Necessity: An Essay on the Natural Philosophy of Modern Biology*, trans. Austryn Wainhouse (New York: Vintage Books, 1972), 180.

30. Steven Weinberg, *The First Three Minutes: A Modern View of the Origin of the Universe* (London: Andre Deutch, 1977), 154.

31. Richard Dawkins, *The Selfish Gene*, new ed. (Oxford: Oxford University Press, 1989), 198, 330.

32. Ibid., 198.

33. Ibid., 330–31. For a similar polemical discourse, see Daniel C. Dennett, *Darwin's Dangerous Idea: Evolution and the Meanings of Life* (London: Penguin Books, 1996), especially 514–16, 519–20.

34. See, e.g., "Faith and evolution," *The Tablet*, 17 September 1988, pp. 1064–65; Angela Tilby, "The scientist's Gospel," *The Tablet*, 16 May 1992, pp.

606–7; Mary Midgley, "Can science save its soul?" *New Scientist* 135, no. 1832 (1 August 1992): 24–27; Peter Atkins, "Will science ever fail?" *New Scientist* 135, no. 1833 (8 August 1992): 32–35; Henry Porter, "Mind Over Matter: Faith, hope and clarity," *The Guardian*, 23 September 1996, pp. 1–3.

35. Mikael Stenmark, "What Is Scientism?" *Religious Studies* 33, no. 1 (March 1997): 15.

36. Paul Davies, *God and the New Physics* (London: Penguin Books, 1990), ix.

37. Stephen Hawking, *A Brief History of Time: From the Big Bang to Black Holes* (Toronto: Bantam Books, 1995), 193.

38. Ibid., 192.

39. Ibid., see 156–57.

40. Richard Dawkins, *River out of Eden: A Darwinian View of Life* (London: Phoenix, 1996), 155.

41. Ian G. Barbour, *Religion and Science: Historical and Contemporary Issues* (London: SCM Press, 1998), 78–82, 243–44.

42. See, e.g., Michael Rowan-Robinson, *Ripples in the Cosmos: A view behind the scenes of the new cosmology* (Oxford: W. H. Freeman, 1993), 202–3.

43. See, e.g., Cyril Barrett, "Secular Theologians of Science," *Milltown Studies*, no. 36 (Autumn 1995): 5–16. He singles out Stephen Hawking and Richard Dawkins for particular criticism.

44. Mary Midgley, "Visions, Secular and Sacred," *Milltown Studies*, no. 34 (Autumn 1994): 74–88.

45. Philip E. Devine, "Creation and Evolution," *Religious Studies* 32, no. 3 (September 1996): 333–37.

46. Michael Browne, "Genesis 1 and 2," *The Furrow* [Maynooth, Ireland] 21, no. 6 (June 1970): 346; Edward J. Murphy, "God as Creator," *Position Papers 128–129* (Dublin: Four Courts Press, August–September 1984): 219; George Sim Johnston, "The Genesis Controversy," *Position Paper 203* (November 1990): 385–98; Philip Trower, "The Theory of Evolution: Is evolution true? What does it mean?" *Position Paper 236–237* (August–September 1993): 285–96.

47. James B. Stenson, "Evolution—A Catholic Perspective," *Position Papers 128–129* (August–September 1984): 227, 233; and Dermot Lane, "Theology and Science in Dialogue," *Irish Theological Quarterly* 52, nos. 1 and 2 (1986): 38–39.

48. For a discussion of these points, see P. J. McGrath, "Believing in God," *Irish Theological Quarterly* 42, no. 2 (April 1975): 87–96.

49. James P. Mackey, "Theology, Science and the Imagination: Exploring the Issues," *Irish Theological Quarterly* 52, nos. 1 and 2 (1986): 4.

50. Dawkins, *River out of Eden*, 36.

51. Ibid., 37.

52. Davies, *New Physics*, 6.

53. Douglas J. Futuyma, *Evolutionary Biology*, 2nd ed. (Sunderland, Mass.: Sinauer Associates, 1986), 15–16.

54. See Arthur Peacocke, "Biological Evolution and Christian Theology—

Yesterday and Today," in *Darwinism and Divinity: Essays on Evolution and Religious Belief,* ed. John Durant (Oxford: Basil Blackwell, 1985), 114–15; Michael Denton, *Evolution: A Theory in Crisis* (London: Burnett Books, 1985), 355–57; and Mark Ridley, *The Problems of Evolution* (Oxford: Oxford University Press, 1985), 13–14.

55. *Discourses of the Popes from Pius XI to John Paul II to the Pontifical Academy of Sciences 1936–1986,* ed. Paul Haffner (Vatican City: Pontificia Academia Scientiarum, 1986), 103–4. Subsequent parenthetical references are to this work.

56. G. B. Marini-Bettòlo, *Outlines of the Activity of the Pontifical Academy of Sciences 1936–1986* (Vatican City: Pontificia Academia Scientiarum, 1986), 87–109. The issues studied include cosmology and astrophysics—stellar populations (1957); cosmic radiation in interplanetary space (1962); nuclei of galaxies (1970); astrophysical cosmology and fundamental physics (1981); neurosciences—the brain and conscious experience (1964); nerve cells, transmitters, and behavior (1978); developmental neurobiology in mammals (1985); the structure of matter—macromolecules of biological interest (1961); the origin of life and evolution—molecular aspects of the origin of life (1978); the evolution of primates (1982); biochemical bases of biological processes—cancer (1949); the role of nonspecific immunity in the prevention and treatment of cancer (1977); specificity in biological interactions (concerning enzymes, nucleic acids, proteins, pharmaceuticals, transfer ribonucleic acid, and antibody-antigen interactions); the molecular mechanisms of carcinogenic and anti-tumor activities (1986); econometrics—the econometric approach to developmental planning (1963).

57. Ibid., 110–21. Topics studied include man and the environment—science and the protection of the environment (1970); the impact of chemical "events" on the environment (1983); biological and artificial membranes and desalination of water (1975); natural products and the protection of plants (1976); geophysics (1951); persistent meteo-oceanographic anomalies and teleconnections (1986); the utilization of satellite technology—the impact of space exploration on humankind (1984).

58. Ibid., 122–36. Topics studied include agricultural production—the problem of oligoelements in vegetable and animal life (1955); organic matter and soil fertility (1968); the use of fertilizers in crop production with reference to yields, quality, and economics (1972); the application of modern biology to agriculture (1983); tropical diseases—immunization against parasitic diseases (1981); the interaction of parasitic diseases and nutrition (1985); energy resources—energy in terms of requirements, resources, and aspirations (1980); energy for survival and development (1984); the use of satellite technology—the effects of space exploration on humanity (1984); the impact of remote sensing on developing countries (1986).

59. Ibid., 137–41.

60. Ibid., 142–50. The issues studied include genetic mutations in humans (1974); the effects of ionizing radiation on humans (1975); modern biological

experimentation (1982); *in vitro* techniques to treat human infertility (1984); the artificial prolongation of life and the determination of the exact moment of death (1985).

61. Ibid., 151–56.

62. Ibid., 158–70.

63. Kevin D. O'Rourke and Philip Boyle, *Medical Ethics: Sources of Catholic Teachings*, 2nd ed. (Washington, D.C.: Georgetown University Press, 1993), 81.

64. Lara V. Marks, *Sexual Chemistry: A History of the Contraceptive Pill* (New Haven: Yale University Press, 2001), 218; see also 220.

65. For differing accounts of Wojtyla's role, see Carl Bernstein and Marco Politi, *His Holiness: John Paul II and the hidden history of our time* (London: Bantam Books, 1997), 132–33; and George Weigel, *Witness to Hope: The Biography of Pope John Paul II* (New York: Cliff Street Books, 2001), 207–10.

66. Pope Paul VI, *Humanae Vitae* (25 July 1968), par. 2, in *Vatican Council II: More Postconciliar Documents*, ed. Flannery.

67. Words in quotation marks from Edward Stourton, *Absolute Truth: The Catholic Church in the World Today* (London: Viking, 1998), 44.

68. Richard P. McBrien, *Lives of the Popes: The Pontiffs from St. Peter to John Paul II* (New York: HarperCollins, 2000), 380.

69. Robert Blair Kaiser, *The Encyclical That Never Was: The Story of the Commission on Population, Family and Birth, 1964–1966* (London: Sheed & Ward, 1987), 240–89.

70. Desmond M. Clarke, *Church and State: Essays in Political Philosophy* (Cork, Ireland: Cork University Press, 1985), 47–68.

71. Kaiser, *The Encyclical That Never Was*, 68.

72. Karl Rahner, "The Problem of Genetic Manipulation," in *Theological Investigations*, vol. 9, *Writings of 1965–67 I*, trans. Graham Harrison (London: Darton, Longman & Todd; New York: Seabury Press, 1974–76), 225–52.

73. "Declaration on Procured Abortion" (*Quaestio de Abortu*, 18 November 1974), in *Vatican Council II: More Postconciliar Documents*, ed. Flannery, 447.

10. Pope John Paul II's Philosophy of Science and Faith

1. Richard P. McBrien, *Lives of the Popes: The Pontiffs from St. Peter to John Paul II* (New York: HarperCollins, 2000), 391; and Carl Bernstein and Marco Politi, *His Holiness: John Paul II and the hidden history of our time* (London: Bantam Books, 1997), 462–63.

2. Carl Mitcham, "Signs of Contradiction," in *John Paul II on Science and Religion: Reflections on the New View from Rome*, ed. Robert J. Russell, William R. Stoeger, and George V. Coyne (Vatican City State: Vatican Observatory, 1990), 62.

3. Pope John Paul II, "The problems of science are the problems of man,"

address to the European Physics Society, *L'Osservatore Romano*, no. 576 (9 April 1979): 5, 8. In the following notes all entries for *L'Osservatore Romano* refer to the English edition.

4. *Discourses of the Popes from Pius XI to John Paul II to the Pontifical Academy of Sciences 1936–1986*, ed. Paul Haffner (Vatican City: Pontificia Academia Scientiarum, 1986), 153. Also reported under the title "Deep harmony which unites the truths of science with the truths of faith," *L'Osservatore Romano*, no. 609 (26 November 1979): 9; published under the title "The Galileo Affair," in *The Pope Teaches* 2, no. 4 (October–December 1979): 497–98. See also Tad Szulc, *Pope John Paul II: The Biography* (New York: Scribner, 1995), 440.

5. *Discourses of the Popes*, ed. Haffner, 154–55.

6. Several meetings were held and a number of conferences were organized. A number of books arising from the commission's initiatives were published, some under the imprints of the Pontifical Academy of Sciences and the Vatican Observatory. Members of the commission addressed questions corresponding to their areas of expertise. The Jesuit archbishop of Milan (later Cardinal), Carlo Maria Martini, addressed exegetical questions. Cardinal Paul Poupard, then acting president of the Secretariat for Non-Believers, dealt with cultural issues. Carlo Chagas, professor of biology and biophysics, then president of the Pontifical Academy of Sciences, and the Jesuit priest George Coyne, director of the Vatican Observatory, were especially concerned with scientific and epistemological matters. Juridical and historical questions were addressed by the historian Michele Maccarrone and by either the Jesuit archivist Edmond Lamalle or Professor Mario D'Addio (the latter is mentioned in a later list). Enrico di Rovasenda, the Dominican professor of philosophy and theology, then director of the Chancery of the Pontifical Academy of Sciences, served as secretary of the commission. The above information is derived from Michael Segre, "Critiques and Contentions: Light on the Galileo Case?" *Isis* 88 (1997): 487–88. Segre's information is based on a letter from the Vatican's secretary of state, Cardinal Agostino Casorili, to Paul Poupard on 3 July 1981. The letter in Italian is published with an English translation in Segre, 499–501.

7. Jonathan Kwitny, *Man of the Century: The Life and Times of Pope John Paul II* (New York: Warner Books, 1998), 706 n. 4.

8. "Origins," *NC Documentary Service* 16 (1986): 122, quoted by Robert John Russell, preface to *John Paul II on Science*, ed. Russell, Stoeger, and Coyne, v.

9. Pope John Paul II, "The moral dimension of study and research," address to the "Univ '80" international congress, 1 April 1980; *L'Osservatore Romano*, no. 629 (21 April 1980): 5. See also John Paul's encyclical *Fides et Ratio* (Dublin: Veritas, 1998), par. 81.

10. Pope John Paul II, "Christianity and Culture," 2 June 1980, *The Pope Teaches* 3, no. 2 (April–June 1980): 187–89.

11. Pope John Paul II, "The person, not science, is the measure and criterion of every human manifestation," *L'Osservatore Romano*, no. 658 (17 November 1980): 19–20.

12. Pope John Paul II, "Connection between scientific thought and the power of faith in the search for truth," address to teachers and university students, Cologne Cathedral, 15 November 1980; *L'Osservatore Romano*, no. 659 (24 November 1980): 6–7, 12; and "Science and Faith," *The Pope Teaches* 3, no. 4 (October–December 1980): 335–36.

13. Pope John Paul II, "Every nation has the right to take part in scientific progress," address to scientists at the Marcel Grossman Meeting on Relativistic Astrophysics, 21 June 1985, *L'Osservatore Romano*, no. 894 (15 July 1985): 11–12.

14. The letter from Pope John Paul II to Rev. George V. Coyne, dated 1 June 1988, was published in *L'Osservatore Romano*, no. 1064 (14 November 1988): 3–5, under the heading "Our knowledge of God and nature: Physics, philosophy, and theology," and in *John Paul II on Science*, ed. Russell, Stoeger, and Coyne, pp. M1–M14. Subsequent references to this document are from the second source.

15. John Paul II to Coyne, M5.

16. The implied criticism of Pius XII by John Paul II receives attention in Karl Schmitz-Moormann, "Science and Theology in a Changing Vision of the World: Reading John Paul's Message in Physics, Philosophy and Theology," in *John Paul II on Science*, ed. Russell, Stoeger, and Coyne, 101–2.

17. Ernan McMullin, "A Common Quest for Understanding," in *John Paul II on Science*, ed. Russell, Stoeger, and Coyne, 55.

18. John Paul II to Coyne, M11.

19. John B. Cobb, Jr., "One Step Further," in *John Paul II on Science*, ed. Russell, Stoeger, and Coyne, 5.

20. G. F. R. Ellis, "Critique; The Church and the Scientific Community," in *John Paul II on Science*, ed. Russell, Stoeger, and Coyne, 23.

21. Rosemary Radford Ruether, "Religion and Science in an Unjust World," in *John Paul II on Science*, ed. Russell, Stoeger, and Coyne, 95–98.

22. Schmitz-Moormann, "Science and Theology," 99–100.

23. Richard J. Blackwell, "Science and Religion: The Papal Call for an Open Dialogue," in *John Paul II on Science*, ed. Russell, Stoeger, and Coyne, 3.

24. Ibid., 1.

25. Lindon Eaves, "Autonomy Is Not Enough," in *John Paul II on Science*, ed. Russell, Stoeger, and Coyne, 19–22.

26. Mitcham, "Signs of Contradiction," 62.

27. Wolfhart Pannenberg, "Theology and Philosophy in Interaction with Science: A Response to the Message of Pope John Paul II on the Occasion of the Newton Tricentennial in 1987," in *John Paul II on Science*, ed. Russell, Stoeger, and Coyne, 75–79.

28. Malu wa Kalenga, "Critique of the Message of His Holiness Pope John Paul II," in *John Paul II on Science*, ed. Russell, Stoeger, and Coyne, 41–48.

29. Ellis, "Church and the Scientific Community," 25, 27.

30. Blackwell, "Science and Religion," 4.

31. Elizabeth A. Johnson, "Response to the Message of John Paul II on the

Relationship between the Scientific and Religious Cultures of Our Times," in *John Paul II on Science*, ed. Russell, Stoeger, and Coyne, 39.

32. Jeffrey L. Sheler, "Guarding the Doctrine: Catholic bishops move to rein in academics," *U.S. News & World Report* 130, no. 25 (25 June 2001): 52. See also John Cornwell, *The Pope in Winter: The Dark Face of John Paul II's Papacy* (London: Viking, 2004), 110–11.

33. Tullio Regge, "Comments on 'The Church and the Scientific Communities: A Common Quest for Understanding' by His Holiness John Paul II," in *John Paul II on Science*, ed. Russell, Stoeger, and Coyne, 81–82.

34. Pope John Paul II, "Faith can never conflict with reason," address to the Pontifical Academy of Sciences, 31 October 1992; *L'Osservatore Romano*, no. 1264 (4 November 1992): 2.

35. James Reston, *Galileo: A Life* (London: Cassell, 1994), 284.

36. For bibliographical details, see Maurice A. Finocchiaro, "Science, Religion, and the Historiography of the Galileo Affair: On the Undesirability of Oversimplification," in *Science in Theistic Contexts*, ed. John Hedley Brooke, Margaret J. Osler, and Jitse M. van der Meer, *Osiris* 16 (2001): 122 n. 30; and idem, "Galileo as a 'bad theologian': A formative myth about Galileo's trial," *Studies in History and Philosophy of Science* 33A, no. 4 (2002): 762 n. 33.

37. The English edition was published in 1987. The first publication (1983) was in French, under the title of *Galileo Galilei: 350 ans d'histoire 1633–1983*. This book was edited by Poupard and, from the cardinal's perspective, it had "clarified the past." He presented the collection of essays as a search for truth and understanding, devoid of intentions to justify the 1633 condemnation of Galileo. Paul Poupard, "Introduction: Galileo Galilei: 350 Years of Subsequent History," in *Galileo Galilei: Toward a Resolution of 350 Years of Debate—1633–1983*, ed. Paul Poupard (Pittsburgh, Pa.: Duquesne University Press, 1987), xv.

38. Maurice A. Finocchiaro, "The Galileo Affair from John Milton to John Paul II: Problems and Prospects," *Science and Education* 8 (1999): 202–3.

39. Segre, "Light on the Galileo Case?," 497–98.

40. Finocchiaro, "Galileo Affair," 202.

41. Michael Sharratt, *Galileo: Decisive Innovator* (Cambridge: Cambridge University Press, 1996), 215–16.

42. Maurice A. Finocchiaro, "Introduction," in *The Galileo Affair: A Documentary History*, ed. and trans. Maurice A. Finocchiaro (Berkeley: University of California Press, 1989), 38.

43. Reston, *Galileo: A Life*, 284–85.

44. From a historical point of view the Galileo case was certainly not closed. There was some speculation that some important documents relevant to Galileo might still lie unexamined in the Roman ecclesiastical archives. Annibale Fantoli argued that, even from a religious perspective, the case had to remain "open" to serve as a constant warning not to repeat the errors of the past. Annibale Fantoli,

Galileo: For Copernicanism and for the Church, 2nd ed., trans. George V. Coyne (Vatican City State: Vatican Observatory Publications, 1996), 508–11, and 532 n. 50.

45. George V. Coyne, "The Church in Dialogue with Science: The Wojtyla Years," in *New Catholic Encyclopedia; Jubilee Volume: The Wojtyla Years* (Detroit, Mich.: Gale Group, 2001), 103–4; and idem, "The Church's Most Recent Attempt to Dispel the Galileo Myth," in *The Church and Galileo*, ed. Ernan McMullin (Notre Dame, Ind.: University of Notre Dame Press, 2005), 340–59. In the same volume, see also Michael Sharratt's "Galileo's 'Rehabilitation': Elbow Room in Theology," 332.

46. The conservative newspaper *Il Giornale* announced on its front page, "Pope says that we may descend from monkeys." *La Repubblica* reported that the pope had "made peace with Darwin." The above information from "Pontiff lends his support to theory of evolution," *The Examiner* [Cork, Ireland], 25 October 1996, p. 10.

47. Alison Abbott, "Papal confession: Darwin was right about evolution," *Nature* 383 (31 October 1996): 753.

48. Quotations are from "Message to the Pontifical Academy of Sciences," published in *Evolutionary and Molecular Biology: Scientific Perspectives on Divine Action*, ed. Robert John Russell, William R. Stoeger, and Francisco J. Ayala (Vatican City State: Vatican Observatory Publications; Berkeley, Calif.: Center for Theology and the Natural Sciences, 1998), 2–8. This is a slightly altered version of "Magisterium is concerned with question of evolution, for it involves conception of man," message to the Pontifical Academy of Sciences, 22 October 1996, *L'Osservatore Romano*, no. 1464 (30 October 1996): 3, 7.

49. See Robert John Russell, "Introduction," in *Evolutionary and Molecular Biology*, ed. Russell, Stoeger, and Ayala, iii.

50. Francisco J. Ayala, "The Evolution of Life: An Overview," in *Evolutionary and Molecular Biology*, ed. Russell, Stoeger, and Ayala, 28.

51. Francisco J. Ayala, "Darwin's Devolution: Design Without Designer," in *Evolutionary and Molecular Biology*, ed. Russell, Stoeger, and Ayala, 102, 109, 113.

52. Ibid., 108.

53. See, e.g., Pat Shipman, "Being Stalked by Intelligent Design," *American Scientist* 93, no. 6 (November–December 2005): 500–502.

54. Richard Dawkins, *The Blind Watchmaker* (London: Penguin Books, 1991), 21.

55. "Foreword" to William A. Dembski, Stephen C. Meyer, and Michael J. Behe, *Science and Evidence for Design in the Universe* (San Francisco: Ignatius Press, 2000), 12. This book is based on papers presented by the three authors at a conference in New York on 25 September 1999. The conference was sponsored by the Wethersfield Institute, whose mission it is "to promote a clear understanding of Catholic teaching and practice and to explore the cultural and intellectual dimensions of the Catholic Faith."

56. John F. Haught, *Deeper than Darwin: The Prospect for Religion in the Age of*

Evolution (Boulder, Colo.: Westview Press, 2004), 88–89. The hardcover edition of this book was published in 2003.

57. Michael J. Behe, *Darwin's Black Box: The Biochemical Challenge to Evolution* (New York: Touchstone, 1996), 232–33.

58. There was a strong tendency among scientists to castigate the opinion that intelligent design has a legitimate place, or a useful function, in scientific discourse. For a scathing review of *Darwin's Black Box*, see Jerry A. Coyne's "God in the details," *Nature* 383 (19 September 1996): 227–28.

59. Behe, *Darwin's Black Box*, 30.

60. George V. Coyne, "Evolution and the Human Person: The Pope in Dialogue," in *Evolutionary and Molecular Biology*, ed. Russell, Stoeger, and Ayala, 16–17.

61. John F. Haught, "Darwin's Gift to Theology," in *Evolutionary and Molecular Biology*, ed. Russell, Stoeger, and Ayala, 401.

62. Ibid., 404–5.

63. John F. Haught, *God After Darwin: A Theology of Evolution* (Boulder, Colo.: Westview Press, 2000), 4, 14–15.

64. Ibid., 190.

65. John F. Haught, "Darwin, Design and the Promise of Nature," 19–20, The Boyle Lecture given at the Parish Church of St. Mary-le-Bow, Cheapside, London, 4 February 2004, http://www.stmarylebow.co.uk/news/boyle2004.htm.

66. Members of the subcommission included Very Rev. J. Augustine Di Noia, O.P.; Most Rev. Jean-Louis Bruguès, Msgr. Anton Strukelj, Rev. Tanios Bou Mansour, O.L.M., Rev. Adolpe Gesché, Most Rev. Willem Jacobus Eijk, Rev. Fadel Sidarouss, S.J., and Rev. Shun ichi Takayanagi, S.J.

67. The International Theological Commission, *Communion and Stewardship: Human Persons Created in the Image of God* [23 July 2004], par. 67, http://www.vatican.va/roman_curia/congregations/cfaith/cti_documents/rc_con_cfaith_doc_20040723_communion-stewardship_en.html#t.

68. Lawrence M. Krauss, "School Boards Want to 'Teach the Controversy.' What Controversy?" *The New York Times*, 17 May 2005, http://genesis1.phys.cwru.edu/~krauss/17comm2.html.

69. Christoph Schönborn, "Finding Design in Nature," *The New York Times*, 7 July 2005, http://www.millerandlevine.com/km/evol/catholic/schonborn-NYTimes.html.

70. Ibid.

71. National Center for Science Education, "Reactions to Schoenborn on the air," 28 July 2005, http://www.ncseweb.org/resources/news/2005/US/17_reactions_to_schoenborn_on_the_7_28_2005.asp.

72. Ibid. See also Kenneth R. Miller's "Darwin, Design, and the Catholic Faith," n.d., http://www.millerandlevine.com/km/evol/catholic/op-ed-krm.html.

73. Lawrence M. Krauss, Francisco Ayala, and Kenneth Miller, letter to His Holiness Pope Benedict XVI, and copied to His Eminence Cardinal Christoph

Schönborn and His Excellency William J. Levada, 12 July 2005, http://genesis1 .phys.cwru.edu/~krauss/papalletttxt.htm.

74. Cornelia Dean and Laurie Goodstein, "Leading Cardinal Redefines Church's View on Evolution," *The New York Times*, 9 July 2005, http://www.herald tribune.com/apps/pbcs.dll/article?AID=/20050709/ZNYT02/507090678. Pope Benedict XVI stated in his inaugural ceremony that "we are not some casual and meaningless product of evolution. Each of us is the result of a thought of God." "Homily of His Holiness Benedict XVI," St. Peter's Square, 24 April 2005, http://www.vatican.va/holy_father/benedict_xvi/homilies/documents/hf_ben-xvi_hom_20050424_inzio-pontificato_en.html.

75. Schönborn was "not just any cardinal." He was one of the church's leading theologians and was one the "grand electors" in the conclave a few months earlier which had elevated Cardinal Ratzinger to the position of supreme pontiff. Nevertheless, there were 180 other cardinals. Schönborn's views, therefore, could hardly be seen as a redefinition of the church's position. For a discussion of this, see John L. Allen, "Catholic experts urge caution in evolution debate," *National Catholic Reporter*, 29 July 2005, http://natcath.org/NCR_Online/archives2/ 2005c/072905/072905h.php.

76. Frank Bentayou, "Evolution of a clash," *Plain Dealer*, 20 August 2005, http: //genesis1.phys.cwru.edu/~krauss/pdaugevolution.html.

77. *Tidings Online*, "Scientific data supports design in evolution, says cardinal," 15 July 2005, http://www.the-tidings.com/2005/0716/evolution.htm. The *Tidings Online* article gives the name of the institute as the International Institute of Theology in Gaming, Austria. The correct name for the institute is the "International Theological Institute for Studies on Marriage and the Family." The institute's Web site reveals that it is supported by a group of Austrian and U.S. bishops, and by many private sources. The founding of the institute arose from the initiatives of Pope John Paul II. Schönborn was appointed Grand Chancellor of the institute by the pope.

78. Dean and Goodstein, "Leading Cardinal Redefines Church's View."

79. John L. Allen, "Interview with Professor Nicola Cabibbo," *National Catholic Reporter*, 21 July 2005, http://ncronline.org/mainpage/specialdocuments/ cabibbo.htm.

80. John L. Allen, "Schönborn and science vs. theology . . . ," *National Catholic Reporter* 4, no. 41 (22 July 2005), http://www.nationalcatholicreporter.org/word/ pfw072205.htm.

81. John L. Allen, "Follow up news: Schönborn and evolution . . . ," *National Catholic Reporter* 4, no. 43 (5 August 2005), http://www.nationalcatholicreporter .org/word/pfw080505.htm.

82. George Coyne, "God's chance creation," *The Tablet*, 6 August 2005, http: //www.thetablet.co.uk/cgi-bin/register.cgi/tablet-01063.

83. "World Church News – 3 September 2005: Europe: Schönborn urges creation debate," *The Tablet*, 5 September 2005, http://www.thetablet.co.uk/cgi-bin/citw.cgi/past-00246.

84. "Bush Intensifies Evolution Debate," *International Herald Tribune*, 4 August 2005, http://www.technewsworld.com/story/45222.html.

85. Claudia Wallis et al., "The Evolution Wars," *Time* 166, no. 7 (15 August 2005): 26–35, http://search.epnet.com/login.aspx?direct=true&db=buh&an=17848763.

86. A Harris opinion poll in July 2005 indicated that 64 percent of adults believed that humans were created directly by God, and 45 percent did not accept general evolutionary theory applied to plants and animals. Only 22 percent of adults believed that humans had evolved from earlier species. When asked about the teaching of evolution, intelligent design, and creationism in public schools (regardless of one's personal beliefs), only 12 percent believed that evolution alone should be taught; 23 percent favored creationism alone, and 4 percent favored intelligent design alone. A majority—55 percent—supported the teaching of all three. The Harris Poll, number 52, "Nearly Two-thirds of U.S. Adults Believe Human Beings Were Created by God" (6 July 2005), http://www.harrisinteractive.com/harris_poll/index.asp?PID=581.

A CBS News poll in October 2005 indicated the following: 51 percent of Americans did not believe in human evolution; 30 percent believed in human evolution under divine guidance; and 15 percent accepted human evolution without any direct input from God. CBS News, "Poll: Majority Reject Evolution," 23 October 2005, http://www.cbsnews.com/stories/2005/10/22/opinion/polls/main965223.shtml.

In February 2001 a Gallup poll indicated that 45 percent of U.S. adults did not believe in human evolution, 37 percent believed that God guided the evolutionary process, and 12 percent believed that humans evolved from earlier species without any divine intervention. David Quammen, "Darwin's Big Idea," *National Geographic* 206, no. 5 (November 2004): 6.

87. John Paul II, "Every nation has the right to take part in scientific progress," p. 12.

88. Pope John Paul II, "That we be more responsible for ourselves, our neighbours, institutions and our planet," address to participants at a conference organized by the Vatican Observatory on "The Frontiers of Cosmology," 6 July 1985; *L'Osservatore Romano*, no. 895 (22 July 1985): 3.

89. John Paul II to Coyne, M9.

90. Pope John Paul II, "Proofs for God's existence are many and convergent," weekly general audience in St. Peter's Square, 10 July 1985; *L'Osservatore Romano*, no. 894 (15 July 1985): 1.

91. John Paul II, "Faith can never conflict with reason," 1.

92. Pope John Paul II, "Scientists and God," general audience, 17 July 1985; *L'Osservatore Romano*, no. 895 (22 July 1985): 1.

93. Ibid.

94. Pope John Paul II, "The Perennial Philosophy," 17 November 1979, *The Pope Teaches* 3, no. 1 (January–March 1980): 1–11; and idem, "A Model for Theologians," 13 September 1980, *The Pope Teaches* 3, no. 4 (October–December 1980): 289–93.

95. Pope John Paul II, "Proofs for God's existence," 1.

96. Pius XII, *Humani Generis* (1950), par. 2–4, in *The Popes against Modern Errors: 16 Papal Documents*, ed. Anthony J. Mioni (Rockford, Ill.: Tan Books, 1999).

97. Pope John Paul II, "Scientists and God," 1.

98. David S. Toolan, "Praying in a Post-Einsteinian Universe," *Cross Currents* 46, no. 4 (Winter 1996–97): 448.

99. For enlightenment on this issue the pope asserted that one had to look above and beyond physics and astronomy—to metaphysics and God's revelation. *Discourses of the Popes*, ed. Haffner, 162.

100. Pope John Paul II, "Proofs for God's existence," 1.

101. John Polkinghorne, *Reason and Reality: The relationship between science and theology* (London: SPCK, 1991), 51.

102. Richard Elliott Friedman, *The Disappearance of God: A Divine Mystery* (Boston: Little, Brown & Co., 1995).

103. John Leslie, "How to Draw Conclusions from a Fine-Tuned Cosmos," in *Physics, Philosophy and Theology: A Common Quest for Understanding*, ed. Robert J. Russell, William R. Stoeger, and George V. Coyne (Vatican City State: Vatican Observatory, 1988), 297–311.

104. John Paul II, *Crossing the Threshold of Hope* (London: Jonathan Cape, 1994), 37–41.

11. Bioethics

1. See *Gaudium et Spes*, pars. 9, 12, 33, 34; and *Lumen Gentium*, par. 36; both in *Vatican Council II: The Conciliar and Post Conciliar Documents*, new rev. ed., ed. Austin Flannery (Dublin: Dominican Publications, 1992).

2. For a discussion of Catholic environmental theology, see John Hart, *What Are They Saying about Environmental Theology?* (New York: Paulist Press, 2004).

3. Seán Fagan, *Does Morality Change?* (Dublin: Columba Press, 2003), 226–27.

4. Seán Fagan, "*Humanae Vitae* 30 Years On," *Doctrine and Life* [Dublin] 49, no. 1 (January 1999): 53.

5. Fagan, *Does Morality Change?*, 210.

6. Richard A. McCormick, *Notes on Moral Theology 1965 through 1980* (Lanham, Md.: University Press of America, 1981), 796–97.

7. Charles E. Curran, *Moral Theology: A Continuing Journey* (Notre Dame, Ind.: University of Notre Dame Press, 1982), 125–28.

8. McCormick disagreed with the church's teachings against artificial contra-

ception, voluntary sterilization, and some reproductive interventions. James F. Childress, "Reproductive Interventions: Theology, Ethics, and Public Policy," in *Moral Theology: Challenges for the Future*, ed. Charles E. Curran (New York: Paulist Press, 1990), 287.

9. Benedict M. Ashley and Kevin D. O'Rourke, *Health Care Ethics: A Theological Analysis*, 4th ed. (Washington, D.C.: Georgetown University Press, 1997), 186.

10. The Congregation for the Doctrine of the Faith, *Instruction on Respect for Human Life in Its Origin and on the Dignity of Procreation*, 22 February 1987 (Dublin: Veritas, 1987), introduction. Subsequent parenthetical references refer to this document.

11. *Catechism of the Catholic Church* (Dublin: Veritas, 1995), par. 2377–78.

12. Congregation for the Doctrine of the Faith, *Instruction on Respect for Human Life*, 11–12.

13. Fagan, *Does Morality Change?*, 211.

14. For an indication of this difference in outlook between hierarchy and laity, see the document "In Vitro Fertilisation: Statement of Bishops' Commission for Doctrine of the Irish Episcopal Conference," *The Furrow* 37, no. 3 (March 1986): 197.

15. See Fagan, *Does Morality Change?*, 211–12.

16. See, e.g., Richard P. McBrien, "Theologians Under Fire," in *Readings in Moral Theology No. 6: Dissent in the Church*, ed. Charles E. Curran and Richard A. McCormick (New York: Paulist Press, 1988), 484–90.

17. A pre-embryo may be defined as an entity or organism composed of developing cells from the division of the zygote until the formation of the primitive streak about 14 days after fertilization.

18. The Congregation for the Doctrine of the Faith stated: "From the time that the ovum is fertilized, a new life is begun, which is neither that of the father nor of the mother; it is rather the life of a new human being . . . modern genetic science brings valuable confirmation. It has demonstrated that, from the first instant, the program is fixed as to what this living being will be: a man, this individual man with his characteristic aspects already well determined." Congregation for the Doctrine of the Faith, *Instruction on Respect for Human Life*, 4.

19. Norman Ford, "We don't have to clone," *The Tablet*, 9 December 2000, http://www.thetablet.co.uk/cgi-bin/register.cgi/tablet-00502.

20. Lisa Sowle Cahill, "The Embryo and the Fetus: New Moral Contexts," *Theological Studies* 54, no. 1 (March 1993): 127.

21. Ibid.

22. The embryonic disc is a group of cells from which the embryo will develop. The primitive streak is located at the caudal end of the embryonic disc and is present about fourteen or fifteen days after fertilization. In rare cases the primitive streak may divide to form two centers of development that lead to the formation of separate embryos. Divisions or splits in the pre-embryo, or later in the primi-

tive streak, may be incomplete, leading to the creation of conjoined twins. Medical intervention here may be subject to complex ethical and legal issues. See M. Cathleen Kaveny, "The Case of Conjoined Twins: Embodiment, Individuality, and Dependence," *Theological Studies* 62, no. 4 (December 2001): 753–86.

23. Cahill, "Embryo and the Fetus," 129–32. Bedate and Cefalo observe that some zygotes with normal genotypes fail to develop into fetuses because they are deprived of complementary genetic information arising from sources such as maternal mitochondria or messenger RNA (ribonucleic acid). In these circumstances nonpersonal biological structures (such as tumours or hydratidiform moles) are formed.

24. Mark Johnson, "Delayed Hominization," *Theological Studies* 56, no. 4 (December 1995): 762–63. See also Johnson's "Delayed Hominization: A Rejoinder to Thomas Shannon," *Theological Studies* 58, no. 4 (December 1997): 708–14.

25. Johnson, "Delayed Hominization" (1995), 759.

26. Jean Porter, "Individuality, personal identity, and the moral status of the preembryo: A Response to Mark Johnson," *Theological Studies* 56, no. 4 (December 1995): 767–70.

27. Thomas A. Shannon, "Delayed Hominization: A Response to Mark Johnson," *Theological Studies* 57, no. 4 (December 1996): 731–34.

28. Thomas A. Shannon, "Delayed Hominization: A Further Postscript to Mark Johnson," *Theological Studies* 58, no. 4 (December 1997): 715.

29. Thomas A. Shannon, "Human Embryonic Stem Cell Therapy," *Theological Studies* 62, no. 4 (December 2001): 816–19.

30. Grace MacKinnon, "Theologians Argue Frozen Embryos' Fate," http://www.catholicdoctors.org.uk/CMQ/Nov_2001/frozen_embryos.htm. Article published in the *Catholic Medical Quarterly* (November 2001), and reproduced from an article published in *HLI Reports* 19, no. 8 (August 2001), published by Human Life International. See also Mary Geach and Helen Watt, "Are there any circumstances in which it would be morally admirable for a woman to seek to have an orphan embryo implanted in her womb?" in *Issues for a Catholic Bioethic*, ed. Luke Gormally (London: Linacre Centre, 1999), 341–52.

31. For an indication of this, see Thomas A. Shannon, "Ethical Issues in Genetics," *Theological Studies* 60, no. 1 (March 1999): 123. In reference to "the exponentially rapid rate of scientific and technological development," Shannon states: "One can barely keep up with the reports, much less think through the issues. And the pace will continue."

32. Quotations from Pope John Paul II's encyclical *Evangelium Vitae: The Value and Inviolability of Human Life* (London: Catholic Truth Society, 1995), parr. 26 and 14 respectively.

33. George Weigel, *Witness to Hope: The Biography of Pope John Paul II* (New York: Cliff Street Books, 2001), 756.

34. The Catholic theologian George Weigel stated that "it would be claiming too much to suggest that John Paul's deeper analysis of the 'culture of death' was

seriously engaged by the public in the older democracies, but his defense of the dignity of life . . . struck a chord" (*Witness to Hope*, 759).

35. Simon Mills, *Clinical Practice and the Law* (Dublin: Butterworths, 2002), 413.

36. Pontifical Academy for Life, *Reflections on Cloning* (Vatican City: Libreria Editrice Vaticana, 1997).

37. Sylvia Pagán Westphal and Philip Cohen, "Cloned cells today: Where tomorrow?" *New Scientist* 181, no. 2435 (21 February 2004): 6–7.

38. Robert Lanza and Nadia Rosenthal, "The Stem Cell Challenge," *Scientific American* 290, no. 6 (June 2004): 99.

39. Archbishop Renato Martino, Apostolic Nuncio and Vatican permanent observer to the United Nations, addressed an ad hoc committee of the International Convention Against the Reproductive Cloning of Human Beings. See Renato Martino, "An Affront to the Dignity of the Person," *Position Paper 348* (Dublin, December 2002): 348–50. A copy of this document was also published through the Vatican's official Web site under the heading: "Intervention by the Holy See Delegation at the Special Committee of the 57th General Assembly of the United Nations on Human Embryonic Cloning," dated 23 September 2002.

40. Sylvia Pagán Westphal, "Virgin birth method could found stem cell dynasties," *New Scientist* 178, no. 2392 (26 April 2003): 17.

41. Michael Le Page, "All forms of infertility will be treatable," *New Scientist* 180, no. 2426 (20 December 2003): 17.

42. Sylvia Pagán Westphal, "The mouse with two mothers: Dawn of a new kind of parenthood," *New Scientist* 182, no. 2444 (24 April 2004): 8–10.

43. Philip Cohen, "Rabbit-human stem cell claims provoke controversy and doubt," *New Scientist* 179, no. 2409 (23 August 2003): 14; and Sylvia Pagán Westphal, "Growing human organs on the farm," *New Scientist* 180, no. 2426–2428 (20 December 2003–3 January 2004): 4. See also Shannon, "Ethical Issues in Genetics," 121. Nuclei from rats, sheep, pigs, and rhesus monkeys were inserted into the ova of cows the nuclei of which had been previously removed.

44. Pontifical Academy for Life, *Prospects for Xenotransplantation: Scientific Aspects and Ethical Considerations* (n.d.). This document was accessed through the Vatican's official Web site.

45. Ibid., parr. 10–11, and 20–21 n. 61.

46. "Cloning palaver," *New Scientist* 180, no. 2419 (1 November 2003): 4.

47. Claire Ainsworth et al., "Human cloning: If not today, tomorrow," *New Scientist* 177, no. 2377 (11 January 2003): 8–11.

48. Andy Coghlan, "Race is on to stop human cloning," *New Scientist* 175, no. 2362 (28 September 2002): 11; and Alan Trounson, "A crime against humanity," *New Scientist* 180, no. 2422 (22 November 2003): 23.

49. Christine Soares, "Politics: The biggest obstacle of all," *Scientific American* 290, no. 6 (June 2004): 97.

50. Ainsworth et al., "Human cloning," 11.

51. Editorial, "Beyond Clones," *New Scientist* 181, no. 2435 (21 February 2004): 3.

52. Andreas Frew, "Washington diary," *New Scientist* 176, no. 2366 (28 October 2002): 55.

53. Ainsworth et al., "Human cloning," 11.

54. The leading scientist of "the Dolly team," Ian Wilmut, argued that the potential benefits of therapeutic cloning are so great that it would be immoral not to do it. Wilmut's opinion is probably shared by many scientists. See his article "The moral imperative of human cloning," *New Scientist* 181, no. 2435 (21 February 2004): 16–17.

55. Andy Coghlan, "Are all human embryos equal?" *New Scientist*, no. 2522 (22 October 2005): 10.

56. Editorial, "The lessons of Eve," *New Scientist* 177, no. 2377 (11 January 2003): 3. Ova cells from other species could be used as recipients for human nuclei in generating stem cells. However, this would introduce nonhuman mitochondrial DNA into the genetic composition of the cells.

57. See Celia E. Deane-Drummond, "Biotechnology, ecology and wisdom," *Priests & People* 13, no. 10 (October 1999): 364–68.

58. Pope John Paul II, "Conflict of interest and its significance in science and medicine," *Position Paper 349* (Dublin, January 2003): 5–7, 12.

59. See John Kenneth Galbraith, *The Culture of Contentment* (London: Sinclair-Stevenson, 1992).

12. Reflections

1. Words in quotation marks from The Nicene Creed, in *Catechism of the Catholic Church* (Dublin: Veritas, 1995), 47

2. Blaise Pascal, *Pensées*, rev. ed., trans. A. J. Krailsheimer (London: Penguin Books, 1995), par. 198.

3. Ibid., par. 189; see also par. 190.

4. P. J. McGrath, "Believing in God," *Irish Theological Quarterly* 42, no. 2 (April 1975): 87.

5. In *Vatican Council II: The Conciliar and Post Conciliar Documents*, new rev. ed., ed. Austin Flannery (Dublin: Dominican Publications, 1992), 751–53 parr. 3, 6.

6. Quotations from St. George Mivart, *The Genesis of Species*, 2nd ed. (London: Macmillan, 1871), 309–10.

7. At its most extreme this tendency manifested itself in so-called scientific creationism. Scientific creationists set out to expose the problems and deficiencies of evolutionary theory, and they attempted to demonstrate that creationism represented a better explanation of the scientific evidence. Creationism served as a protective barrier for their religious beliefs, and they were convinced that their position was intellectually respectable and justified. See Eileen Barker, "Let There

Be Light: Scientific Creationism in the Twentieth Century," in *Darwinism and Divinity: Essays on Evolution and Religious Belief*, ed. John Durant (Oxford: Basil Blackwell, 1985), 181–204.

8. The anthropic cosmological principle is discussed in detail in John Houghton's *The Search for God: Can Science Help?* (Oxford: Lion Publishing, 1995), chapter 3.

9. The anthropic principle is discussed here mainly with reference to Stephen T. Davis, *God, Reason and Theistic Proofs* (Edinburgh: Edinburgh University Press, 1997), 111–15; Mark Wynn, "Design arguments," in *Philosophy of Religion: A guide to the subject*, ed. Brian Davies (London: Cassell, 1998), 59–63; and J. J. C. Smart and J. J. Haldane, *Atheism and Theism*, 2nd ed. (Malden, Mass.: Blackwell Publishing, 2003), especially Smart's "Atheism and Theism," 15–26.

10. Alister E. McGrath, *Science and Religion: An Introduction* (Oxford: Blackwell Publishers, 1999), 181–84; quotation from 183.

11. Ernan McMullin, "Natural Science and Belief in a Creator: Historical Notes," in *Physics, Philosophy and Theology: A Common Quest for Understanding*, ed. Robert J. Russell, William R. Stoeger, and George V. Coyne (Vatican City State: Vatican Observatory, 1988), 71.

12. James A. Wiseman, *Theology and Modern Science: Quest for coherence* (New York: Continuum, 2002), 43–44.

13. Richard Dawkins, *The Blind Watchmaker* (London: Penguin Books, 1991), 316–17.

14. Richard Swinburne, "Arguments for the Existence of God," *Milltown Studies*, no. 33 (Spring 1994): 28–32.

15. Stephen Hawking, *A Brief History of Time: From the Big Bang to Black Holes* (Toronto: Bantam Books, 1995), 193.

16. Davis, *God, Reason and Theistic Proofs*, 101.

17. Such an idea has been put forward for consideration on the basis of highly speculative and abstruse philosophical arguments. See Quentin Smith, "The Reason the Universe Exists Is That It Caused Itself to Exist," *Philosophy* 74, no. 290 (October 1999): 579–86.

18. Lee Smolin, "Atoms of Space and Time," *Scientific American* 290, no. 1 (January 2004): 68.

19. Gabriele Veneziano, "The Myth of the Beginning of Time," *Scientific American* 290, no. 5 (May 2004): 66–73.

20. Étienne Gilson, *God and Philosophy* (New Haven: Yale University Press, 1941), 126–27, 130, referred to by John C. Greene, *Darwin and the Modern World View* (Baton Rouge: Louisiana State University Press, 1961), 64–65.

21. *Discourses of the Popes from Pius XI to John Paul II to the Pontifical Academy of Sciences 1936–1986*, ed. Paul Haffner (Vatican City: Pontificia Academia Scientiarum, 1986), 120–21.

22. Pius XII, *Humani Generis* (1950), par. 2–4, in *The Popes against Modern Errors: 16 Papal Documents*, edited and arranged by Anthony J. Mioni (Rockford, Ill.: Tan Books, 1999).

23. Pope John Paul II, *Fides et Ratio* (Dublin: Veritas Publications, 1998), par. 20.

24. Bishop Hedley, *Evolution and Faith with Other Essays* (London: Sheed & Ward, 1931), 240.

25. Owen Chadwick, *The Secularization of the European Mind in the Nineteenth Century* (Cambridge: Cambridge University Press, 1975), 167.

26. See John A. O'Brien, *Evolution and Religion: A Study of the Bearing of Evolution upon the Philosophy of Religion* (New York: Century Co., 1932), 36–37.

27. Antonio Romaña, "The World: Its Origin and Structure in the Light of Science and Faith," in *God, Man and the Universe: A Christian answer to modern materialism*, ed. Jacques de Bivort de la Saudée (London: Burns & Oates, 1954), 61–62.

28. Alfred Loisy argued that there was no such thing as a book that was absolutely true—"a book absolutely true for all times, if it could exist, would be unintelligible for all times." He observed that the Bible was written to serve the religious needs of a particular time and was influenced by scientific and historical opinions that changed from generation to generation. Therefore, in his opinion, the Bible did contain errors arising from discredited ideas about history and science. See James Tunstead Burtchaell, *Catholic Theories of Biblical Inspiration since 1810: A Review and Critique* (London: Cambridge University Press, 1969), 223–24.

29. Jacob W. Gruber, *A Conscience in Conflict: The Life of St. George Jackson Mivart* (Westport, Conn.: Greenwood Press, 1960), 189–90.

30. See Bernard F. Batto, "Creation Theology in Genesis," in *Creation in the Biblical Traditions*, ed. Richard J. Clifford and John J. Collins (Washington, D.C.: Catholic Biblical Association of America, 1992), 16–38.

31. J. Murphy, "Faith and Evolution," *Irish Ecclesiastical Record* 3rd ser. 6 (1885): 487.

32. J. Murphy, "Evolution and Faith," *Irish Ecclesiastical Record* 3rd ser. 5 (1884): 761. Scriptural passages quoted in this context were (1) Genesis 2:7, "And the Lord God formed man out of the slime of the earth"; (2) Job 10:8, "Thy hands have made me, and fashioned me."

33. St. George Mivart, "Roman Congregations and Modern Thought," *North American Review* 170 (1900): 573. The Old Testament stories Mivart is referring to are to be found in chapter 6 of Tobias (Tobit) and chapter 14 of Daniel.

34. St. George Mivart, "Scripture and Roman Catholicism," *Nineteenth Century* 47 (March 1900): 437. The stories in question are in chapters 1 and 2 of Jonah and in Joshua 10—especially verses 12–13.

35. *The Essence of T.H. Huxley: Selections from his writings*, ed. Cyril Bibby (London: Macmillan; New York: St. Martin's Press, 1967), 118–19, 124–25.

36. Pope Paul VI, "The Credo of the People of God" (*Solemni hac liturgia*, 30 June 1968), in *Vatican Council II: More Postconciliar Documents*, 1st ed., ed. Austin Flannery (Collegeville, Minn.: Liturgical Press, 1982), 2:391.

37. Dom Cuthbert Butler, "Introduction," in Hedley, *Evolution and Faith*, xxiv.

38. For a recent presentation of the isolationist theme in religion and science, see Cardinal Cahal B. Daly's book *The Minding of Planet Earth* (Dublin: Veritas, 2004), 89–90. Cardinal Daly conceded that the possibility of conflict between science and faith exists because both "exist in the same world and relate to the same empirical and historical events." But he then proceeded to defend some of the central dogmas of the Catholic faith by viewing them in splendid isolation from the sciences. He argued that the virgin birth of Jesus Christ is not rendered intellectually untenable by the fact that parthenogenesis (in humans) is irreconcilable with the established findings of biology. Another cherished dogma, insulated from scientific enquiry, is the resurrection of the dead, which, although "scientifically impossible," is, nevertheless, eminently believable. The risen body of Jesus Christ is present in the bread of the Eucharist. But the most penetrating scientific examination would be capable of detecting only bread, because "the Risen Body of Christ is outside the laws and limits of space and time and therefore . . . is, by definition, beyond the limits of science."

39. See Tord Simonsson, *Logical and Semantic Structures in Christian Discourses* (Oslo: Universitetsforlaget, 1971), especially 16–17, 24–31.

40. Paschal Scotti, "Wilfrid Ward: A Religious Fabius Maximus," *Catholic Historical Review* 88, no. 1 (January 2002): 49–50.

41. Jerome J. Langford, *Galileo, Science and the Church*, 3rd ed. (Ann Arbor: University of Michigan Press, 1992), 185.

42. Ibid., 185–86.

43. Richard Blackwell, "Could there be another Galileo Case?" in *The Cambridge Companion to Galileo*, ed. Peter Machamer (Cambridge: Cambridge University Press, 1998), 359.

44. Marcello Pera, "The god of theologians and the god of astronomers: An apology of Bellarmine," in *Cambridge Companion to Galileo*, ed. Machamer, 380–81, 384.

45. See chapter 2. Tyndall was speaking here on the subject of "Scientific Materialism," to the Mathematical and Physical Section of the British Association for the Advancement of Science at Norwich in 1868. John Tyndall, *Fragments of Science: A Series of Detached Essays, Addresses, and Reviews* (New York: D. Appleton & Co., 1896), 2:86–88.

Bibliography

Primary Sources

Bibby, Cyril, ed. *The Essence of T.H. Huxley: Selections from his writings*. London: Macmillan; New York: St. Martin's Press, 1967.

Bible, The. New International Version.

Bishops' Commission for Doctrine of the Irish Episcopal Conference. "In Vitro Fertilisation: Statement of Bishops' Commission for Doctrine of the Irish Episcopal Conference." *The Furrow* 37, no. 3 (March 1986): 197–200.

Catechism of the Catholic Church. Dublin:Veritas. 1995.

Congregation for the Doctrine of the Faith. *Instruction on Respect for Human Life in Its Origin and on the Dignity of Procreation*, 22 February 1987. Dublin: Veritas, 1987.

Darwin, Francis, ed. *The Autobiography of Charles Darwin and Selected Letters*. New York: Dover Publications, 1958.

Dessain, Charles Stephen, ed. *The Letters and Diaries of John Henry Newman*. Vol. 16, *Founding a University January 1854 to September 1855*. London: Nelson, 1965.

———. *The Letters and Diaries of John Henry Newman*. Vol. 17, *Opposition in Dublin and London October 1855 to March 1857*. London: Nelson, 1967.

Drake, Stillman, ed. and trans. *Discoveries and Opinions of Galileo*. New York: Anchor Books, 1957.

Figgis, John Neville, and Reginald Vere Laurence, eds. *Selections from the Correspondence of the First Lord Acton*. Vol. 1, *Correspondence with Cardinal Newman, Lady Blennerhassett, W.E. Gladstone and Others*. London: Longmans, Green and Co., 1917.

Finocchiaro, Maurice A., ed. and trans. *The Galileo Affair: A Documentary History*. Berkeley: University of California Press, 1989.

Flannery, Austin, general ed. *Vatican Council II: More Postconciliar Documents*. 1st ed. Collegeville, Minn.: Liturgical Press, 1982.

———, ed. *Vatican Council II: The Conciliar and Post Conciliar Documents*. New rev. ed. Dublin: Dominican Publications, 1992.

Gasquet, Abbot, ed. *Lord Acton and his Circle: Letters of Lord Acton.* London: George Allen, Burns & Oates, 1906.

Haffner, Paul, ed. *Discourses of the Popes from Pius XI to John Paul II to the Pontifical Academy of Sciences 1936–1986.* Vatican City: Pontificia Academia Scientiarum, 1986.

Huxley, Leonard. *Life and Letters of Thomas Henry Huxley.* 3 vols. London: Macmillan, 1903.

International Theological Commission. *Communion and Stewardship: Human Persons Created in the Image of God* [23 July 2004]. http://www.vatican.va/roman_curia/congregations/cfaith/cti_documents/rc_con_cfaith_doc_2004 0723_communion-stewardship_en.html#t.

John Paul II. "Address to Nobel Prize Winners," 22 December 1980, *The Pope Teaches* 3, no. 4 (October–December 1980): 357–61.

———. "Christianity and Culture," 2 June 1980, *The Pope Teaches* 3, no. 2 (April–June 1980): 179–89.

———. "Conflict of interest and its significance in science and medicine." *Position Paper 349* (Dublin, January 2003): 5–7, 12.

———. "Connection between scientific thought and the power of faith in the search for truth," address to teachers and university students, Cologne Cathedral, 15 November 1980; *L'Osservatore Romano*, no. 659 (24 November 1980): 6–7, 12.

———. *Crossing the Threshold of Hope.* London: Jonathan Cape, 1994.

———. "Deep harmony which unites the truths of science with the truths of faith," address to the Pontifical Academy of Sciences, 10 November 1979, *L'Osservatore Romano*, no. 609 (26 November 1979): 9–10.

———. *Evangelium Vitae: The Value and Inviolability of Human Life.* London: Catholic Truth Society, 1995.

———. "Every nation has the right to take part in scientific progress," address to scientists at the Marcel Grossman Meeting on Relativistic Astrophysics, 21 June 1985; *L'Osservatore Romano*, no. 894 (15 July 1985): 11–12.

———. "Faith can never conflict with reason," address to the Pontifical Academy of Sciences, 31 October 1992; *L'Osservatore Romano*, no. 1264 (4 November 1992): 1–2.

———. *Fides et Ratio.* English ed. Dublin: Veritas, 1998.

———. "The human person must be the beginning, subject and goal of all scientific research," address to the Pontifical Academy of Sciences, 28 October 1994, *L'Osservatore Romano*, no. 1365 (9 November 1994): 3, 15.

———. "Magisterium is concerned with question of evolution, for it involves conception of man," message to the Pontifical Academy of Sciences, 22 October 1996; *L'Osservatore Romano*, no. 1464 (30 October 1996): 3, 7.

———. Message on his behalf sent by Agostino Casaroli, Cardinal Secretary of the Vatican State, to Archbishop Paul Poupard, "Teilhard de Chardin," 12 May 1981, *The Pope Teaches* 4, nos. 4–6 (April–June 1981): 159–60.

———. "A Model for Theologians," 13 September 1980, *The Pope Teaches* 3, no. 4 (October–December 1980): 289–93.

———. "The moral dimension of study and research," address to the "Univ '80" international congress, 1 April 1980; *L'Osservatore Romano*, no. 629 (21 April 1980): 5.

———. "Our knowledge of God and nature: physics, philosophy, and theology," letter to Rev. George V. Coyne, Director of the Vatican Observatory, 1 June 1988; *L'Osservatore Romano*, no. 1064 (14 November 1988): 3–5.

———. "The Perennial Philosophy," 17 November 1979, *The Pope Teaches* 3, no. 1 (January–March 1980): 1–11.

———. "The person, not science is the measure and criterion of every human manifestation," *L'Osservatore Romano*, no. 658 (17 November 1980): 19–20.

———. "The problems of science are the problems of man," address to members of the European Physics Society on 30 March 1979; *L'Osservatore Romano*, no. 576 (9 April 1979), English edition, pp. 5, 8. All entries for *L'Osservatore Romano* refer to the English edition.

———. "Proofs for God's existence are many and convergent," weekly general audience in St. Peter's Square, 10 July 1985; *L'Osservatore Romano*, no. 894 (15 July 1985): 1.

———. "Science and Creation," 3 October 1981, *The Pope Teaches* 4, nos. 10–12 (October–December 1981): 285–88.

———. "Science and Faith." *The Pope Teaches* 3, no. 4 (October–December 1980): 335–36.

———. "Science and religion can renew culture," address to a symposium sponsored by the Pontifical Academy of Sciences and the Pontifical Council of Culture, 4 October 1991; *L'Osservatore Romano*, no. 1211 (14 October 1991): 3.

———. "Scientists and God," general audience, 17 July 1985; *L'Osservatore Romano*, no. 895 (22 July 1985): 1, 12.

———. "That we be more responsible for ourselves, our neighbours, institutions and our planet," address to participants in a conference organized by the Vatican Observatory on "The Frontiers of Cosmology," 6 July 1985; *L'Osservatore Romano*, no. 895 (22 July 1985): 3.

Leo XIII. *The Great Encyclical Letters of Pope Leo XIII.* New York: Benziger Brothers, 1903.

———. *The Pope and the People: Select Letters and Addresses on Social Questions by Pope Leo XIII.* Rev. ed. London: Catholic Truth Society, 1920.

Mioni, Anthony J., ed. *The Popes against Modern Errors: 16 Papal Documents.* Rockford, Ill.: Tan Books, 1999.

Mivart, St. George, and Herbert Vaughan. *Under the Ban: A Correspondence between Dr. St. George Mivart and Herbert Cardinal Vaughan.* New York: Tucker Publishing Co., 1900.

Moran, Patrick Francis, ed. *Pastoral Letters and Other Writings of Cardinal Cullen.* Dublin: Browne & Nolan, 1882.

Norman, E. R. *Anti-Catholicism in Victorian England.* London: George Allen and Unwin, 1968.

O'Rourke, Kevin D., and Philip Boyle. *Medical Ethics: Sources of Catholic Teachings.* 2nd ed. Washington, D.C.: Georgetown University Press, 1993.

"Pastoral Address of the Archbishops and Bishops of Ireland," 20 September 1875, *Irish Ecclesiastical Record*, n.s., 12 (October 1875): 1–19.

Pontifical Academy for Life. *Prospects for Xenotransplantation: Scientific Aspects and Ethical Considerations* (n.d.). This document was accessed through the Vatican's official Web site.

———. *Reflections on Cloning.* Vatican City: Libreria Editrice Vaticana, 1997.

Rome and the Study of Scripture: A Collection of Papal Enactments on the Study of Holy Scripture together with the Decisions of the Biblical Commission. 7th ed. St. Meinrad, Ind.: Abbey Press, 1964.

Tanner, Norman P., ed. *Decrees of the Ecumenical Councils.* Vol. 2, *Trent to Vatican II.* London: Sheed & Ward; Washington D.C.: Georgetown University Press, 1990.

Tyrrell, George. *Letters from a "Modernist": The Letters of George Tyrrell to Wilfrid Ward 1893–1908.* Introduced and annotated by Mary Jo Weaver. Shepherdstown, W.V.: Patmos Press; London: Sheed & Ward, 1981.

Secondary Sources

Abbott, Alison. "Papal confession: Darwin was right about evolution." *Nature* 383 (31 October 1996): 753.

Agar, William M. *Catholicism and the Progress of Science.* New York: Macmillan, 1940.

Ahearn, John. "From Anathema to Acceptance: The Development of Roman Catholic Thought on Evolution from Humani Generis to Pierre Teilhard de Chardin." Master of Arts thesis, Northern Arizona University, 1968.

Ainsworth, Claire, et al. "Human cloning: If not today, tomorrow." *New Scientist* 177, no. 2377 (11 January 2003): 8–11.

Alberigo, Giuseppe, and Joseph A. Komonchak, eds. *History of Vatican II.* Vol. 1, *Announcing and Preparing Vatican Council II toward a New Era in Catholicism.* Maryknoll, N.Y.: Orbis, 1995.

Allen, John L. "Catholic experts urge caution in evolution debate." *National Catholic Reporter*, 29 July 2005, http://natcath.org/NCR_Online/archives2/2005c/072905/072905h.php.

———. "Follow up news: Schönborn and evolution . . . ." *National Catholic Reporter* 4, no. 43 (5 August 2005), http://www.nationalcatholicreporter.org/word/pfw080505.htm.

———. "Interview with Professor Nicola Cabibbo." *National Catholic Reporter*, 21 July 2005, http://ncronline.org/mainpage/specialdocuments/cabibbo.htm.

————. "Schönborn and science vs. theology. . . ." *National Catholic Reporter* 4, no. 41 (22 July 2005), http://www.nationalcatholicreporter.org/word/pfw 072205.htm.

Allitt, Patrick. *Catholic Converts: British and American Intellectuals Turn to Rome.* Ithaca, N.Y., and London: Cornell University Press, 1997.

Altholz, Josef L. *The Churches in the Nineteenth Century.* Indianapolis: Bobbs-Merrill, 1967.

————. "The Vatican Decrees Controversy, 1874–1875." *Catholic Historical Review* 57, no. 4 (January 1972): 593–605.

Arbez, Edward P. "Genesis I–XI and Prehistory." Parts 1–3. *American Ecclesiastical Review* 123 (1950): 81–92, 202–13, 284–94.

Arnstein, Walter L. *Protestant versus Catholic in Mid-Victorian England: Mr. Newdegate and the Nuns.* Columbia and London: University of Missouri Press, 1982.

————. "Victorian Prejudice Reexamined." *Victorian Studies* 12 (June 1969): 452–57.

Ashley, Benedict M., and Kevin D. O'Rourke. *Health Care Ethics: A Theological Analysis.* 4th ed. Washington, D.C.: Georgetown University Press, 1997.

Ashton, J. "Evolution as a Theory of Ascent." *Dublin Review* 180 (1927): 53–72.

Ashworth, Allan. "Cardano's Solution." *History Today* 49, no. 1 (January 1999): 46–51.

Astore, William J. "Gentle Skeptics? American Catholic Encounters with Polygenism, Geology, and Evolutionary Theories from 1845 to 1875." *Catholic Historical Review* 82 (January 1996): 40–76.

Atkins, Peter. "Will science ever fail?" *New Scientist* 135, no. 1833 (8 August 1992): 32–35.

Barbour, Ian G. *Religion and Science: Historical and Contemporary Issues.* London: SCM Press, 1998.

Barlow, Connie, ed. *Evolution Extended: Biological Debates on the Meaning of Life.* Cambridge, Mass.: MIT Press, 1995.

Barrett, Cyril. "Secular Theologians of Science." *Milltown Studies* [Milltown Institute of Theology and Philosophy, Dublin] no. 36 (Autumn 1995): 5–16.

Barry, William. *Memories and Opinions.* London: G. P. Putnam's Sons, 1926.

Barton, Ruth. "'An Influential Set of Chaps': The X-Club and Royal Society Politics 1864–1885." *British Journal for the History of Science* 23, no. 76 (March 1990): 53–81.

Behe, Michael J. *Darwin's Black Box: The Biochemical Challenge to Evolution.* New York: Touchstone, 1996.

Belloc, Hilaire. "A Few Words with Mr. Wells." *Dublin Review* 166, no. 333 (April–June 1920): 182–202.

Bentayou, Frank. "Evolution of a clash." *Plain Dealer*, 20 August 2005, http://genesis1.phys.cwru.edu/~krauss/pdaugevolution.html.

Bernstein, Carl, and Marco Politi. *His Holiness: John Paul II and the hidden history of our time.* London: Bantam Books, 1997.

Betts, John Rickards. "Darwinism, Evolution, and American Catholic Thought, 1860–1900." *Catholic Historical Review* 45 (April 1959–January 1960): 161–85.

Bibby, Cyril, ed. *T.H. Huxley on Education: A selection from his writings*. Cambridge: Cambridge University Press, 1971.

Blanning, T. C. W., ed. *The Oxford Illustrated History of Modern Europe*. Oxford: Oxford University Press, 1998.

Bowler, Peter J. *Charles Darwin: The Man and His Influence*. Cambridge: Cambridge University Press, 1996.

———. *The Eclipse of Darwinism: Anti-Darwinian Evolution Theories in the Decades around 1900*. Baltimore: Johns Hopkins University Press, 1983.

———. *Evolution: The History of an Idea*. 3rd ed. Berkeley: University of California Press, 2003.

———. *Reconciling Science and Religion: The Debate in Early Twentieth-Century Britain*. Chicago: University of Chicago Press, 2001.

Bowler, Peter J., and Iwan Rhys Morus. *Making Modern Science: A Historical Survey*. Chicago: University of Chicago Press, 2005.

Bowler, Peter J., and Nicholas Whyte, eds. *Science and Society in Ireland: The Social Context of Science and Technology in Ireland, 1800–1950*. Belfast: Institute of Irish Studies, The Queen's University of Belfast, 1997.

Brennan, Martin. "Adam and the Biological Sciences." *Irish Theological Quarterly* 35, no. 2 (April 1968): 152–53.

———. "From Matter to Man: The Evolutionism of Teilhard de Chardin." *University Review* [Dublin] 5, no. 2 (Summer 1968): 223–33.

Brock, W. H., N. D. McMillan, and R. C. Mollan, eds. *John Tyndall: Essays on a Natural Philosopher*. Dublin: Royal Dublin Society, 1981.

Brooke, John, and Geoffrey Cantor. *Reconstructing Nature: The Engagement of Science and Religion*. Edinburgh: T&T Clark, 1998.

Brooke, John Hedley. *Science and Religion: Some Historical Perspectives*. Cambridge: Cambridge University Press, 1991.

Brooke, John Hedley, Margaret J. Osler, and Jitse M. van der Meer, eds. *Science in Theistic Contexts: Cognitive Dimensions*, special edition of *Osiris* 16 (2001).

Browne, Michael. "Genesis 1 and 2." *The Furrow* (Maynooth, Ireland) 21, no. 6 (June 1970): 344–46.

Brundell, Barry. "Catholic Church politics and evolution theory, 1894–1902." *British Journal for the History of Science* 34 (2001): 81–95.

Bruce, Steve. *Choice and Religion: A Critique of Rational Choice Theory*. Oxford: Oxford University Press, 1999.

———. *God Save Ulster: The Religion and Politics of Paisleyism*. Oxford: Oxford University Press, 1986.

Brush, Stephen G. "The Nebular Hypothesis and the Evolutionary Worldview." *History of Science* 25, no. 3 (1987): 245–78.

Burke, John Butler. "Mr. Wells and Modern Science." *Dublin Review* 169, no. 339 (October–December 1921): 222–36.

Burrow, J. W. *The Crisis of Reason: European Thought, 1848–1914.* New Haven: Yale University Press, 2000.

Burtchaell, James Tunstead. "The Biblical Question and the English Liberal Catholics." *Review of Politics* 31, no. 1 (January 1969): 108–20.

———. *Catholic Theories of Biblical Inspiration since 1810: A Review and Critique.* London: Cambridge University Press, 1969.

Bury, J. B. *History of the Papacy in the 19th Century (1864–1878).* London: Macmillan, 1930.

"Bush Intensifies Evolution Debate." *International Herald Tribune,* 4 August 2005, http://www.technewsworld.com/story/45222.html.

Butler, Dom Cuthbert. *The Vatican Council: The story told from inside in Bishop Ullathorne's letters.* 2 vols. London: Longmans, Green and Co., 1930.

C., J. G. "Darwinism." *Irish Ecclesiastical Record* n.s. 9 (May 1873): 337–61.

Cahill, Lisa Sowle. "The Embryo and the Fetus: New Moral Contexts." *Theological Studies* 54, no. 1 (March 1993): 124–42.

Camp, Richard L. *The Papal Ideology of Social Reform.* Leiden: E. J. Brill, 1969.

CBS News. "Poll: Majority Reject Evolution." 23 October 2005, http://www.cbsnews.com/stories/2005/10/22/opinion/polls/main965223.shtml.

Chadwick, Owen. *The Secularization of the European Mind in the Nineteenth Century.* Cambridge: Cambridge University Press, 1975.

Clark, Martin. "The Theology of Catholic Modernism." *Church Quarterly Review* 164 (1963): 458–70.

Clarke, Desmond M. *Church and State: Essays in Political Philosophy.* Cork, Ireland: Cork University Press, 1985.

Clarke, R. F. "Dr. Mivart on the Continuity of Catholicism." *Nineteenth Century* 47 (February 1900): 244–59.

Clifford, Anne M. "Creation." In *Systematic Theology: Roman Catholic Perspectives,* edited by Francis Schüssler Fiorenza and John P. Galvin, 195–248. Dublin: Gill and Macmillan, 1992.

Clifford, Richard J., and John J. Collins, eds. *Creation in the Biblical Traditions.* Washington D.C.: Catholic Biblical Association of America, 1992.

Clifford, William. "The Days of Creation: A Reply." *Dublin Review* 3rd ser. 6 (October 1881): 498–507.

———. "The Days of Creation: Some Further Observations." *Dublin Review* 3rd ser. 9 (1883): 397–417.

———. "The Days of the Week, and the Works of Creation." *Dublin Review* 3rd ser. 5 (April 1881): 311–32.

Coghlan, Andy. "Are all human embryos equal?" *New Scientist,* no. 2522 (22 October 2005): 10.

———. "Race is on to stop human cloning." *New Scientist* 175, no. 2362 (28 September 2002): 11.

Cohen, Philip. "Rabbit-human stem cell claims provoke controversy and doubt." *New Scientist* 179, no. 2409 (23 August 2003): 14.

Collin, Rémy. *Evolution: Hypotheses and Problems*. London: Burns & Oates, 1959.

Conzemius, Victor. "Acton: The Lay Theologian." *Cristianesimo Nella Storia* 21, no. 3 (2000): 565–85.

Conway, Martin. *Catholic Politics in Europe 1918–1945*. London: Routledge, 1997.

Cornwell, John. "In their own image." *The Tablet*, 21 August 2004: 6–7.

———. *The Pope in Winter: The Dark Face of John Paul II's Papacy*. London: Viking, 2004.

Corrigan, Raymond. *The Church and the Nineteenth Century*. Milwaukee: Bruce Publishing Company, 1938.

Cosslett, Tess, ed. *Science and Religion in the Nineteenth Century*. Cambridge: Cambridge University Press, 1984.

Coyne, George V. "The Church in Dialogue with Science: The Wojtyla Years," in *New Catholic Encyclopedia; Jubilee Volume: The Wojtyla Years*. Detroit, Mich.: Gale Group, 2001.

———. "God's chance creation." *The Tablet*, 6 August 2005, http://www.thetablet.co.uk/cgi-bin/register.cgi/tablet-01063.

Coyne, Jerry A. "God in the details." *Nature* 383 (19 September 1996): 227–28.

Curran, Charles E. *Moral Theology: A Continuing Journey*. Notre Dame, Ind.: University of Notre Dame Press, 1982.

———, ed. *Moral Theology: Challenges for the Future*. New York: Paulist Press, 1990.

Curran, Charles E., and Richard A. McCormick, eds. *Readings in Moral Theology No. 6: Dissent in the Church*. New York: Paulist Press, 1988.

Curtis, Perry. *Apes and Angels: The Irishman in Victorian Caricature*. Rev. ed. Washington: Smithsonian Institution Press, 1997.

Daly, Cardinal Cahal B. *The Minding of Planet Earth*. Dublin: Veritas, 2004.

Daniel-Rops, Henri. *A Fight for God: 1870–1939*. London: J. M. Dent; New York: E. P. Dutton, 1966.

Darwin, Charles. *The Descent of Man and Selection in Relation to Sex*. 2 vols. 1871. Reprint (2 vols. in 1), with an introduction by John Tyler Bonner and Robert M. May, Princeton, N.J.: Princeton University Press, 1981.

———. *The Origin of Species by Means of Natural Selection or The Preservation of Favoured Races in the Struggle for Life*. 1859. Reprint, edited with an introduction by J. W. Burrow, London: Penguin Books, 1985.

Davies, Brian, ed. *Philosophy of Religion: A guide to the subject*. London: Cassell, 1998.

Davies, Norman. *Europe: A History*. Oxford: Oxford University Press, 1996.

Davies, Paul. *God and the New Physics*. London: Penguin Books, 1990.

Davis, Stephen T. *God, Reason and Theistic Proofs*. Edinburgh: Edinburgh University Press, 1997.

Dawkins, Richard. *The Blind Watchmaker*. London: Penguin Books, 1991.

———. *River out of Eden: A Darwinian View of Life*. London: Phoenix, 1996.

————. *The Selfish Gene*. New ed. Oxford: Oxford University Press, 1989.

Dean, Cornelia, and Laurie Goodstein. "Leading Cardinal Redefines Church's View on Evolution." *New York Times*, 9 July 2005, http://www.herald tribune.com/apps/pbcs.dll/article?AID=/20050709/ZNYT02/507090678.

Deane-Drummond, Celia E. "Biotechnology, ecology and wisdom." *Priests & People* 13, no. 10 (October 1999): 364–68.

De Beer, Gavin, ed. *Autobiographies: Charles Darwin, Thomas Henry Huxley*. London: Oxford University Press, 1974.

de Bivort de la Saudée, Jacques, ed. *God, Man and the Universe: A Christian answer to modern materialism*. London: Burns & Oates, 1954.

Deedy, John, *Retrospect: The Origin of Catholic Beliefs and Practices*. Cork and Dublin: Mercier Press, 1990.

Deely, John N., and Raymond J. Nogar. *The Problem of Evolution: A study of the philosophical repercussions of evolutionary science*. New York: Appleton-Century-Crofts, 1973.

de Fraine, Jean. *The Bible and the Origin of Man*. New York: Desclee Company, 1962.

Dell, Robert Edward. "A Liberal Catholic View of the Case of Dr. Mivart." *Nineteenth Century* 47, no. 278 (April 1900): 669–84.

Dembski, William A., Stephen C. Meyer, and Michael J. Behe. *Science and Evidence for Design in the Universe*. San Francisco: Ignatius Press, 2000.

Dennett, Daniel C. *Darwin's Dangerous Idea: Evolution and the Meanings of Life*. London: Penguin Books, 1996.

Denton, Michael. *Evolution: A Theory in Crisis*. London: Burnett Books, 1985.

Desmond, Adrian. *Huxley: From Devil's Disciple to Evolution's High Priest*. London: Penguin Books, 1998.

de Solages, Bruno. "Christianity and Evolution." Translated by Harry Blair. *Cross Currents* 1 (1951): 26–37. First published in *Bulletin de Litterature Ecclesiastique*, no. 4 (1947).

Devillers, Charles, and Jean Chaline. *Evolution: An Evolving Theory*. Berlin: Springer-Verlag, 1993.

Devine, Philip E. "Creation and Evolution." *Religious Studies* 32, no. 3 (September 1996): 325–37.

Dorlodot, Canon. *Darwinism and Catholic Thought*. Translated by Ernest Messenger. New York: Benziger Brothers, 1925.

Draper, John William. *History of the Conflict between Religion and Science*. 10th ed. London: Henry S. King & Co., 1877.

Dru, Alexander. "Modernism and the Present Position of the Church." *Downside Review* 82 (1964): 103–10.

Duddy, Thomas. *A History of Irish Thought*. London: Routledge, 2002.

Duffy, Eamon. *Saints and Sinners: A History of the Popes*. New Haven: Yale University Press and S4C, 1997.

Durant, John, ed. *Darwinism and Divinity: Essays on Evolution and Religious Belief.* Oxford: Basil Blackwell, 1985.

Ebenstein, William. "The Early Reception of the Doctrine of Evolution in the United States." *Annals of Science* 4 (1939): 306–18.

Eisen, Sydney, and Bernard V. Lightman. *Victorian Science and Religion: A Bibliography with Emphasis on Evolution, Belief and Unbelief, Comprised of Works Published from c. 1900–1975.* Hamden, Conn.: Archon Books, 1984.

Ellegård, Alvar. *Darwin and the General Reader: The Reception of Darwin's Theory of Evolution in the British Periodical Press, 1859–1872.* 1958. Reprint, with a foreword by David L. Hull, Chicago: University of Chicago Press, 1990.

Eve, A. S., and C. H. Creasey. *Life and Work of John Tyndall.* London: Macmillan, 1945.

Ewing, J. Franklin. "Darwin Today." *America* (21 March 1959): 709–11.

———. "Human Evolution–1956." *Anthropological Quarterly* 29 (1956): 91–139.

Fagan, Seán. *Does Morality Change?* Dublin: Columba Press, 2003.

———. "*Humanae Vitae* 30 Years On." *Doctrine and Life* [Dublin] 49, no. 1 (January 1999): 51–54.

Fallona, Michael John Anthony. "Polygenism and Theology: Humani Generis and Some Subsequent Developments." Master of Arts thesis, University of St. Michael's College, Toronto, 1967.

Fantoli, Annibale. *Galileo: For Copernicanism and for the Church.* 2nd ed. Translated by George V. Coyne. Vatican City State: Vatican Observatory Publications, 1996.

Fernández-Armestro, Felipe. *Millennium: A History of the Last Thousand Years.* New York: Touchstone, 1995.

Finocchiaro, Maurice A. "The Galileo Affair from John Milton to John Paul II: Problems and Prospects." *Science and Education* 8 (1999): 189–209.

———. "Galileo as a 'bad theologian': A formative myth about Galileo's trial." *Studies in History and Philosophy of Science* 33A, no. 4 (December 2002): 753–91.

Fitzgerald, Percy. *Fifty Years of Catholic Life and Social Progress: Under Cardinals Wiseman, Manning, Vaughan, and Newman.* 2 vols. London: T. Fisher Unwin, 1901.

Ford, Norman. "We don't have to clone." *The Tablet,* 9 December 2000, http://www.thetablet.co.uk/cgi-bin/register.cgi/tablet-00502.

Forestell, J. T. "The Limitation of Inerrancy." *Catholic Biblical Quarterly* 20 (1958): 9–18.

Foster, John Wilson. *Recoveries: Neglected Episodes in Irish Cultural History 1860–1912.* Dublin: University College Dublin Press, 2002.

Foster, John Wilson, and Helena C. G. Chesney, eds. *Nature in Ireland: A Scientific and Cultural History.* Dublin: Lilliput Press, 1997.

Fothergill, Philip G. *Evolution and Christians.* London: Longmans, Green and Co., 1961.

Frank, Karl. *The Theory of Evolution in the Light of Facts*. London: Kegan Paul, Trench, Trübner & Co.; St. Louis: B. Herder, 1913.

Frederick, Sister Mary. *Religion and Evolution since 1859: Some Effects of the Theory of Evolution on the Philosophy of Religion*. Chicago: Loyola University Press, 1934.

Friday, James R., Roy M. MacLeod, and Philippa Shepherd. *John Tyndall Natural Philosopher, 1820–1893: Catalogue of Correspondence, Journals and Collected Papers*. London: Mansell, 1974.

Friedman, Richard Elliott. *The Disappearance of God: A Divine Mystery*. Boston: Little, Brown & Co., 1995.

Fullerton, R. "Basis of Monism—Evolution." *Irish Ecclesiastical Record* 4th ser. 28 (August 1910): 161–74.

Futuyma, Douglas J. *Evolutionary Biology*. 2nd ed. Sunderland, Mass.: Sinauer Associates, 1986.

Galbraith, John Kenneth. *The Culture of Contentment*. London: Sinclair-Stevenson, 1992.

Gill, Henry V. "Entropy, Life and Evolution." *Studies* [Dublin] 22 (March 1933): 129–38.

———. *Fact and Fiction in Modern Science*. Dublin: M. H. Gill and Son, 1944.

Gliboff, Sander. "Evolution, Revolution, and Reform in Vienna: Franz Unger's Ideas on Descent and Their Post-1848 Reception." *Journal of the History of Biology* 31 (1998): 179–209.

Glick, Thomas F., ed. *The Comparative Reception of Darwinism*. Chicago: University of Chicago Press, 1988.

Godkin, Edwin Lawrence. "Tyndall and the Theologians." In *Reflections and Comments: 1865–1895*, 129–37. Westminster: Archibald Constable, 1896.

Gormally, Luke, ed. *Issues for a Catholic Bioethic*. London: Linacre Centre, 1999.

Gould, Stephen Jay. *Ever Since Darwin*. London: Penguin Books, 1991.

Granfield, Patrick. *The Limits of the Papacy: Authority and Autonomy in the Church*. London: Darton, Longman and Todd, 1987.

Greene, John C. *Darwin and the Modern World View*. Baton Rouge: Louisiana State University Press, 1961.

Gregersen, Niels Henrik, and Ulf Görman, eds. *Design and Disorder: Perspectives from Science and Theology*. London: T&T Clark, 2002.

Grenz, Stanley J., and Roger E. Olson. *Twentieth-Century Theology: God and the World in a Transitional Age*. Milton Keynes, U.K.: Paternoster Press, 1992.

Gruber, Jacob W. *A Conscience in Conflict: The Life of St. George Jackson Mivart*. Westport, Conn.: Greenwood Press, 1960.

Gruenthaner, Michael J. "Evolution and the Scriptures." *Catholic Biblical Quarterly* 13 (1951): 21–27.

H., J.C. "The Bishop of Newport's Rejoinder." *Dublin Review* 3rd ser. 19 (January–April 1888): 188–89.

Hales, E. E. Y. *Pio Nono: A study in European politics and religion in the nineteenth century.* London: Eyre & Spottiswoode, 1954.

Hammond, Michael. "Anthropology as a Weapon of Social Combat in Late-Nineteenth-Century France." *Journal of the History of the Behavioural Sciences* 16 (1980): 118–32.

Harris Poll, number 52. "Nearly Two-thirds of U.S. Adults Believe Human Beings Were Created by God." 6 July 2005, http://www.harrisinteractive .com/harris_poll/index.asp?PID=581.

Hart, John. *What Are They Saying about Environmental Theology?* New York: Paulist Press, 2004.

Hauber, W. A. "Evolution and Catholic Thought." *Ecclesiastical Review* 106, no. 3 (March 1942): 161–77.

Haught, John F. "Darwin, Design and the Promise of Nature." The Boyle Lecture given at the Parish Church of St. Mary-le-Bow, Cheapside, London, 4 February 2004, http://www.stmarylebow.co.uk/news/boyle2004.htm.

———. *Deeper than Darwin: The Prospect for Religion in the Age of Evolution.* Boulder, Colo.: Westview Press, 2004.

———. *God After Darwin: A Theology of Evolution.* Boulder, Colo.: Westview Press, 2000.

Hawking, Stephen. *A Brief History of Time: From the Big Bang to Black Holes.* Toronto: Bantam Books, 1995.

Healy, John. "Cardinal Newman on the Inspiration of Scripture." *Irish Ecclesiastical Record* 3rd ser. 5 (March 1884): 137–49.

Hedley, John Cuthbert. "Can the Scriptures Err?" *Dublin Review* 3rd ser. 20 (1888): 144–65.

———. [Bishop]. *Evolution and Faith with Other Essays.* London: Sheed & Ward, 1931.

———. "Physical Science and Faith." *Dublin Review* 4th ser., no. 28 (October 1898): 241–61.

Helmstadter, Richard. *Freedom and Religion in the Nineteenth Century.* Stanford, Calif.: Stanford University Press, 1997.

Helmstadter, Richard J., and Bernard Lightman, eds. *Victorian Faith in Crisis: Essays on Continuity and Change in Nineteenth-Century Religious Belief.* Stanford, Calif.: Stanford University Press, 1990.

Hill, Harvey. "Leo XIII, Loisy, and the 'Broad School': An Early Round of the Modernist Crisis." *Catholic Historical Review* 89, no. 1 (January 2003): 39–59.

Himmelfarb, Gertrude. *Lord Acton: A Study in Conscience and Politics.* San Francisco: Institute for Contemporary Studies, 1993.

Holmes, J. Derek. "Newman and Mivart—Two Attitudes to a Nineteenth-Century Problem." *Clergy Review* n.s. 50, no. 11 (November 1965): 852–67.

———. "Some Notes on Liberal Catholicism and Catholic Modernism." *Irish Theological Quarterly* n.s. 38, no. 4 (October 1971): 348–57.

Hoppen, K. Theodore. "The First Vatican Council." *History Today* 19, no. 10 (1969): 713–20.

Houghton, John. *The Search for God: Can Science Help?* Oxford: Lion Publishing, 1995.

Howell, Kenneth J. *God's Two Books: Copernican Cosmology and Biblical Interpretation in Early Modern Science.* Notre Dame, Ind.: University of Notre Dame Press, 2002.

Hoyt, Robert S., and Stanley Chodorow. *Europe in the Middle Ages.* 3rd ed. San Diego, Calif.: Harcourt Brace Jovanovich, 1976.

Hull, David L. *Darwin and His Critics: The Reception of Darwin's Theory of Evolution by the Scientific Community.* Cambridge, Mass.: Harvard University Press, 1973.

Jedin, Hubert, and John Dolan, eds. *History of the Church.* Vol. 8, *The Church in the Age of Liberalism.* London: Burns and Oates, 1981.

———. *History of the Church.* Vol. 9, *The Church in the Industrial Age.* London: Burns and Oates, 1981.

Jedin, Hubert, Konrad Repgen, and John Dolan, eds. *History of the Church.* Vol. 10, *The Church in the Modern Age.* London: Burns and Oates, 1981.

Jensen, J. Vernon. "Return to the Wilberforce-Huxley Debate." *British Journal for the History of Science* 21, no. 69 (June 1988): 161–79.

———. "The X Club: Fraternity of Victorian Scientists." *British Journal for the History of Science* 5, no. 17 (1970): 63–72.

Johnson, Elizabeth A. "The Legitimacy of the God Question: Pannenberg's New Anthropology." *Irish Theological Quarterly* 52 (1986): 289–303.

Johnson, George. *Fire in the Mind: Science, Faith and the Search for Order.* London: Viking, 1996.

Johnson, Humphrey J. T. *Anthropology and the Fall.* Oxford: Basil Blackwell, 1923.

———. *The Bible and the Early History of Mankind.* London: Burns Oates, 1943.

———. "Leo XIII, Cardinal Newman and the Inerrancy of Scripture." *Downside Review* 69 (1951): 411–27.

Johnson, Mark. "Delayed Hominization." *Theological Studies* 56, no. 4 (December 1995): 743–63.

———. "Delayed Hominization: A Rejoinder to Thomas Shannon." *Theological Studies* 58, no. 4 (December 1997): 708–14.

Johnston, George Sim. "The Genesis Controversy." *Position Paper 203* (Dublin: Four Courts Press, November 1990): 385–98.

Joll, James. *Europe Since 1870: An International History.* 4th ed. London: Penguin Books, 1990.

Jurmain, Robert, and Harry Nelson. *Introduction to Physical Anthropology.* 6th ed. Minneapolis: West Publishing Co., 1994.

Kaiser, Robert Blair. *The Encyclical That Never Was: The Story of the Commission on Population, Family and Birth, 1964–1966.* London: Sheed & Ward, 1987.

Kaveny, M. Cathleen. "The Case of Conjoined Twins: Embodiment, Individuality, and Dependence." *Theological Studies* 62, no. 4 (December 2001): 753–86.

Kenny, Anthony, ed. *The Oxford Illustrated History of Western Philosophy.* Oxford: Oxford University Press, 1994.

————. *What Is Faith? Essays in the philosophy of religion*. Oxford: Oxford University Press, 1992.

Kneller, Karl Alois. *Christianity and the Leaders of Modern Science: A Contribution to the History of Culture in the Nineteenth Century*. Translated by T. M. Kettle. London: B. Herder, 1911.

Krauss, Lawrence M. "School Boards Want to 'Teach the Controversy.' What Controversy?" *The New York Times*, 17 May 2005, http://genesis1.phys.cwru.edu/~krauss/17comm2.html.

Krauss, Lawrence M., Francisco Ayala, and Kenneth Miller. Letter to His Holiness Pope Benedict XVI, and copied to His Eminence Cardinal Christoph Schönborn and His Excellency William J. Levada, 12 July 2005. http://genesis1.phys.cwru.edu/~krauss/papalletttxt.htm.

Kuhn, Thomas S. *The Structure of Scientific Revolutions*, 2nd ed. Chicago: University of Chicago Press, 1970.

Kwitny, Jonathan. *Man of the Century: The Life and Times of Pope John Paul II*. New York: Warner Books, 1998.

Lane, Dermot. "Theology and Science in Dialogue." *Irish Theological Quarterly* 52, nos. 1 and 2 (1986): 31–53.

Langford, Jerome J. *Galileo, Science and the Church*. 3rd ed. Ann Arbor: Ann Arbor Paperbacks, University of Michigan Press, 1992.

Lanza, Robert, and Nadia Rosenthal. "The Stem Cell Challenge." *Scientific American* 290, no. 6 (June 2004): 92–99.

Larkin, Emmet. *The Historical Dimensions of Irish Catholicism*. Washington, D.C.: Catholic University of America Press; Dublin: Four Courts Press, 1984.

Latourette, Kenneth Scott. *Christianity in a Revolutionary Age: A History of Christianity in the Nineteenth and Twentieth Centuries*. Vol. 1, *The Nineteenth Century in Europe: Background and the Roman Catholic Phase*. London: Eyre & Spottiswoode, 1959.

Lemius, J. B. *A Catechism of Modernism*. 1908. Reprint, Rockford, Ill.: Tan Books, 1981.

Le Page, Michael. "All forms of infertility will be treatable." *New Scientist* 180, no. 2426 (20 December 2003): 17.

Levine, George. "Huxley, the Most Powerful Sage of Them All." *Victorian Studies* 42, no. 1 (Autumn 1998–99): 101–19.

Lightman, Bernard. *The Origins of Agnosticism: Victorian Unbelief and the Limits of Knowledge*. Baltimore: Johns Hopkins University Press, 1987.

Lindberg, David C., and Ronald L. Numbers, eds. *God and Nature: Historical Essays on the Encounter between Christianity and Science*. Berkeley: University of California Press, 1986.

————, eds. *When Science and Christianity Meet*. Chicago: University of Chicago Press, 2003.

Livingstone, David N. *Darwin's Forgotten Defenders: The Encounter between Evangelical Theology and Evolutionary Thought*. Grand Rapids: William B. Eerdmans; Edinburgh: Scottish Academic Press, 1987.

Lyng, Stephen G., and Lester R. Kurtz. "Bureaucratic Insurgency: The Vatican and the Crisis of Modernism." *Social Forces* 63, no. 4 (June 1985): 901–22.

Lyon, John. "Immediate Reactions to Darwin: The English Catholic Press' First Reviews of the 'Origin of Species.'" *Church History* 41 (March 1972): 78–93.

Machamer, Peter, ed. *The Cambridge Companion to Galileo*. Cambridge: Cambridge University Press, 1998.

Mackey, James P. "Theology, Science and the Imagination: Exploring the Issues." *Irish Theological Quarterly* 52, nos. 1 and 2 (1986): 1–18.

Marini-Bettòlo, G. B. *Outlines of the Activity of the Pontifical Academy of Sciences 1936–1986*. Vatican City: Pontificia Academia Scientiarum, 1986.

Marks, Lara V. *Sexual Chemistry: A History of the Contraceptive Pill*. New Haven: Yale University Press, 2001.

Marks, Louis S. "Darwin: 100 Years After." *Fordham Life* 4, no. 2 (Summer 1959): 2–5.

Martino, Renato. "An Affront to the Dignity of the Person." *Position Paper 348* (Dublin, December 2002): 348–50.

Mathew, David. *Lord Acton and His Times*. London: Eyre & Spottiswoode, 1968.

Mazhar, Noor Giovanni. *Catholic Attitudes to Evolution in Nineteenth-Century Italian Literature*. Venice: Istituto Veneto di Scienze, Lettere ed Arti, 1995.

Mazzotti, Massimo. "For science and for the Pope-King: Writing the history of the exact sciences in nineteenth-century Rome." *British Journal for the History of Science* 33 (2000): 257–82.

McBrien, Richard P. *Catholicism*. New ed. San Francisco: Harper, 1994.

———. *Lives of the Popes: The Pontiffs from St. Peter to John Paul II*. New York: HarperCollins, 2000.

McCool, Gerald A. *Catholic Theology in the Nineteenth Century: The Quest for a Unitary Method*. New York: Seabury Press, 1977.

McCormick, Richard A. *Notes on Moral Theology 1965 through 1980*. Lanham, Md.: University Press of America, 1981.

McDonald, Walter. *Reminiscences of a Maynooth Professor*. Edited with a memoir by Denis Gwynn. Cork, Ireland: Mercier Press, 1967.

McElrath, Damian. "Richard Simpson and John Henry Newman: The Rambler, Laymen, and Theology." *Catholic Historical Review* 52 (April 1966–January 1967): 509–33.

McGarrigle, Francis J. "Could the World Have Had No Beginning?" *Irish Ecclesiastical Record* 5th ser. 41 (January 1933): 1–12.

McGrath, Alister E. *Christian Theology: An Introduction*. 2nd ed. Oxford: Blackwell Publishers, 1997.

———. *Science and Religion: An Introduction*. Oxford: Blackwell Publishers, 1999.

McGrath, P. J. "Believing in God." *Irish Theological Quarterly* 42, no. 2 (April 1975): 87–96.

McLeod, Hugh. *Religion and the People of Western Europe 1789–1970*. Oxford: Oxford University Press, 1981.

————. *Secularisation in Western Europe 1848–1914*. Basingstoke [United Kingdom]: Macmillan Press; New York: St. Martin's Press, 2000.

McManners, John, ed. *The Oxford Illustrated History of Christianity*. Oxford: Oxford University Press, 1992.

McMillan, N. D., and J. Meehan. *John Tyndall: 'X'emplar of scientific and technological education*. Edited by Pauric Hogan. Dublin: N.C.E.A., 1980.

McMillan, Norman. "Tyndall the philosopher: John Tyndall (1820?–1893)." *Carloviana* [County Carlow, Ireland], no. 40 (1992–93): 25–29.

McMullin, Ernan, ed. *The Church and Galileo*. Notre Dame, Ind.: University of Notre Dame Press, 2005.

————, ed. *Evolution and Creation*. Notre Dame, Ind.: University of Notre Dame Press, 1985.

————. *Science and the Catholic Tradition*. New York: America Press, 1960.

McNeil, Maureen. "Clerical Legacies and Secular Snares: Patriarchal Science and Patriarchal Science Studies." *The European Legacy* 1, no. 5 (1996): 1728–39.

McNulty, T. Michael. "Evolution and Complexity." *American Catholic Philosophical Quarterly* 72 (1999): 435–48.

McOuat, Gordon, and Mary P. Winsor. "J.B.S. Haldane's Darwinism in its religious context." *British Journal for the History of Science* 28, no. 97 (June 1995): 227–31.

McSweeney, Bill. *Roman Catholicism: The Search for Relevance*. Oxford: Basil Blackwell, 1980.

Merriman, John. *A History of Modern Europe: From the Renaissance to the Present*. New York: W. W. Norton & Co., 1996.

Messenger, Ernest C. *Evolution and Theology: The Problem of Man's Origin*. London: Burns, Oates & Washbourne, 1931.

Messenger, E. C., ed. *Theology and Evolution: A Sequel to Evolution and Theology*. London: Sands & Co., 1951.

Middleton, W. E. Knowles. "Science in Rome, 1675–1700, and the Accademia Fisicomatematica of Giovanni Giustino Ciampini." *British Journal for the History of Science* 8, no. 29 (July 1975): 138–54.

Midgley, Mary. "Can science save its soul?" *New Scientist* 135, no. 1832 (1 August 1992): 24–27.

————. "Visions, Secular and Sacred." *Milltown Studies* [Milltown Institute of Theology and Philosophy, Dublin] no. 34 (Autumn 1994): 74–93.

Miller, Kenneth R. "Darwin, Design, and the Catholic Faith," n.d., http://www.millerandlevine.com/km/evol/catholic/op-ed-krm.html.

Mills, Simon. *Clinical Practice and the Law*. Dublin: Butterworths, 2002.

Mivart, St. George. "The Catholic Church and Biblical Criticism." *Nineteenth Century* 22 (July 1887): 31–51.

———. "Catholicity and Reason." *Nineteenth Century* 22 (December 1887): 850–70.

———. "The Continuity of Catholicism." *Nineteenth Century* 47 (January 1900): 51–72.

———. *The Genesis of Species*. 2nd ed. London: Macmillan, 1871.

———. "Modern Catholics and Scientific Freedom." *Nineteenth Century* 18 (July 1885): 30–47.

———. "Letter from Dr. Mivart on the Bishop of Newport's Article in Our Last Number." *Dublin Review* 3d ser. 19 (January–April 1888): 180–87.

———. "Roman Congregations and Modern Thought." *North American Review* 170 (1900): 562–74.

———. "Scripture and Roman Catholicism." *Nineteenth Century* 47 (March 1900): 425–42.

———. "Some Recent Catholic Apologists." *Fortnightly Review* 67 (1900): 24–44.

———. "Some Reminiscences of Thomas Henry Huxley." *Nineteenth Century* 42 (December 1897): 985–98.

[Molloy, Gerald]. "Geology and Revelation." Parts 1–9. *Irish Ecclesiastical Record* 3 (1867): 121–34, 241–61, 358–74, 448–67; 4 (1868): 49–66, 169–87, 326–41, 373–85; 5 (1869): 49–73, 193–223.

Molloy, Gerald. *Geology and Revelation: or The Ancient History of the Earth considered in the light of geological facts and revealed religion*. London: Longmans, Green, Reader, and Dyer; Dublin; McGlashan and Gill, and W. B. Kelly, 1870.

Molloy, [Gerald]. "The Historical Character of the First Chapter of Genesis." *Record of the Maynooth Union* [Ireland], 1895–1896: 30–35.

Monod, Jacques. *Chance and Necessity: An Essay on the Natural Philosophy of Modern Biology*. Translated by Austryn Wainhouse. New York: Vintage Books, 1972.

Moore, James R. *The Post-Darwinian Controversies: A study of the Protestant struggle to come to terms with Darwin in Great Britain and America 1870–1900*. Cambridge: Cambridge University Press, 1979.

Moore, Walter. *Shrödinger: Life and thought*. Cambridge: Cambridge University Press, 1992.

Morrison, John L. "William Seton   A Catholic Darwinist." *Review of Politics* 21, no. 3 (1959): 566–84.

Moss, Jean Dietz. "Galileo's Letter to Christina: Some Rhetorical Considerations." *Renaissance Quarterly* 36, no. 4 (Winter 1983): 547–76.

Muckermann, H. *Attitude of Catholics towards Darwinism and Evolution*. 4th ed. St. Louis: B. Herder, 1924.

Murphy, Edward J. "God as Creator." *Position Papers 128–129* (Dublin: Four Courts Press, August–September 1984): 214–22.

Murphy, Francis Xavier. *The Papacy Today*. London: Weidenfeld and Nicolson, 1981.

Murphy, J. "The Case of Galileo." *Nineteenth Century* 19 (May 1886): 722–39.

———. "Evolution and Faith." *Irish Ecclesiastical Record* 3rd ser. 5 (1884): 756–67.

——. "Faith and Evolution." *Irish Ecclesiastical Record* 3rd ser. 6 (1885): 481–96, 723–36.

National Center for Science Education. "Reactions to Schoenborn on the air." 28 July 2005. http://www.ncseweb.org/resources/news/2005/US/17_ reactions _to_schoenborn_on_the_7_28_2005.asp.

Neuhaus, Richard John, ed. *Biblical Interpretation in Crisis: The Ratzinger Conference on Bible and Church*. Grand Rapids: William B. Eerdmans, 1989.

Newman, Elizabeth. "Theology and Science without Dualism." *Cross Currents* 48, no. 1 (Spring 1998): 34–48.

Newman, John H. Cardinal. *The Idea of a University*. Edited, with introduction and notes by I. T. Ker. London: Oxford University Press, 1976.

——. "On the Inspiration of Scripture." *Nineteenth Century* 15, no. 84 (February 1884): 185–99.

Noether, Emiliana P. "Vatican Council I: Its Political and Religious Setting." *Journal of Modern History* 40, no. 1 (March 1968): 218–33.

Norman, Edward R. *The English Catholic Church in the Nineteenth Century*. Oxford: Clarendon Press, 1984.

Norman, E. R. *Anti-Catholicism in Victorian England*. London: George Allen and Unwin, 1968.

Numbers, Ronald L., and John Stenhouse, eds. *Disseminating Darwinism: The Role of Place, Race, Religion and Gender*. Cambridge: Cambridge University Press, 1999.

Nye, Mary Jo. "The Moral Freedom of Man and the Determinism of Nature: The Catholic Synthesis of Science and History in the *Revue des Questions Scientifiques*." *British Journal for the History of Science* 9, no. 33 (November 1976): 274–92.

O'Brien, John A. *Evolution and Religion: A Study of the Bearing of Evolution upon the Philosophy of Religion*. New York: Century Co., 1932.

Oldroyd, David, and Ian Langham, eds. *The Wider Domain of Evolutionary Thought*. Dordrecht, Holland: D. Reidel Publishing Company, 1983.

O'Leary, Don. *Vocationalism and Social Catholicism in Twentieth-Century Ireland: The Search for a Christian Social Order*. Dublin: Irish Academic Press, 2000.

Ong, Walter J., ed. *Darwin's Vision and Christian Perspectives*. New York: Macmillan, 1960.

O'Rourke, Kevin D., and Philip Boyle. *Medical Ethics: Sources of Catholic Teachings*. 2nd ed. Washington, D.C.: Georgetown University Press, 1993.

O'Sullivan, Wayne M. "Henry Nutcombe Oxenham: *Enfant Terrible* of the Liberal Catholic Movement in Mid-Victorian England." *Catholic Historical Review* 82 (1996): 637–60.

Pancaldi, Giuliano. *Darwin in Italy: Science across Cultural Frontiers*. Translated by Ruey Brodine Morelli. Bloomington: Indiana University Press, 1991.

Papers of the Working Group on Roman Catholic Modernism of The American Academy of Religion. New Orleans: 1990.

Parry, J. P. *Democracy and Religion: Gladstone and the Liberal Party, 1867–1875.* Cambridge: Cambridge University Press, 1986.

Pascal, Blaise. *Pensées.* Rev. ed. Translated with an introduction by A. J. Krailsheimer. London: Penguin Books, 1995.

Paul, Harry W. "The Crucifix and the Crucible: Catholic Scientists in the Third Republic." *Catholic Historical Review* 58 (April 1972–January 1973): 195–219.

———. *The Edge of Contingency: French Catholic Reaction to Scientific Change from Darwin to Duhem.* Gainesville: University Presses of Florida, 1979.

———. "Science and the Catholic Institutes in Nineteenth-Century France." *Societas–A Review of Social History* 1, no. 4 (1971): 271–85.

Peters, Ted. "Theology and the Natural Sciences." In *The Modern Theologians: An introduction to Christian theology in the twentieth century*, 2nd ed., edited by David F. Ford, 649–68. Malden, Mass.: Blackwell Publishers, 1997.

Pierse, Garrett. "Evolution and Creation: A New Argument for the Latter." *Irish Theological Quarterly* 15 (1920).

"Pius IX and the 'Civilta Cattolica.'" *Dublin Review* n.s. 7, no. 14 (1866): 414–32.

Polkinghorne, John. *Reason and Reality: The relationship between science and theology.* London: SPCK, 1991.

Poole, Michael. *Beliefs and Values in Science Education.* Buckingham: Open University Press, 1995.

Porter, Henry. "Mind over Matter: Faith, hope and clarity." *The Guardian* (23 September 1996), pp. 1–3.

Porter, Jean. "Individuality, personal identity, and the moral status of the preembryo: A Response to Mark Johnson." *Theological Studies* 56, no. 4 (December 1995): 763–70.

Poupard, Paul, ed. *Galileo Galilei: Toward a Resolution of 350 Years of Debate—1633–1983.* Translated by Ian Campbell. Pittsburgh, Pa.: Duquesne University Press, 1987.

Pyenson, Lewis, and Susan Sheets-Pyenson. *Servants of Nature: A History of Scientific Institutions, Enterprises and Sensibilities.* London: Fontana Press, 1999.

Quammen, David. "Darwin's Big Idea." *National Geographic* 206, no. 5 (November 2004): 2–35.

Rádl, Emanuel. *The History of Biological Theories.* Translated by E. J. Hatfield. London: Oxford University Press, 1930.

Rahner, Karl. "The Problem of Genetic Manipulation." In *Theological Investigations.* Vol. 9, *Writings of 1965–67 I.* Translated by Graham Harrison. London: Darton, Longman & Todd; New York: Seabury Press, [1974–1976].

Rappaport, Rhoda. "Geology and Orthodoxy: The Case of Noah's Flood in Eighteenth-Century Thought." *British Journal for the History of Science* 11, no. 37 (March 1978): 1–18.

Reardon, Bernard M. G. *Roman Catholic Modernism.* London: Adam and Charles Black, 1970.

Reston, James. *Galileo: A Life.* London: Cassell, 1994.

Richardson, Alan, and John Bowden, eds. *A New Dictionary of Christian Theology.* London: SCM Press, 1989.

Richardson, W. Mark, and Wesley J. Wildman, eds. *Religion and Science: History, Method, Dialogue.* New York: Routledge, 1996.

Ridley, Mark. *The Problems of Evolution.* Oxford: Oxford University Press, 1985.

Roberts, J. M. *A History of Europe.* Oxford: Helicon, 1996.

———. *The Penguin History of the World.* 3rd ed. London: Penguin Books, 1995.

Root, John D. "English Catholic Modernism and Science: The Case of George Tyrrell." *Heythrop Journal* 18 (July 1977): 271–88.

———. "The Final Apostasy of St. George Jackson Mivart." *Catholic Historical Review* 71, no. 1 (January 1985): 1–25.

Rowan-Robinson, Michael. *Ripples in the Cosmos: A view behind the scenes of the new cosmology.* Oxford: W. H. Freeman, 1993.

Ruse, Michael. "The Changing Face of Darwinism." *Victorian Studies* 45, no. 2 (Winter 2003): 305–17.

———. *The Darwinian Revolution.* Chicago: University of Chicago Press, 1979.

Russell, Robert J., William R. Stoeger, and George V. Coyne, eds. *John Paul II on Science and Religion: Reflections on the New View from Rome.* Vatican City State: Vatican Observatory, 1990.

———. *Physics, Philosophy and Theology: A Common Quest for Understanding.* Vatican City State: Vatican Observatory, 1988.

Russell, Robert John, William R. Stoeger, and Francisco J. Ayala, eds. *Evolutionary and Molecular Biology: Scientific Perspectives on Divine Action.* Vatican City State: Vatican Observatory Publications; Berkeley, Calif.: Center for Theology and the Natural Sciences, 1998.

Sasse, Hermann. "Inspiration and Inerrancy—Some Preliminary Thoughts." *Reformed Theological Review* 19, no. 2 (July 1960): 33–48.

———. "Rome and the Inspiration of Scripture." *The Reformed Theological Review* 22, no. 2 (June 1963): 33–45.

Schoenl, William J. *The Intellectual Crisis in English Catholicism: Liberal Catholics, Modernists, and the Vatican in the Late Nineteenth and Early Twentieth Centuries.* New York: Garland Publishing, 1982.

Schönborn, Christoph. "Finding Design in Nature." *New York Times,* 7 July 2005, http://www.millerandlevine.com/km/evol/catholic/schonborn-NYTimes.html.

Schoof, Mark. *A Survey of Catholic Theology, 1800–1970.* Paramus, N.J.: Paulist Newman Press, 1970.

Schultenover, David G. *A View from Rome: On the Eve of the Modernist Crisis.* New York: Fordham University Press, 1993.

Scotti, Dom Paschal. "Happiness in Hell: The Case of Dr. Mivart." *Downside Review* 119, part 416 (2001): 177–90.

Scotti, Paschal. "Wilfrid Ward: A Religious Fabius Maximus." *Catholic Historical Review* 88, no. 1 (January 2002): 42–64.

Segre, Michael. "Critiques and Contentions: Light on the Galileo Case?" *Isis* 88 (1997): 484–504.

Shannon, Thomas A. "Delayed Hominization: A Further Postscript to Mark Johnson." *Theological Studies* 58, no. 4 (December 1997): 715–17.

———. "Delayed Hominization: A Response to Mark Johnson." *Theological Studies* 57, no. 4 (December 1996): 731–34.

———. "Ethical Issues in Genetics." *Theological Studies* 60, no. 1 (March 1999): 111–23.

———. "Human Embryonic Stem Cell Therapy." *Theological Studies* 62, no. 4 (December 2001): 811–24.

Sharratt, Michael. *Galileo: Decisive Innovator.* Cambridge: Cambridge University Press, 1996.

Sheler, Jeffery L. "Guarding the Doctrine: Catholic bishops move to rein in academics." *U.S. News & World Report* 130, no. 25 (25 June 2001): 52.

Shipman, Pat. "Being Stalked by Intelligent Design." *American Scientist* 93, no. 6 (November–December 2005): 500–502.

Simonsson, Tord. *Logical and Semantic Structures in Christian Discourses.* Oslo: Universitetsforlaget, 1971.

Smart, J. J. C., and J. J. Haldane. *Atheism and Theism.* 2nd ed. Malden, Mass.: Blackwell Publishing, 2003.

Smith, Huston. "The Ambiguity of Matter." *Cross Currents* 48, no. 1 (Spring 1998): 49–60.

Smith, Quentin. "The Reason the Universe Exists Is That It Caused Itself to Exist." *Philosophy* 74, no. 290 (October 1999): 579–86.

Smolin, Lee. "Atoms of Space and Time." *Scientific American* 290, no. 1 (January 2004): 66–75.

Smyth, John. *Genesis and Science: Inspiration of the Mosaic Ideas of Creative Work.* London: Burns & Oates, 1898.

Soares, Christine. "Politics: The biggest obstacle of all." *Scientific American* 290, no. 6 (June 2004): 97.

Speaight, Robert. *Teilhard de Chardin: A Biography.* London: Collins, 1967.

Stenhouse, John. "Catholicism, Science, and Modernity: The Case of William Miles Maskell." *Journal of Religious History* 22, no. 1 (February 1998): 59–82.

Stenmark, Mikael. "What Is Scientism?" *Religious Studies* 33, no. 1 (March 1997): 15–32.

Stenson, James B. "Evolution—A Catholic Perspective." *Position Papers 128–129* (Dublin: Four Courts Press, August–September 1984): 222–33.

Stephen, J. F. "Mr. Mivart's Modern Catholicism." *Nineteenth Century* 22 (October 1887): 581–600.

Stourton, Edward. *Absolute Truth: The Catholic Church in the World Today.* London: Viking, 1998.

Studer, James N. "Consciousness and Reality: Our Entry into Creation." *Cross Currents* 48, no. 1 (Spring 1998): 15–33.

Stuhlmueller, Carroll. "Catholic Biblical Scholarship and College Theology." *The Thomist* 23, no. 4 (October 1960): 533–63.

Swinburne, Richard. "Arguments for the Existence of God." *Milltown Studies*, no. 33 (Spring 1994): 28–32.

Szulc, Tad. *Pope John Paul II: The Biography*. New York: Scribner, 1995.

Thomson, David. *Europe Since Napoleon*. Rev. ed. London: Pelican Books, 1966.

Tidings Online. "Scientific data supports design in evolution, says cardinal." 15 July 2005. http://www.the-tidings.com/2005/0716/evolution.htm.

Tilby, Angela. "The scientist's gospel." *The Tablet* (16 May 1992): 606–7.

Tolbert, Jane T. "Peiresc and Censorship: The Inquisition and the New Science, 1610–1637." *Catholic Historical Review* 89, no. 1 (January 2003): 24–38.

Toolan, David S. "Praying in a Post-Einsteinian Universe." *Cross Currents* 46, no. 4 (Winter 1996–97): 437–70.

Tracey, Alice. "Professor John Tyndall." *Carloviana* [County Carlow, Ireland] 1, no. 3 (January 1949): 127–43.

Trounson, Alan. "A crime against humanity." *New Scientist* 180, no. 2422 (22 November 2003): 23.

Trower, Philip. "The Theory of Evolution: Is evolution true? What does it mean?" *Position Paper 236–237* (Dublin: Four Courts Press, August–September 1993): 285–96.

Turner, Frank Miller. *Between Science and Religion: The Reaction to Scientific Naturalism in Late Victorian England*. New Haven: Yale University Press, 1974.

———. *Contesting Cultural Authority: Essays in Victorian Intellectual Life*. Cambridge: Cambridge University Press, 1993.

———. "Science and Religious Freedom." In *Freedom and Religion in the Nineteenth Century*, edited by Richard Helmstadter, 54–86. Stanford, Calif.: Stanford University Press, 1997.

Tyndall, John. *Fragments of Science: A Series of Detached Essays, Addresses, and Reviews*. Vol. 1. 6th ed. London: Longmans, Green & Co., 1879.

———. *Fragments of Science: A Series of Detached Essays, Addresses, and Reviews*. Vol. 2. New York: D. Appleton & Co., 1896.

Vasey, Vincent. "The Reasons for Providentissimus Deus." *St. Meinrad Historical Essays* [The Abbey Press, St. Meinrad, Ind.] 6, part 3 (May 1943): 243–54.

Vaughan, John S. "Bishop Clifford's Theory of the Days of Creation." *Dublin Review* 3rd ser. 9 (January 1883): 32–47.

———. "Faith and Evolution: A Further Consideration of the Question." *Irish Ecclesiastical Record* 3rd ser. 6 (1885): 413–24.

———. "Faith and Evolution: A Reply." *Irish Ecclesiastical Record* 3rd ser. 6 (1885): 651–64.

Veneziano, Gabriele. "The Myth of the Beginning of Time." *Scientific American* 290, no. 5 (May 2004): 66–73.

Vidler, Alec R. *The Modernist Movement in the Roman Church: Its Origins & Outcome*. London: Cambridge University Press, 1934.

Vidler, A. R. *A Century of Social Catholicism 1820–1920*. London: S.P.C.K., 1964.

Vollert, Cyril. "Humani Generis and the Limits of Theology." *Theological Studies* 12 (March 1951): 3–23.

von Aretin, Karl Otmar. *The Papacy and the Modern World*. London: Weidenfeld and Nicolson, 1970.

von Arx, Jeffrey Paul. "Interpreting the Council: Archbishop Manning and the Vatican Decrees Controversy." *Recusant History* 26, no. 1 (2002): 229–42.

———. *Progress and Pessimism: Religion, Politics and History in Late Nineteenth Century Britain*. Cambridge, Mass.: Harvard University Press, 1985.

Wallis, Claudia, et al. "The Evolution Wars." *Time* 166, no. 7 (15 August 2005): 26–35, http://search.epnet.com/login.aspx?direct=true&db=buh&an=178 48763.

Walsh, James J. *The Popes and Science: The History of the Papal Relations to Science during the Middle Ages and down to Our Time*. New York: Fordham University Press, 1908.

Ward, Wilfrid. "Liberalism and Intransigeance." *Nineteenth Century* 47 (June 1900): 960–73.

———. *The Life of John Henry Cardinal Newman: Based on His Private Journals and Correspondence*. 2 vols. London: Longmans, Green and Co., 1921.

———. *Problems and Persons*. London: Longmans, Green and Co., 1903.

Weber, A. S. *Nineteenth Century Science: A Selection of Original Texts*. Ontario: Broadview Press, 2000.

Weber, Ralph E. *Notre Dame's John Zahm: American Catholic Apologist and Educator*. Notre Dame, Ind.: University of Notre Dame Press, 1961.

Weigel, George. "Catholicism and Democracy: The Other Twentieth-Century Revolution." *The Washington Quarterly* 12, no. 4 (autumn 1989): 5–25.

———. *Witness to Hope: The Biography of Pope John Paul II*. New York: Cliff Street Books, 2001.

Weigel, Gustave. "Current Theology: Gleanings from the Commentaries on Humani Generis." *Theological Studies* 12 (1951): 520–49.

Weinberg, Steven. *The First Three Minutes: A Modern View of the Origin of the Universe*. London: Andre Deutsch, 1977.

Weisengoff, John P. "Inerrancy of the Old Testament in Religious Matters." *Catholic Biblical Quarterly* 17 (1955): 248–57.

Wells, David F. *Revolution in Rome*. Downers Grove, Ill.: Intervarsity Press, 1972.

Westphal, Sylvia Pagán. "Growing human organs on the farm." *New Scientist* 180, no. 2426–2428 (20 December 2003–3 January 2004): 4–5.

———. "The mouse with two mothers: Dawn of a new kind of parenthood." *New Scientist* 182, no. 2444 (24 April 2004): 8–10.

———. "Virgin birth method could found stem cell dynasties." *New Scientist* 178, no. 2392 (26 April 2003): 17.

Westphal, Sylvia Pagán, and Philip Cohen. "Cloned cells today. Where tomorrow?" *New Scientist* 181, no. 2435 (21 February 2004): 6–7.

White, Andrew D. *A History of the Warfare of Science with Theology in Christendom.* 2 vols. 1896. Reprint (2 vols. in 1), New York: George Braziller, 1955.

Wilmut, Ian. "The moral imperative of human cloning." *New Scientist* 181, no. 2435 (21 February 2004): 16–17.

Wilson, J. Anselm. *The Life of Bishop Hedley.* London: Burns, Oates & Washbourne, 1930.

Wiltgen, Ralph M. *The Rhine Flows into the Tiber: A History of Vatican II.* Rockford, Ill.: Tan Books, 1985.

Windle, Bertram C. A. *The Catholic Church and its Reactions with Science.* London: Burns, Oates & Washbourne, 1927.

———. *A Century of Scientific Thought & Other Essays.* London: Burns & Oates, 1915.

———. *The Church and Science.* London: Catholic Truth Society, 1920.

———. *The Evolutionary Problem as It Is Today.* New York: Joseph F. Wagner; London: B. Herder, 1927.

———. *What Is Life? A Study of Vitalism and Neo-vitalism.* London: Sands and Co.; St. Louis: B. Herder, 1908.

Wiseman, James A. *Theology and Modern Science: Quest for coherence.* New York: Continuum, 2002.

"World Church News: Europe: Schönborn urges creation debate." *The Tablet,* 3 September 2005, http://www.thetablet.co.uk/cgi-bin/citw.cgi/past-00246.

Young, David. *The Discovery of Evolution.* Cambridge: Cambridge University Press, 1992.

Zahm, John Augustine. *Bible, Science, and Faith.* Baltimore: John Murphy & Co., 1894.

———. *Evolution and Dogma.* 1898. Reprint, with a new introduction by Thomas J. Schlereth, New York: Arno Press, 1978.

Zerafa, P. "The Limits of Biblical Inerrancy." *Angelicum* 39 (1962): 92–119.

Index